Forestry Sector Intervention

Forestry Sector

The Impacts of

ROY G. BOYD

Intervention

Public Regulation on Social Welfare

WILLIAM F. HYDE

OWA STATE UNIVERSITY PRESS / AMES

Dedicated to Robert Fallon (1957–1985)
a promising young economist and good personal friend

333.75
B78†

ROY G. BOYD is an economist at the Resources and Technology Division, Economic Research Service, United States Department of Agriculture.
WILLIAM F. HYDE is an associate professor at the School of Forestry and Environmental Studies and Acting Director, Center for Resource and Environmental Policy Research, Duke University.

©1989 Iowa State University Press, Ames, Iowa 50010
All rights reserved

Composed by Iowa State University Press from author-provided disks
Printed in the United States of America

First edition, 1989

Library of Congress Cataloging-in-Publication Data

Boyd, Roy.
    Forestry sector intervention.

    Includes index.
    1. Forest policy—United States.   2. Forest policy—Economic aspects—United States.   3. Forests and forestry—Economic aspects—United States.   I. Hyde, William F.   II. Title.
SD565.B68   1989   333.75′0973   88–619
ISBN 0–8138–1447–2

CONTENTS

FOREWORD *by Roger A. Sedjo, vii*

PREFACE, *ix*

1 / Introduction, 3

2 / State Forest Practice Acts, 24

3 / Comparing the Effectiveness of Cost Sharing
and Technical Assistance Programs, 48

4 / Price Reporting Services, 90

5 / Minimum Wage and Occupational
Safety and Health, 120

6 / The Jones Act, 162

7 / Taxation, 190

8 / Public Ownership of Forestlands, 217

9 / Summary, Conclusions, and
Policy Implications, 264

Index of Symbols and Abbreviations, 285

INDEX, 291

FOREWORD

In this study, Roy Boyd and William Hyde have added a valuable dimension to the ongoing inquiry into the effect of public regulation on the natural resource sector in general and the forestry sector in particular. Two types of audience will benefit from a reading of this book. First, individuals interested in forestry, the forest sector, and the influence of public forestry programs will find that this volume provides a useful assessment of the empirical impact of a wide array of public programs that apply specifically to the forest sector. The study examines a large number of forest-directed regulations and programs, including state forest practice acts, technical assistance programs, price reporting services, minimum wage and occupational safety and health regulations, the Jones Act, taxation, and public ownership of forestlands. The impacts of these various programs and activities are empirically estimated and an assessment is made of their effects on economic efficiency, positive or negative.

In addition, readers interested in the broader social issue of the role and usefulness of public regulation in improving market outcomes in a largely private economy will find this book's analysis of forestry sector programs insightful. The view of the efficacy of public regulation of the American forests has been a debating point not just for decades but for at least a century. Are forests a resource that can be properly regulated by the forces of the market, or does this sector contain special features that ensure that the market will fail to provide appropriate regulation to achieve socially desirable outcomes? The widespread lack of confidence in the market discipline led the Congress to set aside the federal Forest Reserves in the late nineteenth century and establish, at the beginning of the twentieth century, the Forest Service as the agency to oversee and manage these public forests. Furthermore, a lack of confidence in market processes is the justification for a wide array of public programs, past and present, that are designed to intervene in the market with the intention of rectifying market failures that are believed to lead persistently to nonefficient resource allocations.

This controversy over the role of government in an essentially market economy, which of course encompasses a much wider range of participants than simply those interested in the forest sector or even natural resources more generally, has a long and contentious history that shows no sign of abating. Philosophical positions have been developed by both those espousing widespread government interventions and those arguing for essentially market-determined outcomes. At various times, one group or the other appears to have the upper hand. The New Deal and early postwar period was clearly the high water mark for the view that markets commonly "failed" and therefore could not be trusted to generate desirable outcomes. Hence, public agencies were needed to monitor, oversee, and regulate a wide variety of previously unregulated private economic activity. The 1960s, however, saw the beginning of the erosion in confidence that government could optimally intervene. This erosion continued and grew through the 1970s and into the Reagan era of the 1980s.

With the theories of the various schools of thought well developed, the issue of the desirability of various government regulations becomes ultimately an empirical question. Philosophical and theoretical arguments aside, do regulations and publicly sponsored programs generally achieve their stated goals and enhance the public welfare broadly defined? In this volume, Boyd and Hyde address the issue head on. They examine and estimate empirically the impact of a wide array of different types of public policies, ranging from various timber management policies to endangered species protection, designed to improve the performance of the forestry sector. Their examination includes public land management but features the numerous policies affecting private forest management. While their findings provide little evidence that individual government programs generally improve the overall performance of the forestry sector, there are some important exceptions.

The results of these studies cannot be directly applied to other sectors. Nevertheless, they do provide food for thought regarding broader philosophical issues that extend well beyond the forestry sector. Natural resources in general, and forestry in particular, have traditionally been viewed as sectors replete with externalities and hence prime candidates for regulation and public ownership. Forestry then should be a sector in which the effects of public programs are predominantly positive. This is not what Boyd and Hyde find.

In summary, the lessons from this book are both practical and philosophical, and its findings add a new dimension to an old and ongoing debate. There is a tremendous amount of work in this book. I applaud the effort and encourage further sound empirical work on the topic.

ROGER A. SEDJO

Senior Fellow and Director,
Forest Economics and Policy Program,
Resources for the Future

PREFACE

There has been very little empirical analysis of public regulations and other government interventions in the markets for many primary natural resource commodities and almost no empirical analysis of regulatory effects in forestry. The high policy profile of many interventions begs more serious attention and this book is our "first-cut" response. We focus on regulations affecting private forestlands but also include chapters on taxation and public ownership in forestry, because the impacts of taxation and public ownership can be very large and nonneutral on the economic development of the forestry sector.

The first steps in any analysis like ours are to identify the perspective from which it originates and the audience to which it addresses itself. Our perspective is that of the policymaker, perhaps a member of Congress or senior public agency official, who asks, "What are the gains to society from this regulation? Can it accomplish what its proponents desire? Should I support and encourage it?"

We are not so naive as to believe that members of congress and public agency administrators will have either the time or the inclination to immerse themselves in the detail of our analyses. Rather, the detailed analysis of each example regulation in this book provides the background necessary for technically proficient congressional aides and the policy analysis staffs of public agencies to trace our reasoning and reproduce our results. The introduction and conclusion of each analysis, each chapter, can stand alone in a way we hope is brief yet meaningful. Alternately, that policymaker may choose to go straight to the summary chapter, which also was written to stand on its own.

Meanwhile, we hope that our effort provides insight and, better yet, that our effort encourages others to reexamine the same regulations we examine and to examine for the first time other, perhaps even more important, public market interventions affecting forestry. We also hope that our effort shows other foresters the strength of applied welfare economics in assessing such policy issues. In particular, we hope that some of our analyses competently follow Clark Binkley's lead in promoting the use of general equilibrium analyses in the economics of forestry.

George Dutrow and our entire group of colleagues at the Southeastern Center for Forest Economics Research encouraged our research (with funding from the Southeastern Forest Experiment Station, USDA Forest Service, and from Duke and North Carolina State Universities). George brought us all together and, simply said, his efforts made this book possible. Skip Hyberg, from North Carolina State University and also a member of this group, is using similar general equilibrium approaches in forestry. Vern Robinson, Fred Cubbage, Jan Laarman, Lou Silver, Ed deSteiguer, and Dudley Wallace reviewed our manuscripts. Each has done notable work on topics related to one or more of our chapters. Lester Holley also reviewed manuscripts. His example provides us all with the best working model of a modern forest economist. Mike Vasievich, who may be the best data source in forestry, provided basic data and insight as to where to obtain more basic data. Jack Royer is the most knowledgeable person we know on nonindustrial forest landowners. We relied on his insights in at least four different chapters. Lou Eckstein provided valuable insight into the structure of local stumpage markets. His own research goes further than ours in displaying the value of price information to nonindustrial landowners. Wilma McInturff provided continued good cheer — and assistance in finding our colleagues when they tired of our questions.

Our graduate students at Duke University and various other colleagues made substantial inputs to one or another of the specific chapters. Harold Olinger, Virginia Division of Forestry, Leo Wilson, Oregon State University Department of Forestry, Arden Olson, Washington Department of Natural Resources, provided data; and Carol Dahl, Louisiana State University, provided econometric advice for the chapter on state forest practice acts. Rob Fallon, University of Wisconsin-Milwaukee, assisted us on this chapter and the FIP chapter. Rob was a promising young economist and good personal friend who died in an automobile accident before completion of this manuscript. Much of the most difficult work in these two chapters is a credit to his outstanding effort.

Bill Schworm, University of British Columbia, and Dave Hoaas and Dave Newman, Duke University, collaborated on various versions and parts of the price variation chapter. Joe Chang, University of Kentucky, and Karl Lofgren, Swedish University of Agricultural Sciences, also provided their usual first-rate economic insight and encouragement on this chapter. Jim Neal, U.S. Forest Service, provided information on Timber Mart-South for the price variation chapter. Marsha Courchane, North Carolina State University, prepared an early version of the minimum wage chapter; and Mike Moore and George Tauchen of Duke University, Jim Granskog, U.S. Forest Service, and Brian Greber, Oregon State University, made important review comments. John Austin of Weyerhaeuser, Drew Chad of MacMillan Bloedel, and especially Dick King of North Carolina State University helped with our Jones Act analysis. Jeff Turnbull, Louisiana State University, cowrote an earlier version of the property tax section and Jeff Stier, University of Wisconsin, and D. E. Mills, University of Virginia, provided their usual outstanding reviews. Steve Daniels, Randy Strait, Pat Hepner, and Dierdre Woods, Duke University; Dave Wear and Dave Jackson, University of Montana; Mike Lennartz, Mel Hopkins, and John Hendee, U.S. Forest Service Southeastern Forest Experiment Station; Ron Cox, Jeannette Price, Chuck Spoon, and Laura Tinsley, Lolo National Forest; Rich Bishop, University of Wisconsin; Kerry Smith, Vanderbilt University; and Jonna Kincaid and Darius Adams, University of Washington—all contributed to the public lands chapter. Kerry Krutilla, Duke University, and Roger Sedjo of Resources for the Future carefully reviewed and suggested important revisions in the summary chapter. The idea for this book developed while Bill was working with Roger at Resources for the Future. Many of these colleagues also advised on other chapters. Every one of them made contributions of real substance.

Clearly, a large amount of insight other than our own went into this volume. Most notable of all, however, was that of Barbara Daniels, our research associate throughout this five-year effort. Barb obtained virtually all of the data and participated in virtually all of the analysis. She is responsible for more analytical corrections and improvements than we can identify. She also wrote early drafts for some partial chapters. There can be no harder worker or better associate—and friend.

Gretchen Van Houten always provided cheerful and timely editorial advice. Bill Silag provided more technical assistance than any senior editor could have anticipated. We are pleased for our relationship with Gretchen, Bill, and ISU Press.

Finally, we must thank Sara Boyd and Pamela Bellin. Without Sara's understanding Roy would not have had the time to accomplish this undertaking and without her hospitality Bill would not have had the Washington, D.C., haven from which he and Roy attacked many of the technical problems of this book. Bill would have been much less happy and the manuscript revisions of both Bill and Roy would have been less timely without Pam's assistance.

Much of the merit of this book is due to the thoughtful attention and friendly comment of all these people.

R.G.B.
W.F.H.

Forestry Sector Intervention

CHAPTER 1

Introduction

Regulation and the distortion of economic incentives is once again an important public policy issue. The Reagan Administration has made a daily news item of deregulation for the transportation industries, for utilities and energy, and of environmental health and safety restrictions on general industrial production. The administration argues that the current collection of industrial regulations contributes in an important way to our economic malaise, restricting industrial output and contributing to inflation. Regulation is no less an issue among people interested in natural resources. Witness the Sagebrush Rebellion, the many recent state forest practice acts, herbicide-use restrictions, and current debates over minerals exploration and timber harvest restrictions on the public lands. This book is an empirical inquiry into these issues, into natural resource regulation and deregulation on the forests and rangelands that are one-third of our nation's lands. Its objective is to examine such regulations, their impacts on resource production and pricing, and also the question of who bears the burden of these impacts.

The usual argument against regulation is that its costs exceed its benefits; therefore, there are gains to be obtained from deregulation. The Civil Aeronautics Board is the popular successful example. Deregulation of airfares and schedules resulted in both decreased ticket prices and expanded service. The argument proceeds, explaining that deregulatory efforts would be even more successful except that changes in regulatory policies affect vested interests (Stigler 1971, Posner 1974). Therefore, a few potentially large losers often argue successfully against the multitude of small, even unidentified, gainers from deregulation. The counterargument for regulation is that its benefits, instead, exceed its costs. Distributive arguments often support regulation as well. For example, regulation ensures minimal levels of health, safety, and environmental quality, levels that may be critical to our social well-being but that would not be forthcoming if industry

3

were allowed to single-mindedly pursue its own advantage.

These arguments, both for and against regulation, in general are well rehearsed but often are void of empirical content. This is why there can be two opinions on relative benefits and costs. The absence of empirical content certainly typifies most discussions of regulations of primary natural resources (energy and agriculture are occasional exceptions) and is surprising in light of continued concern with natural resource scarcity and the potential for regulation to distort market incentives to overcome scarcity. Consider environmental restrictions that raise the cost of timber production. Consider the Jones Act, which restricts timber shipments by sea, effectively reducing the production incentives facing coastal area foresters. Or consider federal timber production incentives, those market distorting counterparts of regulation, which are often wasted on landowners who have no intention of ever harvesting their timber. All these examples are from public timber policy. Additional examples can be found for timber, and others can be found for range, recreation, fish and wildlife, water, and minerals as well.

Our intent in this book is to sharpen understanding of the justifications for regulation or deregulation in natural resources and to provide the empirical content necessary for regulatory judgement. We apply a broad definition of regulation to include restrictions on both production and consumption as well as specialized market incentives. It is clear that restrictions are a form of regulation. It should also be clear that public agency market interventions for the purpose of providing production incentives constitute a form of regulation insofar as they modify the workings of a freely operating market and divert funds from other, potentially more productive, investments.

We would like to make a general assessment of the aggregate impacts of all regulations affecting forests and rangelands. This would require an understanding of very many specific regulations, too many for reasonable examination within one volume and more than enough to allow for some conclusive generalizations. Therefore, we approach our problem by initially reviewing the conceptual justifications for public market intervention and for developing a working taxonomy of intervention. This first step relies on the standard economic arguments of allocation, distribution, and stabilization. The second tests these justifications empirically for cases chosen from the taxonomic classes; that is, from illustrative cases of public market interventions affecting forests and rangelands. We exclude agriculture and energy resources on the grounds that they have been discussed by others more knowledgeable than we. (See Schultz 1978 for a general reference and any of several publications from the Energy Division of Resources for the Future. Also see Haveman 1972.) We expect to find that some regulations can be justified, and others cannot be, whereas in still other situations new regulations may be justified where none currently exist. Finally, we relate findings from these illustrative cases to the broader group of all regulations of forests and rangelands in general, and we suggest the policy implications of these findings. We will find that many regulations have substantial localized impacts on the level of resource use or on special producer or consumer groups. Furthermore, we will find that public ownership and nonneutral taxation are special regulatory forms with important aggregate economic effects.

The remainder of this chapter provides background for our analysis. The next section considers the historical progression of regulation as a natural resource policy topic. Certainly, we can trace it to the Eisenhower Administration and perhaps we can trace it as far back as the 1781 Articles of Confederation, which justified the initial federal policy role in this country. A third section, the bulk of this chapter, reviews the standard economic arguments for market intervention and uses them to develop our working taxonomy of intervention. A final section introduces the remainder of the book, empirical chapters on specific regulations chosen to represent the taxonomic classes and to display their implications to resource regulation in general.

 Historical Background

Public agency market intervention and its economic justifications are not new issues. Indeed, they recur throughout the history of natural resource management in the United States (see Hibbard 1965). The arguments and assumptions that led to the earliest interventions are the historical antecedents of many modern arguments for public intervention. Their review, therefore, provides useful background for our analysis. It serves to place current policy issues in a timely perspective.

According to the standard argument, governments exist because there are goods and services, such as roads and national defense, that are better provided communally than with the independent encouragement of a freely working market. The optimal magnitudes of provision for such communal goods and services are debatable, however, because their benefits are often difficult to quantify. Moreover, the level of government responsible for their provision has never been a certain thing in the United States. The degree of government centralization has been a constant issue. Indeed, our Constitution itself is the product of debate over an earlier and much less centralized organization under the Articles of Confederation. This all suggests themes of public entry where the market fails to provide socially valuable goods and services, yet uncertainty as to the appropriate magnitude of public activity and level of government centralization. These themes apply to natural resource management throughout its public history in the United States — as well as to other classes of public activity.

We can trace the formation of resource management agencies to the perception of market failure. The Environmental Protection Agency and the U.S. Forest Service are examples. We can argue that the EPA was created to correct the market failure to charge individual pollutors in accordance with the level of costs their pollution imposes on society. The Forest Service is an older and less obvious case. Nineteenth century forest practices consisted primarily of clearcutting the timber and either hauling it to market or burning it in order to clear the land for agriculture. There was little or no encouragement for reforestation and forested land was not actively managed for its future yield of timber. This created an expectation of timber famine among early professional foresters. Failure of the forest industry to plan now for future timber demands was the topic of a major paper at the 1873 annual meeting of the American Association for the Advancement of Science and the founding cause of the American Forestry Association in 1875. These organizations argued that, since the market apparently provided insufficient incentive for private investment in continued timber production, public intervention was the only means for assuring a supply of timber sufficient to satisfy future national needs. Therefore, they encouraged the federal government to retain its western forestlands as a hedge against the forecasted timber famine. The federal government studied the question and eventually, in 1891, created the Forest Reserves, forerunner to today's national forests managed by the U.S. Forest Service (Clepper 1971, 17ff.).

Neoclassical economics argues that the expectation of timber famine probably is an invalid justification for public agency participation in the timber market. Timber does trade in a satisfactory market. Timber prices increase in response to an expected shortage (or famine) and induce the current investment in timber growing necessary to prevent the expected shortage.[1] Neoclassical economics does recognize market failures in the associated forestland production of water and recreational services as continuing justifications for public agency involvement in forest management. These latter market failures, however, were not identified in the earliest arguments for public intervention.

Decentralization, deregulation, and even dispersal are important current policy issues for the Forest Service and the Bureau of Land Management. They are not new issues. From 1911 to 1920, cession of the national forests to the states and even their dispersal among private owners were important issues. The arguments against federal agency management were that the Forest Service blocked development of good agricultural land within the forests and that much national forestland was more valuable in private management for mining and water power. There was also an undercurrent of conflict with stockmen (Clepper 1971, 69ff.). Dispersal of public rangeland among homesteaders was the sole purpose of BLM's forerunner agency. (Does this all sound familiar to the Sagebrush Rebellion of 1980s?)

Regulation was the central policy issue in the 1920s and 1930s. For ranchers, the term *regulation* referred to attempts to control overgrazing of public lands. For foresters, *regulation* referred to public restrictions on private industrial forest management in order to ensure a future timber supply and, thereby, to prevent timber famine. The policy issue, the most devisive policy issue in the history of American forestry, was not "whether regulation" but "who." Should state or should federal agencies regulate the industry? The rise of state forest agencies and the timely fading of a few old debators decided this issue in favor of the states — many of which found industrial regulation unnecessary until the environmental movement of the 1970s encouraged various states to pass state forest practice acts (Clepper 1971, 152ff.).

Of course, the "partnership" theme of the Eisenhower Administration directed some attention away from private land regulation and toward public resource management. In its best light, partnership, which was more relevant to water management agencies, argued for private concessions managing marketable public resources and continuing public management of nonmarketable resources (Krutilla & Eckstein 1958).

This background leaves us with the opinion that basic questions never change. They may apply to new problems, as new market failures are found or old ones decrease in importance. Or they may remain unresolved, perhaps due to the absence of objective measures for their inquiry. We attempt to rectify the latter problem beginning in the next section. Our approach is that of marginal economic analysis. It, too, has good historical precedent, if less historical application than we might wish. President Washington's Secretary of Treasury, Albert Gallatin, recommended a rudimentary form of benefit–cost analysis to judge the efficiency of public canal and roadbuilding activities. Perhaps, we can trace our origin to him.

Approach

The theory of political economy contains three justifications for public agency intervention in a market economy: *allocation, distribution,* and *stabilization.* Our historical discussion focused on market failure, an allocational argument. Distribution and stabilization have not been traditional justifications for intervention in resource management — with the notable exception of agriculture. These latter justifications are becoming more prevalent, however, as arguments for contemporary public intervention in forest and rangeland management. We consider all three justifications for market intervention in turn, and then discuss the optimal level of intervention associated with each. This approach prepares the foundation for our taxonomic classification of regulations and the chapter organization for the remainder of this book.

The allocation argument justifies intervention in the presence of market failure; that is, where a freely operating market fails to arrive at a socially efficient price-quantity equilibrium. Social efficiency is defined by the equality of incremental benefits with incremental costs. Failure of the market to achieve this equality can be the result of either natural monopolies, such as public utilities, or externalities. Externalities describe cases where socially valued goods or services, such as clean air, fail to exchange at any price.

Natural monopolies must be managed by single owners in order to capture all the production cost decreases due to agglomeration. Evidence that they occur infrequently in the markets for timber, range, recreational lands, or wetland resources resides in our observations that the property rights for these resources are well defined and readily transferable, yet the ownership of these resources remains unconcentrated and widely distributed throughout the country.

Externalities occur where the relevant market is either absent or where it is interdependent with the market for another good or service. There is some argument that the borrowers' market for long-term capital provides an example of an absent market affecting nonindustrial private forestry (NIPF). There is social value to having financial markets for any amount of capital lent or borrowed and for any length of time. The financial markets fail, however, and intervention may be justified if financial institutions stop short of lending the small amounts of capital required by NIPF landowners for the long periods necessary for growing timber. This issue received considerable attention through the years before the 1958 committee report on *Forest Credit in the United States*. The committee, appointed by Resources for the Future and composed mostly of prominent bankers and foresters, concluded that there is no failure in the capital market; adequate financial markets are present. Timber returns are just too low and timber investments too risky to justify lending to or borrowing by the smaller NIPF landowners.

The sources of dispersed outdoor recreation, such as wilderness areas, are further examples of goods and services that possess social value but that do not readily exchange in the market. It is difficult or impossible to assign title or deed to them; they cannot be owned in any restrictive sense. No one denies the value of wilderness recreation, for example, but attempts to ration it through a system of charges would be easily avoided because there is no way to exclude access to most wilderness areas. In such cases, the public may intervene, setting regulations on production and consumption that, while possibly increasing costs, result in improved allocation of these nonmarket goods and services.

Externalities due to interdependent markets refer to cases where activities germane to the production or consumption of a good or service affect other, unrelated goods and services. For example, logging activities require roads that also open forests to recreational users (a positive interdependency) but simultaneously increase stream sediment flow (a negative interdependency with downstream users). Logs exchange in the market for a price but their production impacts on recreation and downstream water users are external to existing markets. Only public regulation of timber roadbuilding or joint management for timber, recreation, and downstream uses by a single landowner can bring about roads built with consideration for all three of these forestland uses. Such impacts on unrelated goods and services are the most frequent justification for allocative public intervention in free markets. They are common to both production from forests and rangeland and consumption of resource services. Special public laws providing for water and air pollution control, multiple use public land management, fish and wildlife protection, and tax advantages for green space around some cities give explicit recognition to the externality case on forestlands.

Distribution, the second justification for public agency market intervention, implies an ethical commitment to some minimum standard of material well-being. Accordingly, typical recipients of distributive benefits come from financially poorer population groups or geographic regions, populations such as teenagers with high unemployment and regions such as Appalachia where small and dispersed populations experience difficulty supporting minimal levels of social services. In addition, distributive benefits may be designed to overcome the social and economic disadvantage unfairly confronting groups like women, minorities, and the handicapped.

The purpose of distributive benefits is to remove whatever distinguishes the economic opportunity (or lack thereof) of these groups from that of the rest of society. That is, the objective is to permit these groups the freedom to integrate with the rest of society if they choose. The tools for and time period of distributive relief must be defined accordingly. Abstracting from the very important set of distributive benefits justified in order to overcome biases in basic civil liberties, then, the tools of distributive relief consist of direct transfer payments and subsidized social services. Economic arguments confine distributive relief to the period it takes the disadvantaged group to adjust; therefore, there may always be distributive programs for the aged, but programs for minorities and residents of Appalachia may only last one generation because the second generation is fully mobile and trainable. Those in the second generation who fail to respond to distributive incentives are demonstrating a personal preference with full knowledge of its consequences and, therefore, can no longer be thought of as disadvantaged.[2]

Distributive programs are generally the responsibility of social welfare agencies, such as the federal Departments of Labor, Education, or Health and Human Services, but resource management agencies are also occasionally called upon to support distributive objectives. Food stamp programs in the Department of Agriculture and Forest Service–managed Job Corps centers, timber production incentives restricted to small private landowners and special federal timber sales set aside for small loggers and millowners provide examples. Some argue that such programs only confuse the efficiency objectives of resource management agencies (LeMaster 1975; Haigh & Krutilla 1980) and may even decrease income equality (Herendeen 1966). Others respond that general social welfare programs often favor the urban poor and overlook the special needs of the rural poor, thereby deferring some distributive concerns to resource management agencies like the Department of Agriculture or the U.S. Forest Service (Bryant et al. 1981).

Stabilization, the final justification for market intervention, has to do with moderating the cyclic nature of the economy in general and with tempering price fluctuations and maintaining high levels of employment in particular. It has its origins as a justification for market intervention in the Great Depression and in the Employment Act of 1946. Stabilizing intervention usually involves macroeconomic fiscal policies (e.g., changes in public expenditure or taxation levels) or Federal Reserve monetary policies (e.g., changing interest rates or money supply). These policies are often designed for their moderating influences on employment and prices in specific activities like construction that tend to act as leading indicators of general macroeconomic activity. This is important to us because of the link between construction and its primary materials, basic natural resources like timber.

Stabilization is also an argument for intervention where geographic regions are confronted arbitrarily with economic hardship due to either natural disasters or widely fluctuating local prices and production levels. The boom-or-bust nature of extractive resource-based communities, like Rocky Mountain communities dependent on local timber production, is an example of the latter. Some recent microeconomic attention has been directed toward this problem (Haveman & Krutilla 1968; Krutilla, Fisher & Rice 1978; Bender & Schwiff 1982). It should be clear that stabilizing intervention in this case can be confined to a period defined by the lifetime of location-fixed capital equipment and by local labor immobility. Furthermore, employment for temporary workers attracted from outside the region is not a microeconomic (local) stability concern because these workers enter the region fully aware of its fluctuating nature and, therefore, fully compensated for its negative effects.

OPTIMAL INTERVENTION

The unresolved and underlying question has to do with the optimal mix of market incentives and public interventions. Where market failure occurs, the optimal level of intervention and the "perfect" regulation, in some sense, are defined by output levels equating incremental unit-output benefits, including nonmarket benefits, with incremental unit costs, including nonmarket costs. Nonmarket benefits and costs are due to the externalities previously discussed.

Figure 1.1 describes the characteristics of this rule graphically. Consider the market for timber and the downstream sediment deposition originating from the roadbuilding and harvesting activities associated with timber production. The function D describes market demand for timber, S describes timber supply, and the market equilibrates at point a where q_1 Mbf (million board feet) of timber exchange at price p_1 per Mbf. The market fails to compensate downstream landowners for the impact of the sedimentation caused by timber production. If this impact is a cost equal to the difference between S and S', then we can correct the joint market for timber and sediment by taxing or regulating so as to impose an additional burden on the timber producer equal to this difference. The producer either pays the cost of correcting the negative sedimentation externality imposed on downstream landowners or transfers to the public treasury (by means of a license fee, a tax, or a fine) the means to pay for it. As a result, the timber supply function shifts to S' and the market now clears at a socially optimal q_2 Mbf of timber trading at price p_2 per Mbf. The optimal tax or the impact of the optimal regulation is $(b-c)$ per Mbf for the last board foot of timber. The area dab describes the net social gain from this optimal tax or regulation.[3] (Figure 1.1 reflects a partial equilibrium solution. General equilibrium extends the assessment to those sectors of the economy affected indirectly by the intervention; for example, the construction sector, which redirects equipment from other productive activities in order to produce the forest roads.)

Discussions and applications of this rule for optimal intervention focus on the costs of either compensating unwilling consumers of the negative externality, downstream landowners, or producing the physical correction, either rapid regeneration or sediment ponds or better roads and buffer strips between the harvest operations and streambanks. These discussions tend to overlook the transactions costs associated with the intervention itself. Yet, if these transactions costs exceed the net social gains from the

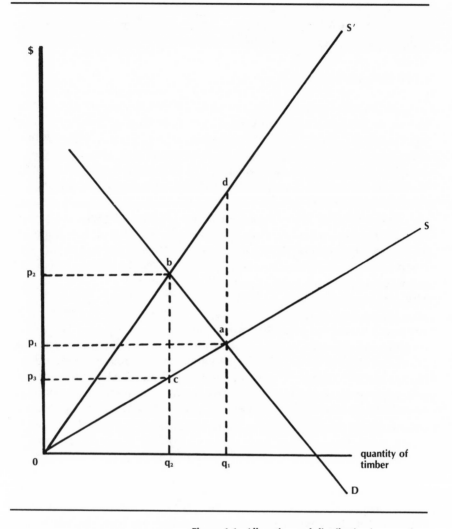

Figure 1.1. Allocative and distributive intervention.

intervention, then there is no point to the regulation or tax. The most obvious transactions costs are the administrative costs of the regulating authority and the monitoring and additional legal costs that, in our example, incur to both the forest landowners and the downstream landowners. It is not difficult to imagine reasonable administrative costs alone exceeding the benefits of regulatory improvement. In this case, "no regulation," despite uncorrected market failure, is preferable to "perfect" regulation.

In addition to these static costs to and gains from regulation, there are two dynamic costs of regulation: the costs imposed by new regulations as

they alter future expectations and the costs imposed by the general inflex-
ibility of regulations once imposed. Consider that current investments are
induced by expected future returns. Where subsequent regulations alter
investment expectations, immobile investments in capital and labor become
unemployed. This unemployment represents an additional opportunity cost
that must be charged against regulatory gains. Furthermore, regulations are
often set at fixed physical standards, such as the number of parts of dis-
solved solids per million parts of potable water or a maximum time period
for and minimum level of acceptable regeneration following timber harvest. These are levels that our political system finds difficult to adjust in
order to accommodate changes in both technology and relative social valuation over time. Such changes suggest that initial expectations of gains
from regulation may not continue unaltered over time. Accordingly, expected future gains should be adjusted for anticipated future changes in
taste and technology. Of course, the empirical problem lies in *ex ante* estimation of these intertemporal adjustments. Perhaps, the best we can hope
for is flexible attitudes toward given regulations. (And herein lies the explanation behind proposals for sliding regulations that encourage flexibility
and sunshine laws that put temporal limits on regulations and regulating
agencies.)

Thus, the summary rule for regulation designed to make optimal corrections for market failure sets the level of market intervention such that
expected incremental social gains from regulation, including nonmarket
gains, properly discounted, equal incremental production losses, including
nonmarket losses, plus incremental costs due to dynamic changes in tastes
and technology, plus regulatory transactions costs, all properly discounted.

The optimality criteria for distribution- and stabilization-justified regulations are less clear. Economists feel that they are unable to comment
scientifically on distribution. They can report the distributive impact of a
regulation; that is, who pays and who benefits. Furthermore, if we make
the reasonable assumption that our society prefers a more-rather-than-less
egalitarian distribution of income, then we can reject distributive arguments for regulations that return more benefits to higher- than to lower-
income populations. Similarly, we can query arguments for distributive
benefits accruing to those who are well employed and receiving income well
above some accepted poverty level.

Reference to Figure 1.1 also describes certain distributive impacts. Recall the example of timber production causing downstream sediment deposition, a negative externality. Public market intervention shifts the supply
from S to S'. Consumers of timber (i.e., sawmills) lose a value equal to
p_2bap_1, producers of timber (forest landowners) lose p_1acp_3, and the regulating authority or other institution providing means to satisfy the regulation and to correct the externality gains p_2bcp_3 from the transfer. Consider

the case where roadbuilding and tree planting contractors receive the amount p_2bcp_3 to prevent the sediment flow. Distributive arguments might be made for the regulation if these contractors are poorer, according to some acceptable measure, than the sawmill operators and forest landowners from whom they receive the transfer. Even then, we might not choose to redistribute to the contractors, if their well-being exceeds some minimum social standard.

The optimal level of stability is also uncertain. Stabilizing regulations reduce economic fluctuations but only at a cost in terms of forgone regional product (or allocative gains). Dividing economic cycles into peaks and troughs, an acceptable stabilizing regulation, therefore, restricts the cyclical troughs of employment, prices, and production more than enough to offset the combination of its decreasing allocative impact on cyclical peaks plus its transaction costs.

Figure 1.2 provides a graphic description of the impact of a stabilization policy. In this case, instability is due to stochastic variations in supply and there is no net long-term allocative loss other than (unidentified) transactions costs. The market clearing price-quantity combinations vary between p_1, q_1 and p_2, q_2 with each describing the market half of the time. After stabilization p_s, q_s describes the market all the time. Consumers suffer a net loss from stabilization equal to $[A + B - (C + D + G)]/2$. Producers obtain a net gain equal to $[(C + D - F) + (D + E - A)]/2$. It can easily be shown that producer gains exceed consumer losses; therefore, overlooking transactions costs, society as a whole obtains net gains from stability.[4] Instability due to variation in demand is analogous, except that consumers gain and producers lose. In both cases (supply and demand variations), there are net social gains from stability if the costs of administering the stabilizing mechanism are sufficiently low.

Empirical tests of stabilizing interventions may be difficult, because they rely on projections of economic cycles, both with and without the regulation. We may have to be satisfied with simply observing whether prices and quantities have been unusually unstable for forestry in comparison with its competitors.

(The rule for stabilizing interventions may have to be modified in exceptional cases to include the concept of intergenerational equity. Intergenerational equity requires that the troughs of certain cycles not dip below some minimum level. Applications of intergenerational equity usually refer to specific resources that may be abundant now but that may not be abundant at some moment in the future. Resources such as potentially endangered species provide an example.)

Empirical literature suggesting even the direction (that is, more or less) of optimal intervention in forest and rangeland markets has been sparse. Indeed, that is one of our reasons for this research and this book. What

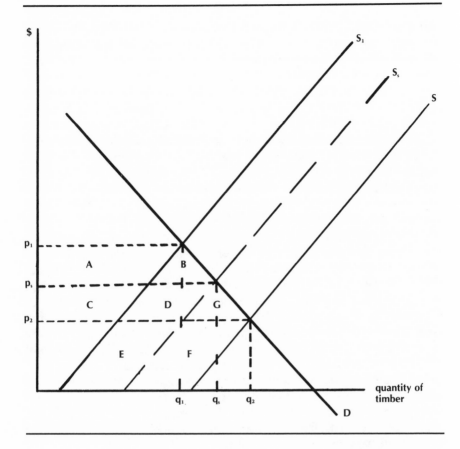

Figure 1.2. Stabilizing intervention.

literature exists tends to focus on allocative intervention — and there is considerable disagreement within it. Johnson (1983) argues that, rather than compensating for a lack of market efficiency, regulations that dictate forestland use and timber harvest strategies to the private landowner work against allocative efficiency. He attributes this to the fact that these regulations are designed and endorsed by a primarily urban public, whose interest in forests as timber producers is overshadowed by its interest in the recreational and aesthetic value of forested areas (an unproved hypothesis itself). Johnson's observation of corporate stock prices over time suggests to him that the passage of various state forest practice acts caused the value of private timber holdings to decline. Of course, Johnson's observation of correlation is no proof of causation. Furthermore, there is no evidence that such a decline is not optimal and that the state forest practice acts do not, in fact, protect more important nonmarket forest values that compete with timber production. Indeed, Vaux (1983) examines the net financial impacts of various state of California interventions in private timber production. His observations are based on a wealth of experience but admittedly weak data and casual empiricism. Vaux concludes that "the potential net economic gain to all sectors of the California economy is clearly far in excess of the costs." Others (e.g., Gould 1975) simply argue that not enough is done to preserve or to provide those nonmarket amenities associated with forested lands. They prefer, instead, increased regulation and subsidization.

In sum, there are many public programs assisting private forest landowners that may be justified partially or wholly on the basis of nonmarket benefits.[5] There is, however, virtually no empirical evidence, of their economic impacts or their efficacy in providing an optimal mix of both timber and nonmarket forest resource services.

The empirical literature on the stabilization and distribution justifications for market intervention is, to our knowledge, composed entirely of two articles by Wiseman and Sedjo (1981, 1983) and one by Gallagher (1980). Wiseman and Sedjo examine supply and demand functions for logs and lumber and observe the price and social welfare impacts associated with shifts in these functions due to the imposition of log export restrictions. They find the lumber price impact small both absolutely and relative to the log price impact. They also find net social welfare losses but local welfare gains to producers of export logs and processors of lumber. Gallagher's analysis and results are similar. The Gallagher and the Wiseman and Sedjo analyses are wholly consistent with both our objective in this volume and our analytical approach described by Figure 1.1. It is our contention only that there are both too few analyses of this sort and none for most of the important forest policy issues of our times.

A TAXONOMY OF MARKET INTERVENTION

With this background we can turn our attention to the regulations of forests and rangelands themselves. They provide a broad topic, including both renewable and nonrenewable resource products like timber and minerals, and services like recreation. An exhaustive discussion of all current and potential natural resource regulations would be tedious and repetitive as the analytical and policy characteristics of one regulation are repeated again and again for the same and other resources in similar situations. Alternatively, we might propose a taxonomy of market intervention and then closely examine detailed cases within each taxonomic class. Ideally, the chosen cases would be symptomatic of other regulatory policies within the taxonomic class and, therefore, demonstrative of the class as a whole.

One such classification might divide regulations as they modify market resource management decisions for purposes of allocation, distribution, or stabilization and as they are directed at either supply or demand for the basic in situ resource. Each regulation may have other, even more important, impacts, but all regulations share in their common reference to demand or supply of the in situ resource; that is, their impacts on its equilibrium price–quantity relationship; and their implications to the welfare of consumers and producers of the resource and suppliers of other productive inputs. Thus we have a 2 × 3 matrix with six classes of regulations (Table 1.1).

Table 1.1. Six classes of regulations

	Allocation	Distribution	Stabilization
Demand	x	x	x
Supply	x	x	x

This classification includes the bulk of what we normally consider regulation of private markets. For example, the Endangered Species Act, which responds to nonmarket demands (or the allocative justification), and state forest practice acts, which also respond to various perceived market failures, make the production of a given volume of timber more expensive, thereby affecting its supply. Restrictions on timber roads and bridge culverts imposed because of the nonmarket potential for downstream sediment deposition similarly raise costs, thereby affecting supply. Minimum wage and occupational health and safety requirements for millworkers raise processing costs, thereby decreasing the derived demand for the basic resource, sawtimber or pulpwood.

On the other hand, this classification is not wholly satisfactory. It too narrowly characterizes many specific regulations that are justified on multiple grounds. For example, price reporting may keep producers better informed, thereby causing them to sell timber when they know prices are high and to withhold timber when prices are low. This is a stabilization argument, but a distributive argument supplements it because the producers who benefit most are small private growers of timber. Large operations have the means to keep themselves better informed of the market. Occasionally, nonindustrial private forest incentives, another example, are justified on all three grounds: allocation because of a perceived inability of the market to encourage investment in timber production; distribution because the recipients of the incentive payments are generally smaller and presumably poorer landowners; and stabilization because the physical result of the incentives may be to smooth out long-term flows of timber production.

Table 1.2 shows the impact of a further sample of regulations on forest and rangeland management according to their justifications as we understand them.

Table 1.2. Regulations affecting rural natural resources by justifications for market intervention

Impact on in situ resource	Allocation	Distribution	Stabilization
Demand	Building codes Jones Act	Occupational safety and health restrictions in processing mills Minimum wage requirements in processing mills	Macroeconomic stabilization policies affecting basic resources Jones Act
Supply	Herbicide use restrictions State forest practice acts Nonindustrial private forest production incentives Acid rain restrictions Forest protection (fire and insect) assistance	Price reporting Nonindustrial private forest production incentives	Stockpiling Nonindustrial private forest production incentives Price reporting
Public ownership	Multiple-use public land management Harvest restrictions on clearcutting National Park Service Fish and Wildlife Service Wilderness protection Endangered species protection BLM range improvements Recreation costs	Small business set aside of public timber sales 16th section lands supporting state schools Youth and Young Adult Conservation Corps	Community stability – U.S. Forest Service Sustained yield management
Taxation	Favorable taxation of agricultural and forestland as green space Favorable capital gains taxation Depletion allowances	Inheritance taxes Payments in-lieu-of-taxes (payments to counties for roads and schools from public timber sale receipts)	Property taxes on timberland rather than less regularly occuring severance and yield taxes

Space in this one volume precludes an exhaustive review of all regulations pertaining to the management of forests and rangelands. Furthermore, we have seen that our taxonomy is not a fully satisfactory guide for choosing illustrative regulations for discussion. Therefore, we choose, for the body of our book, illustrative regulations designed to satisfy each cell in our taxonomic system, while anticipating that, due to overlap, the total number of regulations to be examined will be fewer than the six cells. We also attempt to constrain our choice by the dual criteria of current policy importance and analytical interest.

The result of our choice is the remainder of this book. Chapter 2, the first empirical chapter, addresses state forest practice acts. These acts generally reflect either of two moments in our history. Some state forest practice acts developed out of a concern for timber supply, particularly the failure of private timber landowners or market signals to reflect anticipated future supply shortfalls. This is a perceived market failure problem. Other state forest practice acts are a development of the last fifteen years of environmental concerns. These are designed to overcome water quality and deforestation concerns emanating from unattractive timber harvest practices, another market failure problem. Forest practice acts vary from state to state but eighteen states have such laws, and when industrial foresters object to government regulation these laws are what they generally have in mind. Chapter 3 features federal programs designed to provide incentives for nonindustrial private forest landowners to grow and harvest timber. These programs, or their predecessors, represent the longest history of public interventions in private timber markets. They are also the most recognizable part of the important current question regarding federal assistance to state and private forestry.

Chapter 4 addresses the question of price stability. No current public program is designed to stabilize timber prices, but one argument for prospective price reporting services is that timber prices are more volatile than the prices of most other basic resources. Perhaps, more complete price information will cause a reduction in instability. (Another argument is that nonindustrial private landowners suffer from poor market information more than other landowners and that public price reporting services help correct this distributive imbalance.)

The next two chapters feature demand impacts. Minimum wage and occupational health and safety requirements restricting mill operations are the subject of Chapter 5. These regulations may have positive distributive impacts; but when they constrain the choices of mill managers, then they also have a negative impact on mill profitability and productivity levels. Decreases in mill output imply decreases in demand for mill inputs, including inputs like sawlogs and pulpwood. The Jones Act is the subject of

Chapter 6. It restricts shipping between American ports to more expensive American built, owned, and operated vessels, thereby encouraging the maintenance of a large merchant fleet thought necessary for national security (a nonmarket value). One of its impacts is to make coastal Canadian lumber producers, who do not have to abide by the Jones Act, relatively better competitors in the domestic U.S. market.

Our effort would be incomplete, however, if we stopped here. Public ownership and nonneutral taxation are two special forms of public intervention, whose impacts may outweigh the impacts of all other regulations combined. It is not our intent to feature public ownership and nonneutral taxation, but we cannot disregard their importance. Therefore, we have included two survey chapters, one reviewing various programs departing from market provision of goods and services originating from the *public lands,* the other reviewing two important *tax* impacts on forest and range management.

These two special forms of market intervention possess the same fundamental economic justifications—allocation, distribution, and stabilization—as the previous regulations. However, the managers of publicly owned resources—national forests, national parks, national resource lands (BLM), and various state lands—are in a position to affect only the supply and not the demand of resources from these lands. Furthermore, allocation is arguably the only justification for public resource ownership, with distribution and stabilization being the responsibility of other agencies. Nevertheless, we observe public land management agencies using the distribution and stabilization arguments as justification for some of their production activities. Therefore, the entire second (supply) row of our classification matrix is relevant for an examination of public ownership. Similarly, we find nonneutrality in tax law justified on allocational, distributive, and stabilization grounds. The final two rows of Table 1.2 identify some of the relevant public ownership and tax adjustments.

We will find some cases where there is a paucity of basic empirical research providing solid insight—regardless of current public policies that implicitly presume such knowledge. This is true notably for distributive questions, where we find several public programs designed to assist small, and presumably poor, landowners, but no real evidence as to who the poor are or where they reside. In these cases, it is incumbent upon us to inquire into empirical characteristics identifying the relative wealth of rural resource-based populations before drawing conclusions regarding the success of specific public programs. By itself, such inquiry may suggest new programs for previously untargeted recipients. It may also identify old programs with inappropriate (nonpoor) target populations.

Expectations

A final chapter summarizes our results from previous chapters and draws conclusions and policy implications. We attempt to comment on each regulation and to relate it to others in its taxonomic class. We expect difficulties with the empirical evaluations. A paucity of data forces some of our observations to be imprecise, regardless of current public policies that may implicitly presume better knowledge. Neither the optimal regulation nor a complete comparison of benefits and costs can be found for each existing regulation. We can always draw conclusions, however, about the cost of a given regulation and, therefore, the minimum social benefit necessary to justify it. Even this level of information is sufficient to focus reasonable choice among policy alternatives. We can also reject outright some regulations as not accomplishing their intended purposes, and we may be able to suggest more effective or more direct ways to accomplish the purposes of other regulations. We can also determine which regulations have a measurable impact on the market for the in situ resource, stumpage. Finally, when we are through, we will have examined enough regulations to suggest conclusions about whether public intervention in forest and rangeland management is a significant deterrent to growth in that sector. We will also have used enough different tools of economic analysis to have provided a sort of methodological survey and guide useful for further evaluation of natural resource regulations by others interested in these issues.

In brief, we expect to reject some regulations as too costly or as not accomplishing their objectives, to accept some others, and to recommend variations or wholly new regulations in still other cases. Our alternatives often will not be between regulation or no regulation or perfect regulation, rather they will be among regulations of varying flexibility managed at alternative levels of government. We intend for our conclusions to suggest general orders of magnitude, pervasive costs, and methods for further analysis for various natural resource regulation problems.

Notes

1. Libecap and Johnson (1978) and Berck (1978) challenge the famine arguments empirically. They find that private rates of return in timber management and harvest were similar to rates of return for the rest of the economy; therefore, there is no evidence of underinvestment in timber production. Of course, we have observed no timber famine. Hyde (1981) provides the historical context for the famine arguments of nineteenth century professional foresters.

2. They may prefer to live in a "disadvantaged" region because, in their judgements, the environmental amenities of the region, for example, more than compensate for the lower income. Stated another way, per capita money income is not a sufficient measure of economic well being, and economic growth and growth in social welfare may not be closely linked. Power (1980) tests these hypotheses empirically, attempting to correlate regional wage differentials with measures of the quality of life. He finds that wage differentials of 5–35 percent are insufficient to induce mobile workers into industrial urban regions. This should not surprise us. Consider that, in spite of lower wages in Appalachia, rural Montana, or Michigan's Upper Peninsula, there is great regional pride and preference to remain in the region. There may even be net in-migration even though better paying jobs exist elsewhere.

3. The same general calculations can be made for either parallel shifts in the supply functions or for nonlinear functions.

4. $A + B < C + D + G$, by inspection. Therefore, consumer gains are negative. $C + D > A$ and $D + E > F$; therefore, producer gains, which are equal to $[(C + D - F) + (D + E - A)]/2$, are positive. Net social gains, which are the sum of consumer and producer gains, are positive.

Proof:
$$[A + B - (C + D + G)]/2 + [(C + D - F)$$
$$+ (D + E - A)]/2 > 0$$
$$(C + D - F) + (D + E - A) > (A + B) - (C + D + G)$$
$$2C + 3D + E + G > 2A + B + F$$
$$E = F, D > B,; (C + D + G/2) > A \text{ by inspection} \qquad \text{(Q.E.D.)}.$$

Therefore, producer gains exceed consumer losses, and society's net gain is positive. Turnovsky (1978) proves this for the more general case, where supply and demand functions may not be linear.

5. Consider, for example, the various state forest practice acts and many of the State and Private Forestry programs of the U.S. Forest Service: forest insect and disease management, urban forestry assistance, Dutch elm disease demonstration, rural fire prevention and control, river basin surveys, watershed planning, etc.

 References

Bender, Bruce, and Steven Shwiff. 1982. The appropriation of rents by boomtown governments. *Economic Inquiry* 20(1):84–103.

Berck, Peter. 1978. The economics of timber. *Bell Journal of Economics* 9(2):147–62.

Bryant, W. K., et al. 1981. Economics of rural poverty. In *A survey of the agricultural economics literature,* vol. III, ed. L. R. Martin. pp. 3–152. Minneapolis: University of Minnesota.

Clepper, Henry. 1971. *Professional forestry in the United States.* Baltimore: Johns Hopkins University Press.

Forest credit in the United States. 1958. Washington, D.C.: Resources for the Future.

Gallagher, Paul. 1980. *An analysis of the softwood log trade between the United States and Japan.* St. Paul: University of Minnesota Agricultural Experiment Station Technical Bulletin 330. Forestry Series No. 34.

Gould, Ernest M. 1975. The search for parity. *Journal of Forestry* 73(4):217–21.

Haigh, John A., and John V. Krutilla. 1980. Clarifying policy directives; a case of national forest management. *Policy Analysis* 6(4):409–39.

Haveman, Robert H. 1972. *The economic performance of public investments.* Baltimore: Johns Hopkins University Press.

Haveman, Robert H., and John V. Krutilla. 1968. *Unemployment, idle capacity, and the evaluation of public expenditures.* Baltimore: Johns Hopkins University Press.

Herendeen, John B. 1966. Farm programs and income distribution in agriculture by economic class of farm and by area. In *Income distribution analysis with special reference to problems of rural people,* ed. W. B. Black et al. Raleigh: North Carolina State University, AP1 Series 23:223–47.

Hibbard, Benjamin H. 1965. *A history of the public land policies.* Madison: University of Wisconsin Press.

Hyde, William F. 1981. Volume or value maximization in forestry. *Annals of Regional Science* 15(2):55–71.

Johnson, M. Bruce. 1983. Regulation of private forestlands: The taking issue. In *Government interventions, social needs, and the management of U.S. forests,* ed. R. Sedjo. Washington, D.C.: Resources for the Future.

Krutilla, John V., and Otto Eckstein. 1958. *Multiple purpose river development,* Chapter 1. Baltimore: Johns Hopkins University Press.

Krutilla, John V., and Anthony C. Fisher, with Richard E. Rice. 1978. *Economic and fiscal impacts of coal development.* Baltimore: Johns Hopkins University Press.

LeMaster, Dennis A. 1975. Focus on the issues: A comment on the Forest Services' alternative goals. *Journal of Forestry* 72(7):398–435.

Libecap, Gary A., and Ronald N. Johnson. 1978. Property rights, nineteenth century federal timber policy and the conservation movement. *Journal of Economic History* 39(1):129–42.

Posner, Richard A. 1974. Theories of economic regulation. *Bell Journal of Economics* 5(2):335–58.

Power, Thomas. 1980. *The economic value of the quality of life.* Boulder, Colo.: Westview.

Schultz, Theodore W. 1980. *Distortions of agricultural incentives.* Bloomington: Indiana University Press.

Sedjo, Roger A., and A. Clark Wiseman. 1983. The effectiveness of an export restriction on logs. *American Journal of Agricultural Economics* 65(1): 113–16.

Stigler, George J. 1971. The theory of economic regulation. *Bell Journal of Economics* 2(1):3–21.

Turnovsky, Stephen J. 1978. The distribution of welfare gains from price stabilization: A survey of some theoretical issues. In *Stabilizing world commodity markets,* ed. F. G. Adams and S. A. Klein. Lexington, Mass.: Lexington Books.

Vaux, Henry J. 1983. State interventions on private forests in California. In *Government interventions, social needs, and the management of U.S. forest,* ed. R. Sedjo. Washington, D.C.: Resources for the Future.

Wiseman, A. Clark, and Roger A. Sedjo. 1981. Effects of an export embargo on related goods: Logs and lumber. *American Journal of Agricultural Economics* 63(3):424–29.

CHAPTER 2

State Forest
Practice Acts

State forest practice acts (SFPAs) are the best known and most frequently identified public regulations of private forestlands. Eighteen states presently enforce them and many other states have considered them. Their general impact is a requirement for private landowners to maintain a minimum level of standing timber inventory, a requirement that usually comes in the form of a rule about either regeneration or postharvest stocking density.

There have been two historical periods of interest in SFPAs. The older laws reflect the concern in the 1930s and 1940s for an anticipated timber famine. In terms of our Chapter 1 taxonomy, this is the same as a perceived failure of market prices to reflect anticipated future timber scarcity and, thereby, to induce sufficient current investment in timber. Required regeneration and stocking levels are a means of providing current inventories and guaranteeing future supplies; therefore, they are a means of limiting future scarcity. We can examine the empirical impact of such requirements by contrasting inventories in two adjacent states, both of which have similar forestry conditions but only one of which has a forest practice act.

The greater discussion today focuses on the SFPAs of the 1970s. These are a response to environmental concerns. They reflect public recognition of the nonmarket values generated by forests and the potential for environmental degradation caused by timber harvesting. These, too, are market failure or externality arguments. The more recent SFPAs are more difficult to examine, because the short time since their origin means that their impacts on standing inventories, as yet, are difficult to measure in the field. Our alternative approach is to examine the general determinants of private forestry investment with the intent of hypothesizing which legal approaches have the more cost-effective impacts on regeneration and stocking, therefore which foci are most meaningful for these environmentally justified SFPAs.

The chapter itself begins with a historical review of the various state forest practice acts and continues with a conceptual model of their impacts.[1] Our empirical assessment of the older laws contrasts Virginia, which has had a forest practice act since 1950, with North Carolina, which never has had one. We observe that a stocking level requirement in Virginia has not succeeded in creating a significant difference between the forests of the two states. Our empirical assessment continues with data from Oregon and Washington, states with more recent forest practice acts, (1971 and 1974, respectively). We observe that their cost-effective focus is inconsistent with early environmentalist focus on industrial forestlands.

Historical Review

The cut-and-get-out experience of the Great Lakes states and their forest industries in the 1880s fostered continuing concern over the effects of deforestation and the possibility of a timber famine in the United States.[2] By the early 1900s, leaders of the U.S. Forest Service were calling for restrictions on cutting practices on private lands. At the same time, the Society of American Foresters formed a committee to recommend ways of preventing widespread deforestation. Like the Forest Service, the committee advocated strict regulation of private forestry practices. The culmination of these concerns was a bill submitted in Congress promoting national regulation of private forestry practices. The forest industry was able to block this bill, however, and it was replaced by the compromise Clarke-McNary Act of 1924, which provides for federal-state cooperation in forestry extension, fire prevention, and tree planting but which omits any mention of private forestry regulation.

Earle Clapp became Chief of the Forest Service in 1939. He was a strong advocate of regulation and his vigorous efforts prompted congressional action. The forest industry, in turn, increased its counteremphasis on the states as the appropriate regulatory authorities. Sixteen states passed forest practice acts by 1950 (Table 2.1). Much of this early state legislation provides for prompt establishment of a minimum number of desirable trees on the harvested areas. Cutting regulations are infrequent. Most acts prescribe minimum cutting diameters or a minimum number of seed trees to be left per acre. Seed tree requirements may specify species, size, number, and the period over which the seed trees must remain uncut. The penalties for noncompliance, however, are not severe under most of these acts (Ellefson & Cubbage 1980). Testing the effectiveness of these early SFPAs in inducing greater regeneration and higher levels of standing inventory is the objective of our empirical comparison of Virginia with North Carolina.

Table 2.1. States with forest practice laws

Early laws (pre-1950)	Revisions or new laws
1903 Nevada	1969 Maine[a]
1922 Louisiana[a]	1971 Nevada[a]
1937 Idaho	1971 Oregon[a]
1939 New Mexico[a]	1973 California[a]
1941 Oregon	1974 Washington[a]
1943 Florida[a]	1974 Idaho[a]
1943 Massachusetts	1977 Maryland[a]
1943 Minnesota	1978 Alaska[a]
1944 Mississippi[a]	1982 Massachusetts[a]
1945 California	
1945 Missouri[a]	
1945 Vermont[a]	
1945 Washington	
1946 New York[a]	
1949 New Hampshire[a]	
1950 Virginia[a]	

[a]Law presently in force.

The interest in regulation deteriorated by 1950 due to the combination of the strength of the forest industry, the retirement of the Forest Service personnel who were the strongest advocates for regulation, and no further evidence of a need for regulation. There were no new SFPAs for approximately twenty years.

The early 1970s witnessed a dramatic increase in environmental concerns and forest regulation again became a topic of public debate. Environmentalists opposed clearcutting as an unaesthetic harvest practice. At the same time, both the Federal Water Pollution Control Acts of 1972 and 1977 and the Environmental Protection Agency called on timber-producing states to enact legislation to control the deleterious impacts on water quality caused by extensive logging roads and both pesticide and fertilizer applications on private forestlands.

There are nine revised or new SFPAs, six in western states. The laws in California, Oregon, and Washington, all major timber-producing states, have specific provisions worth noting. The laws in all three states establish forest practice boards to recommend, administer, and enforce environmentally sensitive forestry activities on private lands. The laws in California and Oregon permit forest practices to vary across independently administered geographic regions. The Washington law, on the other hand, varies statewide requirements according to the category in which a potentially harmful forest practice fits. These approaches provide the background for one of our empirical inquiries.

The revised laws in these three states and in Nevada and Idaho tighten restrictions on harvesting and reforestation. These laws still require a specific number of seedlings or seed trees per acre and they also restrict activities like harvesting close to streams, skidding, slash disposal, and logging road construction. The new laws often require submission of a harvest plan to the state forestry agency and, in all cases, provide for more substantial penalties and more rigorous enforcement policies than the earlier laws.

The various SFPAs have generated debate over both the advisability of regulation and the most effective form of regulation. Clearly, regulation of any form is inadvisable if its administration and enforcement costs outweigh its environmental and timber production benefits. Ellefson (1974), LeMaster (1975), and Weible (1980) point to an additional perverse effect of SFPAs: These regulations increase timber production costs, thereby raising the offer price for timber and causing previously marginally profitable operations to close.

Even if SFPAs are advisable, Nelson (1976) and Nyland (1978) question whether other measures are more likely to have the desired impacts on private harvest and reforestation practices. The American Forestry Association (1976) suggests that other public policy tools, such as voluntary guidelines, extension forestry, subsidies (like the Forestry Incentives Program), and tax incentives (like preferential capital gains treatment of timber) are more effective. The heart of these arguments lies in the notion that restrictive regulations create incentives to avoid compliance. Methods such as incentive payments and tax advantages, it is argued, avoid this problem by inducing reforestation through the market mechanism.[3] Testing the effectiveness of existing laws in inducing higher levels of standing inventory and greater regeneration is the objective of our empirical comparisons.

Conceptual Model

This section introduces the conceptual model underlying our analyses of both the earlier and the more recent SFPAs. We first consider the basic market conditions for stumpage, then introduce the anticipated negative externality caused by timber harvesting. Social and market adjustment for this externality—either a perceived market failure to anticipate a future timber supply shortfall in the case of the older laws or an aesthetic or environmental value damaged in the harvest process in the case of the more recent laws—is the purpose of these laws. The market adjustment shows us the impact of such laws on individual timber producers and their production functions.

Figure 2.1, which corresponds closely to Figure 1.1, describes the stumpage market. The function D describes the demand for stumpage and the function S describes aggregate production costs and supply. In the absence of public intervention, the market clears at q_1 Mbf of stumpage and price p_1 per Mbf. Timber harvests, however, create negative social values, or externalities, that the market fails to reflect. Adding the social costs of these externalities to the private production costs raises the function describing full social opportunity costs. Policymakers can correct this market imperfection by taxing either producers or consumers of stumpage an amount equal to the difference between the two functions S and S'. The result is a new market equilibrium at the lower quantity q_2 and higher stumpage price p_2. The lower harvest level also means less environmental destruction, reduced impact on aesthetic values, and a larger standing timber inventory remaining to satisfy future demand.

Alternately, policymakers might introduce a harvest restriction that, like a tax, is an imposition on production. This is the case of state forest practice acts. The restriction is the required minimum stocking or regeneration level. If effective, it can only raise production costs and decrease forest landowners' willingness to produce.

Figure 2.1 reflects aggregate production. To add further to our understanding of the production restriction, we can consider its impact on the generalized case of an individual timber landowner with a fixed area of forestland in one uniform productivity class. We begin with the assumption of profit-maximizing behavior and trace the impact through the landowner's production function. The correct form of this expression involves complex discounting terms well known in the forestry literature (e.g., Hyde 1980, Chapter 3). We can simplify by abstracting from these terms and this form, yet without altering our basic point regarding the impact of a required minimum stocking or regeneration level. That is, the stocking or

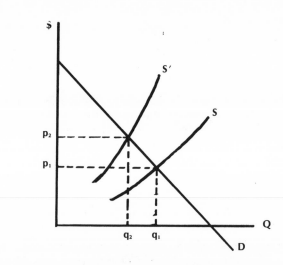

Figure 2.1. The timber market in the presence of an externality.

regeneration constraint exists regardless of the optimal timing of any harvest.

The problem facing the individual producer in a competitive market is to maximize

$$\pi = pQ(K,L) - rK - wL \tag{2.1}$$

subject to $\overline{K} - K \geq 0$, where Q, K, and L denote quantities of stumpage, capital (in the form of standing timber), and labor, and p, r, and w are their respective prices. Our timber landowner is a price taker with respect to the stumpage market at the expected time of harvest. $\overline{K}$ refers to the fixed amount of capital (minimum standing timber inventory) the law constrains the landowner to maintain.

Expressing equation (2.1) in a Lagrangian form and differentiating with respect to K, L, and the Lagrangian multiplier λ yields the first order conditions:

$$\frac{\delta\pi}{\delta K} = p\frac{\delta Q}{\delta K} - r + \lambda = 0 \tag{2.2a}$$

$$\frac{\delta\pi}{\delta L} = p\frac{Q}{L} - w = 0 \tag{2.2b}$$

and

$$\frac{\delta\pi}{\delta\lambda} = K - \overline{K} = 0 \tag{2.2c}$$

Expression (2.2c) is an equality if the constraint is binding. Where it is binding, we can rearrange terms to obtain

$$p\frac{\delta Q}{\delta L} = w \tag{2.3a}$$

and

$$p\frac{\delta Q}{\delta K} = r - \lambda \tag{2.3b}$$

or

$$\frac{MP_K}{MP_L} = \frac{r - \lambda}{w} \tag{2.4}$$

where MP_K and MP_L refer to the marginal products of capital and labor, respectively. The Lagrangian multiplier λ is the shadow price of the capital constraint.

Figure 2.2 depicts this situation where the constraint is binding. The vertical axis measures the rate of return on investment in capital and r_0 is the rate of return on the next best investment. The horizontal axis measures investment in capital, which, in our case, is additional standing timber inventory. In the absence of an SFPA, the private timber landowner invests I_0, or until the value of the marginal product of capital, VMP_K, falls to r_0. The intention of the SFPA is to require the landowner to invest I_1 or until the social value of the marginal product of capital, $SVMP_K$, equals r_0.

The state forest practice act *intends* that λ, the difference between the private and social VMP_K, measures the cost to society of the harvest externality. This cost also equals the gain to society from preventing the externality. We have no true measure of the social gain, however, without knowledge of a social welfare function with an argument for the externality. We do know for sure that the difference between the social and private VMP_K is an imposition on the private timber producer in the form of legally required additional investment (increased standing timber inventory).

In the aggregate of many landowners and many acres, the SFPA may or may not be effective. If it has no impact on the investment in standing timber inventory, then the law is ineffective, λ is zero and the administration of the law is a real resource cost without any corresponding benefit. Apparently, either the law requires an investment that private landowners would make anyway or the law is not enforced. If, on the other hand, the law causes an increased investment in standing timber inventory, then the

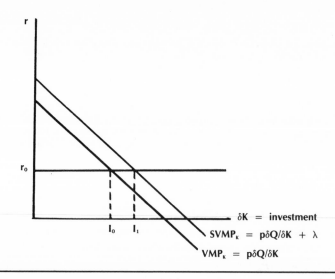

Figure 2.2. The return on capital.

costs to private landowners of holding the additional inventory plus the public agency administrative costs must be compared with the unknown social gain in order to determine the law's social efficiency.[4] Measuring the inventory cost of the law is the focus of our subsequent empirical inquiry.

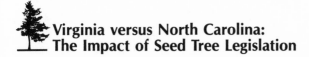# Virginia versus North Carolina:
The Impact of Seed Tree Legislation

Seed tree laws requiring landowners to leave a few mature trees as seed sources after timber harvests are common among the older state forest practice acts. Virginia passed a law of this type in 1950 and has enforced it ever since. The thirty-five year history of the law provides ample time for observations of its biological and economic impacts and, therefore, makes it attractive for statistical analysis.

The present Virginia law requires that

> Every landowner who cuts . . . for commercial purposes, timber from one acre of land on any acre on which loblolly pine (*Pinus taeda*), shortleaf pine (*Pinus echinata*), pond pine (*Pinus scrotina*), or white pine (*Pinus strobus*), singly or together, occur and constitute ten per- cent or more of the live trees on each acre or acres shall . . . reserve and leave uncut and uninjured not less that eight cone-bearing loblolly, shortleaf, pond or white pine trees fourteen inches or larger in diameter on each acre thus cut (Virginia Division of Forestry 1979).

The law goes on to stipulate that, "Such pine trees shall be left uncut for the purpose of reseeding the land and shall be healthy, windfirm, and of well developed crowns, evidencing seed bearing ability by the presence of cones in the crown." Pines left as seed trees "shall be the property of the land- owner but shall not be cut until at least three years have elapsed." The state forester may enforce these restrictions and violators are liable for fines up to $80 per acre.

Unlike Virginia, the neighboring state of North Carolina has never had any kind of forest practice act and has never required landowners to leave seed trees. Virginia and North Carolina are similar in topography, climate, species, and government administrative policies. Neither state has a large amount of publicly held forestland. Finally, the relevant data from the two states' forestlands are collected in a comparable manner and at a compara- ble time. Stumpage prices tend to be somewhat lower in Virginia but our econometric analysis can separate out that distinction. Virginia may also be different from North Carolina in that it has a state reforestation incentive program that, if effective, increases inventories on Virginia's private forestlands. The program is small, however, and its impact cannot be substantial. Thus, we can argue that North Carolina's forestlands are an approximate mimic of what Virginia's forestlands would look like without the latter's forest practice act. Contrasting timber investments in the two states permits an empirical measure of the effectiveness of Virginia's law.

ANALYSIS

We can test the hypothesis that the difference in forest investment between Virginia and North Carolina is a function of the Virginia forest practice act with observations of forest inventories per acre from 199 counties in both states after first removing explanatory variables other than the Virginia seed tree law. The anticipated difference in inventory is a function of biological and economic variables and a state dummy variable. Site productivity is the important biological variable. Stumpage price and the county property tax rate are the economic variables. The anticipated site productivity and stumpage price effects are positive because they raise the schedule for the value of the marginal product of capital. The anticipated tax effect is uncertain. Property taxes on standing timber increase the cost of holding the inventory and encourage its earlier harvest and, therefore, smaller inventories. On the other hand, tax administration varies from county to county (although all tax laws are set by the state). Therefore, local tax differences may mask the theoretical impact. Furthermore, forestland is notoriously poorly appraised relative to higher valued properties, a fact that may allow for unanticipated inventory increases.

Ownership behavior, too, may make a difference in the investment level. Public land inventories are generally greater than those on industry lands, which, in turn, are generally greater than those on nonindustrial private lands. The public lands are often managed for larger timber as well as for the nontimber values which may be consistent with mature forests. Nonindustrial private forest landowners may have comparative advantages elsewhere. Therefore, they tend to make the least investments in their forestlands and often harvest earlier than industrial landowners or public managers.[5]

DATA

The dependent variable is softwood inventory per acre of commercial forestland as reported in various resource bulletins published by the U.S. Forest Service's Southeastern Forest Experiment Station (Bechtold 1985; Knight and McClure 1978).[6] This is better than a measure of the total softwood and hardwood inventory per acre for two reasons. First, the purpose of Virginia's seed tree law is to increase the regeneration and stocking of relatively higher value softwood species and not lower value hardwood species. Second, poor quality hardwoods often grow naturally as unintended residuals on poorer quality lands.

The conceptual discussion argues for an independent variable measuring net investment or the change in capital or change in inventory—all of which are the same thing—in a known period. In our case, net investment equals timber growth minus removal minus mortality for the time period in question. Data expressing this measure are difficult to obtain.

We use standing timber, a stock variable, as a proxy for net investment, a flow variable, with the following justification. A renewable resource stock S at any time t is a series of n past net investments I. That is, $S_t = I_{t-n}(1 + r)^{t-n} + I_{t-n-1}(1 + r)^{t-n-1} + \ldots + I_t$, where r is the return on those investments. If this return is constant over time and n is sufficiently large, then $S_t/r = I$. Therefore, S is a constant multiple of I. As such, it can serve as proxy for I. An n of twenty-seven years, the time between imposition of the Virginia seed tree law and the 1977 Virginia forest inventory, is sufficiently large because twenty-seven years is approximately one full softwood timber rotation, or the minimum period for full reflection of the law's impact on the total softwood inventory.

This point is important. It means that there has been one full economic adjustment period. (A timber rotation is the "economic long run" in forestry.) Therefore, once we have adjusted for other economic and biological factors, the existence of an SFPA can explain an inventory difference. In particular, there is no time-related reason to expect that Virginia's and North Carolina's inventories would be of different age structures and, therefore, of different timber volumes.

The independent variables are the state dummy (NC = 0, VA = 1), site productivity, price, tax, and ownership. The Forest Service resource bulletins provide the numbers of acres in each of five potential biological productivity classes. County productivity indices, PI, derive from the formula

$$PI = 1/A \sum_i A_i M_i \qquad i = 1,2 \ldots 5$$

where A is acres and M is the midpoint of the productivity class.

Price data originate from Timber Mart-South (Norris 1977–1984). Timber Mart-South is a recent service that reports monthly stumpage prices for six regions in the two states. We average the regional prices for the seven-year period in order to restrict bias from short-term variation and assign the regional prices to each county in the region.

The tax data are countywide observations reported by the Virginia and North Carolina Departments of Taxation (1965–1975). Counties levy taxes on the assessed property value. This value is less than the appraised value and its share of appraised value may vary across counties. The tax rate itself varies over time as county appropriations vary. Therefore, we use the 1964–1974 average county tax divided by the assessed property value.

Ownership data also originate from the Forest Service resource bulletins. The ownership measures are public acreage and industrial acreage as a percent of all commercial forestland in the county. (Inclusion of a similar measure of nonindustrial private forestland, the third broad inventory category collected by the U.S. Forest Service, would create perfect collinearity. It is omitted for that reason.)

RESULTS

Table 2.2 records the variables, their acronyms, and expected signs. Table 2.3 shows the estimated coefficients for four variations on the empirical model. The terms below the coefficients are t statistics and the terms to the right of the coefficients are the summary equation statistics. The first equation is the full empirical model discussed throughout this section. The second, third, and fourth equations drop independent variables with insignificant coefficients from the first equation. The F statistics indicate that all four equations are significant at the .01 level and that the combined independent variables explain a significant amount of variation in the dependent variables. The relatively low R^2s, however, show that much variation remains unexplained. This could be because the model overlooks other biological variables or because it inadequately reflects the nonmarket production of nonindustrial private landowners (see Chapter 3).

The empirical findings rely on linear OLS techniques. The forestry sector is often modeled as log linear (e.g., Adams & Haynes 1980; Considine 1978; Wallace 1977) but a Box-Cox search for the best statistical fit strongly supports our use of a simple linear model (see Appendix 2A). The coastal plain regions of both states have larger proportions of softwood, larger shares of industrial lands, and higher productivity sites than the

Table 2.2. Identification of variables

Variable	Acronym	Expected sign VA/NC	Expected sign OR/WA
Volume per acre (public and private)	VOL		
Volume per acre (private only)	VOLP		
State dummy	SD	+	?
Productivity index	PI	+	+
Price	PR	+	+
Property tax	TX	?	?
Percentage industry owned	IND	−	−,+
Percentage publicly owned	PUB	+	+
Percentage hardwood	HW		−
Intercept	C	?	?

Table 2.3. Virginia–North Carolina results, total

LnVOL	Independent variables							Summary statistics			
	SD	PI	PR	TX	IND	PUB	C	F	R²	Degrees of freedom	Standard error of estimate
One	.0129 (.3968)	.0099 (6.4872)[b]	.0056 (6.6664)[b]	.1704 (.215)	−.0082 (−.5519)	.1199 (1.2809)	−.5172 (−4.4863)[b]	30.085[c]	.4685	192	.1768
Two	.0104 (.3461)	.0093 (6.4258)[b]	.0053 (8.2824)[b]	.0346 (.4481)	—	—	−.5782 (−5.5347)[b]	44.788[c]	.4649	194	.1767
Three	.0121 (.3731)	.0092 (6.4034)[b]	.0054 (6.5316)[b]	.0327 (.417)	−.2112 (−.1416)	—	−.579 (−5.52)[b]	35.653[c]	.4667	193	.1771
Four	.0123 (.4065)	.0099 (6.5139)[b]	.0056 (8.3236)[b]	.0177 (.2269)	—	.1203 (1.2909)[a]	−.5167 (−4.5078)[b]	36.287[c]	.4712	193	.1764

[a]Significant at .10 level.
[b]Significant at .05 level.
[c]Significant at .01 level.

piedmont or less accessible mountain regions. The coastal plain regions also support more mills. All this suggests better access from the forest to the mill in the coastal plain. These factors might also suggest that a larger share of harvests are clearcut than selectively harvested, and on shorter rotations, in the coastal plain. This, in turn, implies greater regional variation in standing inventory. Nevertheless, an ANOVA fails to detect heteroscedasticity in any of the four equations (see Appendix 2B). Therefore, GLS estimation procedures are unnecessary.

Turn now to the specific results for the four equations. Table 2.3 reveals that both the productivity index and the stumpage price have the expected positive influence on standing inventory and, therefore, on net investment in timber. Both are highly significant and remain so in all equations. Furthermore, their coefficients change little no matter which other variables are included.

The tax coefficient is positive but insignificant in all equations. We cannot rule out any hypothesis regarding its impact. It is possible that both tax administration and the appraisal of forestlands vary so greatly from county to county that there is no consistent property tax impact on standing inventory or net investment.

The coefficient on the industrial ownership share has the anticipated sign but is always insignificant. When the industrial ownership variable is dropped from equation four, then the coefficient on the public ownership share becomes significant. The public coefficient always has the anticipated positive sign. Taken together, this evidence suggests that the public–all private acreage split is important, but that the industrial–nonindustrial split among private landowners is not.[7]

The primary objective of this exercise is to estimate the value of the capital constraint, the λ in equation 2.1. Table 2.3 shows that, although the coefficient on the state dummy does have the right sign in all cases, in no case is this variable significant. (Indeed, the small positive coefficient, even if it were significant, might be due to Virginia's reforestation incentive program and not its forest practice act.) Therefore, we cannot reject the hypothesis that the Virginia seed tree law has no effect on restocking and reforestation. Virginia's landowners may avoid the capital constraint by leaving only the least valuable trees for regeneration. Where landowners cannot avoid the constraint, then the increased cost may cause the removal of marginal lands from active softwood timber production.

In sum, our statistical tests suggest confidence in the equations as a whole and in the predictive power of the important independent variables. The insignificance of the coefficient on the state dummy implies that there is no evidence that the law is effective. That is, the law may encourage no net addition whatsoever to standing timber inventory. Therefore, both the private costs for Virginia's timber landowners and the social gains from an additional inventory of seed trees are zero. This does not mean, however, that the Virginia law has no welfare effects. The state Division of Forestry estimates that it spends up to $150,000 per year ($0.01 per acre) on enforcement and administration of this seed tree law (Olinger 1985). To the extent that the law has no significant inventory effect, these resources can be spent more productively elsewhere.

Oregon and Washington: The Impact of Environmental Legislation

Recent environmental concerns have led to new, more vigorous, state forest practice acts. The most important and most controversial of these are in California, Oregon, and Washington. We might choose those in Oregon and Washington for statistical examination because of the proximity of the two states and the fundamental similarities in their topography, climate, species, and ownership patterns. Both new laws are complex and expensive in their administration and both are more severe in their enforcement than most of the older SFPAs. The 1971 Oregon law features minimum acceptable forest practices for several intrastate regions. The State Forester and State Forestry Board certify private timber operations and enforce regional practices with the threat of fines up to $1000, imprisonment for a year, or both. Annual administrative costs were $1.3 million (or $0.14 per acre) in 1980 (Wilson 1985).

The 1974 Washington law involves three state agencies, a Forest Practices Board, and the county governments.[8] It regulates forest practices similar to those regulated in Oregon, but across four environmental and administrative land classes and five water quality classes. Violation of the law can subject Washington landowners to the same maximum penalties as in Oregon. The Washington administration and enforcement budget is high, approximately $1.5 million (or $0.17 per acre) in 1977 (Olson 1985).

The relatively short period of the existence of these laws suggests that results from statistical tests similar to those for Virginia and North Carolina cannot indicate either real or perceived differences between the Oregon and Washington laws. Rather, such tests reflect longer standing differences between the states. Nevertheless, these tests can be useful to our assessment of the more recent SFPAs. To the extent that they can display significant determinants of investment in timberland, then they can isolate cost-effective focal points for the administration and enforcement of these laws.

ANALYSIS AND DATA

Our Oregon–Washington analysis proceeds in much the same manner as the Virginia–North Carolina comparison. We search for the impact of various biological and economic variables on long-term timber investment, which is measured as total standing volume per acre. The public sector in Oregon and Washington is much larger than in North Carolina and Virginia. Furthermore, it is not generally thought to be as responsive to economic factors as the private sector and, finally, the new SFPAs do not pertain to it. Therefore, we consider a second set of regressions with standing private volume per acre as the dependent variable. The expected sign on the industry coefficient changes to positive for the second set of equations in anticipation that industrial managers prefer shorter rotations, therefore less inventory, than public land managers, but industrial managers invest more, therefore hold greater inventories, than nonindustrial private landowners.

We remove the property tax rate as an independent variable because the tax situation in Oregon and Washington is even more complex than in North Carolina and Virginia and because preliminary regressions show it to have no more significance than it did in the earlier case. Finally, we introduce hardwood acreage as an independent variable rather than removing hardwood volume from the dependent variable as in the North Carolina–Virginia case. The Oregon and Washington hardwood acreage is more distinct and the species are of less economic importance than in North Carolina and Virginia. Hardwood volume per acre in Oregon and Washington is generally less than softwood volume per acre. Therefore, the expected sign on the hardwood coefficient is negative.

The data sources are various Forest Service resource bulletins for Oregon and Washington as they report standing inventory and its allocation among ownerships, species types, and site productivity classes for each of seventy counties in the two states (Bassett & Oswald 1981a; 1981b; 1982; 1983; Farrenkopf 1982; Gedney 1982). We calculate the site productivity index as earlier. Price data originate from public sales of timber from U.S. Forest Service lands (Ruderman 1983).

RESULTS

Table 2.2 records the variables, their acronyms and expected signs. Tables 2.4 and 2.5 show the regression results for the total volume per acre and private volume per acre, respectively.

The Box-Cox test strongly favors a log linear form for the regressions of total volume per acre.[9] The F and R^2 statistics indicate that all three equations are significant at the .01 percent level and that the combined independent variables explain over 90 percent of all variation in the dependent variables. The signs on all coefficients satisfy our expectations with one notable exception, the insignificant negative sign on stumpage price. Perhaps, this negative price coefficient is due to the large influence of public land (58 percent of all forestlands). These lands are generally

Table 2.4. Washington–Oregon results, total

			Independent variables					Summary statistics		
LnVOL	SD	LnPI	LnPR	LnIND	LnPUB	C	F	R^2	Degrees of freedom	Standard error of estimate
One	.0313 (.422)	1.3324 (22.367)[b]	.013 (−.6415)	−.0606 (−2.0148)[b]	.0629 (1.4203)[a]	−4.5054 (−5.2089)[b]	201.145[c]	.9355	64	.24585
Two	.0386 (.5958)	1.327 (24.016)[b]	−.798 (−.4519)	—	.1411 (3.3423)[b]	−4.5719 (−6.3036)[b]	270.891[c]	.9399	65	.23726
Three	.0192 (.298)	1.3292 (23.211)[b]	−.0636 (−.3482)	−.079 (−2.6935)[b]	—	−4.8811 (−6.3081)[b]	256.124[c]	.9367	65	.2436

[a]Significant at .10 level.
[b]Significant at .05 level.
[c]Significant at .01 level.

Table 2.5. Washington–Oregon results, private

			Independent variables					Summary statistics		
LnVOL	SD	PI	PR	IND	HW	C	F	R^2	Degrees of freedom	Standard error of estimate
One	.4076 (2.2392)[b]	.0153 (3.8079)[b]	.0132 (3.0624)[b]	.9485 (2.5081)[b]	−.0766 (−1.6886)[b]	−.7722 (−2.0372)[b]	62.011[c]	.8155	64	.4532
Two	.6304 (5.0808)[b]	.0101 (3.8517)[b]	.0117 (2.7281)[b]	.885 (2.3191)[b]	—	−.5004 (−1.4379)[a]	74.67[c]	.803	65	.4596

[a]Significant at .10 level.
[b]Significant at .05 level.
[c]Significant at .01 level.

thought to be unresponsive to price (see, for example, Adams & Haynes 1980).

The Box-Cox test is ambiguous regarding the form of the regressions of private volume per acre. A slightly smaller maximum likelihood recommends the linear form although linear and log linear forms obtain similar specifications. The F and R^2 statistics indicate that both equations are significant at the .01 percent level and that the combined independent variables explain over 80 percent of all variation in the dependent variables. The signs on all coefficients, including price, confirm our expectations and are highly significant. Indeed, these equations display better fits than the Virginia–North Carolina equations. Perhaps this is because the less predictable nonindustrial share of all private lands is smaller in Oregon–Washington (41 percent) than in Virginia–North Carolina (over 65 percent). The sign on the industrial land share coefficient continues to behave as expected, changing from negative in Table 2.4 to positive in Table 2.5.

The state dummy is positive in all equations in both tables and is highly significant in the more satisfying private volume regressions in Table 2.5. This argues that Washington has greater inventories per acre than Oregon. The difference cannot be due to the difference in forest practice acts because there has been too little time since the introduction of the new Oregon and Washington laws for empirical observation of the laws' impacts. A more likely explanation lies in the harvest histories of the two states. Washington was harvested earlier and has recovered more completely. That is, both states are in their second forests but Washington is further along. Consequently, the Washington inventory per acre is greater.[10]

Our Oregon and Washington equations suggest no categorical implications regarding the effectiveness of the newer, environmentally sensitive SFPAs. The equations do imply strongly, however, that the act of holding private forest inventories is price responsive, that industrial ownerships maintain greater inventories than nonindustrial private ownerships, and that site productivity is an important determinant of the inventory level for all private owners. (All these observations are consistent with our findings for Virginia and North Carolina.)

Together, these arguments suggest that the forest industry responds to incentives to restock quickly on high-productivity land in high-price regions. Forest practice act enforcement is probably unnecessary on these acres. The same arguments also anticipate environmental and forest practice act gains from directing enforcement attention to the opposite class of acres, low-productivity nonindustrial acres in low-price regions. Focus on seed tree, reforestation, and other stocking level results following harvests on the latter class of lands is a more fruitful area for forest practice administration and enforcement than is the requirement for landowners to specify forest plans on the former class of acres. This suggests potential support for (1) the regional feature of the Oregon law, although Oregon's regional forest practice boards are composed of private timber owners who cannot be expected to recommend against their own best interests, and (2) the site productivity feature of the Washington law.

 Summary and Conclusions

There is little point to independent examination of every SFPA from the 1930s and 1940s—if that were possible. We choose instead to examine one representative state law, Virginia's, for the comparison between forest inventories in the presence of the law with what they might have been in the absence of such a law. Forest inventory in the adjacent state of North Carolina, which has never passed forest practice legislation, provides basis for the comparison. Our approach is to contrast county inventories in the two states after removal of the impacts of various biological and economic factors.

We find no statistical significance between the adjusted inventories per acre in the two states. Although our empirical models may contain some specification biases we feel reasonably confident that Virginia's forest practice act does not have the intended impact. That is, if the legislation causes no addition to inventory, then it can have no impact on future timber supply and no contribution to social gain. The legislation imposes no additional cost on forest landowners, either because they avoid enforcement or because the legislation only requires action that the landowners undertake even in the absence of the forest practice act. Thus, the administrative costs (approximately $150,000 per year minus fines collected, or $0.01 per acre of private commercial forestland) are the only costs of the Virginia legislation and there are no corresponding benefits. In conclusion, there are no apparent redeeming features in Virginia's forest practice act and North Carolina has been the wiser in avoiding the public expenditures of a similar law.

A different, and more effective, Virginia law might be designed. Perhaps, because of industry opposition, it has not been. The facts of industry and other opposition, existing laws, and our empirical evidence all suggest a burden of proof for proponents of other state forest practice acts. Proponents should demonstrate that there are, in fact, additional inventories resulting from imposition of their forest practice acts. If they can show this conclusively, then they must also show that these additional inventories produce net additions to the future timber supplies equal in value to (1) the additional production costs imposed by the legislation plus (2) the states' administrative and enforcement costs.

The SFPAs of the 1970s create additional problems for analysis. We cannot assess the impacts of any of these laws with confidence because there has been insufficient time for the laws to induce measurable differences in forest inventories. As an alternative, we can review two states, Oregon and Washington, with newer, environmentally sensitive, forest practice acts and with the intention of observing the determinants of previous forest investments in these states. Legislation that intends to alter forest inventories, whether for environmental or other reasons, might reasonably focus on forestlands where the natural investment incentives are weakest.

Our statistical results suggest that the most fruitful focus for the Oregon and Washington forest practice acts is on poorer site nonindustrial forestlands in regions where stocking per acre is relatively low—and, obviously, in the period immediately surrounding the timber harvest. Such focus would yield cost-effective administration and enforcement. These laws remain expensive, approximately $1.3 million per year in Oregon and $1.5 million per year in Washington, or $0.14 per acre and $0.17 per acre, respectively. These are public funds. There are additional costs to private forest landowners for maintaining additional inventories—where the law is effective. Whether the laws are socially efficient is something we cannot estimate without knowledge of the environmental and aesthetic gains they produce and the production costs they impose, but we know that social efficiency requires that the net gains must exceed $0.14 per acre per year across all private forestlands in these states.

We also know that focus on poorer site nonindustrial forestlands was not the intention of the environmental movement, which originally encouraged the Oregon and Washington laws. Their intention to focus (less effectively) on industrial forestlands throws further doubt on the merit of existing SFPAs in general.

 Statistical Appendices

2A. BOX-COX TESTS

The natural logs of the input data for the dependent and independent variables are simple transformations of the data. A more general transformation developed by Box and Cox is the power transformation defined as

$$X(\tau)_i = \frac{X_i^\tau - 1}{\tau}, \quad \tau = 0$$

where i refers to the ith observation of the dependent or independent variable. (Bolch & Huang [1974] show that when $\tau \to 0$, then the power transformation is equivalent to a natural log transformation; and when $\tau \to 1$, then the power transformation is equivalent to a simple untransformed linear model.)

Running a Box-Cox regression involves a nonlinear search for the value of τ that provides the best fit of the data in the sense that it maximizes the log of the likelihood function. Using the log likelihood test described in Bolch and Huang, we cannot reject the null hypothesis that $\tau = 1$ in the case of Virginia and North Carolina. On the other hand, we cannot reject the null hypothesis that $\tau = 0$ for the initial regressions on Washington and Oregon (total inventory per acre). The test displays no preference for the second Washington and Oregon regressions (private inventory per acre). We choose the linear regression form in this final case on the basis of a higher log likelihood value. In this case, the Box-Cox test yields a value of $\tau = 0.4$. Table 2.6 provides the actual estimates for the two regressions reported in Table 2.5. The data transformation has little effect on either the signs or the significance of any of the independent variables.

2B. TESTS FOR HETEROSCEDASTICITY

The test for heteroscedasticity in the Virginia–North Carolina OLS residuals is a one-way analysis of variance test (Freund 1971, 395–400). Our question is whether the residual variances in the regressions X^2_{ij} differ on average across the three geographic regions in both states; $\alpha_1 = $ mountains, $\alpha_2 = $ piedmont, and $\alpha_3 = $ coastal plain, where the j's index treatments and i's index observations.

More formally,

$$X_{ij} = \mu + \alpha_1 + \alpha_2 + \alpha_3 + \epsilon_{ij} \qquad (2B.1)$$

where X_{ij} is a normal random variable (μ, σ^2) and the ϵ_{ij}'s are normal (0, σ^2) with neither serial correlation nor heteroscedasticity. We test the hypothesis

$$H_0 = \alpha_1 = \alpha_2 = \alpha_3 = 0 \qquad (2B.2)$$

Our test statistic is

$$\frac{\sum_{j=1}^{J} n_j \, (\overline{X}^2_j - \overline{X}^2)^2 / (J - 1)}{\sum_{j=1}^{J} \sum_{i=1}^{n_j} (X^2_{ij} - \overline{X}^2_j)^2 / (n_1 + n_2 + n_3 - J)} \sim F^{J-1}_{n_1+n_2+n_3-J} \qquad (2B.3)$$

Table 2.6. Box–Cox results on private forestland stocking in Washington and Oregon (all estimates given are of elasticities at the mean)

LnVOLP	Variables						Value of τ	Log of likelihood function
	SD	PI	PR	IND	HW	C		
One	.1203 (3.905)[b]	.8225 (2.913)[b]	.4105 (1.581)[a]	.0579 (1.684)[b]	-.1169 (-1.473)[a]	Not Applicable	.4	-42.258
Two	.1478 (5.86)[b]	.4413 (3.374)[b]	.54719 (2.2347)[b]	.066 (1.425)[a]	—	Not Applicable	.3	-43.4195

[a]Significant at .10 level.
[b]Significant at .05 level.

where n_j refers to the number of elements in the jth treatment, $\overline{X}{}^2_j$ is the mean variance within the jth treatment and $\overline{X}{}^2$ is the estimated mean variance. The expression in the numerator of (2B.3) is the sum of squared errors of the variance between treatments. The expression in the denominator of (2B.3) is the sum of squared errors of the variance within each treatment. A high value for the test statistic indicates the likelihood of heteroscedasticity. Its value is never statistically significant in our regressions testing the differences between Virginia and North Carolina. Therefore, we accept the null hypothesis that there is no regional difference.

Notes

1. This review draws heavily upon Cubbage and Siegel (1985). Also see Siegel (1974) for further review.

2. Libecap and Johnson (1978) provide an economic evaluation of this experience.

3. Chapter 3 provides an empirical measure of the impact of the Forestry Incentives Program. Chapter 7 provides the same for both capital gains and preferential land use taxation in forestry.

4. An effective law also drives some previously marginal timberlands from production. If these lands have no other market valued use, as is the case for much timberland, then the (newly noncommercial) inventory on these lands continues to increase. This continuing increase is a result of timber's natural biological growth process and it further satisfies the aesthetic and environmental objectives of some SFPAs. Although removing marginal land from timber production may cause some addition to inventories, it still conflicts with the future timber supply objectives of older SFPAs because marginal production is removed from supply and the natural addition to (noncommercial) inventory is unavailable to an economic market.

5. Chapter 3 considers the motives of nonindustrial private landowners in greater detail.

6. The Virginia data are for 1977 whereas the North Carolina data are for 1984. The moderate southern pine stumpage price increases of the late 1970s might have attracted more North Carolina timber to the market, thereby decreasing 1984 North Carolina inventories relative to 1977 inventories. This would reinforce the SFPA-induced likelihood that our regression results will show larger inventories in Virginia.

7. The results to this point are consistent with Considine's (1978) log linear specification for Virginia alone, except that Considine also found diameter and stocking to be important biological variables. Considine did not include price and tax variables. As an aside, the most theoretically satisfying production relationships known to us (Wallace 1977; Wallace & Newman 1986) are Cobb-Douglas functions of biological and ownership variables regressed on North Carolina (1) volume plus cut and (2) growth plus removals.

8. The "capture" theory of regulation (Stigler 1971) may explain the large and relatively inflexible administrative structure in Washington. According to this theory, small and well-organized groups, like Washington's environmentalists in the early 1970s, have the best chance of obtaining their preferred kind of regulation.

Furthermore, environmentalists may encourage the disparate administration of the law in many hands. They, thereby, thwart expected attempts by regulated landowners to "cozy up" to the regulating authority and to avoid compliance. Similarly, statewide administration of the law can be seen as an attempt to restrict landowners from appeals to potentially more understanding local regulatory administrators.

9. The results from regressions of the linear form do not change the nature of our findings.

10. A separate test shows no difference between the inventory levels for private forests in eastern Oregon and in eastern Washington. Apparently, the entire difference is restricted to private forests in western Washington.

 References

Adams, D. M., and R. W. Haynes. 1980. *The 1980 softwood timber assessment market model: Structure, projections, and policy simulations.* Forest Science Monograph 22.

American Forestry Association. 1976. *Final project report on the American Forestry Association workshops on forest practices and water quality.* Washington, D.C.: American Forestry Association.

Bassett, P. M., and D. D Oswald. 1981a. *Timber resource statistics for southwest Washington.* Resource Bulletin PNW-91. Portland, Ore.: USDA Forest Service Pacific Northwest Forest and Range Experiment Station.

_____. 1981b. *Timber resource statistics for the Olympic Peninsula, Washington.* Resource Bulletin PNW-93. Portland, Ore.: USDA Forest Service Pacific Northwest Forest and Range Experiment Station.

_____. 1982. *Timber resource statistics for the Puget Sound area, Washington.* Resource Bulletin PNW-96. Portland, Ore.: USDA Forest Service Pacific Northwest Forest and Range Experiment Station.

_____. 1983. *Timber resource statistics for eastern Washington.* Resource Bulletin PNW-104. Portland, Ore.: USDA Forest Service Pacific Northwest Forest and Range Experiment Station.

Bechtold, W. A. 1985. *Forest statistics for North Carolina, 1984.* Resource Bulletin SE-78. Asheville, N.C.: USDA Forest Service Southeastern Forest Experiment Station.

Bolch, J., and C. Huang. 1974. *Multivariate statistical methods for business and economics.* Englewood Cliffs, N.J.: Prentice-Hall.

Considine, T. 1978. Forest productivity in Virginia: Using forest survey data. Master's thesis, Duke University School of Forestry and Environmental Studies, Durham, N.C.

Cubbage, F. W., and W. Siegel. 1985. The law regulating private forest practices. *Journal of Forestry* 83:537–45.

Ellefson, P. 1974. Focus on issues—State forest practice acts. *Journal of Forestry* 72:196–97.

Ellefson, P., and F. W. Cubbage. 1980. *State forest practice laws and regulations: A review and case study for Minnesota.* Station Bulletin 536-1980. Minneapolis: University of Minnesota Agricultural Experiment Station.

Farrenkopf, T. O. 1982. *Forest statistics for eastern Oregon, 1977.* Resource Bulletin PNW-94. Portland, Ore.: USDA Forest Service Pacific Northwest Forest and Range Experiment Station.

Freund, J. 1971. *Mathematical statistics.* Englewood Cliffs, N.J.: Prentice-Hall.

Gedney, D. R. 1982. *The timber resources of western Oregon—Highlights and statistics.* Resource Bulletin PNW-97. Portland, Ore.: USDA Forest Service Pacific Northwest Forest and Range Experiment Station.

Hyde, W. F. 1980. *Timber supply land allocation and economic efficiency.* Baltimore: Johns Hopkins University Press for Resources for the Future.

Knight, H. A., and J. P. McClure. 1978. *Virginia's timber, 1977.* Resource Bulletin SE-44. Asheville, N.C.: USDA Forest Service Southeastern Forest Experiment Station.

LeMaster, D. 1975. Focus on the issues—EPA's suggested state forest practices act: Questions about timber harvesting plans. *Journal of Forestry* 73:121.

Libecap, G., and R. Johnson. 1978. Property rights, nineteenth century federal timber policy and the conservation movement. *Journal of Economic History* 39:129–42.

Nelson, A. W. 1976. Private forest practices: How much regulation is too much? In *Proceedings, 1975 National Convention, Society of American Foresters,* pp. 66–68. Bethesda, Md.: Society of American Foresters.

Norris, F. 1977–1984. *Timber Mart-South.* 2(1)–8(12). Highlands, N.C.: Timber Mart-South Incorporated.

North Carolina Department of Tax Research. 1965–1975. *Statistics of taxation.* Raleigh: North Carolina Department of Tax Research.

Nyland, R. D. 1978. Voluntary guidelines instead of government regulation in New York. *Journal of Forestry* 76:188–89.

Olinger, H. L. 1985. Personal communication with Harold Olinger, Assistant Chief of Administration, Commonwealth of Virginia Division of Forestry, 28 October 1985.

Olson, A. 1985. Personal communication with Arden Olson, Division Manager, Washington Department of Natural Resources Private Forestry Assistance and Regulations. September 1985.

Ruderman, F. K. 1983. *Production, prices, employment and trade in Northwest forest industries, first quarter 1983.* Resource Bulletin PNW-106. Portland, Ore.: USDA Forest Service Pacific Northwest Forest and Range Experiment Station.

Siegel, W. C. 1974. State forest practice laws today. *Journal of Forestry* 72:208–11.

Stigler, G. J. 1971. The theory of economic regulation. *Bell Journal of Economics* 2:3–21.

Virginia Department of Taxation. 1965–1975. *Virginia assessment/sales ratio study.* Richmond, Va.: Virginia Department of Taxation.

Virginia Division of Forestry. 1979. *Leave pine and poplar seed trees.* Publication 59.

Wallace, T. D. 1977. A tentative look at forest productivity in North Carolina using secondary data. Duke University Economics Department, Durham, N.C. Manuscript.

Wallace, T. D., and D. Newman. 1985. Measurement of ownership effects of forest productivity in North Carolina, 1974–84. *Canadian Journal of Forest Research* 16:733–38.

Weible, R. E. 1980. The economics of managing nonpoint forestry sources of water pollutants. Master's thesis, University of Minnesota College of Forestry, St. Paul.

Wilson, L. 1985. Personal communication with Leo Wilson, Forest Practices Director, Oregon State Department of Forestry, 7 November 1985.

CHAPTER 3

Comparing the Effectiveness of Cost Sharing and Technical Assistance Programs

After the various state forest practice acts, probably the best-known market interventions in forestry are the assistance programs for nonindustrial private forest landowners, which are intended to encourage the planting, growth, and harvesting of timber. These market interventions are often overlooked by those foresters with objections to the general concept of regulation because they provide an incentive rather than a deterrent to foresters' professional interests and activities. Nevertheless, they do represent a long-term, large scale federal commitment to influence the market for stumpage. Federal programs began as long ago as 1924. The budget for the current version, the Forestry Incentives Program, was $12.5 million in 1984 and some states made additional expenditures for their own related programs. The federal government allocated another $2.5 million to forestry extension with essentially the same objective; that is, to convince nonindustrial private forest landowners of the merit of growing and harvesting timber and to provide technical assistance for these landowners toward this end (Continuing Resolution to PL 98-107, October 1, 1983).

Forestry assistance programs began with the Clarke-McNary Act of 1924, which authorized farm forestry extension work, and continued in one form or another with the Agriculture Conservation Program (ACP) of 1936 (and its current version, the Rural Environmental Assistance Program), and the Norris-Doxey Act of 1937 (and its successor, the Cooperative Forest Management Act of 1950). The Forestry Incentives Program (the current federal program, commonly known as FIP) began in 1974. It provides up to 75 percent of all reforestation and timber stand improvement (TSI) costs for nonindustrial private landowners, who own between 50 and 500 acres of forestland. The benefactors of the FIP program are concentrated in the South and Southeast, where there are a large number of relatively small private and rural forest landowners and where the forest products industry that purchases timber from nonindustrial private forest landowners is also important. Nevertheless, landowners from almost every state in the country receive some amount of FIP assistance.

The basic justification for these various forestry assistance programs has its roots in the longstanding expectation of market failure to prevent a forthcoming timber famine. More recently, there is a general understanding that famine is an unreasonable expectation. Rather, producers and consumers adjust to any demand and supply disequilibrium, thereby creating a new equilibrium stumpage price and quantity. Nevertheless, this new equilibrium may be at a higher price if, in some sense, there is an insufficient future availability of timber. Recognizing this, one modern justification for FIP is a market failure argument: market failure to provide the information about anticipated future higher prices that would induce current investments in timber and, thereby, yield the necessary expansion in future timber harvests and restrict anticipated future price increases as well as their negative impact on the quantity of forest products demanded.

FIP focuses on nonindustrial private forest (NIPF) landowners because this is the class of landowners from which many professional foresters think a positive timber production response is most likely. They argue that the current growth rate on NIPF lands may not correspond to the lands' biological potential (President's Advisory Panel on Timber and the Environment 1973, 35–36).[1] Furthermore, they argue that there may be good opportunities for financial gain from investments in forestry on these lands (Adams et al. 1982; USDA 1982, 246). Moreover, many professional foresters do not think that the other two broad landowner classes, industrial and public, possess the same timber investment potential. The foresters' argument seems to be that industrial owners are well aware of the future market and responsive to it. The argument continues that a cadre of professional foresters manage the public lands. These professionals are better prepared to understand good forest management than are most NIPF landowners. Furthermore, the public lands are subject to other budget allocations, and seeking budget expansion is another, different issue for professional foresters.

Focus on NIPF landowners raises a second justification sometimes given for FIP. The small size and rural location of eligible ownerships suggest that the landowners themselves may be less well off in some sense. Therefore, they may be candidates for redistributive gains from society as a whole. FIP may provide such gains.

The purpose of this chapter is to examine FIP in view of these two justifications. The case for market failure in timber investment and supply has not been shown convincingly—in our judgement. Timber trades in a satisfactory market, NIPF landowners have free access to capital markets, and there is no evidence that a shortage of reliable information regarding future prices restricts planting, therefore timber inventories, on NIPF lands.

Indeed, a prestigious committee assembled in 1958 to report on Forest Credit in the United States concluded that there is no market failure. In the absence of convincing evidence to the contrary there is every reason to accept the committee's judgement. Furthermore, whether uncertainty regarding future prices causes a risk-averse decision by NIP timber producers to underinvest is an unresolved, empirical question. However, even if true, surely it must be rejected as a source of market failure because, as the harvest date approaches, prices rise anticipating any impending shortage and (1) some NIPF landowners begin planting and improving their existing timber stands in response to the market signal and (2) some NIPF landowners who had no original plans to harvest their (aesthetically valued) timber stands respond to the change in relative price structure.

Altogether, this means that there is no reason, in our opinion and in this chapter, to establish a value for the presumed externality, the market failure. Rather, our analysis is concerned strictly with showing the welfare and distributive impacts of FIP on consumers and nonindustrial private producers of timber. Our eventual conclusion will be that those impacts do not justify the public intervention.

Approach

The welfare and distributive impacts of FIP can be described conceptually with reference to Figure 3.1. (Figure 3.1 contrasts with Figure 1.1 only in that it reflects a subsidy, not a restrictive market intervention.) The function D describes market demand for timber. The function S describes timber supply without the incentive (or the sum of public transfers and nonindustrial private investments in timber in the presence of the incentive) while S' describes the expansion in timber supply due to the incentive (or strictly nonindustrial private investment in timber in the presence of the incentive). The market clears at point a in absence of the incentive and at point b in presence of the incentive. FIP causes transfers from NIPF landowners to sawmills and pulp mills equal to $p_1 abp_2$ (some of these gains pass on to final product consumers) and transfers from the public treasury to the NIPF landowners who produce timber for harvest equal to $0db$ (of which acb is passed on to consumers). Area $0cb$ remains with producers, thereby enabling cost decreases from p_1 to p_2 and production increases from q_1 to q_2. There is a deadweight social cost (payment from the treasury unmatched by economic gain) equal to adb.[2]

The full social costs, however, are in excess of adb. Figure 3.1 only reflects FIP payments that (1) are effective in increasing timber supply. In addition, there are (2) those FIP payments made to landowners who never harvest their timber, and (3) the transactions costs associated with administering the program. The first two are transfers to NIPF landowners that add to the landowners' private gains, but the second does not add to aggregate social gain. The market reflects neither of the final two public costs; therefore, neither shows up in Figure 3.1. The misallocation of resources to FIP exceeds *adb* by the sum of the latter two public costs.[3]

Transforming this conceptual argument into an empirical argument requires (1) an understanding of the impacts of FIP on NIPF landowner behavior and, therefore, on the level of eventual timber harvests due to FIP payments and (2) knowledge of the nonindustrial private share of the sup-

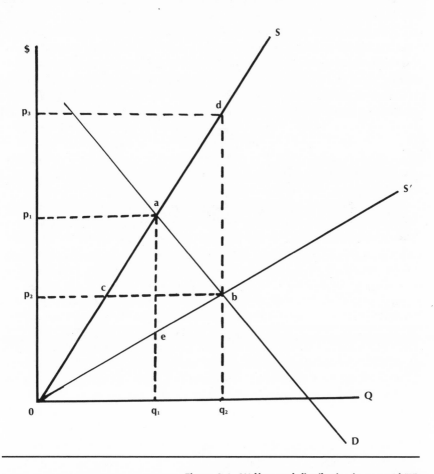

Figure 3.1. Welfare and distributive impacts of FIP.

ply of timber. The remainder of this chapter develops the conceptual and empirical devices necessary to provide this understanding.

We begin with a short background statement focusing on the motives of NIPF landowners and then turn to a conceptual model of landowner behavior. Our premise is that these landowners maximize their utility from both timber and nontimber uses of their land. This premise is consistent with a large body of literature, which finds that NIPF landowners have multiple objectives for owning land and often have personal comparative advantage in professional activities different from forestry.[4] Similar models have been developed before (e.g., Binkley 1981), but ours is unique in that it accounts explicitly for technical change and permits independent roles for capital and labor in the production process. Royer's (1981) survey of NIPF landowners in North Carolina provides the data for an empirical test of the model. Its North Carolina focus is particularly fortunate from our perspective, because North Carolina is part of those southern and southeastern regions where current FIP programs are concentrated. Royer's survey also provides additional data permitting the comparison of cost sharing programs like FIP with technical assistance programs like extension forestry.

In an appendix to this chapter, we estimate demand and supply functions for North Carolina stumpage. Valid models of individual landowner behavior and knowledge of the aggregate stumpage demand and supply for all landowners together permit us to estimate the welfare impacts of both the FIP and extension forestry in North Carolina. Finally, Royer's data also permit us to reason through arguments about the distributive impacts of these programs.

Our results indicate that FIP stimulates planting but not harvesting. This is not surprising. Planting is FIP's major objective—although not its economic justification. Technical assistance, on the other hand, stimulates both planting and harvesting. Nevertheless, as Figure 3.1 anticipates, both FIP and technical assistance create net social welfare losses, FIP more than technical assistance. Our results also show that both fail on distributive grounds as well. A concluding section generalizes these observations on technical assistance and cost sharing programs beyond the political boundaries of FIP and the geographic boundaries of North Carolina.

 Nonindustrial Private Forests

Nonindustrial private forests account for a substantial portion of all U.S. forestlands and timber resources. In 1977, the NIPF lands included roughly 15 percent of the total "commercial" forestlands and 42 percent of the standing timber volume in the United States.[5] Approximately one-third of annual softwood harvest and three-quarters of annual hardwood harvest originate from these lands (USDA 1982, 424).

NIPF landowners are a diverse group, consequently they possess a diversity of motives for property ownership and the production of timber may be only of minor importance for a great many of them. For the farmers who own 116 million acres of forestland, timber management may be only of peripheral concern when compared with the business of managing a farm. Nonfarmers own the remaining 162 million acres (USDA 1982). A few of these are industrial landowners who are not vertically integrated in the wood products industry but whose objective is to produce timber for a profit. Burlington Northern Railroad (BN) with 1.5 million acres of forestland is an example (Burlington Northern 1983). Programs like FIP generally impose acreage limitations that restrict participation by very large landowners like BN. Remaining nonfarm forest landowners have a variety of reasons for ownership, including recreation (second homes, hunting clubs, etc.), speculation, and mining, and here again, profitable timber management may be of little concern to many of them.

NIPF landowners face a host of technical and economic problems, even where profitable timber management is an objective. Most know little of forestry and many are absentee landowners. They have little time to manage for timber. The small size of their landholdings causes them to harvest infrequently and, thereby, creates small incentive for them to become fully aware of the market for stumpage. Furthermore, NIPF landowners often deal with only one buyer and, therefore, they have no basis for judging how good the prospective buyer's purchase offer may be.[6] In light of these factors, it is understandable that professional foresters see considerable opportunity for profitable timber management on nonindustrial private forest lands.

 A Model of Landowner Behavior

This background argues that managing and harvesting timber on nonindustrial private forestlands is only one component of the larger problem of maximizing landowner utility. It encourages us to approach the landowner utility problem from the perspective of a two-factor, two-sector, general equilibrium model, in which one sector reflects timber management and the second reflects other landowner objectives.[7] We develop such a model and determine its comparative static conditions before turning to its empirical estimation. The comparative static conditions anticipate the empirical impacts of exogenous inputs like FIP payments and forestry extension on nonindustrial private timber output. (Readers who are uninterested in detailed mathematics and who have good intuition regarding NIPF land-owner incentives may choose to forego reading this section and move directly to the empirical tests.)

THE TWO-SECTOR MODEL

The nonindustrial private landowner seeks to maximize a (strictly quasi-concave, locally nonsatiated, continuous and differentiable) utility function consisting of two arguments, income and production intended for consumption in the landowner's own household:

$$U(y,x_1) \quad \text{where } U_{x_1} > 0, \, U_y > 0. \tag{3.1}$$

The term x_1 refers to the amount of household produced consumption and represents the satisfaction derived from land uses such as recreation. The term y refers to the aggregate money income of the landowner or, alter-nately, it can be considered a composite good purchased with that income. We assume that both x_1 and y are normal; that is, they increase less than proportionally with increases in landowner utility.

After discounting future harvest values to the present and setting the market price of timber equal to 1, both for ease of exposition only, then the statement for the landowner's aggregate income is

$$y = M + x_2 \tag{3.2}$$

M represents the level of exogenous income and x_2 is the value (and volume) of timber harvests.

For any given level of technology, the nonindustrial private landowner combines labor L with capital K to produce both timber x_2 and nontimber x_1 outputs from the land.

$$x_1 = \beta_1 \times f(L_1, K_1) \tag{3.3}$$
and
$$x_2 = \beta_2 \times g(L_2, K_2) \tag{3.4}$$

where L_i and K_i ($i = 1,2$) refer to the quantities of labor and capital applied in the ith sector and the β_is are Hicks neutral technology parameters. (The timber sector does not gain from labor and capital inputs to the household consumption sector.) We assume that both functions exhibit constant re-turns to scale and that, initially, the aggregate levels of capital and labor are fixed at $\overline{K}$ and $\overline{L}$, respectively. Combining equations (3.2) and (3.4) yields an expression for income as a function of capital and labor:

$$y = M + \beta_2 \times g(L_2, K_2) \tag{3.5}$$

The landowner's problem is to allocate capital and labor so as to maximize total utility. The maximization procedure is understood more easily with reference to Figure 3.2. In this figure, the vertical axis represents total money income received by the landowner and the horizontal axis represents total household consumption produced on the land. If timber management and harvesting fully consumes $\bar{K}$ and $\bar{L}$, then there can be no production for household consumption and total income equals $0c$. If, on the other hand, household consumption fully consumes all capital and labor, then there can be no timber harvesting and no income from it. In this latter case, total monetary income is exogenous and equals $0b$. Household consumption equals $0e$. Therefore, with no commercial timber management, the landowner ends up at point d on his or her production possibilities frontier.

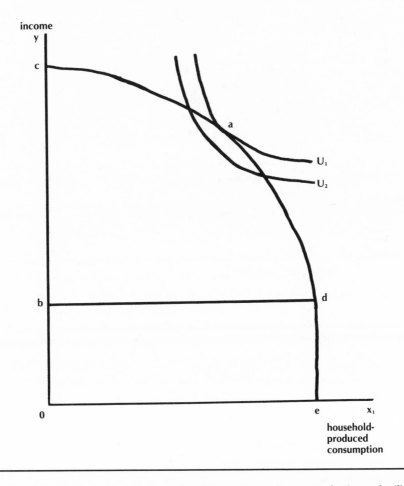

Figure 3.2. Landowner production and utility.

The landowner's indifference curves between timber and nontimber, the U_i, are convex because he or she derives utility (i.e., real income) from both uses of the land. Optimal land use implies maximizing landowner utility subject to the production possibilities constraint. In Figure 3.2, the maximum occurs at point a, where commercial timber production and nontimber household production are both partial uses of the land. Some harvests occur, but utility from the forestland, rather than profits from timber sales, is maximized.

In the analysis that follows, we assume that no optimal solution occurs along segment de (where there are no timber harvests). Therefore, we can ignore exogenous income M and, without loss of generality, use x_2 (timber income) as the measure of monetary income in our arguments.

A GENERAL EQUILIBRIUM SOLUTION. Solution to this general equilibrium problem requires examination of the landowner's outputs of x_1 and x_2. We initially direct our attention to the technology and production tradeoffs in the two output sectors and derive the general equilibrium solution for real income on the production possibilities frontier. Subsequently, we examine the role of utility in output choice and obtain four equations describing the landowner's supply of and demand for the household services and timber provided by x_1 and x_2, respectively. Our interest is in the impact of incentive payments like FIP on landowner behavior. Therefore, our discussion features the general equilibrium effects of changes in exogenous parameters like subsidies and their opposites, taxes, on the optimal outputs of timber and household services.

Rather than totally differentiating the entire general equilibrium system and solving for the derivatives, we follow a less mechanical approach first suggested by Caves and Jones (1973), which considers the different elements of the process characterized by the "equations of change."

The nonindustrial landowner, at any given time, faces a set of factor prices, r and w, and taxes (or subsidies) T_{Ki} and T_{Li}, on capital and labor. Assuming cost minimization and competitive pricing (i.e., output price P_i equals marginal cost MC_i), then output price is a function of tax (subsidy) inclusive factor prices. Thus, for a particular level of technology β_i,

$$P_i = P_i(rT_{Ki}, wT_{Li})\big|_\beta \tag{3.6}$$

Equation (3.6) describes price (and marginal cost) in the ith output sector.[8] Differentiating equation (3.6) logarithmically at the point where $T_{Ki} = T_{Li} = 1$, or where there are no taxes or subsidies, then

$$\hat{P}_i = -\hat{\beta}_i + \theta_{Li}\hat{w}T_{Li} + (1 - \theta_{Li})\hat{r}T_{Ki} \tag{3.7}$$

A "hat" over a variable indicates a log differential (i.e., $\hat{\beta}_i = d\beta_i/\beta_i$). Equation (3.7) describes the percentage change in marginal costs where $\theta_{Li} \equiv (wT_{Li}L_i/x_iP_i)$ represents labor's share of the ith output sector's production. If timber management requires relatively more labor and less capital (mature timber) than required for, say, recreational management for household consumption, then θ_{L2} is greater than θ_{L1}. (It may be absolutely small in both sectors, however.)

Equation (3.7) can be simplified by defining a variable T_i as $\hat{T}_i \equiv \theta_{Li}\hat{T}_{Li} + (1 - \theta_{Li})\hat{T}_{Ki}$, or the factor share weighted sum of the input taxes. $\hat{T}_i$ is equivalent to the tax (subsidy) on output in the ith sector. Integrating this definition into equation (3.7) yields

$$\hat{P}_i = \hat{T}_i - \hat{\beta}_i + \theta_{Li}\hat{w} + (1 - \theta_{Li})\hat{r} \tag{3.8}$$

which isolates the effects of taxes, technology, and factor prices on each sector's marginal costs. Clearly, technical change acts to decrease both the wage and the capital cost. Furthermore, the impact of taxes on marginal costs is the opposite of the similar impacts of subsidies and technical improvements.

Consider now, equilibrium real income or the value of all goods consumed, including recreation and other forms of household consumption as well as goods purchased with money income. The value of total landowner output is

$$x = x_1P_1 + x_2P_2 \tag{3.9}$$

Alternately, total output is the rental income collected by the landowner on his or her physical and human capital. Therefore,

$$x = w(T_{L1}L_1 + T_{L2}L_2) + r(T_{K1}K_1 + T_{K2}K_2) \tag{3.10}$$

which expresses real income as a function of labor, capital, and their tax inclusive prices in each sector.

Equation (3.9) implicitly normalizes the price index P for total output and sets it equal to 1. Therefore, the logarithmic derivative of the price index is

$$\hat{P} = \mu_1\hat{P}_1 + \mu_2\hat{P}_2 = 0 \tag{3.11}$$

where μ_i is the expenditure share for the ith sector, $\mu_i \equiv [x_iP_i/(x_1P_1 + x_2P_2)]$.

Combining equation (3.11) and the sum of the marginal cost differentials for the two sectors, from equation (3.8), yields

$$0 = \mu_1 \hat{T}_1 - \mu_1 \beta_1 + \mu_1 \theta_{L1} \hat{w} + \mu_1 (1 - \theta_L) \hat{r} + \mu_2 \hat{T}_2 - \mu_2 \beta_2$$
$$+ \mu_2 \theta_{L2} \hat{w} + \mu_2 (1 - \theta_{L2}) \hat{r} \qquad (3.12)$$

Equation (3.12) relates changes in output prices to changes in factor prices. It can be rewritten as

$$0 = \hat{T} - \hat{\beta} + \theta_L \hat{w} + (1 - \theta_L) \hat{r} \qquad (3.13)$$

where $\hat{T}$ is the implicit tax factor on aggregate output resulting from input taxes,

$$\hat{T} \equiv \mu_1 \hat{T}_1 + \mu_2 \hat{T}_2;$$

$\hat{\beta}$ is the composite index of factor neutral technical change,

$$\hat{\beta} \equiv \mu_1 \hat{\beta}_1 + \mu_2 \hat{\beta}_2;$$

and θ_L is labor's share of total income,

$$\theta_L \equiv \mu_1 \theta_{L1} + \mu_2 \theta_{L2}.$$

Now, differentiating equation (3.10) logarithmically and substituting the result in equation (3.13) yields

$$\hat{x} = \theta_L \hat{w} + (1 - \theta_L) \hat{r} + \hat{T} + \theta_L \hat{L} + (1 - \theta_L) \hat{K}$$
$$= \theta_L \hat{L} + (1 - \theta_L) \hat{K} + \hat{\beta} \qquad (3.14)$$

which describes percentage changes in income $\hat{x}$ as a function of exogenous parameters. The tax factors do not appear in this general equilibrium solution for $\hat{x}$ because maximization occurs where these factors are equal to one—as we assumed when differentiating equation (3.6).

It remains for us to determine the landowner's general equilibrium demand and supply equations. Nonindustrial private landowners trade timber for household service activities so as to maximize utility. Demand relationships involving relative prices and income can describe this trade-off along the landowner's isoquant. Totally differentiating the landowner's demand equations for the products of both sectors yields

$$\hat{x}_i = \eta_i \hat{x} - \sigma \hat{P}_i \qquad (3.15)$$

where η_i and σ are the real income and compensated substitution (price) elasticities for the product of the ith sector. Combining equations (3.14) and (3.15), yields

$$\hat{x}_i = \eta_i [\theta_L \hat{L} + (1 - \theta_L)\hat{K} + \hat{\beta}] - \sigma \hat{P}_i \tag{3.16}$$

which is the ith sector's general equilibrium demand.

The two demands described by equation (3.16) are insufficient to uniquely determine the nonindustrial landowner's output of timber and household services. We also need knowledge of the supply relationships that describe the timber–household service trade-off along the production possibility frontier as functions of inputs, technology, and relative prices. Derivation of these supply relationships is lengthy and even more technical. We relegate it to an appendix. The final supply relationships themselves for each of the two output sectors are

$$\hat{x}_i = \hat{\beta}_i + s(\widehat{\beta_i P_i}T/\beta T_i) + \theta_L \hat{L} + (1 - \theta_L)\hat{K}$$
$$+ [\theta_L(1 - \theta_L)(\theta_L - \theta_{Li})/\mu_1\mu_2(\theta_{L1} - \theta_{L2})^2](\hat{K}/\hat{L})$$
$$+ \mu_i(\theta_{Li} - \theta_{Lj})s [\mu_1\theta_{L1}(1 - \theta_{L1}) \hat{\gamma}_1 + \mu_2\theta_{L2}(1 - \theta_{L2}) \hat{\gamma}_2] \tag{3.17}$$

where s is the elasticity of supply and the γ_is describe the impact of relative input taxes (subsidies) in the ith sector.[9]

COMPARATIVE STATICS. At the outset of this section, we stated that our purpose is to examine the reaction of nonindustrial private landowners to changes in economic factors such as a cost sharing subsidy. In terms of the general equilibrium model just outlined, this means using equations (3.16) and (3.17) to determine the impacts of various exogenous parameters on nonindustrial private timber output x_2. The parameters in which we are interested include the levels of labor, capital, technology, and subsidies, with the latter two being more important for our purpose.

Consider first an increase in the exogenous level of labor L. Such change shifts the production possibilities frontier toward the relatively labor-intensive sector, thereby increasing the length of segment bc in Figure 3.2. For the algebraic derivation of the impact of this shift on timber production, it is notationally convenient to define a parameter Z such that $Z \equiv -[(1 - \theta_L)(\theta_L - \theta_{L2})]/[\mu_1\mu_2(\theta_{L1} - \theta_{L2})^2]$. We can determine the change in nonindustrial private timber output due to an exogenous increase in labor by substituting Z for its identity in the demand and supply equations, (3.16) and (3.17), respectively, and setting them equal to one another. In this manner,

$$\hat{x}_2 = \theta_L\{[s\eta_2 + \sigma(1 + Z)]/[s + \sigma]\}\hat{L} \tag{3.18}$$

which is positive under our assumptions about the relative labor intensiveness of timber growing and the normality of monetary income. In general, the anticipated size of the coefficient $\theta_L[\bullet]$ rises with the level of the aggregate labor share θ_L, the relative labor share θ_{L2}, and the real income elasticity μ_2. The role of the supply and demand elasticities, however, is much more ambiguous and depends on the values of η_2 and Z. The effect of an increase in the supply elasticity s is to move the value of the coefficient closer to $\theta_L\eta_2$ whereas an increase in the demand elasticity σ moves it closer to $\theta_L(1 + Z)$. Thus, if $\eta_2 > 1 + Z$, then a rise in s or a drop in σ serves to increase timber output. If, on the other hand, $\eta_2 < 1 + Z$, then the opposite is true and x_2 rises in response to an increase in σ or a decrease in s.

The impact on timber output changes somewhat when an increase in exogenous labor L accompanies an equal percentage increase in the level of exogenous capital K. The result, with reference to Figure 3.2, is a parallel shift in the production possibilities frontier above the level of exogenous income $0b$. The effect of such a shift on timber production is given algebraically by

$$\hat{x}_2 = [(\sigma + s\eta_2)/(\sigma + s)]\hat{Q} \tag{3.19}$$

where $\hat{Q} = \hat{K} = \hat{L}$.

As before, the supply and demand elasticities s and σ, respectively, enter into the analysis ambiguously, and again assuming the normality of both goods, equation (3.19) is positive and increases with the real income elasticity η_2. Furthermore, if $\eta_2 > 1$, then the coefficient of $\hat{Q}$ is greater than 1. This implies that timber harvests increase both absolutely and relative to household consumption. The size of the coefficient does not depend on the size of the relative and aggregate labor shares, θ_{L2} and θ_L, as it did in equation (3.18), because the expansions of labor and capital are proportional.

Let us shift our focus somewhat and consider now the impact on timber output of a change in commercial timber growing technology $\hat{\beta}_2$. That is, consider the effect of an improvement in technology that, although factor neutral, is specific to the commercial timber sector and has no impact on the household (recreation) sector. This is the intent of federal forestry assistance programs. In terms of Figure 3.2, such a change is represented by a pivotal outward shift in the production possibilities frontier to a level above the level of exogenous income. There is no change in household consumption bd in the absence of commercial timber production. With commercial timber production, however, timber-related income bc increases, thereby permitting relatively greater consumption of x_2 than with an equivalent parallel shift in the production possibilities frontier. Equation (3.20) shows the algebraic derivation of this technical change:

$$\hat{x}_2 = [(\sigma + \sigma s\mu_1 + \eta_2\mu_2 s)/(\sigma + s)]\hat{\beta}_2 \tag{3.20}$$

It, like equations (3.18) and (3.19), is positive and, because of $\hat{\beta}_2$'s factor neutrality, independent of all labor and capital factor shares. Therefore, increases in $\hat{\beta}_2$ are effective in increasing both relatively capital-intensive activities, like timber stand improvement, and relatively labor-intensive activities, like harvesting.

Finally, let us consider the comparative static impacts of output and input subsidies on nonindustrial private timber production. (FIP is an input subsidy.) As with a factor-neutral, sector-specific technical change, the effect of a subsidy is to pivot outward the production possibilities frontier in Figure 3.2. This shift implies an increase in the maximum value earned from timber output while leaving unchanged the maximum level of household production. Unlike technical change, however, subsidies do not change the maximum timber output volume. Therefore, our algebraic analysis initially holds the production possibilities frontier constant and examines the change in relative timber output resulting from changes in relative timber and household subsidies. Subsequently, we consider how a simultaneous increase in real income alters things. Looking first at an increase in output subsidies and using equations (3.16) and (3.17), we have

$$\hat{x}_2 = [s\sigma\mu_1/(\sigma + s)]\hat{T}_2 \tag{3.21}$$

which is clearly positive. This result is intuitive: Timber output increases in response to an input subsidy. Output increases require, furthermore, that the income elasticity η_1 is less than the substitution (demand price) elasticity σ, because the value of timber has increased.[10] While this condition should be met in most cases, the net effect of a subsidy on timber output could be substantially less than the substitution effect alone.

Derivation of the impacts of increases in input subsidies like FIP on commercial timber outputs is similar.

$$\hat{x}_2 = [s\sigma\mu_1/(\sigma + s)] \quad [(1 - \theta_{L2}) + (\theta_{L2} - \theta_{L1})\mu_2]\hat{T}_{K2} \tag{3.22}$$

Equation (3.22) differs from equation (3.21) by the second bracketed term (involving labor and capital shares). Like changes in T_2, the changes in T_{K2} increase timber output, but since they must do this primarily through increases in the amount of capital used in growing timber, their impact must be less than that of an equivalent harvest subsidy by at least θ_{L1} (because $\mu_1 < 1$). Therefore, we expect that policies like FIP are more successful at increasing relative capital use (through timber investments) than at stimulating timber harvests. Indeed, we anticipate that the impact of a capital subsidy on harvest activities is rather small, especially when compared with an equivalent change in the level of technology β_2.

EMPIRICAL TESTS

Available data are from single event surveys. They do not provide the continuous measure of timber production necessary for the dependent variable in the utility maximization model. Therefore, existing techniques and data permit us neither to estimate utility empirically nor to work through a comparative static application of the utility model. Existing techniques and data do permit us to test whether the propensities to harvest and to introduce timber stand improvements (TSI) bear the relationships to economic and demographic parameters of landowner behavior predicted by the model. Therefore, rather than ordinary least squares, our empirical solution is a nonlinear qualitative response model (Amemiya 1981; Lee 1978; Wu 1965).

Our concern is with the impact of certain economic parameters on nonindustrial private timber output x_2. The data include no explicit measure of x_2 for individual landowners but they do include information on whether a particular landowner harvested trees or made timber-related improvements. Both the decision to harvest and the decision to make timber stand improvements are important aspects of timber supply, now and in the future, and the probability attached to each of these decisions is closely related to the comparative static results from our general equilibrium model. If, for example, a rise in an economic variable such as technology increases optimal timber output, then it should increase the landowner's propensity to harvest timber. Similarly, it should increase the landowner's propensity for TSI. More formally, following Amemiya's notation,

$$y^*_{iH} = \beta_{1H} + x'_{iH}\beta_{2H} + \xi_{iH} \tag{3.23}$$

where y^*_{iH} represents the propensity of the ith landowner to harvest timber, x'_{iH} is a vector of economic and demographic characteristics and ξ_{iH} is an error term. Similarly, for TSI,

$$y^*_{iI} = \beta_{1I} + x'_{iI}\beta_{2I} + \xi_{iI} \tag{3.24}$$

where x'_{iI} contains largely the same variables as x'_{iH}. (This procedure has the advantage of requiring no explicit reference to the maximization of an indirect utility function.) Following Lee (1978), we assume normal distributions for both ξ_{iH} and ξ_{iI} and estimate the parameters by the probit maximum likelihood estimator.

DATA. Royer's 1981 survey of commercial forest landowners in North Carolina provides the necessary data for the empirical tests. Table 3.1 summarizes our choice of variables and indicates the anticipated directions of the relationships between dependent and independent variables.

Table 3.1. Summary of variables

Acronym	Variable	Expected significance (all tests)
HST	Probability of harvest	
IMP	Probability of timber stand improvement, including reforestation	
C	Constant	
INC	Income in hundreds of dollars	?
ED	Years of formal education	+
FIP	Dummy variable for cost sharing	+
TEC	Dummy variable for level of technology	+
PR1	1980 sawtimber price/Mbf	+
PR2	1976–1980 sawtimber price/Mbf (1977 dollars)	+
DIST	Distance from land, miles	−
FRM	Dummy variable for farm–nonfarm distinction	?
FOR	Forested area owned, acres	+

The dependent variables are timber harvest and TSI activities, including reforestation. Both represent decisions that increase timber supply. Therefore, we anticipate that the landowner's propensity for either is closely related to those independent variables that our general equilibrium–comparative static results identify as affecting timber supply. In the two probit empirical tests, values of one denote harvest or TSI whereas values of zero denote no harvest or no TSI. In Royer's survey, harvest refers to harvest in 1980 whereas TSI refers to activities in the period 1976–1980.[11]

The Royer data have the additional merit of permitting us to consider the relative impact of forestry extension — the timber management advice provided to the landowner by extension foresters and other public agents. The additional timber management information provided by forestry extension is akin to raising the level of technology available to the landowner, therefore the comparative static results suggest that extension, like the technology variable, has a positive impact on timber supply.

Royer's data make no reference to price. We obtained price data for each of three timber producing regions in North Carolina from Timber Mart-South (Norris 1981) and associated the prices from each region with the landowners in Royer's sample from that region. Harvest prices are for 1980, corresponding to the harvest year in Royer's survey. The correct price to associate with TSI activities is more problematic. We chose the five-year average price (1976–1980) with the justification that it, or a multiple of it, should reflect landowners' future price expectations. Price increases affect output much like a timber harvest or management subsidy affects output. Therefore, the comparative static results suggest that price has a positive impact on timber supply.

We discuss the anticipated effects of the remaining independent variables together with our empirical observations of them in the next section.

GENERAL RESULTS. Tables 3.2 and 3.3 present the results for the probit estimates for TSI (including reforestation) and timber harvest, respectively. The format of the two tables is the same. The numbers in parentheses are estimates for the asymptotic t statistics for each explanatory variable. Also included with each regression is a number equal to -2 times the logarithm of the likelihood ratio. This number, which is distributed as χ^2_{k-1} (where k equals number of regressors), is conceptually equivalent to the F statistic used in linear tests and its large values here indicate that our tests on both TSI and timber harvest are highly significant. Finally, the numbers denoted by Cor. indicate the high percentage of correct predictions made on the sample data from our estimates.[12]

In the first TSI equation (Table 3.2), all independent variables have the correct signs and all except income, distance, and the farm–nonfarm proxy are significant at the 5 percent level. Only income is not significant at the 20 percent level. Consequently, we remove it from the second equation with little effect on the other regressors. The comparative static results argue that increases in exogenous income tend to contract timber supply. Perhaps this effect is offset somewhat by the increase in business acumen usually associated with an increase in income and that, therefore, might tend to expand timber supply.

As distance between the landowner's residence and his or her forestland increases, the labor he or she can devote to forest management decreases. The comparative static results predict and our empirical tests confirm (weakly) that a reduction in labor and its corollary, greater distance, decrease timber supply.

The comparative static results predict nothing about the impacts of either the landowner's level of education or the farm–nonfarm distinction among landowners. We might anticipate, however, that education increases awareness of technical and market opportunities, and therefore, that education has a positive effect on timber supply. The impact of farmer forest landowners versus that of nonfarmer forest landowners is more difficult to anticipate. Royer included the farm–nonfarm distinction in his survey. We include it in our regressions because the landholding motives of these two ownership classes may vary considerably, and these different motives may have a differential influence on timber supply. Our empirical results confirm that there is a differential impact, although not a highly significant one. Farmers participate less often than their nonfarmer counterparts in those TSI activities that eventually expand timber supply.

Consider now the timber harvest equations themselves in Table 3.3. The income variable becomes negative in the first equation but it remains insignificant. The education variable also becomes insignificant, indicating that the number of years of education is less a factor in the decision to harvest mature timber than it was in the TSI decision. If timber manage-

Table 3.2. Estimated coefficients for IMP

C	INC	ED	FIP	TEC	PR2	DIST	FRM	FOR	χ^2_8	% Cor.
-3.01 (-5.7)ᵇ	.00047 (.807)	.0388 (1.85)ᵇ	.6285 (3.314)ᵇ	.6285 (3.314)ᵇ	.0076 (1.636)ᵃ	-.001 (-1.383)ᵃ	-.4078 (-1.389)ᵇ	.00049 (2.805)ᵇ	90.1	87.4

C	INC	ED	FIP	TEC	PR2	DIST	FRM	FOR	χ^2_7	% Cor.
-2.989 (-5.69)ᵇ	—	.0456 (2.389)ᵇ	.6038 (3.221)ᵇ	.7994 (3.96)ᵇ	.0077 (1.659)ᵃ	-.0009 (-1.288)ᵃ	-.3908 (-1.34)ᵃ	.0053 (3.095)ᵇ	89.4	87.8

ᵃIndicates significance at the .2 level.
ᵇIndicates significance at the .05 level.

Table 3.3. Estimated coefficients for HST

C	INC	ED	FIP	TEC	PR1	DIST	FRM	FOR	χ^2_8	% Cor.
-2.63 (-4.425)ᵇ	-.0002 (-.357)	.0076 (.283)	.182 (.775)	.862 (3.164)ᵇ	.0101 (1.964)ᵇ	-.0025 (-1.45)ᵃ	.7837 (2.933)ᵇ	.0007 (3.192)ᵇ	50.6	89.2

C	INC	ED	FIP	TEC	PR1	DIST	FRM	FOR	χ^2_6	% Cor.
-2.5771 (-4.989)ᵇ	—	—	.1904 (.802)	.8638 (3.338)ᵇ	.0099 (1.938)ᵇ	-.0024 (-1.457)ᵃ	.7785 (2.967)ᵇ	.0007 (3.19)ᵇ	50.5	89.5

ᵃIndicates significance at the .2 level.
ᵇIndicates significance at the .05 level.

ment plans can be associated with better educated landowners, then our observation on education, coupled with the greater significance of the price variable in these timber harvest regressions, supports the argument that nonindustrial private timber harvests are more often due to a good purchase offer than to any preconceived timber management plan. Moreover, the significance of the price variable also suggests that a publicly sponsored program to report regional prices to interested landowners might be effective in increasing timber supply from nonindustrial private forestlands. (We follow up on this idea in Chapter 4.) Both insignificant variables, income and education, are dropped from the second timber harvest regression with little effect on the other regressors.

The farm–nonfarm distinction has a significant and positive impact on timber harvest, which contrasts with its impact on TSI. Farmers, it would seem, though less inclined to TSI, are more willing to harvest their mature timber than are their nonfarmer counterparts.

The acreage variable remains for comment. Its impact is statistically significant in all four TSI and harvest regressions and its sign is consistent with our comparative static results. Landowners increase their total stock of capital by acquiring larger forestland holdings. Larger land holdings also require an increase in the total use of labor. Expansions of either capital or labor suggest expanding timber supply.[13]

A COMMENT ON COST SHARING AND TECHNICAL ASSISTANCE

We have constructed a conceptual model of nonindustrial private forest landowner behavior, discussed the data necessary to test this model, and commented on the general empirical results. Our primary interest remains, however, in the impact of public cost sharing programs like the FIP on these landowners and, therefore, on timber supply. Where the means are available for such an evaluation, we are also interested in the contrast between cost sharing and forestry assistance programs with regard to their impacts on timber supply.

The impacts of such programs are best seen in our analysis to this point by examining the changes in probabilities of TSI or timber harvests brought about by landowner awareness of cost sharing and technical assistance. Measuring this change in probability, when all other variables are measured at their means, we find that $\delta y^*_{iI}/\delta \text{FIP} = 0.055$, which means that an awareness of cost sharing increases the probability of TSI by 5.5 percent. Cost sharing has a much smaller impact on timber harvests. Indeed, we cannot reject the hypothesis that it has no impact whatsoever.

Once again, measuring the change in probability when all remaining variables are measured at their means, we find that $\delta y^*_{iI}/\delta \text{TEC} = 0.073$ and $\delta y^*_{iH}/\delta \text{TEC} = 0.071$, which means that technical assistance increases the probability of TSI by 7.3 percent and increases the probability of timber harvest by 7.1 percent. That is, technical assistance, due to its factor neutrality, has a significant effect on both the TSI and the immediate timber harvest aspects of supply. In contrast, cost sharing, which affects supply primarily through its impact on capital costs, has little or no impact on the probability of timber harvests.

Influencing nonindustrial timber productivity is not a simple matter and, unlike profit-maximizing firms, landowners with multiple objectives often react poorly to specialized economic incentives. In our conceptual model, we find that the real income effect on household consumption reduces the impact of subsidies on timber supply. Furthermore, input subsidy programs like FIP are distortionary, affecting capital improvements (TSI activities) far more than they affect harvests of mature timber. In contrast, in both our conceptual and empirical models, technical changes brought about by forestry extension unambiguously lead to increases in both TSI and current harvest aspects of timber supply. This result, combined with our other empirical findings, suggests that government policies that rely more on the dissemination of technical and market information to private landowners are probably a better means of increasing timber supply than are policies involving large-scale reforestation subsidies. We pursue this hypothesis further in the remainder of the chapter as we inquire into the costs and benefits of both FIP and forestry extension as these programs are administered in North Carolina.

 ## Welfare and Redistributive Implications

FIP has an empirically significant impact on TSI, therefore on inventory, and technical assistance has an empirically significant impact on both TSI and current harvests. Each suggests a downward shift in either the anticipated future (TSI) or current (harvest) market supply of stumpage, as from S to S' in Figure 3.1. It remains for us to estimate the supply shifts and the expected shifts in the North Carolina demand and supply equilibrium.[14] We can estimate the size of the welfare triangles (previously described with reference to Figure 3.1) from knowledge of market conditions both with and without both FIP and technical assistance. These estimates provide measures of how close their beneficial impacts come to justifying the costs of the FIP and technical assistance programs in North Carolina.

The procedure for calculating the welfare triangles:

(1) Find the initial price-quantity equilibrium, $a(p_1, q_1)$ in Figure 3.1,

using the supply (3B.6) and demand (3B.7) equations from Appendix B;

(2) Find the incremental inventory effect due to the FIP or the technical assistance program;

(3) Add the results from step 2 to the base inventory in equation (3B.6) and re-solve for the the new price-quantity equilibrium, $b(p_2,q_2)$ in Figure 3.1;

(4) Find points c, d, and e in Figure 3.1 as

c: initial supply at p_2

d: initial supply at q_2

e: incremented supply at q_1;

(5) Calculate the welfare triangles from knowledge of points a–e.

Estimates of the welfare triangles also show one measure of the redistribution of wealth from the public treasury through FIP payments and technical assistance to NIPF producers and eventually to consumers of stumpage. We make these estimates with reference to the landowners' future expectations in 1980. Finally, Royer's survey permits inquiry into the income classes of NIPF landowners who receive either FIP or technical assistance, thereby also permitting us to make a further statement about the overall equity of these programs.

COST SHARING

FIP encourages 5.5 percent of all NIPF landowners to conduct TSI of which reforestation accounts for more than 95 percent. Assuming the entire impact is on reforestation and that 5.5 percent of landowners also means that 5.5 percent of all NIPF land is affected, then it is a fairly simple step to anticipate the future timber yield due to FIP.

The calculation for the anticipated future yield due to the 1980 FIP program in North Carolina is

program yield = FIP impact × NIPF acreage × yield/acre
             = (0.055) (14.03 million acres) (2549 ft³/acre)

Representative plantation yields might originate from thirty-year pine plantations on fifty-year site index 65 (McClure and Knight 1984).[15] One hundred percent pine plantations, thirty-year rotations, and all FIP payments directed to regeneration are generous assumptions that produce an upward bias on our physical yields and eventual economic benefits.[16] Yields might be adjusted upward another 20 percent over the rotation (to 3059 ft³/acre) in order to reflect the historical and expected rate of increase in all North Carolina plantation growth (Wallace & Newman 1986). This latter increase is probably due to the expansion of managerial knowledge over time and probably should not be considered truly a return to the FIP input. Including it provides yet additional upward bias in eventual estimates of returns to FIP.

The result is a measure of the increase in standing forest inventory in thirty years. This inventory increase shifts the stumpage supply function described in Appendix 3B, thereby providing an anticipated future decrease in the equilibrium North Carolina stumpage price of less than $6.38 per Mcf and an anticipated future harvest increase of less than 787 Mcf—both compared with 1980 market values.

The price effect suggests that industrial timber landowners (who are ineligible for FIP) might recognize that one impact of FIP is to decrease anticipated stumpage prices and, therefore, to decrease the profitability of all forestlands including their own. For this reason, they might oppose FIP. Vertically integrated firms also might see the advantage of disposing of their timberlands, thereby avoiding the price decreasing impact of FIP on their own lands yet gaining from the availability of lower-priced NIPF stumpage for their mills. If they are able to dispose quickly enough of a large enough share of their timberlands, then integrated firms may favor FIP.

Table 3.4 records the final estimates. The total federal and state expenditures for FIP in North Carolina in 1980 were $1.6 million (USDA ASCS 1980). Of this, 9 percent or $147.1 thousand was for administration, less than $673.4 thousand was effective payment to NIPF landowners, and more than the $798.0 thousand residual was ineffective payments to landowners. Effective payments are those for TSI, including regeneration, which decrease landowner costs and cause an anticipated increase in future harvests. These payments are equal to p_3dbp_2 in Figure 3.1. The remaining, ineffective, payments are those for TSI, including regeneration, for which there is no anticipated future harvest due to the recreation or the other nonmarket timber production objectives of landowners.

The FIP program redistributes from the the public treasury to three general groups. The bulk of administrative costs may be redistributed as wages to the public servants who manage the FIP program. The anticipated price decrease (due to FIP induced inventories that increase eventual harvests) yields an eventual total redistributive gain for all consumers equal to p_1abp_2 in Figure 3.1 or from $162.4 thousand to $873.7 thousand depending on the discount rate applied to these future benefits.[17] (Consumers range from mill owners to final product consumers. The gains of each depend on the supply and demand elasticities of their respective intermediate or final wood products.) NIPF landowners receive $1,471.4 thousand in transfers from the U.S. Treasury, but the anticipated market redistribution to consumers leaves all landowners—public, industrial, and nonindustrial—with a smaller net gain of between $598.1 thousand and $1,309.0 thousand.

This provides some insight as to why timber producing NIPF land-

Table 3.4. Comparative welfare impacts of FIP and technical assistance under various discount rates (in thousands of 1980 dollars)

	FIP 4%	FIP 7%	FIP 10%	Technical assistance 4%	Technical assistance 7%	Technical assistance 10%
Costs to public treasury						
1. Administrative	↓	147.1	↑	↓	106.1	↑
2. Direct transfers to landowners						
a. Effective (p_3dbp_2 in Figure 3.1)	↓	673.4	↑	↓	868.6[a]	↑
b. Ineffective $(3 - 1 - 2a)$	↓	798.0	↑	↓	192.7	↑
3. Total	↓	1618.5	↑	↓	1167.4	↑
Transfers to						
4. Public servants	↓	147.1	↑	↓	106.1	↑
5. Consumers (p_1abp_2 in Figure 3.1)	873.7	372.2	162.4	1134.7[a]	490.6[a]	220.7[a]
6. Landowners $(2 - 5)$	598.1	1099.1	1309.0	−73.4	570.7	840.6
Welfare						
7. Deadweight welfare loss (abd in Figure 3.1)	↓	2.7	↑	↓	4.5[a]	↑
8. Net public losses for entire program $(3 - 2a + 7)$	↓	947.8	↑	↓	303.3	↑

[a]The individual breakdown is

		TSI	Harvest
effective costs		865.3	3.3
transfers to consumers	4%	1121.5	13.2
	7%	477.9	12.7
	10%	208.5	12.7
deadweight loss		4.5	<0.05

owners may not aggressively pursue their opportunities to receive FIP payments. They, too, retransfer some of their gains to consumers. If we consider that NIPF landowners are probably perfect competitors in the factor markets, then they must pay an amount nearly equalling their FIP receipts for FIP-associated labor and capital inputs. Landowners retain only the returns to land and managerial inputs. Therefore, transfers to consumers in the form of lower stumpage prices might easily exceed the returns to these latter inputs and timber producing landowners could be net losers.

The only landowners who receive unambiguous gains from FIP are those with recreation or other nontimber objectives for their forestlands. These landowners receive "ineffective" FIP payments, some share of which become payments to labor and capital inputs for timber stand improvements. These landowners, however, intend to retain the entire shares due to land and managerial inputs because they do not anticipate selling their timber and, thereby, transferring some of their benefits to consumers in the form of lower stumpage prices. Of course, gains for landowners with nontimber objectives are not part of the original intention of the FIP program.

The standard measure of net social welfare loss corresponds to *adb* in Figure 3.1. This measure is the amount of FIP payments effective in increasing anticipated timber supply but for which the public opportunity costs exceed the public gain. This is a transfer from the general public to NIPF landowners and consumers, for which there is no offsetting aggregate gain to either landowners or the general public. This deadweight loss ranges up to $2,700. This measure is an underestimate, however, to the extent that it overlooks administrative costs and FIP payments ineffective in increasing the anticipated timber supply. The full measure of the net social welfare loss attached to the 1980 FIP program in North Carolina is at least $947,800.

TECHNICAL ASSISTANCE

The costs of forestry extension are for the program as a whole. The transfers to particular citizen groups can be distinguished, however, according to the technical assistance impact on either TSI or current harvests.

The calculations for the transfers and the deadweight welfare loss associated with the technical assistance impact on TSI are similar to those for the FIP impact. Technical assistance provides information that encourages 7.3 percent of NIPF landowners in North Carolina to conduct TSI, of which reforestation probably accounts for the largest share. The anticipated future inventory calculation is

program yield = TEC impact × NIPF acreage × yield/acre
= (0.073)(14.03 million acres)(3059ft³/acre)[18]

Integrating this anticipated inventory effect with the demand and supply functions from Appendix 3B provides the new equilibrium price and quantity. Anticipated future stumpage prices decline up to $8.18 per Mcf and harvests increase up to 1.0 MMcf.

The calculations for transfers and the deadweight welfare loss associated with the technical assistance impact on current harvests are somewhat different. Technical assistance provides information that encourages 7.1 percent of landowners to harvest from mature current inventories within a four-year period or

annual harvests = 0.071(mature standing inventory)/4

If we generously assume that the standing forest for the aggregate of all NIPF landowners in North Carolina is a regulated forest, then

mature inventory = (current inventory)2/30

Current standing inventory is multiplied by 2 to account for growth of a regulated forest before its eventual harvest and divided by 30 for the assumed thirty-year rotation.

The harvest measure from the preceding paragraph corresponds to an increase in equilibrium quantity of 1.13 Mcf. This increase can be interpreted as a supply shift along the demand function described in Appendix 3B. The equilibrium stumpage price, in this case, decreases $0.01 per Mcf. Thus, the beneficial impact of technical assistance on current harvests is very small.[19] Further assumptions about this supply shift are necessary in order to estimate the transfers and the deadweight welfare loss. One reasonable assumption is that the supply shift is parallel throughout. This is the same as assuming that technical assistance provides information that causes all landowners to decrease their stumpage reservation prices a similar amount.

Table 3.4 records our final estimates. Costs are total costs for both impacts of technical assistance. Transfers are for the separate TSI and harvest impacts. Since costs are combined, the net final social welfare loss must be the loss for the combination of both technical assistance program impacts. The comments regarding the attraction of FIP to consumers, industrial landowners, and nonindustrial landowners hold for the attraction of technical assistance. At very low discount rates, consumers may gain more from lower prices than NIPF landowners gain in valuable information obtained from technical assistance programs. The result can be a net loss to landowners.

In sum, many gains from technical assistance to NIPF landowners with timber objectives pass on to consumers or to the various factors of timber production. Industrial landowners ineligible for technical assistance may even lose as a function of a dominating price effect. The only NIPF landowners who achieve unambiguous gains from technical assistance are those with recreation or other nontimber objectives. These landowners suffer no retransfers (to different final product consumers) through the stumpage price effect. The social contribution of technical assistance is greater than that of FIP; that is, its contribution to the volume of timber supplied is greater (1.0 MMcf to 0.787 MMcf) and its net social cost is smaller ($303,300 to $747,800) because technical assistance yields both current and anticipated future harvest impacts and the likelihood of each of these impacts for any NIPF landowner is greater than the likelihood of the one (statistically significant) inventory or anticipated future harvest impact of FIP.

FURTHER THOUGHTS ON REDISTRIBUTION

Table 3.4 shows the redistributive effects of FIP and technical assistance for public servants, landowners, and consumers as well as the welfare costs to society as a whole. We can add another perspective on redistribution by considering the income distribution of recipients of FIP and technical assistance. One argument for both of these programs is that they aid small landowners who, presumably, are poorer members of our society. This latter perspective is a test of that argument.

Table 3.5 compares the income classes of all households nationwide with the income classes of all NIPF landowners, of all landowners receiving FIP, and of all landowners receiving technical assistance. The all-households measure is representative of the taxpayers who fund both public programs. The landowner measures are for North Carolina alone and originate from Royer's survey. We further divide landowners by (1) landowners in each income class regardless of acreage owned and (2) acres in each landowner income class.

The all-household income observations show the expected bell-shaped distribution. All the various NIPF landowner observations show bimodal distributions with one mode in the $15–25,000 class and one in the $45,000+ class. In any case, the great majority of both landowners and acres receiving the advantage of either FIP or technical assistance are associated with income classes in excess of $15,000. Fifty-five percent of acres receiving FIP and 57 percent of acres receiving technical assistance are held by landowners with annual incomes greater than $45,000. Finally, we make the general observation that NIPF landowner incomes are greater than all-household incomes throughout the distributions. The incomes of landowners receiving technical assistance are greater and the incomes of those receiving FIP are greater yet. These results unambiguously reject any argument that either direct FIP payments or technical assistance have redistributive merit for landowners in North Carolina.

Table 3.5. Redistributive effects of FIP and technical assistance (by percent of population in income class)

Population category	Annual income (in $1000s, 1980)							Gini coefficient
	0–5	5–10	10–15	15–25	25–35	35–45	45+	
All households, nationwide[a]	10.6	14.5	13.7	24.0	17.5	12.4[b]	7.3[c]	0.218
All NIPF landowners	10.0	15.0	15.7	23.3	12.6	8.1	15.2	0.246
All NIPF acres, by income of landowner	9.0	6.1	11.8	8.2	9.4	9.4	47.4	-0.072
All NIPF landowners receiving FIP[d]	0	13.2	5.3	21.0	13.2	15.8	31.5	0.052
All NIPF acres receiving FIP, by income of landowner[d]	0	4.5	1.8	12.0	5.9	21.0	54.9	-0.328
All NIPF landowners receiving technical assistance[e]	4.1	9.2	10.2	19.4	15.3	9.2	32.6	0.076
All NIPF acres receiving technical assistance, by income of landowner[e]	0.7	8.9	6.7	10.1	8.6	7.8	57.3	-0.236

[a]*Statistical Abstract of the U.S. 1982–83*, p. 429.
[b]Annual income, $35–50,000.
[c]Annual income greater than $50,000.
[d]Sample size, 38.
[e]Sample size, 98.

Summary and Conclusions

The purpose of this chapter is to examine public cost sharing programs. Cost sharing programs provide incentives for nonindustrial private landowners to grow timber. In particular, the current program, FIP, pays a share of regeneration or timber stand improvement costs for eligible landowners.

Forestry incentives are an appropriate topic of inquiry for this volume on public regulation because they represent a large-scale, long-term public market intervention. Their basic justification has its roots in the expectation of market failure to prevent a forthcoming timber famine. More recent justifications are the restrictive effort of cost sharing on anticipated future stumpage price increases and the redistributive gain for less–well-off citizens who happen to be NIPF landowners.

We restrict our examination to the impacts of FIP on North Carolina landowners because the best available data source refers to that population. That same data source also permits us to examine the impact of technical assistance, the extension forestry alternative to cost sharing. We begin our analysis with a conceptual model of landowner behavior which permits both timber and recreation or other nontimber landowner objectives and then test the model with the survey data from North Carolina.

Our most general observation is that output subsidies (on harvests) are more effective than input subsidies (on regeneration or timber stand improvement) because (1) input subsidies focus primarily on only one factor of production (capital) and (2) some share of input subsidies never result in the desired output. Therefore, we expect that cost sharing programs like FIP are more successful at increasing relative capital use than at stimulating harvests. Indeed, FIP has no statistically significant impact on North Carolina harvests in the survey period available to us. In contrast, technical assistance shows no bias for capital inputs. It leads to significant increases in both timber stand improvements and current harvests. The combination of these results suggests that support for dissemination of technical and market information to private landowners is a better means of increasing timber supply than a dollar equivalent reforestation subsidy like FIP.

The second step of our analysis is to impose our measure of the impacts of FIP and technical assistance on our knowledge of the North Carolina timber supply. This permits us to measure the social welfare benefits and costs of these programs.

We know that if the good in question exchanges in a freely operating and competitive market which includes neither externalities nor nonmarket values, then there can be only net welfare losses from public market intervention. Timber does exchange in a free and competitive market that includes no externalities; therefore our findings of net social welfare losses are unsurprising. NIPF timber producers gain from their FIP receipts or from the information obtained from extension foresters. Much of these gains, however, are passed on as payments to factors. To the extent that these payments and this information lead to harvest expansion, either current or eventual, and harvest expansion causes lower prices, then consumers also gain. Landowners who do not harvest, either now or eventually, contribute no timber value to society but receive an internalized nonmarket gain from the payment or information. This gain is unshared either within or outside the market. Taxpayers make the FIP payments and support the technical assistance. Their losses exceed the transfers to consumers and producers because some of their support of FIP and technical assistance has a greater opportunity return elsewhere.

Redistributive arguments for FIP and technical assistance are apparently no more valid than efficiency arguments. The population distribution of NIPF landowners reflects greater wealth than the population distribution of taxpayers as a whole and the population distribution of landowners receiving FIP reflects greater wealth yet.

Our empirical observations are only valid for North Carolina. We anticipate that evidence from other states would reflect different magnitudes of gains and losses. In particular, NIPF landowners may make greater gains from FIP and technical assistance in the Deep South where foresters generally expect that timber production is a more viable option. The opposite may be true in the Northeast and the Great Lakes states where timber production on NIPF lands may be financially less viable and where the landowners are well known for their nontimber objectives. Program administrators tend to agree with these generalizations and these anticipated regional results are consistent with the regional expenditure pattern for FIP.

Our observations cause us to go a step further, however, and to predict that technical assistance is generally more cost effective (and less inefficient) than an equal amount of cost sharing and that only the magnitudes of impact vary regionally. Nevertheless, both cost sharing and technical assistance have negative net impacts on social welfare regardless of the region. Furthermore, we might anticipate that forest landowners in all regions are generally from income classes undeserving of transfers usually intended for the least–well-off members of society. In sum, technical assistance is probably less undesirable than cost sharing, but neither is a wise use of public funds.

Appendix 3A: Landowner Supply Equations

DERIVATION OF THE INPUT–OUTPUT EQUATIONS AND SUPPLY ELASTICITY

From the definitions of capital and labor in the text we know that $L = L_1 + L_2$ and $K = K_1 + K_2$. The logarithmic differentials of these two equations are

$$L\hat{L} = L_1\hat{L}_1 + L_2\hat{L}_2, \text{ and } K\hat{K} = K_1\hat{K}_1 + K_2\hat{K}_2. \tag{3A.1}$$

Multiplying the first of these by w, the second by r, and dividing each of them by x yields

$$\theta_L L = \mu_1\theta_{L1}\hat{L}_1 + \mu_2\theta_{L2}\hat{L}_2, \text{ and}$$
$$(1 - \theta_L)\hat{K} = \mu_1(1 - \theta_{L1})\hat{K}_1 + \mu_2(1 - \theta_{L2})\hat{K}_2 \tag{3A.2}$$

since $wL/x = \theta_L$, $rK/x = (1 - \theta_L)$, $wL_i/x = \mu_i\theta_{Li}$, and $rK_i/x = \mu_i(1 - \theta_{Li})$. When the costs of production in each sector are minimized, then

$$L_i = L_i(wT_{Li}, rT_{Li}, x_i/\beta_i) \quad i = 1,2 \tag{3A.3}$$

which describes the demand for labor as a function of (tax inclusive) input prices and the level of output. Assuming constant returns to scale, then equation (3A.3) may be rewritten as a function of the factor price ratios or

$$L_i = x_i/\beta_i F_i(wT_{Li}/rT_{Ki}). \tag{3A.4}$$

The logarithmic differential of this factor demand equation is

$$\hat{L}_i = \hat{x}_i - \hat{\beta}_i - (1 - \theta_{Li})s_i(\widehat{w\gamma_i/r}) \tag{3A.5a}$$

where s_i is the elasticity of substitution between L and K in the ith sector's production and $\gamma \equiv T_{Li}/T_{Ki}$. Analogously, for capital

$$\hat{K}_i = \hat{x}_i - \hat{\beta}_i + \theta_{Li}s_i(\widehat{w\gamma_i/r}) \tag{3A.5b}$$

These two equations (3A.5) are the "input–output" equations. They play a major role in derivation of the general equilibrium supplies in the next section of this appendix.

Turning to derivation of the supply elasticity, we note that along the production possibilities frontier, the L, K, the βs, and all taxes are constant. Thus, equations (3A.2) and (3A.5) may be rewritten as

$$0 = \mu_1\theta_{L1}\hat{L}_1 + \mu_2\theta_{L2}\hat{L}_2 = \mu_1(1 - \theta_{L1})\hat{K}_1 + \mu_2(1 - \theta_{L2})\hat{K}_2 \tag{3A.6}$$

and

$$\hat{L}_i = \hat{x}_i - (1 - \theta_{Li})s_i(\widehat{w/r}) \tag{3A.7a}$$

$$\hat{K}_i = \hat{x}_i + \theta_{Li}s_i(\widehat{w/r}) \tag{3A.7b}$$

Inserting equations (3A.7) into (3A.6) and solving for the x_i terms yields

$$\hat{x}_i = \mu_i(\theta_{Li} - \theta_{Lj})s(\widehat{w/r}) \qquad i \neq j \tag{3A.8}$$

where $s = [\mu_1\theta_{L1}(1 - \theta_{L1})s_1 + \mu_2\theta_{L2}(1 - \theta_{L2})s_2]/[\mu_1\mu_2(\theta_{L1} - \theta_{L2})^2]$.

Along the production possibilities frontier, equation (3.8) in the body of the chapter may be rewritten as $\hat{P}_i = \theta_{Li}w + (1 - \theta_{Li})\hat{r}$ from which it follows that

$$(\widehat{P_i/P_j}) = (\theta_{Li} - \theta_{Lj})(\hat{w}/r) \tag{3A.9}$$

This permits us to rewrite equation (3A.8) as

$$\hat{x}_i = \mu_j s(\widehat{P_i/P_j}) \tag{3A.8'}$$

Now, from equation (3.11) in the chapter, we know that $\mu_i(\widehat{P_i/P_j}) = P_i$ so that equation (3A.8) may again be rewritten as

$$\hat{x}_i = s\hat{P}_i \tag{3A.8''}$$

showing that s is the elasticity of supply for each output sector.

GENERAL EQUILIBRIUM OUTPUT SUPPLY EQUATIONS

The input–output equations (3A.5) may be stated equivalently as

$$\hat{L}_i = (\widehat{K_i/\beta_i}) - (1 - \theta_{Li})s_i((\hat{w}/r) + \hat{\gamma}_i) \qquad i = 1,2 \tag{3A.10a}$$

and

$$\hat{K}_i = (\widehat{K_i/\beta_i}) + \theta_{Li}s_i((\hat{w}/r) + \hat{\gamma}_i) \tag{3A.10b}$$

Combining equations (3A.10) with equations (3A.2) for both labor and capital yields

$$\theta_L\hat{L} = \mu_1\theta_{L1}(\widehat{x_1/\beta_1}) + \mu_1\theta_{L1}(\widehat{K_2/\beta_2}) - s\mu_1\mu_2(\theta_{L1} - \theta_{L2})^2 (\widehat{w/r})$$
$$+ \mu_1\theta_{L1}(1 - \theta_{L1}) \hat{\gamma}_1 + \mu_2\theta_{L2}(1 - \theta_{L2}) \hat{\gamma}_2 \tag{3A.11a}$$

and

$$(1 - \theta_L)\hat{K} = \mu_1(1 - \theta_{L1})(\widehat{x_1/\beta_1}) + \mu_2(1 - \theta_{L2})(\widehat{x_2/\beta_2})$$
$$- s\mu_1\mu_2 (\theta_{L1} - \theta_{L2})^2(\widehat{w/r})$$
$$+ \mu_1\theta_{L1}(1 - \theta_{L1}) \hat{\gamma}_1 + \mu_2\theta_{L2}(1 - \theta_{L2}) \hat{\gamma}_2 \tag{3A.11b}$$

Solving these two equations for the endogenous $(\widehat{x_2/\beta_2})$ terms yields

$$\widehat{x_i/\beta_i} = [\mu_j(\theta_{Li} - \theta_{Lj})/\mu_1\mu_2(\theta_{L1} - \theta_{L2})^2]\,[\theta_L(1 - \theta_{Lj})\hat{L}$$
$$- \theta_{Lj}(1 - \theta_L)\hat{K} + s\mu_1\mu_2(\theta_{L1} - \theta_{L2})^2(\hat{w}/r)$$
$$+ s\mu_1\theta_{L1}(1 - \theta_{L1})\,\hat{\gamma}_1 + s\mu_1\theta_{L2}(1 - \theta_{L2})\,\hat{\gamma}_2] \qquad (3A.12)$$

Manipulating terms from this equation, we obtain

$$[\mu_j(\theta_{Li} - \theta_{Lj})/\mu_1\mu_2(\theta_{L1} - \theta_{L2})^2]\,[\theta_L(1 - \theta_{Lj})\hat{L} - \theta_{Lj}(1 - \theta_L)\hat{K}]$$
$$= \theta_L L + (1 - \theta_L)\hat{K} + [\theta_L(1 - \theta_L)(\theta_L - \theta_{Li})/\mu_1\mu_2(\theta_{L1} - \theta_{L2})^2]\hat{K}$$
$$\qquad (3A.13)$$

where $R \equiv (K/L)$.

Equation (3.8) in the chapter describes changes in marginal costs. Rewritten, this becomes

$$(\widehat{\beta_i p_i/T_i}) = \theta_{Li}\hat{w} + (1 - \theta_{Li})\hat{r}$$
$$(\widehat{\beta_i p_j/T_j}) = \theta_{Lj}\hat{w} - (1 - \theta_{Lj})\hat{r}$$

Subtracting the second of these from the first and multiplying by μ_j yields

$$\mu_j(\widehat{\beta_i p_i T_j/\beta_j p_j T_i}) = \mu_j(\theta_{L1} - \theta_{Lj}) \qquad (3A.14)$$

and using the definitions of p, β, and T yields

$$\mu_j(\widehat{\beta_i p_i T/\beta T_i}) = \mu_j(\theta_{Li} - \theta_{Lj}) \qquad (3A.15)$$

Finally, combining equations (3A.15) and (3A.13) with (3A.12) provides the output supplies

$$\hat{x}_i = \beta_i + s(\widehat{\beta_i p_i T/\beta T_i}) + \theta_L\hat{L} + (1 - \theta_L)\hat{K}$$
$$+ [\theta_L(1 - \theta_L)(\theta_L - \theta_{Li})/\mu_2\mu_2(\theta_{L1} - \theta_{L2})^2]\hat{R}$$
$$+ \mu_j(\theta_{Li} - \theta_{Lj})s\,[\mu_1\theta_{L1}(1 - \theta_{L1})\,\hat{\gamma}_1 + \mu_2\theta_{L2}(1 - \theta_{L2})\,\hat{\gamma}_2] \qquad (3A.16)$$

which express each sector's supply totally in terms of exogenous parameters.

Appendix 3B: North Carolina Demand and Supply Equations

The objective of this appendix is to develop aggregate stumpage supply and demand estimates for North Carolina.[20] Lumber and wood products demand estimates are unavailable; therefore, we must reject the derived approach in favor of the direct estimation approach demonstrated by Jackson (1983) in his study of Montana's timber market. The direct estimation approach is attractive for relatively small regional markets such as North Carolina or Montana and has the additional advantage of permitting simultaneous estimation of the supply and demand. The heterogeneity of ownerships and the combination of both softwood and hardwood stumpage, however, make North Carolina's market more complex than Montana's primarily public and primarily softwood market.

The simultaneous equation approach estimates the supply and demand parameters indirectly by solving reduced-form equations. The direct relationships are

$$Q_D = q_1(P_S, P_F) \tag{3B.1}$$
$$Q_S = q_2(P_S, I) \tag{3B.2}$$
$$Q_D = Q_S \tag{3B.3}$$

where Q_D = stumpage quantity demanded;
$\quad\quad Q_S$ = stumpage quantity supplied;
$\quad\quad P_S$ = stumpage price;
$\quad\quad P_F$ = final goods (lumber and wood products) price;
$\quad\quad I$ = stumpage inventory.

We estimate the reduced forms of equations (3B.1) and (3B.2) from time series data. Our actual estimates are in logarithmic form because the logarithmic transformation eliminates the heteroscedasticity found in nonlogarithmic form and because the coefficients in the logarithmic form are the inventory and price elasticities.

DATA

The necessary data are (1) a measure of combined hardwood and softwood stumpage harvest; (2) a weighted average stumpage price; (3) a relative price index for finished goods (lumber and wood products); and (4) the standing timber inventory. All data are on a statewide, all-ownership basis, and are annual for the years 1962–1982.

STUMPAGE HARVEST. In their final form, harvest data are an estimate of the annual softwood and hardwood cut in North Carolina in thousand cubic feet (Mcf).[21] Unfortunately, total state- and ownershipwide harvests are not tabulated each year by either the USDA or North Carolina Forest Services; therefore, this measure must be compiled from several sources. We found the annual production of each major finished forest product (that is, lumber, plywood, and pulpwood, which together account for 95 percent of all harvests) and multiplied each by its conversion factor in order to express the finished volume in Mcf of stumpage input requirements. The sum of stumpage requirements for each product equals the annual stumpage harvest.

The U.S. Department of Labor *Current Industrial Report MA-24T* (1962–1982) provides the softwood and hardwood lumber production data. The USDA Forest Service resource bulletin, *Southern Pulpwood Production* (1962–1982), provides softwood and hardwood pulpwood production data. The American Plywood Association (1983) reports softwood plywood production. Our estimates exclude stumpage inputs to hardwood plywood production because the data are relatively unavailable and also because hardwood plywood accounts for an insignificant share of total stumpage demand.[22]

The U.S. Forest Service reports conversion factors for thousand board feet of lumber (Mbf) and cords of pulpwood to Mcf of stumpage for selected years (USDA Forest Service 1958; 1965; 1973; 1982). We derive conversion factors for million square feet (MMft^2) of plywood to Mcf of stumpage input from plywood output reported in both measures (American Plywood Association 1983; USDA Forest Service 1965; 1973; 1982). For all products, conversion factors for the years not reported are linear interpolations of the known factors.

STUMPAGE PRICE. There is no good stumpage price series that includes stumpage sold from all ownerships for all years in our study period. Our stumpage price series is a weighted average of the reported stumpage prices for softwood and hardwood sawtimber and pulpwood for North Carolina National Forests.[23] The weights are the production proportions found in the previous step. For example, the softwood sawtimber weight is the portion of total harvest accounted for by softwood lumber and plywood production. Reported prices are in units of $/Mbf for sawtimber and $/cord for pulpwood. The previous conversion factors provide the measure to combine all prices into a weighted average price in the common unit of $/Mbf. Finally, this weighted price, divided by the all-commodities price index (U.S. Department of Commerce 1983), creates a real price.

FINAL GOODS PRICE. The proxy for final goods price is the relative national lumber and wood products price index (U.S. Department of Commerce 1983). There is no North Carolina counterpart for this national index, but this is probably not a problem because North Carolina's final goods trade in a national market. Furthermore, truly exogenous variables are driven by broad economywide forces and should not contain endogenous local fluctuations.

INVENTORY. The measure of inventory is the total volume in MMcf of softwood and hardwood growing stock in North Carolina. North Carolina inventories are recorded for the years 1962, 1970, 1974, 1977, and 1983–1984 (USDA Forest Service 1966; 1975; 1982; 1984; 1985). Linear regressions of both softwood and hardwood inventory provide inventory estimates for the intermediate years. The regression results are

Softwood inventory (MMcf) $= 2172.608 + 110.188T$
$$(5.883) \qquad (21.939)$$
$$F = 481.336 \qquad R^2 = .9917$$

Hardwood inventory (MMcf) $= -5939.604 + 279.709T$
$$(-3.013) \qquad (10.435)$$
$$F = 108.892 \qquad R^2 = .9643$$

where T = time in years (1962, 1963 . . . 1982). The numbers in parentheses are t ratios, and both equations are significant at the .01 level of confidence.

These regressions show that inventory is linearly related to time; therefore the inventory variable in the supply and demand equations also serves as the trend variable. No separate trend variable is included for this reason.

RESULTS

Combining these data according to the method previously described yields the following results for the least squares regressions of the reduced form equations:

$$\ln Q = 10.667195 + .459164 \ln P_F + .017873 \ln I \qquad (3B.4)$$
$$(9.698) \qquad (3.992) \qquad (.148)$$
$$F = 10.059 \qquad R^2 = .4753 \qquad DW = 1.463$$
$$\ln P_s = 2.205865 + 1.721184 \ln P_F - .541457 \ln I \qquad (3B.5)$$
$$(.563) \qquad (4.200) \qquad (-1.262)$$
$$F = 8.989 \qquad R^2 = .4441 \qquad DW = 1.980$$

The numbers in parentheses are t ratios, and both equations are significant at the .01 level of confidence. All signs are as anticipated. Upon completing each regression, we tested for, but found no evidence of, either autocorrelation or heteroscedasticity.

Solving for P_F and I and substituting into the supply and demand equations provides estimates for the original demand and supply equations for North Carolina stumpage:

$$\ln Q_S = 10.078732 + .2667722 \ln P_S + .1623186 \ln I \qquad \text{(3B.6)}$$
$$\ln Q_D = 10.740009 + .5159787 \ln P_F - .0330091 \ln P_S \qquad \text{(3B.7)}$$

These results are satisfying despite the weaknesses of our data and the limitations of our approach. That is, we would prefer to derive our demand function from the production function of the stumpage processing industries and, in lieu of that, we would prefer more frequent inventory data. Nevertheless, we are able to determine demand and supply functions for North Carolina's combined output of softwood and hardwood stumpage that show correlations between actual and predicted values of .7362 and .4547, respectively, for the years 1962–1982. Our ability to predict quantity and price, from equations (3B.4) and (3B.5), is even more satisfactory. The correlations between actual and predicted market clearing prices and quantities are .7069 and .7265, respectively. Furthermore, our elasticities are all within a reasonable range of those found elsewhere in the literature for similar situations.

Notes

1. This is no statement whatsoever about economic potential. Furthermore, Clawson (1979) argues that there is no reason to single out the NIPF lands. Industrial and nonindustrial private lands perform similarly with respect to their biological potential if we compare them on a state-by-state basis. Only when we aggregate to the national level does a distinction appear between biological performances on industrial and nonindustrial lands. The distinction is due to better biological performance in the Pacific Northwest than in the Southeast. (This fact itself throws doubt on the usefulness of the biological performance measure.) Industrial lands are relatively predominant in the Pacific Northwest, whereas nonindustrial lands are relatively predominant in the Southeast.

2. DeSteiguer (1984) refers to additional nonindustrial private investment induced by FIP. In this diagram, his induced investment is the area q_1ebq_2. DeSteiguer finds that the incremental private induced investment (q_2b) equals one-fifth the public matching investment (db). In general, the magnitude of induced private investment is a function of the supply and demand elasticities and the federal cost share. The larger the supply and demand elasticities and the smaller the federal share, then the larger the relative private inducement.

3. We might anticipate the argument that the relative price of timber is increasing and that FIP leads to expanding harvests which restrict somewhat the relative price increase. If the anticipated price increase originates from an increase in demand and D in Figure 3.1 fails to reflect this increase, then the appropriate demand function is (unshown) D', which is to the right of the function D. The remaining analysis is analogous to our earlier argument. If, instead, the anticipated price increase originates from an increase in costs, then the appropriate supply functions are above the functions S and S'. The counterpart to S remains above the

counterpart to S' and, once more, the remaining analysis is analogous to our earlier argument. In all cases, there is a net welfare loss equal to or greater than the triangle *abd* or its counterpart.

4. This literature seems almost completely forgotten in current discussions of federal programs for assisting NIPF landowners. This is particularly surprising when we consider that it is arguably the best-placed body of literature in the history of forest economics and that it was written by many of those who are now senior leaders among forest economics and policy professionals (Conklin 1966; Muench 1966; Lord 1963; Quinney & Schallau 1963; Kenniston 1962; James & Schallau 1961; Stoddard 1961; Stoltenberg & Webster 1959; Yoho & James 1958; Stoltenberg 1954; James 1950). (James and Yoho were the dissertation chairmen who provided incentive for much of this literature.) Some recent literature is consistent with these older discussions (Wallace & Silver 1983; Binkley 1981; Gregersen, Houghtaling, & Rubenstein 1979); other recent literature at least is not inconsistent (Mills & Cain 1979; Mills 1978; 1976; 1975). The bulk of recent literature, however, fails to tie landowner objectives with timber harvest expectations and, thereby, arrives at judgements that we believe cannot be substantiated. See, for example, several of the participant papers in *Nonindustrial Private Forests: A Review of Economic and Policy Studies* (Royer & Risbrudt 1983).

5. Commercial forestland consists of acres that are capable of producing in excess of 20 ft^3 of industrial wood fiber per annum. The definition is restricted to a unique unit of measure and void of any changes in mill utilization or market conditions. Furthermore, it only considers species currently growing on the acre—in spite of the fact that other native species (species occurring within the natural successional sequence) may grow at different rates.

6. The next chapter discusses the pricing and satisfactory offer problem further.

7. The model draws on concepts used by modern labor economists and bears similarity with models frequently encountered in the international trade and public finance literature. See, for example, Becker and Lewis (1972) for the labor methodology. See Caves and Jones (1973) and Johnson (1971) for diagrammatic and mathematical presentations of two-sector models similar to the model in this chapter.

8. The prices of all inputs and outputs are shadow prices corresponding to relative values within the model. They should not be confused with exogenous factors like the market price of timber.

9. See Appendix 3A for the derivatives.

10. Letting income rise on the production possibilities frontier with a subsidy, as it would with an increase in β_1, we obtain $x_1 = [s\mu(\eta_1 - \sigma)]/(\sigma + s)T_2$. Therefore, if $\eta_1 > \sigma$, then household consumption from the land x_1 increases at the expense of timber output x_2. But this is an unlikely case. We anticipate that the value of σ is relatively high since other types of recreation are good substitutes for x_1. Furthermore, the anticipated η_1 is low (i.e., $\eta_1 < 1$) since a landowner will be satiated with x_1 long before becoming satiated with all other goods (represented by x_2).

11. Royer mailed 960 inquiries and received 531 replies for a 55 percent response, a good response for this type of survey. A follow-up phone survey indicated that nonrespondent replies did not differ significantly from those of respondents, thereby suggesting that there is little risk of sample selection bias. Of the 531 respondents, 111 are not useful because either the ownership did not qualify as nonindustrial private or the respondent made no reply for one or more key varia-

bles. The remaining 420 respondents provide the sample for our probit analysis of TSI, equation (3.24). The sample for timber harvesting, equation (3.23), is only 298. Some landowners who made TSIs have only immature timber. Only those who own mature timber can have a positive probability to harvest. We examined all 420 observations for landowners who harvested timber in 1980, and from these we searched for the most recent previous harvest by any sample member. This harvest was in 1950 and it suggests an estimate of 30 years for timber rotations. Therefore, we eliminate from the sample of 420 all 122 landowners who harvested in the 30 years immediately prior to 1980, on grounds that their currently standing timber is immature. The effect of this reduction in observations is to make our results less precise (since data were omitted) but to leave them unbiased.

12. For each observation i, $y^*_{it} < 0.5$ predicts a value of 0, and $y^*_{it} > 0.5$ predicts a value of 1.

13. Many suggest that the length of land tenure is positively correlated with timber harvests (e.g., Clawson 1979, Stoddard 1961). Our comparative static results provide no insight to this hypothesis. Furthermore, our regressions with Royer's data never found this relationship to be significant. For both reasons, together, we exclude land tenure from the equations reported in Tables 3.2 and 3.3.

Our own hypothesis that there is no relation between tenure and likelihood of harvest is consistent with our empirical results as well as with the observations of Stoddard, Clawson, and others, if we accept that the length of land tenure historically may have been correlated with timber harvests. Historically, farmers composed a larger share of nonindustrial private landowners. More recently they have sold to industrial and nonfarm private landowners. Industrial lands are not included in either these data or this question. Nonfarm private landowners, though more inclined to TSI, may be less inclined to harvest their timber.

14. We overlook the interdependence of stumpage demand and supply over time. Interdependence is due to the long production and investment periods in timber and the fact that stumpage is both factor and product. This interdependence need not modify our analysis because the physical impacts of FIP and technical assistance on aggregate timber production are very small, even if all accumulated in one year. That is, one year's demand has no significant impact on that very small share of next year's supply induced by FIP or technical assistance.

Nevertheless, our estimates should be treated with caution because they may vary over time (see Cooley & Prescott 1973). Our estimates represent our best knowledge of future markets *at this time.*

15. Average rotations may even be shorter—implying smaller physical yields. Newman (1986) and Lofgren and Johansson (1985, Chapter 9) show that landowners are responsive to pulpwood price but not to sawtimber prices. Pulpwood rotations are shorter than sawtimber rotations.

16. For example, a few gains are from hardwood plantations that yield less in discounted value and in annual volume than pines. For another example, gains from one injection of FIP or TA may accrue over several years only beginning with year 30. We make the assumption—generous to eventual economic welfare implications—that all gains from any public effort accrue immediately in the thirtieth year.

17. Our choice of discount rates is guided by the Office of Management and Budget (OMB)–U.S. Forest Service negotiated rate of 4 percent and the OMB rate of 10 percent for most other federal agency investments.

18. The fully stocked plantation yields per acre are much greater than the yield response (610 ft³/acre) that Cubbage finds for similar technical assistance in Geor-

gia (personal communication, background data for Cubbage, Skinner, & Risbrudt 1985). Cubbage's results suggest an additional reason to believe our results are generous with respect to beneficial impacts of technical assistance. (Cubbage's actual statistic is volume/acre response to technical assistance divided by standing volume/acre. Multiplying this by the standing NIPF softwood volume/acre in North Carolina in 1980 provides the yield response of 610 ft³/acre.)

19. Its size relative to the impacts of either FIP or technical assistance, however, is indeterminate. All we can say is that our estimates of benefits from all three are biased upward.

20. See Daniels and Hyde (1986) for greater detail.

21. FIP and technical assistance affect both species groups. Therefore, the species aggregation is appropriate even if we make the generous assumption of all softwood reforestation in the body of this chapter.

22. Hardwood plywood production data are available for only two years out of the twenty-year study period. In 1964, timber cut for hardwood plywood accounted for 14 percent of the hardwood harvest (.05 percent of the total harvest). In 1973 it accounted for 9 percent and .03 percent of the hardwood and total harvests, respectively.

23. Although these are the prices received for public timber sales, a comparison of these prices for recent private sale stumpage prices reported in Norris (1976–1983) shows that, for the period 1976–1983, public and private prices are highly correlated. Their correlation coefficient is .92. Hence the North Carolina National Forest price series, which extends throughout the entire study period (1962–1982), provides a reasonable proxy for stumpage price data for all North Carolina ownerships.

References

Adams, D. M., R. W. Haynes, G. F. Dutrow, R. L. Barber, and J. M. Vasievich. 1982. Private investment in forest management and the long-term supply of timber. *American Journal of Agricultural Economics* 64(2):232–41.

Amemiya, T. 1981. Qualitative response models: A survey. *Journal of Economic Literature* 19(4):1483–1536.

American Plywood Association. 1983. *Structural panel production statistics.* Management Bulletin No. FA-220. Tacoma, Wash.: Author.

Becker, G. S., and G. H. Lewis. 1972. Interaction between quantity and quality of children. *Journal of Political Economy* (April):5279–88.

Binkley, C. S. 1981. *Timber supply from nonindustrial forests: A microeconomic analysis of landowner behavior.* New Haven, Conn.: Yale University, School of Forestry and Environmental Studies Bulletin No. 92.

Burlington Northern. 1983. *Annual report, 1982.* Seattle, Wash.: Burlington Northern Inc.

Caves, R. E., and R. W. Jones. 1973. *World trade and payments: An introduction.* Boston: Little, Brown.

Clawson, M. 1979. The economics of U.S. private nonindustrial forests. Working Paper R-14. Washington, D.C.: Resources for the Future.

Conklin, H. E. 1966. The new forests of New York. *Land Economics* 42:203–4.

Cooley, T., and E. C. Prescott. 1973. Varying parameter regression: A theory and some applications. *Annals of Economic and Social Measurement* 10(4):463–73.

Cubbage, F. W., T. M. Skinner, and C. D. Risbrudt. 1985. *An economic evaluation of the Georgia rural forestry assistance program.* Research Bulletin 322. Athens: University of Georgia, College of Agriculture Experiment Station.

Daniels, B., and W. F. Hyde. 1986. Demand and supply for North Carolina's timber. *Forest Ecology and Management* 14(2):59–67.

deSteiguer, J. E. 1984. Impact of cost-share programs on private reforestation investment. *Forest Science* 30(3):697–704.

Gregersen, H., T. Houghtaling, and A. Rubenstein. 1979. *Economics of public forestry incentive programs: A case study of cost-sharing in Minnesota.* Agricultural Experiment Station Technical Bulletin No. 315. St. Paul: University of Minnesota.

Jackson, D. H. 1983. Sub-regional timber demand analysis: Remarks and an approach for prediction. *Forest Ecology and Management* 5:109–18.

James, L. M. 1950. Determining forest landownership and its relation to timber management. *Journal of Forestry* 48(4):261–64.

James, L. M., and C. H. Schallau. 1961. Forestry practices under the Agricultural Conservation Program. *Land Economics* 37:142–49.

Johnson, H. G. 1971. *The two sector model of general equilibrium.* London: George Allen and Unwin Ltd.

Kenniston, R. F. 1962. The forest owner—A person. *Journal of Forestry* 60(4):249–53.

Lee, L. F. 1978. Unionism and wage rates: A simultaneous equations model with qualitative and limited dependent variables. *International Economic Review* 19(2):415–34.

Lofgren, K. G., and P. O. Johansson. 1985. *The economics of forestry and natural resources.* Oxford: Basil Blackwell Ltd.

Lord, W. B. 1963. A reconsideration of the farm forestry problem. *Journal of Forestry* 61(4):262–64.

McClure, J. P., and H. A. Knight. 1984. *Empirical yields of timber and forest biomass in the Southeast.* Research Paper SE-245. Asheville, N.C.: USDA Forest Service Southeastern Forest Experiment Station.

Mills, T. J. 1975. Investment priorities for small-owner assistance programs. *Journal of Forestry* 73(4):210–13.

———. 1976. 1974 Forestry Incentives Program: Indicators of cost effectiveness. *Journal of Forestry* 74(10):678–83.

———. 1978. *Timber yield and financial return performances of the 1974 Forestry Incentives Program.* Research Paper RM-204. Washington, D.C.: USDA Forest Service.

Mills, T. J., and D. Cain. 1979. Financial efficiency of the 1974 Forestry Incentives Program. *Journal of Forestry* 77(10):661–66.

Muench, J. 1966. The impact of public versus private ownership on timberland in a rural economy. *Journal of Forestry* 64(11):721–24.

Newman, D. H. 1986. An econometric analysis of aggregate gains from technical change in southern softwood forestry. Ph.D. dissertation. Duke University, Durham, N.C.

Norris, F. 1976–1983. Timber Mart-South. 1(1)–8(12). Highlands, N.C.: Timber Mart-South Incorporated.

President's Advisory Panel on Timber and the Environment. 1973. *Report of the President's Advisory Panel on Timber and the Environment.* Washington, D.C.: U.S. Government Printing Office.

Quinney, D. N., and C. H. Schallau. 1963. Lake states forest lands in a changing economy. *Land Economics* 39:421–28.

Resources for the Future. 1958. *Forest credit in the United States: A survey of needs and facilities.* Washington, D.C.: Resources for the Future.

Royer, J. P. 1981. North Carolina nonindustrial private forest landowner's survey. Durham, N.C.: Duke University School of Forestry and Environmental Studies.

Royer, J. P., and C. D. Risbrudt, eds. 1983. *Nonindustrial Private Forests: A Review of Economic and Policy Studies.* Durham, N.C.: Duke University School of Forestry and Environmental Studies.

Stoddard, C. H. 1961. *The small private forest in the United States.* Washington, D.C.: Resources for the Future.

Stoltenberg, C. H. 1954. Rural zoning in Minnesota. *Land Economics* 30:153.

Stoltenberg, C. H., and H. H. Webster. 1959. What ownership characteristics are useful in predicting response to forestry programs? *Land Economics* 35:292–95.

U.S. Department of Agriculture (USDA), Agricultural Stabilization and Conservation Service (ASCS). 1980. *Annual Statistical Report.* Washington, D.C.: U.S. Government Printing Office.

USDA, Forest Service. 1958. *Timber resources for America's future.* Forest Resource Report No. 14.

_____. 1962–1982. *Southern pulpwood production.* Resource Bulletin SE-(nos. 5–8). Asheville, N.C.: USDA Forest Service Southeastern Forest Experiment Station.

_____. 1965. *Timber trends in the United States.* Forest Resource Report No. 17. Washington, D.C.: Author.

_____. 1966. *North Carolina's timber.* Resource Bulletin SE-5. Asheville, N.C.: USDA Forest Service Southeastern Forest Experiment Station.

_____. 1973. *The outlook for timber in the United States.* Forest Resource Report No. 20. Washington, D.C.: Author.

_____. 1975. *North Carolina's timber, 1974.* Resource Bulletin SE-33. Asheville, N.C.: USDA Forest Service Southeastern Forest Experiment Station.

_____. 1982. *An analysis of the timber situation in the United States 1952–2030.* Forest Resources Report No. 23. Washington, D.C.: Author.

_____. 1984. *Forest statistics for the northern coastal plain of North Carolina, 1984.* Resource Bulletin SE-74. Asheville, N.C.: USDA Forest Service Southeastern Forest Experiment Station.

_____. 1984. *Forest statistics for the southern coastal plain of North Carolina, 1983.* Resource Bulletin SE-72. Asheville, N.C.: USDA Forest Service Southeastern Forest Experiment Station.

_____. 1985. *Forest statistics for the mountains of North Carolina, 1984.* Resource Bulletin SE-77. Asheville, N.C.: USDA Forest Service Southeastern Forest Experiment Station.

_____. 1985. *Forest statistics for the piedmont of North Carolina, 1984.* Resource Bulletin SE-76. Asheville, N.C.: USDA Forest Service Southeastern Forest Experiment Station.

_____. 1985. *Forest statistics for the piedmont of North Carolina, 1984.* Resource Bulletin SE-76. Asheville, N.C.: USDA Forest Service Southeastern Forest Experiment Station.

U.S. Department of Commerce, Bureau of the Census. 1983. *Statistical abstract of the United States*. 104th ed. Washington, D.C.: U.S. Government Printing Office.

U.S. Department of Labor, Bureau of the Census. 1962–1982. *Lumber Production and Mill Stocks*. Current Industrial Reports MA-24T. Washington D.C.: U.S. Government Printing Office.

Wallace, T. D., and D. H. Newman. 1986. Measurement of ownership effects on forest productivity in North Carolina, 1974–84. *Canadian Journal of Forest Research* 16:733–38.

Wallace, T. D., and J. L. Silver. 1983. Public cost-sharing and production in nonindustrial private forests: The case of FIP in coastal Georgia. In *Nonindustrial private forests: A review of economic and policy studies,* ed. J. P. Royer and C. D. Risbrudt, pp. 165–80. Durham, N.C.: Duke University School of Forestry and Environmental Studies.

Wu, D. M. 1965. An empirical analysis of household durable goods expenditures. *Econometrica* 34:761–80.

Yoho, J. G., and L. M. James. 1958. Influence of some public assistance programs on forest landowners in northern Michigan. *Land Economics* 34(4):357–64.

CHAPTER 4

Price Reporting Services

The purpose of this chapter is to consider the stabilization justification for public market intervention. Stabilization is an infrequently heard argument for current or proposed regulation of private forestry.[1] There may be an execption, however, in Timber Mart-South (TMS), a stumpage price reporting service for the southern and southeastern regions of the United States.

TMS currently publishes monthly average prices for sales of stumpage in 38 substate regions throughout the South and Southeast. TMS initially (1977–1980) received public financial assistance from the U.S. Department of Agriculture but is now entirely private and self-supporting. Its success encourages the Department of Agriculture to consider expanding stumpage price reporting services to other regions of the country, in particular the Northeast and the Great Lakes states.

Mill owners and large timber landowners have a good understanding of local stumpage market dynamics. Wood products are their full-time business, therefore they have sufficient incentive to keep themselves informed, and TMS brings them little benefit. The situation is different, however, for the multitude of nonindustrial private forest landowners. These landowners may be farmers and/or absentee landowners, usually with primary business interests and knowledge quite different from forestry. They may have little time to devote to forest management and personal comparative advantage in other pursuits even if some of them have keen interests in their forestlands. For these nonindustrial private forest landowners, TMS may provide the only reliable source of stumpage price information. (They can purchase advice from consulting foresters, but consultants may have some interest in providing a rosy picture of the market in order to convince landowners to sell timber and, thereby, to enhance their own commissions.)

The impact of TMS may be large where its price information actually affects timber management and harvesting decisions. Nonindustrial private forest landowners, although individually small, in the aggregate provide 65 percent of the total timber harvest in the South and Southeast. They provide lesser but still significant shares of total harvests in the Northeast and the Great Lakes states (56 and 59 percent, respectively) to which stumpage price reporting services may expand (USDA 1982, 423). Knowledge of prevailing market prices improves the competitive position of these nonindustrial private forest landowners with respect to other, larger producers of stumpage and with respect to purchasers of nonindustrial private harvests. Knowledge of stumpage prices may also reduce the randomness of nonindustrial private timber sales, encouraging more to be offered when prices are high and fewer when prices are low. The result may be a smoothing of market cycles or, what is the same, a decrease in stumpage price variation.

This price variation is the source of the stabilization justification for publicly supported price reporting services. There is no evidence of—and our ears pick up no argument for—market failure in the exchange of stumpage. There is evidence of redistributive gains from larger consumers of stumpage to smaller nonindustrial private producers, but this redistribution is not central to our interests in this chapter.

Stabilization is a common argument for market intervention in agriculture, where we observe publicly supported price reporting services as well as direct price supports and quantity guarantees, all in response to apparently widely fluctuating agricultural prices and quantities. Stabilization may be a valid argument for public market intervention in forestry as well. It remains for us to inquire whether the social gains from stumpage price stability (or decreases in price variability) outweigh their public administrative costs. TMS is the source of the stabilization gains in our empirical inquiry into this question.

 Approach

Our approach to the stabilization question is divided into two parts, a discussion of the general sources and the empirical magnitude of price variation in forestry and a discussion of the welfare effects associated with the reduced price variation, if any, attributed to TMS price reporting.[2] The sources of price variation in forestry are generally thought to originate with macroeconomic policies, the housing industry, and other demand-side variables. The theory we develop shows that there are supply-side sources of stochastic and unusual stumpage price variation as well. The supply-side sources feature the difficulty of making accurate projections and the likelihood of accumulating projection errors over time. A subsequent section of the chapter examines various empirical measures of price variation – regardless of its source.

The existence of price variation is insufficient evidence to justify market intervention. There is a certain amount of variability in all markets, yet we hear no arguments for universal market intervention or for constant trending prices. Social justification for price stability exists only where the variation causes unusual hardship. For this reason, both our theoretical and empirical inquiries contrast timber price variation with that of other basic materials. The contrast cannot show whether hardship exists, but it can show whether timber price variation is greater than usual for comparable materials. A look ahead shows that our findings are ambiguous. Nevertheless, a final section of this chapter proceeds with an assessment of TMS on grounds that there already has been a public market intervention to support its development. Therefore, assessment of TMS is, at least, an interesting ex post policy question.

A finding that price variation in forestry is unusually large and unexpected would raise several questions: Does price reporting help decrease the price variation and by how much? Do the benefits from price reporting exceed its costs? The answers to these questions require price data from both before and after introduction of a price reporting service. TMS provides "after" data for a case study but there is no good source for "before" data. Indeed, if there were, then there would be no cause for TMS.

We develop an alternate approach to answering these questions but one that provides only impressionistic answers at best. The data available before TMS is southwide and annual. We first find economic measures of the supply and demand for stumpage and the stochastic variation around each from this data. Our second step measures the consumers' and producers' gains from potential decreases in the variation, some of which must result from TMS. Finally, we ask whether it is reasonable that these uncertain gains from TMS exceed its known costs.

 ## Are Stumpage Prices Unstable?

Our purpose in this part of the chapter is first to provide the reasoning to anticipate that price variation in forestry is relatively larger than that for other basic raw materials and then to test this hypothesis empirically. Our reasoning includes demand arguments – but features (previously unidentified) supply arguments.

THEORY

Foresters direct only a modicum of attention to price variation, but we sense that this attention has a demand orientation that might be divided into three arguments: macroeconomic, inventory, and industrial structure effects.

Both building cycles and business cycles have large impacts on forestry. Building cycles are directly related to construction, which has an obvious link with lumber and wood products. Indeed, lumber used for housing, home repair, mobile homes, and nonresidential construction is the end use of 34 percent of all timber harvested (USDA 1982, 27–29). Business cycles may not by themselves have effects on forestry any greater than their impacts on other basic industries. The corrective mechanisms for business cycles, government fiscal and monetary policy, however, may have very important impacts on forestry. Fiscal policy often targets the construction industry as a leading indicator of business cycles. The links with lumber production remain obvious and direct. Monetary policy quickly results in adjustments in the interest rate, a prime determinant of new construction, and once more there is a direct link with lumber production and timber harvests. In conclusion, there are direct vertical market associations between some of the greater macroeconomic sources of demand-induced market instability and forestry.

These arguments for demand-induced instability are tempered, however, by the number of links in the vertical industry structure between the macrovariables and final products and the stumpage market (i.e., lending institutions, real estate agencies, building contractors, lumberyards, sawmills, log yards). Each additional link suggests another inventory available to absorb some of the variation in final product demand. (Furthermore, these inventories absorb quantity variation, which Newbery and Stiglitz [1979] argue is more important than the price variation to which TMS responds.)

Finally, there are opposing industrial structure effects on stumpage market variation. Vertically integrated firms often own insufficient forestland to provide fully for the demands of their own mills. In such cases, they tend to purchase nonindustrial private stumpage in normal times and to conserve their own timber for harvest and internal consumption when prices are high (and their own timber is most valuable). Thus, they deflate the high extremes of market price variation. The relatively greater market power of the mills as opposed to that of the nonindustrial private forest landowners who produce much of their raw material provides a counter effect, however. Those mills with oligosony power can transfer some of the demand-price variation received by them to the smaller, less concentrated and less-well-informed, stumpage producers. In many areas there are only one or two purchasers of stumpage and a nearly unlimited number of nonindustrial private landowners providing stumpage. Market power clearly lies with the mills.[3]

The net effect of demand-oriented impacts on stumpage price variation is uncertain from this discussion. We sense, however, that those with a professional interest in the market would argue that altogether the macroeconomic, inventory, and industrial structure effects tend to increase stumpage price variation.

INTERTEMPORAL PRODUCTION WITH FORECASTING ERROR. Our argument for supply-induced stochastic stumpage price variation depends on the notion that the complexity of forecasting future prices causes forest managers to make harvesting errors.[4] Specifically, producer output decisions are optimal if they are based on expectations conditioned by all available information, including structural information about the economy. This is the concept of rational expectations developed by Muth (1961), Lucas (1976), and Sargent (1978). The problem lies in the inability of producers to assimilate all the information necessary to make optimal decisions.

The argument begins with a simple model of the firm's intertemporal decision making under uncertainty and adds sophistication in its dynamic relationship between current and future decisions until it eventually includes the long-term renewable resource case with forecasting errors that accumulate over time. This is the general case relevant for timber producers. We shall find that, for them, short-term deviations from the optimal output path may have long and systematic impacts.

In the simplest case, commodity price p at time t is a linear function of current supply of the product $Q(t)$ plus a random term $\epsilon(t)$, which is uncorrelated over time. That is,

$$p(t) = \alpha_0 + \alpha_1 Q(t) + \epsilon(t) \tag{4.1}$$

where the α_i are constants. (There may be many varieties of uncertainty, but the price uncertainty represented in equation [4.1] illustrates all the relevant issues. It is unnecessary to explicitly demonstrate any other uncertainty.)

Assume that there are N identical producers in the industry. Therefore,

$$Q(t) = Nq(t) \tag{4.2}$$

where $q(t)$ is the output of a single producer at time t.

Also assume that factor prices are constant over time, and permit us to suppress them in the notation. Therefore, each producer's cost function C

depends on only the rate of output at time t. Making this cost function quadratic in output simplifies the analysis as it creates linear production decision rules.

The present value of one producer's future revenues is

$$V = \sum_{t=0}^{\infty}(1 + r)^{-t} \{p(t)q(t) - C[q(t)]\} \tag{4.3}$$

where r is the discount rate.

The producer chooses the output path that maximizes the expected present value of future revenues, subject to one of three dynamic production constraints. The producer makes production decisions prior to observing the market in period t and, therefore, always faces uncertainty regardless of the specific dynamic production constraint.

A NONDYNAMIC PRODUCTION CONSTRAINT: THE CASE OF AGRICULTURE. The first production constraint places no intertemporal restriction on output, therefore output in period t is unrelated to output in any other period t'. The output function is

$$\tilde{q}(t) = \beta_0 + \beta_1\tilde{p}(t) \tag{4.4}$$

where $\tilde{p}(t)$ is the expectation of $p(t)$ which the producer uses in making the output decision and the β_i are constant. There is no intertemporal problem. Rather, the producer chooses current output at each t so as to maximize expected t-period profit. This may be the relevant specification for agricultural crops and for some manufacturing activities with relatively short production processes.

We can find the producer's optimal expected price by substituting equations (4.2) and (4.4) into equation (4.1)

$$\overset{*}{p}(t) = (\alpha_0 + \alpha_1N\beta_0)/(1 - \alpha_1N\beta_1) \tag{4.5}$$

where the asterisk denotes optimality. The actual and optimal prices at time t are identical since this preliminary form of the model assumes perfect foresight.[5]

The optimal output is

$$\overset{*}{q}(t) = \beta_0 + \beta_1\overset{*}{p}(t) \tag{4.6}$$

The construction of an optimal forecast of the future price requires much information not readily available to producers. Even in this simple case, each producer must know the parameters characterizing the cost and market demand functions. The information requirements for an optimal forecast become enormous in our subsequent cases composed of more complex intertemporal relations and the presence of such requirements begs forecasting and production errors. Producers can avoid the information requirements, and these errors, only where it is possible to hedge against all production risks — as through the purchase of insurance or through forward sales in futures markets. Yet it is not usually possible to hedge so perfectly, therefore we must consider the alternative: imperfect forecasting.

Following Newbery and Stiglitz (1979; 1981; 1982) we permit firms to forecast future prices that differ from those optimal forecasts that are conditional on complete information. In this case the firm's actual price expectations, denoted by $p(t)$, are

$$\tilde{p}(t) = \overset{*}{p}(t) + \eta(t) \tag{4.7}$$

where $\eta(t)$ is the forecast error. The term $\eta(t)$ is not the difference between the forecast and the actual value of a future price; rather, it is the difference between the actual forecast and an optimal forecast. In general, $\eta(t)$ is a function of those exogenous variables relevant to an optimal forecast but absent from the actual forecasts. If the omitted exogenous variables are serially correlated, then the forecast errors will be serially correlated as well.

The relationship between the firm's output decision, equation (4.4), and its optimal output is the difference between equations (4.4) and (4.6)

$$q(t) = \overset{*}{q}(t) + \beta_1 \eta(t) \tag{4.8}$$

Thus, the divergence between actual output $q(t)$ and optimal output $\overset{*}{q}(t)$ is a linear function of the forecast error $\eta(t)$. As a consequence, the divergence between the actual price $p(t)$ and the optimal price $\overset{*}{p}(t)$ is a linear function of the forecast error.

$$p(t) = \overset{*}{p}(t) + \hat{\beta}_1 \eta(t) + \epsilon(t) \tag{4.9}$$

where $\hat{\beta}_1 = \alpha_1 N \beta_1$

We conclude that, in the absence of a complete set of risk markets, deviations of actual prices and quantities from optimal prices and quantities depend on the changes in all the relevant variables that firms omit when constructing their price forecasts. These deviations are serially correlated and the actual forecast prices provide erroneous signals for determining output decisions. Therefore, market allocation in general cannot be Pareto optimal.

DYNAMIC CONSTRAINTS ON OUTPUT: THE CASE OF MINERAL RESOURCES.
The first production constraint was a polar case that places no dynamic restrictions on output decisions. The second production constraint limits the producer's initial resource stock thereby also restricting intertemporal output. Suppose the firm manages resource stock R at time t and that the firm's total output cannot exceed this stock. In this case, the producer maximizes the expected value of equation (4.3) subject to the constraint

$$\sum_{t=0}^{\infty} q(t) \leq R(0) \qquad (4.10)$$

or, equivalently,

$$R(t + 1) = R(t) - q(t), \; R(t + 1) \geq 0 \qquad (4.11)$$

This dynamic constraint describes the general problem confronting producers of nonrenewable resources.

Following Kushner (1971) and Sargent (1978), the output function for this case is

$$\tilde{q}(t) = \beta_0 + \beta_1 \tilde{\lambda}(t) + \beta_2 R(t) \qquad (4.12)$$

where

$$\tilde{\lambda}(t) = \sum_{i=t}^{\infty} \gamma(i)\tilde{p}(i) \qquad (4.13)$$

The tilde continues to denote actual expectations and the $\gamma(i)$ determine the weights on price in each future period; therefore, $\tilde{\lambda}(i)$ is a weighted sum of future price forecasts. The current output decision depends on this weighted sum of future forecasts as well as the current resource stock.

In order to construct optimal forecasts, the producer must know the current price, the previous history of prices, the model structure, and the distribution of resource stocks across producers. Once more, this is a great volume of information and we must allow the possibility that actual forecasts differ from optimal forecasts. Therefore,

$$\tilde{\lambda}(t) = \overset{*}{\lambda}(t) + \eta(t) \qquad (4.14)$$

where $\eta(t)$ is the forecast error. The term $\eta(t)$ is serially correlated even if the omitted variables in the information set are not serially correlated because $\tilde{\lambda}(t)$ and $\tilde{\lambda}(t + 1)$ depend on overlapping forecasts of future prices $\tilde{p}(t)$.

Both the optimal output $\overset{*}{\tilde{q}}(0)$ and the actual output $q(0)$ are conditional on the given initial stock $R(0)$. Therefore, only the nonoptimal forecast causes the actual output to diverge from the optimal output at time t. In all later time periods, however, the divergence between actual and optimal output is considerably more complex. For any later time $t + n$, both the current forecast error and the difference between the actual and optimal stock of the resource cause actual output to diverge from optimal output. To see this, notice that equations (4.12) and (4.14) imply that

$$q(t) = \overset{*}{q}(t) + \beta_1\eta(t) + \beta_2[R(t) - \overset{*}{R}(t)] \tag{4.15}$$

where $\overset{*}{R}(t)$ denotes the optimal stock of resource R at time t. Furthermore, the dynamic constraint on output, equation (4.10), implies that the current divergence betweeen the actual and optimal resource stock depends on all previous divergences betweeen actual and optimal output. That is,

$$R(t) = \overset{*}{R}(t) + \sum_{i=0}^{t-1}[\overset{*}{q}(i) - \tilde{q}(i)] \tag{4.16}$$

Equations (4.15) and (4.16) imply that the period t divergence between actual and optimal output can be written as a function of all previous forecast errors:

$$q(t) = \overset{*}{q}(t) + \sum_{i=0}^{t}\gamma(t - i)\eta(i) \tag{4.17}$$

where γ is defined recursively by

$$\gamma(0) = \beta_1 \quad \text{and} \quad \gamma(N) = -\beta_2\sum_{i=0}^{N-1}(i) \tag{4.18}$$

Equation (4.18) can be readily proved by induction. Since the γ (i) are functions only of the parameters β_1 and β_2, then the divergence between actual and optimal output at any time t is a weighted sum of the forecast errors from time zero to time t.

A similar result derives from the relationship between the actual and optimal resource stocks. Combining equations (4.16), (4.17), and (4.18) yields

$$R(t) = \overset{*}{R}(t) + \sum_{i=0}^{t-1}\delta(i)\eta(i) \tag{4.19}$$

where $\delta(i)$ is defined by

$$\delta(i) = \sum_{j=0}^{t-1-i}(t - 1 - j) \tag{4.20}$$

The divergence between the actual and optimal resource stock at time t is a weighted sum of the previous forecast errors where the weights are complex combinations of the parameters β_1 and β_2 only.

Because of the dynamic constraint on output, forecasting errors accumulate in the resource stocks and, as a consequence, also accumulate in the output decisions. Therefore, the actual paths of output and of the remaining resource stock can diverge from the optimal paths over substantial periods of time. In the first case analyzed, the actual output can diverge systematically from the optimal output only because of serial correlation in the forecast errors. In this second case where there is a dynamic constraint on available stock, actual output diverges systematically from the optimal output not only because there is serial correlation in the forecast error but also because forecast errors accumulate in the resource stock.

DYNAMIC OUTPUT CONSTRAINTS WITH ACCUMULATING AND NONLINEAR STOCK EFFECTS: THE CASE OF FORESTRY. In the final case, the dynamic production constraint is more complex yet. Consider a renewable resource such as timber for which there is a positive rate of growth that depends on the resource stock (i.e., standing timber). The relationship between the resource stock and output is specified as

$$R(t + 1) = f[R(t)] - q(t) \qquad (4.21)$$

where f is positive, increasing, and concave.

Once more, the firm chooses an output path that maximizes the expected value of equation (4.3) subject to equation (4.21). If the function f in equation (4.21) is quadratic, then the linear decision rule, equation (4.12), still describes the forecast errors and equation (4.15) continues to characterize the difference between actual and optimal output.

The difference in impacts between the renewable resource constraint and the simple stock constraint lies in the forecast errors that accumulate in the stocks. In the simple stock case, a forecast error in any period induces a linear change in the resource stock for all later periods. In the renewable resource case with a dynamic constraint (4.21), forecast errors accumulate in a nonlinear fashion since the growth rate depends nonlinearly on the existing stock. The divergence between the actual and optimal stocks is

$$R(t + 1) = \overset{*}{R}(t + 1) + f[R(t)]$$
$$- f[\overset{*}{R}(t)] - \beta_2[R(t) - \overset{*}{R}(t)] + \beta_1\eta(t) \qquad (4.22)$$

which indicates that the divergence at time $t + 1$ depends nonlinearly on the divergence at time t. (The second and third terms on the RHS are nonlinear.) As a consequence, the divergence between the actual and optimal resource stock at time $t + 1$ is a nonlinear function of all previous forecast errors.

Consider, for example, that the firm's forecast error at time zero is $\eta(0)$. The output, $\gamma(0)$ is nonoptimal to the extent of the forecast error. The actual stock at time t is nonoptimal only because of the nonoptimality of the output, $\gamma(0)$. At time $t + 1$, however, actual stock $R(t + 1)$ diverges from optimal stock $\overset{*}{R}(t + 1)$ not only because of the output errors at times t and $t + 1$ but also because of the difference in the growth rates of the actual and the optimal resource stocks.

Further consideration for the age structure of the resource stock and its effect on growth rates would add yet another dimension to the nonoptimality of the residual stock. Forecast errors would affect not only the total resource stock but also its age composition.[6] Altering the age structure affects the growth rate of the stock and therefore the size of the resource stock in the future.

In conclusion, the volume of information required to construct optimal forecasts is large and generally unavailable to producers. Forecasting with restricted information yields forecast errors that cause actual output to diverge from optimal output. If there is no intertemporal restriction on the output path, then the divergence is serially correlated only because of serial correlation in the forecast errors. If there are intertemporal restrictions on the output path, then the actual output and the optimal output can diverge systematically over time. Serial correlation in the divergence is caused not only by the serial correlation in the forecast errors but also by the accumulation of forecast errors in the resource stocks. As a consequence, large and persistent cycles can occur in both output and prices. The complexity of these cycles for renewable resources such as timber can be even greater because of the dependence of growth rates on the size and the age composition of the resource stock.

EMPIRICAL MEASURES

We reviewed briefly the arguments for stumpage price variation originating from demand-induced factors and considered in detail the reasons why supply-related price variation in renewable resources like timber might be greater than price variation for agricultural crops and nonrenewable resources. In what follows we examine empirical evidence relevant to the hypothesis that timber prices are more volatile than the prices of other producer commodities. We consider two data sources with different characteristics: one is recent and monthly, the other annual since 1870; one permits comparison with eleven producer goods each from a processing level similar to lumber or pulp, the other compares more primary but more aggregate resources. We compute and compare several measures of volatility for each data set. Our conclusions are ambiguous. There is unpredictable price variation in forestry but we have little confidence that it exceeds the unpredictable variation in comparable resources.

The first data set is the monthly producer price index (PPI) for selected commodity groups (Citibase 1983). An advantage of this data set is its comprehensive coverage of a wide variety of commodity groups. A disadvantage is the relatively short period of its availability (January 1947–July 1982), which restricts our detection of long-term trends or cycles in price volatility.

Table 4.1 shows the eleven comparable commodity groups. Commodity price indices can be gathered further into five broad categories corresponding to the three categories in our previous conceptual discussion of supply-induced price variation; agriculture, nonrenewable, and renewable resources; plus two manufacturing categories, durable and nondurable products. The renewable resource category includes lumber and wood products and pulp, paper, and allied products—both categories are one production step removed from stumpage. They are closer to demand-induced price variations and more susceptible to variations in processing costs than stumpage. The same is true however for all the commodity groups within the data set. Therefore, differences in price volatility cannot be attributed to different levels of aggregation in the commodity group price indices.

Table 4.1. Measures of variation in the producer price indexes for selected commodity groups (monthly data: January 1947–July 1982)

	S.D. of ln(p)	Average of $\bar{p}$	S.D. of $\bar{p}$	Mean squared error of forecast residual
Agriculture:				
Farm produce	.327	.0021	.0252	.0250
Nondurable manufactured products:				
Textile products & apparel	.215	.0016	.0068	.0044
Chemical & allied products	.342	.0027	.0095	.0066
Rubber and plastic products	.304	.0028	.0121	.0098
Durable manufactured products:				
Machinery & equipment	.415	.0040	.0051	.0035
Furniture & household durables	.247	.0024	.0044	.0034
Nonrenewable resources:				
Fuels & related products	.611	.0054	.0136	.0095
Minerals & metal products	.458	.0041	.0089	.0073
Nonmetallic mineral products	.414	.0038	.0065	.0058
Renewable resources:				
Lumber & wood products	.424	.0034	.0160	.0130
Pulp, paper & allied products	.368	.0033	.0081	.0067

Note: p is the price index; ln(p) is the natural log of the price index; S.D. is the standard deviation; $\bar{p}$ is the first difference of the natural log of the price index; forecast residual is the residual of the ARIMA model specified in Table 4.2.

Table 4.1 compares four measures of price volatility. The first column shows the standard deviation of the natural log of the PPI for each commodity group. It measures the variation about the mean of the log of the price index, and it provides some evidence in support of our hypothesis. The standard deviations for renewable and nonrenewable resources are larger than the standard deviations for other categories. The relatively large standard deviation for nonrenewable resources and the high standard deviation for machinery and equipment may be due to either demand- or market structure–induced price variation.

The second column shows the average percentage changes in the PPI for each commodity group. This measure provides an ordered ranking of price volatility broadly similar to that of column 1. The average percentage changes for renewable and nonrenewable resources are larger than for the other categories. Renewable resource prices are volatile according to this measure, although the price volatility of nonrenewable resources remains larger.

Nevertheless, there is a problem with these two measures of price volatility. Both can be large simply as a consequence of completely predictable long-term trends. For example, suppose the price of lumber increases 20 percent every year while the prices of all other commodities increase 10 percent every year. Both measures will show greater price volatility for lumber than for other commodities. Indeed, the common observation is that lumber prices are increasing more rapidly than the prices of other commodities. Lumber prices also increase more rapidly than the price of pulp (e.g., Barnett & Morse 1963; Manthy 1978). This may wholly explain the relatively greater measures of price volatility for lumber and wood products than for pulp, paper, and allied products. It also argues for alternate measures of price volatility that can abstract from predictable trends. Our third and fourth measures do that.

The third column of Table 4.1 shows the standard deviation of the percentage change of the PPI around its average change. This is a reasonable measure of the volatility of the PPI for each commodity group, if the trends of the percentage change are predictable but the deviations about the trends are not. The interesting observation from this measure is that it shows agriculture to have the most volatile prices. This observation contrasts with the previous measures, which found that both renewable and nonrenewable resources prices were more volatile than agricultural prices. The remaining commodity groups follow our expectations with lumber and wood products prices showing greater volatility than nonrenewable resources prices, which in turn show greater volatility than manufacturing product prices.

The third measure abstracts from constant trends but not from predictable cyclical price variation. The conceptual analysis in the earlier section of this chapter indicates, however, that *unpredictable* price variations cause nonoptimal price forecasts, production errors, and resource misallocation. This suggests that we take a closer look at predictability: most price series lack stationarity, or the affinity for a mean value, yet their nonstationarity often behaves in a homogeneous manner. That is, while the price series is nonstationary, successive price changes, or first differences of prices in a series, are stationary and predictable by market participants.[7] This characteristic of price series argues for regressing the percentage change in the PPI for each commodity group on its own lagged values and a moving average of its past residuals. This mimics the (often only intuitive) insight of market participants regarding future prices. The residual in these regressions measures wholly unpredictable price variation.

This is the approach of ARIMA models (Box & Jenkins 1970; Nelson 1973). Table 4.2 shows our ARIMA regressions for each commodity group. In all cases we include a first order autoregressive term. Most cases show a better fit with additional, higher-order autoregressive, or first-order moving average, terms.

Table 4.2. ARIMA models for the producer price index for selected commodity groups (monthly data: January 1947–July 1982)

Agriculture:
Farm products $\quad \tilde{p}_t = .0021 + .1034\tilde{p}_{t-2} - .1110\tilde{p}_{t-4} + \xi_t$
$\qquad\qquad\qquad\quad (1.75)^b \quad (2.14)^b \quad (-2.29)^b$

Nondurable manufactured products:
Textile products & apparel $\quad \tilde{p}_t = .0018 + .7042\tilde{p}_{t-1} + .0715\tilde{p}_{t-2} + \xi_t$
$\qquad\qquad\qquad\qquad\qquad (1.91)^b \quad (14.52)^b \quad (1.47)^a$

Chemicals & allied products $\quad \tilde{p}_t = .0028 + .5792\tilde{p}_{t-1} + .1796\tilde{p}_{t-2} + \xi_t$
$\qquad\qquad\qquad\qquad\qquad (2.16)^b \quad (12.11)^b \quad (3.75)^b$

Rubber & plastic products $\quad \tilde{p}_t = .0028 + .4918\tilde{p}_{t-1} + .1390\tilde{p}_{t-2} + \xi_t$
$\qquad\qquad\qquad\qquad\qquad (2.20)^b \quad (10.21)^b \quad (2.89)^b$

Durable manufactured products:
Machinery & equipment $\quad \tilde{p}_t = .0039 + .5902\tilde{p}_{t-1} + .1818\tilde{p}_{t-2} + \xi_t$
$\qquad\qquad\qquad\qquad (5.39)^b \quad (12.34)^b \quad (3.80)^b$

Furniture & household durables $\quad \tilde{p}_t = .0024 + .4657\tilde{p}_{t-1} + .2292\tilde{p}_{t-2} + \xi_t$
$\qquad\qquad\qquad\qquad\qquad\quad (4.40)^b \quad (9.84)^b \quad (4.84)^b$

Nonrenewable resources:
Fuels & related products $\quad \tilde{p}_t = .0057 + .7140\tilde{p}_{t-1} + \xi_t$
$\qquad\qquad\qquad\qquad (3.55)^b \quad (20.75)^b$

Metals & metal products $\quad \tilde{p}_t = .0041 + .5752\tilde{p}_{t-1} + \xi_t$
$\qquad\qquad\qquad\qquad (4.91)^b \quad (14.47)^b$

Nonmetallic mineral products $\quad \tilde{p}_t = .0039 + .8954\tilde{p}_{t-1} + .6657\xi_{t-1} + \xi_t$
$\qquad\qquad\qquad\qquad\qquad (4.42)^b \quad (23.39)^b \quad (10.40)^b$

Renewable resources:
Lumber & wood products $\quad \tilde{p}_t = .0035 + .3349\tilde{p}_{t-1} - .3445\xi_{t-1} + \xi_t$
$\qquad\qquad\qquad\qquad (2.75)^b \quad (4.43)^b \quad (-4.56)^b$

Pulp, paper & allied products $\quad \tilde{p}_t = .003 + .4685\tilde{p}_{t-1} + .1575\tilde{p}_{t-2} + \xi_t$
$\qquad\qquad\qquad\qquad\qquad (3.89)^b \quad (9.75)^b \quad (3.28)^b$

Note: $\tilde{p}_t$ is the first difference in the natural log of the price at time t; ξ_t is the error at time t; the terms in parentheses are the t statistics indicated when significant at the (^{b}) .05 and (^{a}) .10 levels.

The fourth column of Table 4.1 shows the standard deviation of the ARIMA residuals. This is the standard deviation of wholly unpredictable price variation. (The arithmetic difference between the third and fourth columns is the predictable cyclical price variation.) Agriculture prices show the largest unpredictable price variation but lumber and wood products also show a large degree of unpredictable variation. The difference between columns 3 and 4 shows that very little of the price variation is predictable for either agriculture or lumber and wood products. Pulp, paper, and allied products; nonrenewable resources; and nondurable manufacturing products show a moderate degree of unpredictable price variation whereas durable manufactured products show the least amount of unpredictable price variation.

We can take this analysis of our first data set one step further and consider how price volatility has changed over time. For one measure we might segregate the first and last ten years of data (1947–1957 and 1972–1982, respectively), convert the standard deviations of the forecast residuals to variances, and calculate F tests in order to determine statistical differences.[8] This measure shows that price volatility (1) decreases for durable and nondurable manufacturing products; (2) increases for agriculture; (3) increases for both lumber and wood products and pulp, paper, and allied products; and (4) showed no significant change for nonrenewable resources.

All observations of changes in price volatility are significant at the 1 percent level, except for pulp, paper, and allied products, which are significant at the 5 percent level. The increase in agriculture price volatility is interesting in that it occurs during a period of generally expanding price reporting, output quota, and inventory control programs, all of which should decrease agricultural price variation.

In conclusion, unpredictable price variation is the favored measure of price variation because it is the lack of predictability that causes resource misallocation. This measure supports the contention that lumber and wood products prices are relatively volatile and are becoming more so. Pulp, paper, and allied products prices have not been as volatile but they too are becoming more volatile. Furthermore, the measure of unpredictable price variation generally follows the ordered ranking for all commodities anticipated by our conceptual analysis of supply price variation—with the exception of the high ranking for agriculture. Apparently demand or, more likely, market structure–induced price variation is much more important than the anticipated lesser degree of supply-induced price variation in agriculture.

Let us turn now to the second data set, a natural resource price series compiled by Potter and Christy (1962) and revised by Manthy (1978). These are annual data for the longer period, 1870–1973, and for unprocessed natural resources: agriculture, minerals, and forest products. The longer time period and lesser amount of processing are advantages over the first data set. The disadvantage is the greater level of aggregation in the second data set.

Table 4.3 shows our results for the same measures of price variation reported in Table 4.1. Table 4.4 shows the underlying ARIMA models necessary for the fourth measure, the standard deviation of the forecast residual. The small t statistics for the ARIMA models are evidence of nonstationarity or a large measure of unpredictability. The rank order of commodity price variation in Table 4.3 differs from that of Table 4.1 for all four measures. Focusing on the measure of unpredictable price variation: agriculture prices are relatively less volatile, mineral prices are relatively more volatile, and forest product prices are of middle rank.

In conclusion, we examine two sets of price data in order to discover if timber prices have been more volatile than the prices of other natural resource commodities. Monthly data since 1947 suggest that lumber and wood products prices have been more volatile than all others except agricultural prices. Pulp, paper, and allied products data show price volatility

Table 4.3. Measures of variation in the natural resource prices compiled by Manthy (annual data: 1870–1973)

	S.D. of ln(p)	Average of $\tilde{p}$	S.D. of $\tilde{p}$	S.D. of forecast residual
Agriculture	.5217	.0141	.1146	.1014
Minerals	.5185	.0028	.1579	.1484
Forest products	.7924	.0238	.1204	.1216[a]

Note: p is the price index; ln(p) is the natural log of the price index; S.D. is the standard deviation; $\tilde{p}$ is the first difference of the natural log of the price index; forecast residual is the residual of the ARIMA model specified in Table 4.4. The p is the actual price (in millions of dollars) for each industry listed.

[a]Rounding error, this figure cannot exceed .1204.

Table 4.4. ARIMA models for the natural resource prices compiled by Manthy (annual data: 1870–1973)

| Agriculture | $\tilde{p}_t = .0145 - .5175\xi_{t-1} + \xi_t$ |
| | $\quad\quad\ \ (.96)\quad (-6.02)^{b}$ |

Minerals	$\tilde{p}_t = .0030 - .6794\tilde{p}_{t-1} - .3691\tilde{p}_{t-2} - .5361\tilde{p}_{t-3}$
	$\quad\quad\ \ (.20)\quad (-2.32)^{b}\quad (-1.22)\quad\ (-2.48)^{b}$
	$\quad\quad\quad\ - .9541\xi_{t-1} - .3923\xi_{t-2} - .2602\xi_{t-3} + \xi_t$
	$\quad\quad\quad\ (-2.97)^{b}\quad (-.96)\quad\quad (-.96)$

| Forest products | $\tilde{p}_t = .0237 - .1823\tilde{p}_{t-1} - .0849\xi_{t-1} + \xi_t$ |
| | $\quad\quad\ \ (2.15)^{b}\quad (-.09)$ |

Note: $\tilde{p}_t$ is the first difference in the natural log of the price at time t; ξ_t is the error at time t; the terms in parentheses are the t statistics indicated when significant at the (^{b}) .05 level.

of middle rank when compared with other natural resource commodities. Annual data since 1870 provide results that contrast with these findings and suggest that agricultural and forest products prices are both relatively less volatile.

These contrasting results are difficult to reconcile but one plausible explanation may be that timber in this country was originally a stock resource and only recently has converted into a renewable resource, as timber plantations—indeed, concern for forest regeneration of any sort—are a feature of only the last thirty years. This explanation suggests that longer timber price series behave more like price series for minerals, although more recent timber price series behave more like price series for agriculture. In any case, we have little justification for arguing that timber prices are more volatile than the prices of other natural resource commodities. Therefore, arguments for public market intervention with the objective of stabilizing timber prices have no more intuitive appeal than those for price stabilizing instruments for comparable resources.

The Social Efficiency of Price Reporting Services: The Case of Timber Mart-South

This examination of price variation provides only uncertain justification for price reporting services in forestry. Nevertheless, Timber Mart-South (TMS) does provide an example of such services and it does receive public financial assistance for its production. We might contrast the potential social gains from TMS with these public costs in order to obtain another measure of the merit of stumpage price reporting services like TMS. The social gains can be read from changes in the familiar welfare triangles introduced in Chapter 1.

Consider Figure 4.1, reflecting a market described by demand function D and supply-originating price variation, causing us to observe either of two supply functions, S_1 or S_2. Consistent with our earlier discussion of Figure 1.2, elimination of this price variation yields a new supply function S_s and corresponding shifts in consumers' and producers' surpluses. Consumers lose area $[(C + D + G) - (A + B)]/2$ and producers gain area $[(F - C + D) + (A - D - E)]/2$. The total effect includes a redistributive payment from consumers to producers and a net social gain.[9] Instability due to variation in demand is analogous except that consumers gain and producers lose. In both cases (supply and demand variations), there are net social gains from stability if the costs of administering the stabilizing mechanism are sufficiently small.

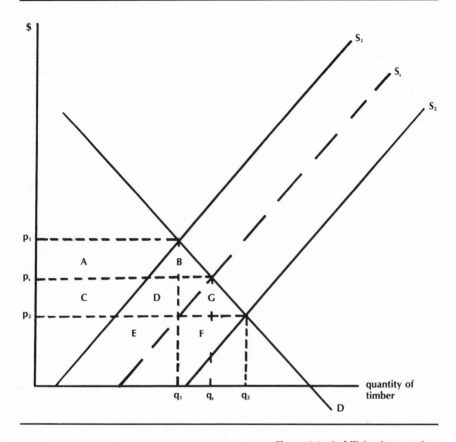

Figure 4.1. Stabilizing intervention.

Figure 4.1 describes an unusual, but diagrammatically simple, linear case where the entire cause of price variation has been corrected. In the more usual case some price variation remains. For example, continuing the supply variation description of Figure 4.1, the old supply functions S_1 and S_2 would be drawn closer to the supply function S_s, together close enough to create the observed decrease in price variation. Corresponding adjustments must be made in the consumers' and producers' surpluses, redistributive payments and net social gain.

There is a second effect of price reporting. Consider a market composed of informed industrial (millowner) consumers and less informed nonindustrial private producers of timber. Price reporting probably improves the competitive position of those who previously had either no price information or only weak price information. This improved market position comes at a relative cost to those who already had good price information. Or, with better information, nonindustrial private producers raise their offer prices as reflected by shifting the supply function from S to S' in Figure 4.2. The result is a smaller market with nonindustrial producers gaining areas $A - C$ and industrial and other consumers losing areas $A + B$.[10] Thus, the effect of the price increase includes a redistributive payment equal to area A from consumers to producers but yields a net social loss equal to $B + C$.

In sum, there are two effects of stumpage price reporting services: a decreased price variation effect, which is the focal point in this chapter; and an income redistributive effect associated with increased nonindustrial private offer prices. Empirical measures of either require observations of demand and supply both before and after the introduction of the price reporting service and at the same level of geographic aggregation as that service. Timber Mart-South was introduced, however, because such prior demand and supply information was unavailable for the thirty-eight substate regions. Therefore, accurate measures of the two effects are impossible.

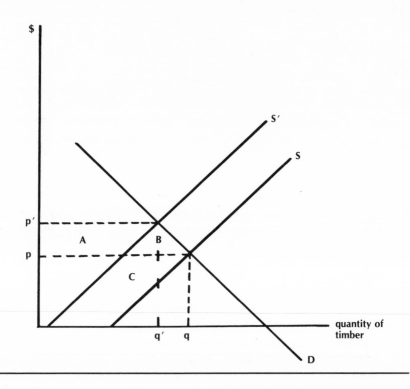

Figure 4.2. Income transfers due to price reporting services.

Our alternative is to seek impressionistic results only. There are annual and southwide price data from 1950. Newman (1986) obtains demand and supply estimates using these data for the period ending with the introduction of TMS in 1977. We use Newman's estimates and follow Turnovsky (1974) in measuring the welfare effects of price variations around Newman's estimates.

The introduction of TMS decreases the price variations around Newman's estimates but by an unknown amount. That is, there is insufficient annual data since 1978 to obtain econometrically satisfying demand and supply functions for comparing estimates of post-1977 price variations with the pre-1977 measures. Our alternative is to contrast the known costs of public support for TMS with the Newman-Turnovsky measures from decreases in demand and supply price variations just necessary to generate an identical gain in social welfare. The final step is to ask whether such decreases in price variations, therefore such gains in social welfare, are reasonable. Clearly, we cannot provide a definitive answer but our opinion is that public expenditure on TMS may be a reasonable investment.

We provide no measure of the redistribution from millowners to nonindustrial private landowners. Nevertheless, the continued existence of paid subscriptions to TMS, many originating with forestry consultants and nonindustrial private landowners, suggests that the transfer must be at least sufficient to cover these subscription fees.

The remainder of this section first reviews the Newman demand and supply estimates, then estimates the decreases in price variation necessary to provide social welfare impacts sufficient to justify public expenditures on TMS, and finally draws our conclusions. An appendix reviews the basic Turnovsky derivation.

SOUTHWIDE DEMAND AND SUPPLY FOR STUMPAGE, 1950–1977

Newman provides 3SLS estimates of southwide demand and supply for both sawtimber and pulpwood stumpage.[11] Table 4.5 shows his preliminary estimates, including their variances, for the time period beginning in 1950 and ending in 1977, when TMS began reporting sawtimber and pulpwood prices.

The lagged quantity variable in Newman's demand equations shows a relationship between stumpage quantity demanded and prior mill capacity. It also reflects the importance of prior period expectations for the subsequent period. (The concept of rational expectations was a theme of the first section of this chapter.) All four equations display good statistical fits. The Durbin-Watson and Durbin's h tests show that autocorrelation is not a great problem with this time series data. With one exception all the signs on the independent variables satistfy expectations, the price elasticities are

Table 4.5. Southwide demand and supply for sawtimber and pulpwood stumpage, 1950–1977

Sawtimber:

$$Q^p_{st} = -1938525 - 3915.9p_{st} + 25314.61p_{lt} + 126291.2w_{lt} + 997100.6r_{lt} + .833833Q_{st-1}$$
$$(-2.1438)^b \quad (-1.7011)^a \quad\quad (2.0821)^b \quad\quad (1.6675) \quad\quad (0.8883) \quad\quad (5.8298)^b$$
$$R^2 = .8771 \quad \text{Durbin's } h = .461 \quad \sigma^2 = 11,455,346,990$$

$$Q^s_{st} = 930106 + 3242.307p_{st} + .006618I_t - 12487.6p_{pt}$$
$$(5.3923)^b \quad (7.7108)^b \quad\quad (3.8511)^b \quad (-6.6251)^a$$
$$R^2 = .8930 \quad \text{Durbin-Watson} = 1.316 \quad \sigma^2 = 9,108,449,870$$

Pulpwood:

$$Q^p_{pt} = 843290.4 - 5742.64p_{pt} - 3606.42p_{at} + 226719.8w_{at} - 2183427r_{at} + 0.573133Q_{at-1}$$
$$(1.111) \quad (-0.8125) \quad\quad (-0.3849) \quad\quad (1.8428)^a \quad\quad (-1.0593) \quad\quad (3.5911)^b$$
$$R^2 = .9366 \quad \text{Durbin's } h = .052 \quad \sigma^2 = 8,652,809,938$$

$$Q^s_{pt} = -918345 + 7088.792p_{pt} + 0.021682I_t + 684.8042p_{st}$$
$$(-5.1860)^b \quad (3.3402)^b \quad\quad (14.7363)^b \quad\quad (2.0012)^a$$
$$R^2 = .9454 \quad \text{Durbin-Watson} = 1.172 \quad \sigma^2 = 6,795,482,204$$

where:
Q^p_{st}, Q^s_{st} = quantities of sawtimber stumpage demanded and supplied in year t (for lumber and plywood, in Mcf)
Q^p_{pt}, Q^s_{pt} = quantities of pulpwood stumpage demanded and supplied in year t (no residues, in Mcf)
$p_{st}, p_{at}, p_{lt}, p_{at}$ = real prices of sawtimber stumpage, pulpwood stumpage, lumber (national index), and paper (national index) in year t
I_t = total standing timber inventory in year t (in Mcf)
w_{lt}, w_{at} = real wages in lumber and paper in year t
r_{lt}, r_{at} = real capital costs in lumber and paper in year t

Note: The numbers in parentheses are t statistics.
[a]Indicates significance at the .10 level.
[b]Indicates significance at the .05 level.

consistent with prior literature, and the coefficients are generally significant.[12] The exception is the sign on paper price in the pulpwood demand equation, and this sign is insignificant. We have no explanation for this sign, but a small coefficient and an inelastic price–quantity relationship is reasonable for demand from the high fixed-cost paper industry.

If we measure all Newman's independent variables except the own-prices at their mean values, then these equations reduce to their Turnovsky forms. That is,

$$Q^D_t = a_0 - a_1 p_t + u_t$$
$$Q^S_t = b_0 + b_1 p_t + v_t$$

where Q^D_t and Q^S_t are the quantities demanded and supplied, respectively; p_t is the own-price; the a_i and b_i are constant coefficients; and u_t, v_t are error terms. In this form, Newman's equations provide the information necessary to estimate the welfare gains from price stabilization.

WELFARE GAINS

Following the equations in the appendix to this chapter, the annual gains in social welfare for decreasing price variation to zero are $2.8 million for sawtimber and $1.2 million for pulpwood. Total reduction in price variation is an unreasonable expectation. Nevertheless, the potential gains are considerably in excess of the approximate $17,000 annual public expenditure for the first three year's support of TMS.[13] Indeed, a very small share of these potential gains covers the public expenditure. It may be quite reasonable that public investment in TMS is socially efficient.

Table 4.6 records these social welfare results. It also records the producer and consumer shares that generate our observation that a larger proportion of the potential gains from price stabilization accrues to the logger and millowner consumers. Finally, Table 4.6 takes one step further our observation that a small share of the potential gains justifies the public intervention. It shows the percentage of the potential decrease in price variation in either market necessary to justify public intervention if the entire decrease accumulates in that market alone. If the sawtimber and pulpwood markets share the responsibility for justifying public intervention, then these percentage decreases would be smaller yet. In all cases the necessary decrease in price variation is very small. Therefore, public support for TMS is potentially reasonable.

Finally, we can consider still further the proposition of efficiency by moving the Newman data three years forward to the period 1953–1980. This includes the first three year's experience with TMS yet maintains a

Table 4.6. Stumpage price variation in the South: 1950-1977

	Sawtimber	Pulpwood	Total
Welfare gains due to total decrease in price variation (1977$)			
Producers' surplus	1,207,616	382,645	1,590,261
Consumers' surplus	1,581,832	786,386	2,368,218
Social welfare	2,789,448	1,169,027	3,958,475
Percentage decrease in price variation sufficient to create annual social welfare gains exceeding the public investment in Timber Mart-South			
Decrease	0.6%	1.5%	

sufficiently long data base for statistical analysis. We anticipate that, if TMS had a price stabilizing effect, then the variations associated with the three additional data years, 1978–1980, would be less than the variations associated with the three absent years, 1950–1952. Therefore, we anticipate that the variations associated with the 1953–1980 equations will be smaller than those associated with 1950–1977 and recorded in Table 4.6. The 1953–1980 equations can reflect only a small part of the full change in price variation due to the introduction of TMS, however, because fourteen of their seventeeen years of data refer to pre-TMS evidence.

Table 4.7 shows the new equations. The 1950–1977 and the 1953–1980 sawtimber equations are similar, except that the latter show better statistical fits as well as the anticipated smaller variances. The 1953–1980 pulpwood equations show a slightly better fit but the demand function shows a greater variance – contrary to expectation. The paper industry was just beginning in the South in the early 1950s. Therefore, there may have been a lower than usual price variation for pulpwood demand at that time and this may explain the one anomaly from among the four functions. In any case, the sawtimber market is bigger and more competitive than the pulpwood market. We anticipate a larger effect and greater importance to price stabilization in the sawtimber market. This anticipation is borne out.

Table 4.7 also shows the welfare gains reflected in the differences between our two sets of equations. These gains are less than the anticipated gain if the general decline in price variation observed between the 1950–1977 equations and the 1953–1980 equations continues for another fourteen years, the period sufficient to permit confident comparison of pre-TMS data with data fully reflecting incorporation of TMS in the market southwide. Nevertheless, even our oberved gains from the short period exceed by thirty times ($538,000/$17,000) those gains necessary to justify the public investment in TMS. This provides further confidence, if not perfect evidence, that the public investment in TMS has been socially efficient.[14]

Summary and Conclusions

There are few public market interventions in private forestry for which stabilization is the justification. The recent public assistance with Timber Mart-South, a southwide stumpage price reporting service, is the exception and there is some discussion of extending this southern experience to other regions of the country. Empirical tests of the welfare impacts of TMS or the potential impacts of other stumpage price reporting services are difficult because even the ideas for these services are so new that there can be little empirical evidence supporting hypotheses about them. Our alternate approach to their analysis is to inquire generally about the justifications for stabilizing interventions in forestry and then to examine what little circumstantial evidence does exist for the evaluation of TMS.

Our inquiry into the justifications for stabilizing interventions begins with a review of demand-side arguments and a development of the concep-

ﬁle 4.7. Welfare gains due to the difference in price variation between the 1950–1977 equations and the ﬁ3–1980 equations (1977$)

	Sawtimber	Pulpwood	Total
ﬤducers' surplus	667,999	−514,715	153,284
﬩nsumers' surplus	178,848	205,968	384,816
ﬤial welfare	846,847	−308,747	538,100

Underlying equations

ﬡtimber equations, 1953–1980:

$$Q^D_{st} = -1964033 - 3831.03p_{st} + 25900.96p_{lt} + 163726.8w_{lt} + 1692907r_{lt} + .668643Q_{st-1}$$
$$(-4.1026)^b \quad (-2.8891)^b \quad (3.9011)^b \quad (3.204)^b \quad (2.0237)^a \quad (4.1241)^b$$
$$R^2 = .9571 \quad \text{Durbin's } h = .975 \quad \sigma^2 = 7,771,806,186$$

$$Q^S_{st} = 673254.2 + 2785.987p_{st} + .009084I_t - 10480.6p_{pt}$$
$$(3.6982)^b \quad (7.9070)^b \quad (4.9765)^b \quad (-6.5712)^b$$
$$R^2 = .9539 \quad \text{Durbin-Watson} = 1.716 \quad \sigma^2 = 6,785,037,557$$

ﬥpwood equations, 1953–1980:

$$Q^D_{pt} = 1341073 - 6789.9p_{pt} - 6746.5p_{at} + 222671.1w_{at} - 1378917r_{at} + .470529Q_{at-1}$$
$$(1.3026) \quad (-1.4377) \quad (-.7051) \quad (3.0190)^b \quad (-1.4531) \quad (3.0944)^b$$
$$R^2 = .8943 \quad \text{Durbin's } h = 1.562 \quad \sigma^2 = 12,945,053,520$$

$$Q^S_{pt} = -741869 + 5322.683p_{pt} + .02114I_t + 703.185p_{st}$$
$$(-3.2542)^b \quad (2.4476)^b \quad (12.4400)^b \quad (2.2804)^b$$
$$R^2 = .9421 \quad \text{Durbin-Watson} = 1.175 \quad \sigma^2 = 6,468,938,917$$

Note: The numbers in parentheses are t statistics.
[a]Indicates significance at the .10 level.
[b]Indicates significance at the .05 level.

tual arguments for supply-side instability. In both cases, it is only unpredictable instability or variation that creates social welfare losses. Producers and consumers anticipate and adjust for predictable variation. In sum, the demand-side arguments are macroeconomic, inventory, and industrial structure in their sources. Their net effects on stability are uncertain. The supply-side arguments for price instability originate from serial correlation in forecast errors and the accumulation of forecast errors over time in resource stocks. Both supply-side arguments are characteristic of renewable resources like timber with long production periods.

Our analysis continues with empirical tests of price instability in two data sets for prices of various commodities or resources. One data set is for eleven partially processed commodities for the period 1947–1982, the other is for three primary resources for the period 1870–1973. Neither empirical test provides convincing evidence that unpredictable variation is unusually great in forestry. Therefore, neither provides strong argument for a stabilization policy.

Nevertheless, there is an explicit stabilizing intervention in the form of TMS, a recent price reporting service. Statistically convincing empirical tests of its impact on price stability must await better data or a longer period of observation. Nevertheless our strong circumstantial evidence suggests (1) that even the smallest decrease in either sawtimber or pulpwood stumpage price variation would justify its costs and (2) that there has been an initial decrease in sawtimber price variation since 1977 and the first issue of TMS. This decrease, if due to TMS, is considerably more than sufficient to justify the public involvement and to encourage further inquiry into the merit of counterpart price reporting services for other regions of the country.

Appendix: Turnovsky's Measures of Welfare Gains from Price Stabilization

Turnovsky's (1974) summary article reviews three well-known earlier articles (Waugh 1944; Oi 1961; Massell 1969) and provides both rigor and generalization for the argument that there are welfare gains to be captured with price stabilization.

Turnovsky begins with a single market in which linear relations describe demand D and supply S.

$$D(p_t) = a_0 - a_1 p_t + u_t \qquad\qquad (4A.1)$$
$$S(p_t) = b_0 + b_1 p_t + v_t \qquad\qquad (4A.2)$$

where p_t equals current price; a_i, b_i are deterministic constants (a_1, $b_1 > 0$); and u_t, v_t are additive stochastic disturbances generated by autoregressive processes.

$$u_t = \varrho_1 u_{t-1} + e_{1t} \tag{4A.3}$$
$$v_t = \varrho_2 v_{t-1} + e_{2t} \tag{4A.4}$$

where $-1 < \varrho_1$, $\varrho_2 < 1$, and e_{1t}, e_{2t} have zero means, and variances σ^2_{e1}, σ^2_{e2} with zero covariance.

Equations (4A.1) and (4A.2) imply that

$$E(u_t) = E(v_t) = 0$$
$$E(u^2_t) = \sigma^2_u = \sigma^2_{e1}/(1 - \sigma^2_1) \tag{4A.5}$$
$$E(v^2_t) = \sigma^2_v = \sigma^2_{e1}/(1 - \sigma^2_2)$$
$$E(u_t v_t) = 0$$

In the absence of price stability, the equilibrium price is

$$p_t = (u_t - v_t + a_0 - b_0)/(a_1 + b_1) \tag{4A.6}$$

and the equilibrium quantity is

$$D(p_t) = S(p_t) = \frac{b_0 a_1 + b_1 a_0}{a_1 + b_1} + \frac{a_1 v_t + b_1 u_t}{a_1 + b_1} \tag{4A.7}$$

In the presence of a price stabilizing mechanism, then p_S is such that

$$E(D_t) = E(S_t) \tag{4A.8}$$

so that the market balances on the average. Stabilization requires continual trade of an amount

$$x_t = v_t - u_t \tag{4A.9}$$

the expected value of which is zero.

Taking the expected value of equation (4A.6) yields

$$E(p_t) = (a_0 - b_0)/(a_1 + b_1) = p_S \tag{4A.10}$$

and the corresponding quantities

$$D(p_S) = u_t + (b_0 a_1 + b_1 a_0)/(a_1 + b_1) \tag{4A.11}$$
$$S(p_S) = v_t + (b_0 a_1 + b_1 a_0)/(a_1 + b_1) \tag{4A.12}$$

Producers' surplus π_t in the absence of price stabilization is

$$\pi_t = \int_{p(0)}^{P_s} S(p')dp' \tag{4A.13}$$

where $p(0)$ is the supply price at zero output. Similarly, producers' surplus π_S at the stabilized price is

$$\pi_s = \int_{p(0)}^{P_s} S(p')dp' \tag{4A.14}$$

The difference, producers' surplus G_P due to stabilization, is

$$G_p = \pi_t - \pi_s = \int_{P_t}^{P_s} S(p')dp' \tag{4A.15}$$

Substituting equation (4A.2), then equation (4A.15) integrates as

$$\begin{aligned}
G_p &= 1/2(p_s - p_t)[S(p_t) + S(p_s)] \\
&= 1/2\frac{(u_t - v_t)}{a_1 + b_1}\left[\frac{2(b_0a_1 + b_1a_0)}{a_1 + b_1}\right. \\
&\quad \left. + \frac{2a_1 + b_1/v_t + b_1u_t}{a_1 + b_1}\right]
\end{aligned} \tag{4A.16}$$

A similar process measures consumers' surplus G_C as

$$G_C = 1/2(p_t - p_s)[D(p_t) + D(p_s)] \tag{4A.17}$$

Furthermore, aggregate social welfare G, the sum of producers' surplus and consumers' surplus, is

$$G = G_P + G_C = 1/2(p_s - p_t)[S(p_s) - D(p_s)] \tag{4A.18}$$

The expected gains in producers' surplus, consumers' surplus, and social welfare are

$$E(G_P) = [-b\,\sigma^2_u + (2a_0 + b_1)\,\sigma^2_v]/2(a_1 + b_1)^2 \tag{4A.19}$$
$$E(G_C) = [(2b_1 + a_1)\,\sigma^2_u - a_1\sigma^2_v]/2(a_1 + b_1)^2 \tag{4A.20}$$
$$E(G) = (\sigma^2_u + \sigma^2_v)/2(a_1 + b_1) \tag{4A.21}$$

Equation (4A.21), the aggregate social gain from price stabilization, is always positive.

Notes

1. Zivnuska (1949) first raised this issue. Scott (1955) also discusses it. To our knowledge it has gone otherwise unnoticed in forestry.

2. The reader who is interested only in the social efficiency contributions of TMS might turn directly to this second section. It was written so that it can stand alone.

3. Kane (1986) shows that market power may not take the form of spatial discrimination and it may be difficult to detect. If the supply elasticities are identical, then the monopsonist mill earns greater profits by paying uniform net prices regardless of supplier location and even if freight costs are significant.

4. This analysis and the results in Tables 4.1 through 4.4 were first discussed by W. Schworm, D. Hoass, and W. Hyde (1983).

5. This is an oversimplification, of course. Perfect foresight is never possible and imperfect foresight is an important source of price variation in agriculture. Nevertheless, agricultural crops have a shorter production period, therefore farmers can have relatively better foresight than producers of other basic resources.

6. Consider cow-calf cycles or, better yet, corn-hog cycles and the economics literature on the cobweb theorem.

7. We can observe that the coefficients of the autoregressive parameters sum to less than 1 for all our subsequent ARIMA models. This means that our price series all do exhibit stationarity (Pindyck & Rubinfeld 1981, pp. 497–508).

8. This is admittedly an ad hoc test, but it is consistent with most tests for heteroscedasticity.

9. See note 4, Chapter 1, for the proof.

10. Not surprisingly, Eckstein (1979) finds that millowners and managers carefully avoid encouraging any organized forum for making general price and quantity information available to nonindustrial private landowners; some actively oppose such suggestions. This behavior is consistent with our observation that millowners and managers are net losers to the (redistributive) price increasing effect of price reporting services.

Some may support price reporting in the hope that it will bring more timber to the market. Figure 4.2 and its adjacent discussion should disabuse us of this notion. Price reporting improves the relative market position of nonindustrial private landowners. It provides additional market information, which causes the nonindustrial private landowners to raise their reservation prices and thereby to shift their aggregate supply curve upward, causing a new market equilibrium at a smaller output level.

11. Brannlund, Johansson, and Lofgren (1985) use a similar model for Sweden.

12. The price elasticities are $e^{D}_{s} = .7030$; $e^{s}_{s} = .5821$; $e^{D}_{p} = .2836$; and $e^{s}_{p} = .3501$; where the superscripts refer to demand or supply and the subscripts refer to sawtimber or pulpwood.

13. Personal communication, James Neal, Regional Extension Forester, USDA Forest Service, February 1986. Timber Mart-South received an initial $50,000 USDA Forest Service grant for subscriptions. The Forest Service distributed 951 TMS subscriptions in the first year and 1051 subscriptions in the second and third years to state foresters and state and county extension offices.

14. There is another potential gain from TMS that is not associated with stabil-

ity. Price data are essential to economic and policy analysis. TMS provides the best stumpage price data in the U.S. and, thereby, can make a large contribution over time to the rational evaluation of public policies. To the extent that this policy analysis leads to more efficient public programs, then TMS contributes to social welfare. We owe this point to D. Newman.

 References

Barnett, H. J., and C. Morse. 1963. *Scarcity and growth: The economics of natural resource availability.* Baltimore: Johns Hopkins University Press.

Box, G. E. P., and G. M. Jenkins. 1970. *Time series analysis: Forecasting and control.* San Francisco: Holden-Day.

Brannlund, R., P. O. Johansson, and K. G. Lofgren. 1985. An econometric analysis of aggregate sawtimber and pulpwood supply in Sweden. *Forest Science* 31(3):595–606.

Citibase/Citibank Economic Department. 1983. CITIBASE: Citibank economic database (machine-readable magnetic data file). New York: Citibank, N.A.

Eckstein, L. W., Jr. 1979. An analysis of vertical market structures in southern timber markets. Ph.D. diss. University of Georgia, Athens.

Kane, S. M. 1986. Spatial price discrimination under monopsony in standing timber markets. Working paper. USDA Economic Research Service.

Kushner, H. 1971. *Introduction to stochastic control.* New York: Holt, Rinehart and Winston.

Lucas, R. E. 1976. Econometric policy evaluation: A crtitique. In *The Phillips curve and labor markets,* ed. K. Brunner and A. H. Meltza. Carnegie-Rochester Conferences on Public Policy 1. New York: North-Holland.

Manthy, R. 1978. *Natural resource commodities: A century of statistics.* Baltimore: Johns Hopkins University Press.

Massell, B. F. 1969. Price stabilization and welfare. *Quarterly Journal of Economics* 83:284–98.

Muth, J. R. 1961. Rational expectations and the theory of price movements. *Econometrica* 29:315–35.

Nelson, C. R. 1973. *Applied time series analysis for managerial forecasting.* San Francisco: Holden-Day.

Newbery, D. M. G., and J. E. Stiglitz. 1979. The theory of commodity price stabilization rules: Welfare impacts and supply responses. *The Economic Journal* 89:799–817.

———. 1981. *The theory of commodity price stabilization: A study in the economics of risk.* New York: Clarendon Press.

———. 1982. The choice of techniques and the optimality of market equilibrium with rational expectations. *Journal of Political Economy* 90(2):223–46.

Newman, D. H. 1986. An econometric analysis of aggregate gains from technical change in southern softwood forestry. Ph.D. diss. Duke University, Durham, N.C.

Oi, W. Y. 1961. The desirability of price instability under perfect competition. *Econometrica* 29:58–64, 248.

Pindyck, R. S., and D. L. Rubinfeld. 1981. *Econometric models and economic forecasts.* New York: McGraw-Hill.

Potter, N., and F. T. Christy, Jr. 1962. *Trends in natural resource commodities: Statistics of prices, output, consumption, foreign trade, and employment in the United States, 1870–1957.* Baltimore: Johns Hopkins University Press.

Sargent, T. J. 1978. Estimation of dynamic labor demand schedules under rational expectations. *Journal of Political Economy* 86:1009–44.

Schworm, W., D. Hoass, and W. Hyde. 1983. An investigation of the price volatility of timber and lumber supplies in the U.S. In *Nonindustrial private forests,* ed. J. Royer and C. Risbrudt. Durham, N.C.: Duke University School of Forestry and Environmental Studies.

Scott, A. 1955. *Natural resources: The economics of conservation.* Carleton Library Series No. 3. Ottawa: Carleton University Press.

Turnovsky, S. J. 1974. Price expectations and the welfare gains from price stabilization. *American Journal of Agricultural Economics* 56:206–216.

USDA Forest Service. 1982. *An analysis of the timber situation in the United States 1952–2030.* Forest Resource Report No. 23. Washington, D.C.: author.

Waugh, F. V. 1944. Does the consumer benefit from price instability? *Quarterly Journal of Economics* 58:602–614.

Zivnuska, J. A. 1949. Commercial forestry in an unstable economy. *Journal of Forestry* 47(1):4–13.

CHAPTER 5

Minimum Wage and Occupational Safety and Health

This chapter and the next focus on regulations that affect the market for in situ resources from the demand side. Included in such regulations might be any that affect the processing of the resource, such as regulations constraining logging and sawmill activities, thereby causing the processing sector to alter its optimal output level or optimal combination of inputs, therefore its derived demand for inputs like stumpage. To our ears, the Occupational Safety and Health Act of 1970 (OSHA) is the most talked about regulation of this sort. It mandates employers to protect employees from "recognized hazards that are causing or are likely to cause death or serious harm" and it provides for fines on employers found to be in noncompliance with the act. There are serious data shortcomings, however, which restrict the analysis of OSHA. Therefore, we selected the federal minimum wage policy as an alternative demand-side regulation. It constrains free choice in factor use by mandating a minimum hourly wage and covers all employees in the forest industries.

The justifications for both OSHA and the minimum wage are distributive, although there is an allocative case for OSHA as well. The distributive argument is that both OSHA and the minimum wage provide minimal protection for the least–well-off members of society. These are the least well informed and the least mobile, therefore the least able to improve their own lot. The allocative argument for OSHA is that employee accidents are costly. Their reduction would create efficiency gains. For example, occupational illness and injury caused a loss of nearly 1 percent of GNP in the 1970s (Freeman 1979).

On the other hand, both OSHA and the minimum wage increase the costs of processing stumpage into final products: OSHA by requiring costly safety protective measures and inspection procedures or by imposing fines; the minimum wage by arguably raising the wage bill for the least skilled and newest employees, thereby increasing the average wage. Managers of both mills and integrated forest product firms might oppose OSHA and the minimum wage because of these implicit production cost increases.

Our primary purpose in this chapter is to examine the welfare and distributive impacts of the minimum wage policy. (Our intention to examine OSHA is satisfied, to the extent possible, in an appendix to this chapter.) Welfare implies inquiry into the burdens on employers and the gains to workers resulting from the minimum wage policy. In this case there are two important classes of workers, those who are covered by the minimum wage law and those who are not covered. Either or both classes of workers may either gain or suffer from changes in employment and income as a result of the law. In general, however, our results will show that a $.25 increase in the statutory minimum wage causes up to a 9.8 percent increase in the wage bill for workers in the forest products industries who are covered by the law. It also causes, in general, a decrease of up to 6.1 percent in the employment of these same workers. The precise wage gain and employment loss depend on the specific forest industry.

Welfare is the more detailed component of our analysis because economic tools are better designed to comment on it. In this case, our inquiry into distributive impacts is a natural outgrowth of the welfare analysis. It consists of a few final observations regarding the income levels of affected employees relative to each other and to society as a whole. The implied questions are: Are these employees the ones whom society would prefer to receive distributive gains? Are the costs of implementation worth the redistributive impacts obtained? Our empirical work will show that the workers who gain the most and who are the least likely to suffer unemployment as a result of an increase in the minimum wage are in the highest paid of the forest products industries. These are not usually thought to be the workers whom society would prefer to receive distributive gains. Furthermore, the minimum wage policy may bring unemployment and wage *decreases* instead to workers in the lowest paid forest products industries. Thus, the impacts of the minimum wage actually run counter to its distributive intentions.

We begin our examination with some background information: a discussion of the law itself and its changes over time with regard to the workers it covers, a review of general observations from the existing empirical literature regarding the law's impact across all industries, and some observations about the law's impact on forest-related industries in particular. A second section develops the conceptual model and a third tests it empirically. We depart somewhat from the one sector model of welfare impacts discussed in Chapter 1 because of the form of available data and in order to examine impacts on the two classes of workers. A two-sector conceptual model, patterned after Mincer (1976) and Wessels (1980) satisfies our purposes. This model is appropriate for industries like logging and for firms in forest products industries like sawmills and planing mills or paper and pulp mills, which are covered by the minimum wage legislation but whose employees have alternate employment opportunities in uncovered industries outside of forestry (Stevens 1980). Our empirical tests of this model follow Boschen and Grossman (1981). These tests feature the lumber and wood products industries and the paper and allied products industries as the Standard Industrial Code breaks them into two- and three-digit industries. A final section draws conclusions and includes summary observations about the distributive questions raised in the preceeding paragraph with respect to those forest products workers affected by the minimum wage requirement.

 ## The Fair Labor Standards Act and the Forest Products Industries

The Fair Labor Standards Act (FLSA) providing for minimum wages went into effect in 1938. It has been subject to frequent amendment and it has spurred voluminous research since then. FLSA initially covered only one-fourth of all private sector employees or 43.4 percent of all nonsupervisory employees in the private, nonagricultural labor force. The manufacturing sector of the economy, including the lumber and wood products and the paper and allied products industries, was among the first covered. With the exception of mining, manufacturing has been the sector most consistently and fully covered. Table 5.1 traces the historical minimum wage, its ratio to the average manufacturing wage, and the percent coverage for the aggregate of all private, nonsupervisory, nonagricultural employees. By 1981 the minimum wage was $3.35 per hour, which was 51.9 percent of the average manufacturing wage. FLSA covered 97 percent of nonsupervisory manufacturing employees and 83.8 percent of all private, nonsupervisory, nonagricultural employees.[1] There has been no increase in the minimum wage since 1981.

Two recent publications survey the empirically based opinion regarding the impacts of the minimum wage, the seven volume report of the Minimum Wage Study Commission (MWSC 1981) established by the U.S. House of Representatives and the proceedings from a minimum wage conference sponsored by the American Enterprise Institute (AEI) (Rottenberg 1981). Combined, the MWSC and AEI publications summarize research on a dozen minimum wage–related topics, including impacts on employment and unemployment, inflation and income distribution, youth and minority employment, employment in low-wage industries, the effects of indexing

Table 5.1. The basic minimum wage and aggregate coverage, 1938–1983

Date of change in minimum wage	Basic minimum changed to	Basic minimum as a % of average (straight time) manufacturing wage	% Covered of all nonsupervisory employees in private, nonagricultural work
10/38	$0.25	41.7	43.4
10/39	0.30	49.5	47.1
10/45	0.40	42.1	55.4
1/50	0.75	54.0	53.4
3/56	1.00	52.9	53.1
9/61	1.15	51.2	62.1
9/63	1.25	52.7	62.1
2/67	1.40	51.5	75.3
2/68	1.60	55.6	72.6
5/74	2.00	47.2	83.7
1/75	2.10	45.1	83.3
1/76	2.30	46.0	83.0
1/78	2.65	48.4[a]	83.8[b]
1/79	2.90	49.7[a]	83.8[b]
1/80	3.10	49.9[a]	83.8[b]
1/81	3.35	51.9[a]	83.8[b]

[a]Manurfacturing wages are extrapolated, based on a log linear trend, 1965–1976. Wages during this period grew at 6.3 percent per year.
[b]Coverage rate under 1977 amendment estimated by Employment Standards Administration.

Source: F. Welch, *Minimum Wages, Fringe Benefits and Working Conditions* (Washington, D.C.: American Enterprise Institute, 1980), p. 3. Copyright 1978 American Enterprise Institute. Reprinted by permission, with updated data.

the minimum wage for inflation and the effects of setting a subminimum wage for younger workers.

Eccles and Freeman (1982) compare the MWSC and AEI publications and find that the observations of each are consistent with current professional consensus regarding the directions, if not the magnitudes, of minimum wage impacts. Table 5.2 is Eccles and Freeman's summary comparison.

Table 5.2. Comparison of minimum wage studies: Minimum Wage Study Commission versus American Enterprise Institute

1. Demographic profiles and compliance

A. MWSC

Gilroy
48% of all minimum wage workers are 16–24 years old, 37% are women 25 years and over, relatively large proportions of minimum wage workers in groups of: teenagers 16–17 (62%), 18–19 (33%), workers over 65 (39%), women (18%), blacks (18%), students (56%), part-time workers (36%), and poverty families (43%); only 9% of adults 20–64.

Institute for Social Research
1980 survey of low-wage establishments finds almost half of near–minimum wage workers under 20, the majority white though higher proportion of nonwhite workers in low-wage work than overall, higher proportion in South.

Sellekaerts & Welch
In 1973–80, found noncompliance consistently higher in low-wage sectors, and in the South, among females, nonwhites and teenagers than in complementary groups. In 1979 violation survey non-South's rate exceeds South's; overtime violations most prevalent. In 1978 *CPS* sample, overtime provisions violated at least in part 73% of the time.

Ehrenberg & Schumann
Considerable noncompliance with overtime pay provisions; overtime pay yields greater benefits to middle and upper-income families than to lower-income families; increases in overtime differential will create modest number of jobs.

B. AEI

Kneisser
Using *CPS,* finds over 60% of all low-wage workers are female; under 40% are teenagers, 30% are in families below the poverty level, tendency to live in the South or Great Plains regions.

Bell
30% of low-wage workers are not household heads; concentration in families above the poverty level.

Fleisher
D.O.L. retail trade surveys in 1962, 1965–66 shows over 90% compliance for U.S., lower rates in South, from 71% in 1962 to 87% in 1966 (in eligible workers covered).

Ehrenberg & Schumann
Same basic conclusions as Ehrenberg and Schumann above.

2. Employment effects – in general

A. MWSC

Abowd & Killingsworth
Under an *ad hoc* model a 2% increase leads to a .2 to 2.4% drop in teenage employment, a .2% rise to a .8% drop for adults. Under a structural model, a 2% increase leads to a .5 to 1% drop for teenagers, a negligible drop for adults.

Madden & Cooper
No statistically significant results as to interstate distribution of sales or employment in wholesale and retail trade.

Table 5.2. (continued)

Brown, Gilroy, Kohen Survey of low-wage sector effects find little conclusive evidence of adverse employment effects.	*Heckman & Sedlockek* Using South Carolina worker data, a 20% minimum wage increase makes over 80% of S.C. workers worse off, either through disemployment or lower wages.

B. AEI

Wessels Minimum wage significantly increases labor-force participation of young adult females and males over 65, significantly decreases labor participation for young males, all with relatively small elasticities.	*Trapani & Moroney* For seasonal cotton farm workers in late 1960s, 63% of large drops in employment attributed to extended minimum wage coverage.
Krumm Significant disemployment effects in all localities on lowest-skill workers as they are replaced by medium-skilled, new labor market entrants.	*Gardner* For farm workers, a rise of 5% in mean hourly wage leads to a minimum 5% reduction in employment.
Fleisher In retail trade in the 1960s, given a labor cost rise of 5%, labor demand dropped 5%; expansion of employment in department stores relative to rest of retail trade.	*Gordon* No significant effects on private household worker employment.

3. Employment effects for youths and youth subminimum

A. MWSC

Meyer & Wise Without minimum wage, employment of nonstudent young men would be up 6% at least, average youth wage lower with the minimum.	*Brown* Size of effects of youth differential on teenage and especially adult employment uncertain; problems with restricted differential.
Brown, Gilroy, Kohen Survey of youth employment studies shows reasonably consistent time-series results that 10% minimum wage increase causes a 1 to 3% reduction in employment for 16–19-year olds, less consistency for 20–24-year olds & subgroups; their runs show a .5 to 1.5% drop.	*Pettengill* Eliminating minimum for youths would increase employment among youth, indeterminate impact on nonyouth low-wage workers.
Hamermesh In private nonfarm sector, a 10% minimum wage increase leads to a 1.2% drop overall; higher in manufacturing, lower in services and retail trade. In private nonfarm sector, a 10% minimum wage increase leads to a 1.2% drop overall; higher in manufacturing, lower in services and retail trade. Estimates that a 25% youth differential would increase employment by about 3%.	*Freeman, Gray, Ichniowski* Student subminimum has led to increase in student person hours worked by perhaps 17% at a cost of perhaps 1% of employment of full-time nonstudent worker hours.

B. AEI

Cunningham For whites, employment is reduced, part-time work discouraged, and school attendance reduced, nonrobust results for blacks.	*Ragan* Legal minimum raises wages in youth intensive sectors; some evidence that manpower programs have raised employment, that minimum reduces employment for some teenage groups.

Table 5.2. (continued)

Al-Salam, Quester & Welch
Expansion of coverage of minimum wages has reduced proportion employed by 0.4 and created a gap between black and white male teenagers of roughly 0.04 as well; cohort size is important determinant of proportion employed.

Fleisher
In retail trade, significant negative impact on employment for young males, inconclusive results for females.

Mattila
For 14–19-year olds, significant results on increase in school enrollments, roughly equal to magnitude of decrease in nonstudent labor force.

Cotterill
Review suggests significant problems of exclusion of other low-wage groups by differential to youth, especially in retail and service areas.

Cotterman
Study of 18–19-year-old males gives insignificant results for disemployment, except for significant in retail trade ($.25 increase leads to 25% drop in black employment, 16% in white); interindustry shifts occur, with high-skilled teens; employment chances improved.

4. Income distribution

A. MWSC
Behrman, Taubman & Sickles
In checking proportions falling below the poverty line, inconclusive results by race; females appear to do slightly better than males; varied results for other age-sex schooling groups.

Johnson & Browning
Through simulations, found even distribution of benefits over all income levels and disemployment effects lowering the benefits, generally small distributional effects, within income classes inequity increases (80% of low-income households lose because of higher prices, 10% of high-income households gain income).

Kohen & Gilroy
Found no strong correlation between individual earnings and family income, and therefore only small "positive" effects on income distribution. Even distribution across income levels of minimum wage workers.

Datcher & Loury
Using *CPS* data, 20% increase in minimum wage causes white family earnings to rise over 1%, black earnings .2%; higher-income families gain absolutely none.

B. AEI
Parsons
Using *NLS,* found small wage gains for low-wage adult females, offset by employment reductions; amount to less than $150 per year.

McCulloch
Using Gini index, net negative effect on equality.

5. Macroeconomics aspects

A. MWSC
Pettengill
1% minimum wage increase leads to a .3 to 1.3% of work force forced out of labor market; average wage rise of 1 to 2%.

Farber
10% change in minimum leads to less than .5% change in union wage.

Table 5.2. (continued)

Boschen & Grossman
Increases in minimum wage depress current employment in some industries, no effect on aggregate employment or average wage rate; effect of indexation uncertain.

Cox & Oaxaca
10% rise leads to a .1% rise in aggregate real wage bill; an increase in high-wage employment, decrease in low-wage and overall.

Sellekaerts
10% minimum wage increase causes a rise of .05% in unemployment rate and .76% rise in average wages; initial impact of indexation uncertain; later effect beneficial (e.g., increased efficiency).

Wolff & Nadiri
Raising minimum wage has positive effect on output due to income distribution, negative on employment, and raises prices more rapidly as minimum rises.

B. AEI
McCulloch
Direct effect on inflation negligible, even if minimum wage is indexed.

6. Nonwage job effects (on the job training, etc.)

A. MWSC
Lazear & Miller
Using NLS, no obvious retardation effects of the minimum wage on wage growth.

B. AEI
Fleisher
Using NLS, while wage rates are higher in covered than noncovered sectors, adding the wage advantage of working to reported wages causes wages in uncovered sector for students and nonstudents to exceed those in covered sector for students and nonstudents.
Wessels
Minimum wages have slight negative or neutral effects on labor participation, slight effects on priors, and a positive or neutral effect on quit rates.

Hashimoto
Using NLS, some reduction in On-the-Job Training (OJT) (2.5%) found for young white males; inconclusive results for blacks.

Leighton & Mincer
Minimum wages discourage OJT especially at lower education levels; mixed results on job turnover.

Data Source: Papers reviewed are contained either in Volumes II–VII of the *Report of the Minimum Wage Study Commission* (MWSC), published in July, 1981; in the American Enterprise Institute's (AEI) conference volume, *The Economics of Legal Minimum Wages* (Simon Rottenberg, ed., published 1981); *Poverty and the Minimum Wage*, by Donald Parsons; *Minimum Wage Regulation in Retail Trades*, by Belton Fleisher; *Minimum Wages and On-the-Job Training*, by Masanori Hashimoto; *Minimum Wages, Fringe Benefits and Working Conditions*, by Walter Wessels; and *The Impact of the Minimum Wage on Regional Labor Markets*, by Ronald Krumm. Studies are referred to by author. NLS refers to the National Longitudinal Survey ("Parnes Survey") funded by the Department of Labor.

Source: M. Eccles and R. Freeman, "What: Another Minimum Wage Study?" *American Economic Review* 72(2):228–29. Reprinted with permission.

The general conclusions originating from neoclassical economic models of employment are that increases in the minimum wage

(1) Raise the entire distribution of wages and prices and reduce aggregate production (assuming no offsetting increase in the money supply and, therefore, no inflation);

(2) Either cause employees to become more productive or, more likely, alter the distribution of employment toward more productive (often older) employees;

(3) Are likely to cause offsetting reductions in both fringe benefits and training programs provided by employers;

(4) Induce substitution away from productive activities requiring large shares of low-skill, low-wage employees;

(5) Have uncertain impacts on aggregate employment and unemployment because, while they reduce employment in the sector covered by the minimum wage, they may also induce employment increases in the sector that is not covered.

How does the minimum wage affect forestry specifically? The lumber and wood products and paper and allied products industries were among the manufacturing industries first significantly covered by the minimum wage provisions of the FLSA in 1938. Employment in some firms in these industries, however, has been and still remains exempt from some coverage. Employees of small logging contractors and small sawmills were exempt specifically from the minimum wage and overtime provisions until 1974 when an amendment to the FLSA repealed their exemption from the former.[2] These employees continue to be exempt from the overtime provision. It should be clear that this legally authorized exemption provides incentive to form the small firms eligible for exemption. Indeed, we observe just this, with large integrated forest products firms often contracting with many small and independent logging contractors and portable sawmills to provide raw material inputs for the integrated firms.

An October 1975 survey by the Bureau of Labor Statistics (BLS) reflects on the importance of minimum wage coverage in the logging and sawmill industries. The survey identified 9806 overtime-exempt independent logging contractors and integrated sawmills and planing mills. These exempt firms employed over 30,000 exempt employees, four-fifths of them working for independent logging contractors. Two-thirds of the exempt employees and 63 percent of the exempt firms were in the South where small firms account for the bulk of the logging and sawmill activities. Moreover, the survey substantiated a seasonality argument for exemption in the logging and sawmill industries. Two-thirds of annual hours worked were accumulated within six months and three-quarters within seven months. Although 14 percent of employees worked in excess of 40 hours during the October survey week, short work weeks dominated with almost half of all employees working fewer than 35 hours (MWSC 1981, vol. IV, 132–34).

The BLS survey finds considerable structural response to statutory opportunities for exemption. We might also inquire whether the degree of labor mobility between forestry and other sectors of the economy and the opportunity for capital-labor substitution, as either the population shifts or the minimum wage increases, permit market adjustments to minimum wage policy.

Stevens (1980) provides the only analysis of labor mobility known to us. He examines labor force mobility in Oregon's forest products industries in general and he finds high labor turnover. Twenty-three percent of the labor force is peripheral, that is, workers who combine forest products industry employment with other employment. This group's average salary was $7938 in 1972, an annual salary halfway between the averages for unskilled and semiskilled workers in general at that time. These peripheral workers spend more time throughout their employment history outside than within the forest products industries. Even among core forest products workers (55 percent of the Oregon labor force) who have current income only from employment within forest products, half the loggers and three-quarters of the mill workers have had previous employment outside the forest products industries. Stevens hypothesizes that a large share of mobility among forest products employees is due to the general rather than firm specific nature of employment in these industries. His evidence suggests that employees do move freely from sectors of the forest products industries covered by the minimum wage provision to sectors not covered. Employees may even depart the forest products industries altogether.

Stier (1980) examines capital–labor substitution in the forest products industries. He found three previous estimates suggesting relative ease of substitution between capital and labor. Four other estimates as well as his own (and a subsequent study by Greber and White [1982]) find an elasticity less than 1 in nine of ten forest products industries. Stier observes, therefore, that factor substitution is more limited in forestry than in other manufacturing industries. Nevertheless, some capital–labor substitution is possible and Stier does not reject labor mobility, particularly labor mobility out of the industry induced by labor-saving technical change.

The existence of labor mobility between nonexempt (forestry) and exempt (nonforestry) sectors and of capital–labor substitution both justify our use of a two-sector model for examining the impacts of the minimum wage provision in the lumber and wood products and paper and allied products industries. Peterson (1981, 54) finds that total related minimum wage impacts exceeded 1 percent of the wage bill for the lumber and wood products industries for some years between 1950 and 1979. He finds no significant impact for the paper and allied products industries for those years. Our results are consistent with his.

The Two-Sector Model

The remainder of this chapter develops our conceptual and empirical tests of minimum wage impacts on the forest products industries. We begin with a few words describing the two-sector model and then match a geometric exposition to them.

In the two-sector model, minimum wage legislation covers one sector but not the other. The aggregate labor supply is the sum of labor supply in the covered sector plus labor supply in the uncovered sector, both of which depend on the return from job search, a decreasing function of labor turnover and the discount rate (Mincer 1976). Basic worker skills are similar and only the willingness to search distinguishes workers in the two sectors. There is no unemployment in the *uncovered* sector, because employers in this sector are free to decrease wages until labor demand equals supply.[3] Therefore, the duration and cost of search in the uncovered sector are zero and the wage in the uncovered sector equals the reservation wage, which is also the reservation return to the search activity. If wages in the covered sector exceed wages in the uncovered sector, then workers are willing to search for employment in the *covered* sector. (This also means that they may stay unemployed longer while they search.) Indeed, the equilibrium wage differential between the two sectors equals the cost of searching for employment in the covered sector. Or, in other words, covered sector equilibrium occurs where demand equals supply for employment in that sector. At this point, workers are indifferent between unemployment together with further search in the covered sector or employment in the uncovered sector.

Increasing the minimum wage causes unemployment in the covered sector which creates a surplus of workers seeking employment in the uncovered sector. This surplus permits employers in the uncovered sector to decrease wages until there is no more unemployment in that sector and both sectors are, once again, in equilibrium. Thus, increases in the minimum wage have both *wage* and *employment* effects in *both sectors*.

Figure 5.1 describes this situation. Demand and supply for labor in the covered sector are D_c and S_c, respectively. The uncovered sector is always in equilibrium — as shown by $D_u = S_u$. In the absence of minimum wage legislation, wages adjust until the covered sector wage w_{c0}, which is also the uncovered sector wage w_{u0}, equals the reservation return to search s_0 and there is no unemployment. The covered sector employs L_{c0} and the uncovered sector employs L_{u0} workers.

Now consider the imposition of a minimum wage w_{m1} greater than w_{c0}. Employment in the covered sector falls from L_{c0} to L_{c1}, turnover decreases as employed covered sector workers have greater incentive to keep their

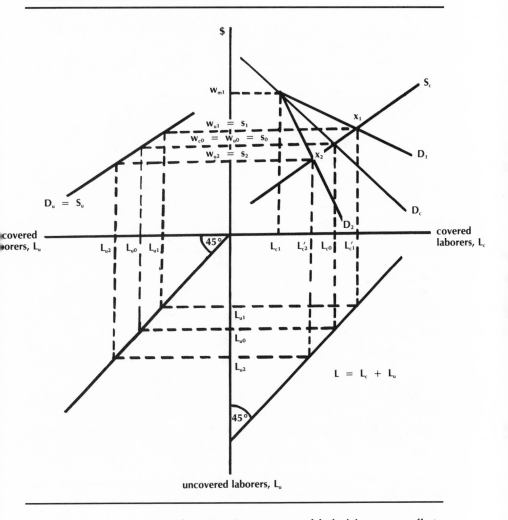

Figure 5.1. A two-sector model of minimum wage effects.

jobs, and the duration and costs of search rise along with unemployment. Therefore the returns to search in the covered sector decrease as the number of unemployed workers in this sector increases. The negatively sloped returns to search schedules D_1 and D_2 relate labor force participation in the covered sector to returns to search in that sector. Participation is a function of the turnover rate and the elasticities with the steeper sloped function D_2 associated with less rapid turnover.

For example, if the number of participants in the covered sector is L_{c1} at w_{m1}, then there is no unemployment in that sector and the return to search is w_{m1}. As unemployment rises in the covered sector, then the returns to search fall along D_1, which becomes the effective demand schedule for covered employment. Equilibrium, in this example, exists at the intersection of the demand and supply schedules for the covered sector, D_1 and S_c, respectively, or at x_1. Employment in the covered sector is L_{c1}, whereas unemployment in that sector is $L_{c1}L'_{c1}$. Employment in the uncovered sector is L_{u1}. The wage in the covered sector is w_{m1}, the minimum wage, while the wage in the uncovered sector is $w_{u1} = s_1$, which is also the return to search in the covered sector.

In this example all labor force participants benefit from the imposition of a minimum wage. Employed covered workers receive w_{m1}, which is greater than their previous wage w_{c0}, whereas both disemployed covered workers and uncovered workers receive $w_{u1} = s_1$, which is greater than their previous wage $w_{u0} = s_0$. Employers in the uncovered sector lose $L_{u0}L_{u1}$ employees to the covered sector and they must bid wages upward from w_{u0} to w_{u1} to prevent further attrition. This general result holds whenever the return to search schedule exceeds (is less steep than) the demand for covered workers, which means that some disemployed covered workers prefer to search for covered employment rather than to seek sure employment in the uncovered sector.

The wage bill in the covered sector decreases (in this example) from the area defined by w_{c0}, L_{c0} to the area defined by w_{m1}, L_{c1}. The wage bill in the uncovered sector falls (in this example) from the area defined by w_{u0}, L_{u0} to the area defined by w_{u1}, L_{u1}. Total wages paid by employers in both sectors depend on substitution and the demand and supply elasticities. Total wages decrease with the imposition of a minimum wage, as we have drawn Figure 5.1.

Now, in the interest of symmetry, consider the alternate case where the return to search schedule, say D_2, is steeper than the demand schedule for covered employees. Some disemployed covered workers move either to the uncovered sector or out of the labor force altogether, thereby bidding the uncovered wage below w_{u0} and decreasing aggregate unemployment. Employees in the covered sector still receive w_{m1}, which exceeds their previous wage $w_{u0} = s_0$, but neither disemployed covered workers nor uncovered workers benefit in this case as they receive $w_{u2} = s_2$, which is less than their previous wage. Employers in the uncovered sector gain $L_{u2}L_{u0}$ employees from the covered sector and the incentive to form small firms which are exempt from minimum wage coverage is probably realized.

In summary, imposing a minimum wage has two effects on the labor force. It affects the wage of some and also affects the value of being employed. Imposing a minimum wage increases the expected return from search in the covered sector; therefore, it increases the value of being unemployed but searching for employment in that sector. It also increases unemployment itself, which means that the expected duration of search is longer, the return to search lesser, and the cost of being unemployed lower. If the net expected return from search is greater and if workers move from the uncovered to the covered sector, then all labor force participants benefit from the minimum wage. If the net expected return from search is lesser, and if workers move from the covered sector to the uncovered sector or out of the labor force altogether, then only employed, covered workers benefit from the imposition of a minimum wage.[4]

 ## An Empirical Assessment

The graphic presentation suggests requirements for several unavailable pieces of data: search time or unemployment in the covered (forest products) sector; the number of minimum wage employees in the forest products sector; and wage and employment measures for the uncovered sectors or, more accurately, for the sum of all those sectors in which disemployed low-wage forest products workers seek alternative employment. Our empirical assessment must make concessions to this data unavailablity.

The average industry wage provides an alternate measure of wages. We anticipate that it reflects increases in the minimum wage, albeit imprecisely. The average wage is composed of both high- and low-wage employment. If there are different demand elasticities for high- and low-wage employment, then their average is not strictly reflective of the minimum wage. Fortunately, the forest products industries generally are low wage industries, therefore this problem is not so great for our analysis as it might be.[5] Furthermore, Tauchen (1981) provides more general evidence that the effect of this spurious aggregation is small.

A solution to the employment data problem is to use observations of forest products employment for the covered sector and to compare them with observations of aggregate employment economywide. Disemployed forest products workers seek new employment in other industries, including both those covered and those not covered by the statutory minimum wage. This is consistent with Stevens's (1980) arguments that training is not industry specific in the forest products industries and also Stevens's observations of labor mobility across industry boundaries. Of course, the aggregate employment measure is a complete measure. It includes both covered and uncovered industries, and it picks up the full effects of changes in the minimum wage, including the displacement effect on covered forest products employees.

Therefore, although Figure 5.1 shows wage and employment effects in both covered and uncovered sectors, we anticipate that our empirical analysis can only comment indirectly on the uncovered sector. For example, if decreases in the ratio of employment in the covered sector (forest products industries) to aggregate employment are functions of increases in the minimum wage, then we can anticipate that a minimum wage increase causes disemployment in forest products and that some disemployed workers find new employment in unidentified uncovered industries elsewhere in the economy. Similarly, if increases in average wages in the forest products industries are functions of increases in the minimum wage, then we know that average workers remaining employed in the covered sector of the forest products industries benefit from the higher minimum wage. We have no information on the aggregate welfare of those workers previously employed in the forest products industries but some of them are now either unemployed or employed outside forestry.

Boschen and Grossman (B&G 1981) develop a general equilibrium model consistent with these variations from the graphic exposition of Figure 5.1 that, with few additional modifications, is appropriate for our specific analysis of the forest products industries. The B&G model requires two labor markets, one covered by the statutory minimum wage and one that attracts disemployed workers from the first, supply and demand functions for the covered market, and an aggregate market clearing assumption for the combination of both markets. The market clearing assumption permits excess workers in the covered market to obtain employment in the second market if they desire.

The B&G model determines direct minimum wage effects as well as the indirect effects deriving from the impact of federal monetary policy on the real minimum wage.[6] This latter is important because inflation caused by an increase in the money supply may explain much, and perhaps all, of the change in the minimum wage. In such cases we would not anticipate large minimum wage effects on either average workers or employment. The B&G model makes one additional set of important, but reasonable, assumptions: the ratios of supply and demand in the covered market to aggregate supply and demand depend on the past ratio of covered to aggregate employment, on current and near future ratios of the average wage to the minimum wage, and on productivity trends.[7]

We redevelop Boschen and Grossman's structural equations for our purposes in appendix A. The original article derives the reduced form equations for wages and employment in both sectors. Our variations on them, in log linear form, are

$$w_{i,t} = \alpha_0 + \alpha_1\Omega_t + \alpha_2\Omega_{t+1} + \alpha_3 M_t + \alpha_4 m_t + \alpha_5 I_t + \epsilon(w)_{i,t} \quad \text{(5.1)}$$
$$A_{i,t} = \beta_0 + \beta_1\Omega_t + \beta_2\Omega_{t+1} + \beta_3 M_t + \beta_4 m_t + \beta_5 I_t + \epsilon(A)_{i,t} \quad \text{(5.2)}$$
$$w_{j,t} = \gamma_0 + \gamma_1\Omega_t + \gamma_2\Omega_{t+1} + \gamma_3 M_t + \gamma_4 m_t + \gamma_5 I_t + \epsilon(w)_{j,t} \quad \text{(5.3)}$$
$$N_{j,t}/A_{i,t} = \delta_0 + \delta_1\Omega_t + \delta_2\Omega_{t+1} + \delta_3 M_t + \delta_4 m_t + \delta_5 I_t$$
$$+ \delta_6 (N_{j,\,t-1}/A_{i,\,t-1}) + \epsilon(N/A)_t \quad \text{(5.4)}$$

where $w_i = $ ln of average wage rate in manufacturing (where manufacturing is a proxy for the total economy);

$A_i = $ ln of actual employment in the total economy;
$w_j = $ ln of average wage rate in forest product industry j;
$N_j = $ ln of actual employment in forest product industry j;
$\Omega_t = $ ln of statutory minimum wage rate at time t;
$M_t = $ ln of money supply at time t;
$m_t = $ ln of growth in the money supply, measured $M_{t+i} - M_{t+i-1}$;
$I_t = $ ln of index of industrial production at time t;
$\epsilon_t = $ a random variable with zero mean; and
$\gamma, \beta, \gamma, \delta = $ constant coefficients.

The employment variables measure fractions of the working age population. The lower case subscripts refer to the particular industry: i for the aggregate of all industries and j for the various SIC designated forest product industries. The log linear specification means that the reduced form coefficients; α, β, γ, and δ; are elasticities with respect to the dependent variables.

Equation (5.1) refers to the average manufacturing wage, a proxy for the average aggregate wage. Equation (5.2) refers to aggregate employment for the total civilian labor force as a percentage of the total working age population. Equation (5.3) determines current forest industry wages and equation (5.4) determines the ratio of current forest industry employment to aggregate employment.

We previously commented on the anticipated signs on each reduced form coefficient. Table 5.8 in the appendix summarizes Boschen and Grossman's discussion of these signs. We anticipate that the current and expected future minimum wage both have positive effects on average wages both in the covered forest products industries and in all manufacturing.[8] This is consistent with our discussion of Figure 5.1. The current minimum wage has a negative effect, however, on actual forest industries employment as well as on aggregate employment because it reduces employer demand in the forest industries and shifts some labor supply away from the uncovered sector. Again, the B&G model expectations are consistent with Figure 5.1.

We anticipate that the money supply has a positive impact throughout, raising nominal average wages but decreasing real average wages in all sectors and, therefore, increasing employer demand for labor and employment in all sectors. The anticipated sign on the monetary policy variable, growth in the money supply, is uncertain. Our uncertainty can be traced through the positive impact of growth in the money supply on expected wages. An increase in expected wages has a positive effect on aggregate labor demand and employment. This employment effect draws down actual wages, however, leaving the net effect on aggregate wages uncertain. Expected wages also have a positive effect on labor demand and employment in the forest industries, therefore a negative effect on forest industry wages, which also leaves the net effect on forest industry wages and on the ratio of aggregate to forest industry employment both uncertain.

The index of industrial production controls for business cycles and trends. Its statistical performance as an independent variable is a slight improvement on the performance of time as a simpler trend variable. In either case the anticipated sign is indeterminate. The sign might be positive if economic growth reflects onto higher wages and employment. It also might be negative for particular sectors as technical change reduces demand for labor or as faster growing sectors attract labor away from the slower growing sector in question.

Finally, we anticipate a generally positive sign on δ_6, the lagged ratio of forest industry employment to aggregate employment. (A negative sign would indicate a declining industry or an industry in transition.)

DATA

Our concessions to available data require that we work first with aggregate data and then with data specific to the forestry sector. The dependent variables are the average wage w_t, and both aggregate employment A_t and employment in the covered sector N_t as shares of the working age population. Our empirical proxy for wage is the average hourly earnings of production or nonsupervisory workers on private payrolls in manufacturing reported in USDL Bureau of Labor Statistics (BLS) (1979, 1984c) Establishment data. Aggregate employment A_t is measured as the aggregate number of employed civilians as reported in BLS (1984b) Household data. The empirical proxies for forest products employees N_t are the number of production and nonsupervisory employees on private payrolls in the SIC two- and three-digit industries for lumber and wood products and for paper and allied products. Table 5.3 identifies these industries. The dates of availability in this table refer to years for which separate data for that industry's wage and employment are available in the BLS Establishment data. All data reflect annual averages. Our measure of working age population, the denominator in the terms N_t and A_t, is the total noninstitutional population 16 years of age and older, also reported in BLS Household data.

The independent variables are the current and subsequent period levels of the statutory minimum wage, Ω_t and Ω_{t+1}, the volume of the current money stock and the change from the preceding period, M_t and m_t, and the index of industrial production, I_t. The Employment Standards Administration provides observations of the minimum wage. The money stock is M1B reported by the U.S. Department of Commerce (1978; 1983). The industrial production index is the aggregate index for all industries reported by the Federal Reserve (1984).

Table 5.3. Forest-based industries

SIC Code	Description	Dates of available data
24	Lumber and wood products, except furniture	1947–1983
241	Logging camps and logging contractors	1972–1983
242	Sawmills and planing mills	1947–1983
243	Millwork, veneer, plywood, and structural wood members	1972–1983
244	Wood containers	1947–1983
245	Wood buildings and mobile homes	1972–1983
249	Miscellaneous wood products	1958–1983
26	Paper and allied products	1947–1983
261,2,6[a]	Paper and pulp mills	1958–1983
262	Paper mills except building paper	1972–1983
263	Paperboard mills	1958–1983
264	Miscellaneous converted paper products	1958–1983
265	Paperboard containers and boxes	1947–1983

[a]The SIC Code combines these three industries for the years 1958–1983.

EMPIRICAL RESULTS

The aggregate equations refer to average manufacturing wage and average employment for the civilian labor force as a percent of the total working age population. We consider the specifications of these equations and their interpretations first, as they provide clues into the expected signs on the explanatory variables for wage and employment equations in the forest products industries. We subsequently review our wage and employment results for each SIC two- and three-digit forest product industry.

The forest products industries are a small component of the aggregate economy but a component with, perhaps, a large share of marginal-wage employees. These marginal-wage employees cause us to inquire more closely into the causal chain from an increase in the minimum wage to disemployment of forest product workers to increased employment of those workers in a noncovered sector of the economy. Therefore, we will also consider the additional measures, agricultural wage and relative agricultural–forestry employment, because agriculture generally is uncovered by the minimum wage and because so many rural forest products employees find in agriculture a viable employment alternative.

The aggregate wage equation is

$$w_{i,t} = -3.575 + .180\Omega_t + .154\Omega_{t+1} + .832M_t - .770m_t + .050I \quad (5.5)$$
$$\phantom{w_{i,t} = } (-.701) \quad (2.84) \quad (2.32) \quad (10.41) \quad (-2.19) \quad (.87)$$
$$\varrho_1 = .5376 \qquad \varrho_2 = -.2126 \qquad R^2 = .9967 \qquad F_e = 1570.56$$
$$ (3.21) \qquad\qquad (-1.27)$$
$$F_\Omega = 7.42 \qquad F_M = 63.29$$

The sample period is 1949–1983. We used OLS and the Yule-Walker (Gallant & Goebel 1976) method to correct for serial correlation and the ϱs are the Yule-Walker autoregressive parameters. The numbers in parentheses are t statistics. They indicate that coefficients on all independent variables except the index of industrial production are significant at the 5 percent level. The signs on all coefficients are consistent with our expectations. The t statistics also indicate that no significant serial correlation remains after the first interative Yule-Walker correction. The F tests examine the hypotheses that F_e, all the equation coefficients are equal to zero; F_Ω, the two minimum wage coefficients are equal to each other and equal to zero; F_M, the two monetary variable coefficients are equal to each other and equal to zero. All three hypotheses can be rejected at the 5 percent level.

The coefficients indicate that raising the statutory minimum wage has a positive effect on the average manufacturing wage. Reflecting on Figure 5.1 shows that an increase in the minimum wage (from w_{c0} to w_{m1}) may attract employees to the covered sectors ($L_{u0} - L_{u1}$) of the aggregate economy and forces uncovered sector employers to bid up the wages they offer (from w_{u0} to w_{u1}) in order to prevent further attrition from their sector. Otherwise a minimum wage increase restricts the exodus of workers from the covered to uncovered sector ($L_{u2} - L_{u1}$) such that the increased covered sector wage more than offsets the decrease in uncovered sector wage (w_{u0} to w_{u2}). The positive effect of the money supply suggests that money has a nonneutral impact on average wages. This is somewhat countered, however, by the negative sign on the monetary policy variable.

The aggregate employment equation is

$$A_{i,t} = -1.007 - .029\Omega_t - .014\Omega_{t+1} + .056M_t + .048m_t + .033I_t \quad (5.6)$$
$$(-3.66) \quad (-.86) \quad (-.40) \quad (1.30) \quad (.26) \quad (1.13)$$
$$\varrho_1 = .5869 \quad \varrho_2 = -.3038 \quad R^2 = .5838 \quad F_e = 7.29$$
$$(3.59) \quad (-1.86)$$
$$F_\Omega = .469 \quad F_M = 1.54$$

These results are weak, perhaps due to the short data period. Nevertheless, the signs on all coefficients are consistent with our expectations. This suggests the equation specification may be correct and, therefore, that our estimates are unbiased. We cannot reject the hypothesis that none of the independent variables alone can predict a share of changes in aggregate employment. On the other hand, we can reject at the 5 percent level the hypothesis that all coefficients are equal to each other and equal to zero.

If we accept this specification, it suggests that the minimum wage has a negative impact. The level of the money supply and monetary policy, as well as the level of industrial production, have positive impacts on aggregate employment. The interpretation for the negative impact of changes in the statutory minimum wage on aggregate employment (reflecting on Figure 5.1) is that an increase in the minimum wage causes a decrease in covered sector employment (from L_{c0} to L_{c1}) but an increase in the number of workers who are unemployed but searching for employment in the covered sector (from zero unemployed workers before the minimum wage increase to $L'_{c2} - L_{c1}$ or $L'_{c1} - L_{c1}$ unemployed workers, depending on the return to search schedule [D_2 or D_1], after the increase). Aggregate unemployment occurs if there is any increase in the number of workers who are unemployed but searching and regardless of the change in employment (to L_{u2} or L_{u1}) in the uncovered sector.

FOREST PRODUCTS INDUSTRIES WAGE AND EMPLOYMENT EFFECTS. Tables 5.4 and 5.5 specify the OLS measures of the effects of minimum wage policies on wages and employment, respectively, in various forest products industries. The digits attached to the wage and employment dependent variables in the left-hand columns of these tables identify the two- and three-digit SIC industries to which each equation refers. The numbers below these digits refer to the sample period.

The wage specifications are similar to the average manufacturing wage specifications (equation 5.5). The signs on all coefficients are consistent with our expectations. The level of the minimum wage has a positive and statistically significant impact for the two-digit SIC industries. It often is significant for the three-digit industries, particularly the higher-wage, more capital-intensive paper and allied products industries. It is always significant where the data series is longer than twelve annual observations. The level of the money supply has a positive impact and is significant at the 5 percent level for all but logging camps and logging contractors (SIC 241) and is significant at the 20 percent level there. The equation F test and the combined F test on the monetary variables are both significant at the 5 percent level for all forest products industries indicating that all the tested coefficients together have an impact different from zero. The combined F test on the minimum wage variables is significant at the 10 percent level for nine of thirteen industries (those with longer time series) indicating that these variables together have an impact different from zero.

Monetary policy and the index of industrial production have mixed impacts that seldom are statistically significant. (We previously anticipated uncertain signs on their coefficients.) The significant negative sign and effect of monetary policy on the lumber and wood products industry (SIC 24) may be explained by the many smaller firms in this industry, small firms that tend to respond today to yesterday's market signals. That is, they do not anticipate the market well. The monetary authority may begin slowing the rate of growth in the money supply while the lumber and wood products industry is still growing, therefore while the average wage in that industry is still growing.

A second explanation may be that growth in the money supply lags

Table 5.4. Wage effects

ln(wage)	Intercept	Independent variables: ln (·)							Summary statistics			
		Ω_t	Ω_{t+1}	M_t	m_t	I_t	ϱ_1	ϱ_2	R^2	F_e	F_Ω	F_M
W24 (1949–1983)	-4.543 (-10.63)[b]	.130 (2.38)[b]	.060 (1.03)	1.021 (14.62)[b]	-.555 (-1.91)[a]	.020 (.39)	.4973 (3.34)[b]		.9962	1416.06[b]	3.84[a]	128.05[b]
W241 (1972–1983)	-2.230 (-.81)	.442 (1.64)	.187 (.84)	.552 (1.73)	.816 (.52)	.058 (.17)	-.0687 (-.24)		.9948	191.31[b]	1.99	8.91[b]
W242 (1949–1983)	-5.200 (-11.30)[b]	.119 (2.09)[b]	.050 (.85)	1.135 (14.56)[b]	-.435 (-1.46)	.024 (.42)	.6030 (4.41)[b]		.9949	1053.42[b]	2.69[a]	126.33[b]
W243 (1972–1983)	-1.287 (-.69)	.390 (2.22)[a]	.228 (1.62)	.523 (2.40)[a]	.784 (.74)	-.151 (-.68)	.0297 (.10)		.9969	321.58[b]	4.05[b]	17.79[b]
W244 (1972–1983)	-2.417 (-1.36)	.312 (1.83)	.208 (1.51)	.619 (2.98)[b]	-1.072 (-1.06)	-.046 (-.22)	-.0042 (-.01)		.9971	343.83[b]	3.13[a]	8.66[b]
W245 (1972–1983)	-3.157 (-1.61)	.218 (1.17)	.116 (.78)	.647 (2.80)[b]	-.661 (-.59)	.146 (.62)	.0346 (.12)		.9955	221.22[b]	1.06	10.18[b]
W249 (1972–1983)	-3.342 (-2.19)[b]	.204 (1.45)	.110 (.99)	.843 (4.57)[b]	-.311 (-.36)	-.061 (-.34)	.1056 (.37)		.9976	415.67[b]	1.53	35.04[b]
W26 (1949–1983)	-4.253 (-7.82)[b]	.184 (2.66)[b]	.104 (1.43)	.972 (10.88)[b]	.737 (2.01)[a]	.042 (.64)	.5145 (3.50)[b]		.9943	941.97[b]	5.20[b]	67.59[b]
W261,2,6 (1958–1983)	-3.518 (-7.16)[b]	.204 (3.34)[b]	.177 (2.85)[a]	1.025 (11.30)[b]	-.185 (-.65)	-.171 (-3.69)[b]	.7372 (4.38)[b]	-.5124 (-3.04)[b]	.9986	2567.83[b]	8.31[b]	73.28[b]
W262 (1972–1983)	-3.950 (-1.73)	.291 (1.36)	.070 (.41)	1.041 (3.87)[b]	.290 (.22)	-.104 (-.39)	.0450 (.16)		.9968	311.50[b]	1.04	31.54[b]
W263 (1958–1983)	-3.835 (-8.33)[b]	.196 (3.46)[b]	.144 (2.51)[b]	1.068 (12.43)[b]	-.238 (-.92)	-.144 (-3.37)[b]	.7781 (4.83)[b]	-.5692 (-3.53)[b]	.9989	3269.13[b]	3.17[b]	86.89[b]
W264 (1958–1983)	-3.847 (-9.46)[b]	.168 (3.36)[b]	.102 (2.00)[a]	.988 (13.24)[b]	-.309 (-1.36)	-.086 (-2.16)[b]	.7550 (4.20)[b]	-.4024 (-2.24)[b]	.9986	2567.83[b]	6.69[b]	100.36[b]
W265 (1949–1983)	-4.167 (-6.90)[b]	.165 (2.12)[a]	.109 (1.32)	.898 (9.19)[b]	-.809 (-1.94)[a]	.093 (1.29)	.4671 (3.08)[b]		.9932	788.72[b]	3.73[a]	47.70[b]

Note: Numbers in parentheses are t statistics.
a Indicates significance at the .10 level.

140

ln(•)	Intercept	Ω_t	Ω_{t+1}	M_t	m_t	I_t	$(N/A)_{t-1}$	ϱ_1	ϱ_2	R^2	F_e	F_Ω	F_M
N24/A (1949–1983)	−.715 (−.88)	−.184 (−1.49)	.080 (.63)	−.075 (−.73)	2.791 (4.72)[b]	−1.46 (−1.84)[a]	.654 (6.95)[b]	−.0729 (−.43)		.9810	215.13[b]	1.12	14.38[b]
N241/A (1972–1983)	−6.501 (−1.33)	.293 (.57)	.385 (.42)	−1.380 (−1.57)	1.421 (.53)	.674 (1.17)	−.448 (−.55)	−.3158 (−1.10)		.9329	6.95[a]	.47	1.34
N242/A (1949–1983)	.142 (.22)	−.239 (−1.99)[a]	.216 (1.69)	−.075 (−.82)	2.749 (4.83)[b]	−.259 (−2.81)[a]	.779 (11.16)[b]	−.2563 (−1.55)[a]		.9950	829.17[b]	2.14[a]	14.49[b]
N243/A (1972–1983)	−4.409 (−1.82)	.201 (.76)	.030 (.11)	−.972 (−5.21)[b]	5.557 (4.53)[b]	.754 (2.49)[a]	.087 (.65)	−.3665 (−1.31)		.9915	58.32[b]	.69	14.61[b]
N244/A (1972–1983)	−7.867 (−2.96)[a]	.036 (.13)	−.512 (−.207)	−.254 (−1.24)	.478 (.32)	1.158 (4.36)[b]	.480 (2.62)[a]	−.2360 (−.81)		.9941	84.25[b]	3.14[a]	.95
N245/A (1972–1983)	−10.594 (−1.71)	−.807 (−1.14)	−.073 (−.11)	−.541 (−.99)	6.971 (2.12)	1.523 (1.88)	.104 (.71)	−.3311 (−1.16)		.9865	36.54[b]	1.03	3.02[b]
N249/A (1972–1983)	−7.984 (−7.70)[b]	−.059 (−.50)	−.375 (−2.94)[a]	−.081 (−1.19)	.326 (.63)	.937 (8.57)[b]	.416 (5.63)[b]	−.6165 (−2.60)[b]		.9984	312.00[b]	13.95[b]	.78
N26/A (1949–1983)	−2.568 (−4.06)[b]	.005 (.09)	−.072 (−1.20)	−.256 (−3.46)[b]	−.144 (−.49)	.173 (3.29)[b]	.368 (2.86)[b]	.0943 (.55)		.9787	191.45[b]	.86	7.01[b]
N261,2,6/A (1958–1983)	−1.701 (−1.40)	.036 (.40)	−.069 (−.72)	−.149 (−.96)	.098 (.20)	−.135 (−1.55)	.494 (1.43)	−.0518 (−.263)	−.1686 (−.86)	.9936	414.00[b]	.26	.51
N262/A (1972–1983)	−8.579 (−4.89)[b]	−.236 (−1.32)	−.519 (−2.64)[a]	.340 (2.61)[a]	−1.914 (−2.93)[a]	.317 (1.52)	.102 (.29)	−.5221 (−2.03)[b]		.9959	121.45[b]	12.70[b]	4.38[b]
N263/A (1958–1983)	−1.361 (−1.44)	.047 (.44)	.002 (.02)	−.256 (−2.29)[a]	.066 (.12)	.056 (.79)	.666 (4.16)[b]	−.1602 (−.80)	.0005 (.01)	.9889	252.42[b]	.17	2.96[b]
N264/A (1958–1983)	−5.588 (−4.50)[b]	.054 (.58)	−.156 (−1.57)	−.136 (−1.38)	−.377 (−.76)	.361 (3.99)[b]	.263 (1.83)[a]	.1580 (.80)	−.1299 (−.66)	.8233	12.42[b]	1.25	1.90
N265/A (1949–1983)	−4.650 (−6.10)[b]	−.009 (−.14)	−.175 (−2.60)[b]	−.417 (−5.02)[b]	−.065 (−.19)	.485 (6.34)[b]	.234 (2.30)[b]	.2650 (1.60)[a]		.9668	121.34[b]	3.91[b]	14.11[b]

Note: Numbers in parentheses are t statistics.
[a] Indicates significance at the .10 level.
[b] Indicates significance at the .05 level.

economic expansion. This is a basic Keynesian hypothesis. If cycles in lumber production are approximately consistent with cycles in aggregate economic activity, then they precede cycles in money supply and the two may be negatively correlated.

The index of industrial production never has a significant impact in the lumber and wood products industries. Its impact is negative and highly significant, however, for three (more capital intensive) pulp and paper industries: paper and pulp mills (SIC 261), paperboard mills (SIC 263), and miscellaneous converted paper products (SIC 264). The explanation may be that these three industries tend to hire more low-wage workers as both the aggregate economy and their own production expands. This activity has a depressing effect on average wages. Examining Table 5.5 confirms that the latter two industries, indeed, expand employment more rapidly than the expansion of aggregate employment as industrial production increases.

In short, the forest products industries wage equations conform well with respect to our expectations. Their statistical significance is greater where there is a longer data series and in the paper and allied products industries, but the signs on the independent variables are as anticipated regardless of the industry or the length of the data series.

Table 5.5 shows that the independent variables are much less reliable predictors of forest products industrial employment relative to aggregate employment — as they were much less reliable predictors of aggregate employment itself. The level of the minimum wage has the anticipated negative impact, as often as not, on relative employment in both the lumber and wood products (SIC 24) and the paper and allied products (SIC 26) industries. Furthermore, where the impact is positive and contrary to our anticipation, then its measure is statistically insignificant. The expected minimum wage has mixed but generally insignificant effects that are consistent with our uncertain anticipations for it.

If we accept as reliable the combined impact of the two minimum wage variables on relative forest products industries employment, it means that an increase in the minimum wage drives down the demand for labor in most forest products industries at a rate even greater than the increasing minimum wage drives down the aggregate economy's demand for labor.[9] This is consistent with an understanding that the aggregate economy has a proportionally larger uncovered sector in which disemployed, formerly covered, forest products workers can seek new employment.

The money supply has a negative impact on relative employment in all but one forest products industry, papermills except building paper (SIC 262). Its impact is more often statistically significant in the paper and allied products industries. The negative impact of the money supply suggests that, as the money supply increases, there is either a corresponding decrease in forest products employment relative to aggregate employment or else forest products employment increases less rapidly than aggregate employment. This impact was not anticipated.[10] It may be reasonable, however, that this negative impact holds across all manufacturing industries and that the retail and service industries, not the manufacturing industries, are the most positive responders to increases in the money supply. Another explanation may be that the negative impact on forest products employment is a function of timing. That is, an increase in the money supply may be a leading indicator of increasing employment but, by the time employment does increase, the monetary authority may be anticipating further rapid economic expansion and, therefore, may decrease the level of money supply.

The impact of the index of industrial production is positive and significant at the 20 percent level with only three exceptions. It has a negative impact on the lumber and wood products industry as a whole and on one industry in each two-digit group, sawmills and planing mills (SIC 242) and paper and pulp mills (SIC 261). The explanation for the negative impact on the lumber and wood products and the sawmill and planing mill industries may be the increasing relative capital intensity observed over the data period for those two industries, which in turn might suggest decreasing relative employment and, particularly, decreasing low-wage employment causing increasing average wages (Stier 1980).

Paper and pulp mills have a decreasing average wage over this period; therefore, we cannot use this argument in this industry. Could it be that there has been relative stagnation in pulp mills? (We cannot argue that there has been stagnation in paper mills, at least in the more recent period beginning with 1972, because the employment equation for paper mills except building paper (SIC 262) shows a positive response to the index of industrial production.) Finally, lagged relative forest products employment has a the anticipated positive impact on employment in twelve of thirteen industries. Its impact is significant at the 10 percent level in eight of the thirteen industries examined.

In short, the coefficients in our employment equations generally are statistically insignificant. Nevertheless, their signs may be reliable. They conform well with expectations and, where the signs are different from expectation, there is always a plausible explanation.

FURTHER EMPIRICAL RESULTS. Examining the forestry–agriculture relationship may lend further support to our developing observation that increasing the minimum wage generally causes employers in the forest products industries to decrease their demand for labor, thereby driving employees from these industries into industries not covered by the statutory minimum wage. The forestry–agriculture relationship is of particular interest because agricultural employment may be the viable alternative for many rural forest products workers.

Table 5.6 shows our specifications for the agricultural wage (WAg) and relative agricultural employment (NAg–A) equations and for the relative SIC two-digit forest products-agricultural employment equations. Recall that all variables are in log form. The wage data are from U.S. Department of Agriculture (1972–1983) and the employment data are from BLS (1984).

The agricultural wage and employment equation specifications are wholly consistent with the aggregate manufacturing results and explanations (equations 5.5 and 5.6). Increasing the minimum wage encourages employees to depart the uncovered agricultural sector in order to search for covered employment. It causes a bidding up of agricultural wages in order for agricultural employers to hold their remaining workers. The relative forestry–agricutural employment equations show that raising the minimum wage probably drives out marginal workers in the relatively low-wage lumber and wood products industries (SIC 24) and, on the whole, drives them to alternate employment in agriculture. The combined effects of the minimum wage variable on paper and allied products employment relative to agricultural employment are approximately offsetting. Therefore, we argue that employment in paper and allied products (SIC 26) and in agriculture decrease at similar rates in response to increasing minimum wages and that employees from both sectors search for new employment in yet a third sector.[11]

Summary and Conclusions

This chapter examines the impact of the statutory minimum wage on the forest products industries. The minimum wage is an example of a regulation affecting the in situ resource from the demand side, specifically a regulation with a social objective of altering income distribution and improving the lot of the least–well-off members of society. We considered the Occupational Safety and Health Act as an example of such a regulation because it is a more discussed regulation regarding impacts on the forest products industries. Data for examining OSHA, however, are unsatisfactory for industry-specific evaluation. Therefore, we chose to direct our attention to the minimum wage requirement.

The chapter begins with a historical review and follows with a graphical exposition of the problem. The Fair Labor Standards Act provides for minimum wage policy. It went into effect in 1938. The forest products industries, as part of the broader manufacturing category of industries, were among the first, most consistent, and fully covered sectors. Employees of the smallest firms are exempt from the overtime provision of FLSA, however, and this exemption provides incentive, particularly in the logging

Table 5.6. Agriculture wage and employment effects and relative forestry–agriculture employment effects

ln(dep. var.)	Intercept	Ω_t	Ω_{t+1}	M_t	m_t	I_t	$(N/A)_{t-1}$	ϱ_1	ϱ_2	R^2	F_e	F_Ω	F_M
										Summary statistics			
				Independent variables: ln (•)									
WAg (1949–1982)	−5.978 (−12.34)[b]	.108 (1.90)[a]	−.002 (−.03)	1.114 (14.24)[b]	−.248 (−.75)	.096 (1.80)[a]	.838 (9.64)[b]	.6543 (3.95)[b]	−.3041 (−1.83)[b]	.9972	1708.71[b]	1.80	118.39[b]
NAg/A (1949–1982)	−.655 (−1.34)	−.116 (−1.99)[a]	−.016 (−.23)	.191 (3.21)[b]	−.699 (−2.06)[a]	−.172 (−1.62)		.0350 (.21)	−.2519 (−1.52)[a]	.9986	2972.02[b]	3.21[b]	5.15[b]
N24/NAg (1949–1983)	−2.969 (−2.43)[b]	−.103 (−.78)	−.117 (−.84)	−.042 (−.30)	2.536 (3.64)[b]	.455 (3.48)[b]	.432 (3.90)[b]	.1729 (1.02)		.9505	83.21[b]	.97	9.55[b]
N26/NAg (1949–1983)	−2.279 (−2.81)[b]	.162 (1.99)[a]	−.159 (−1.69)	−.257 (−3.33)[b]	.105 (.23)	.601 (4.78)[b]	.562 (6.87)[b]	.0263 (.15)		.9936	672.75[b]	2.29[a]	7.23[b]

Note: Numbers in parentheses are t statistics.
[a] Indicates significance at the .10 level.
[b] Indicates significance at the .05 level.

(SIC 241) and sawmill (SIC 242) industries for forming small independent firms that contract to supply their outputs to larger wood products firms. This incentive, of course, introduces the broader problem of obtaining compliance with the law. (Noncompliance, if substantial, can affect our statistical observations.)

The graphical exposition shows that the statutory minimum wage has both wage and employment effects, each of which could be either negative or positive from the perspective of the entire economy. The wage effect for a single covered sector, like the forest products industries, can only be positive. If this positive wage effect in the covered sector accompanies negative employment effects—some newly disemployed, formerly covered workers are forced to seek employment in lower-wage sectors not covered by the minimum wage—then the net effect on the wage bill for the aggregate of all covered and uncovered sectors can be negative.

The bulk of the chapter focuses on empirical measures of the impact of the minimum wage on the various forest products industries. The common approach in the labor economics literature compares minimum wage impacts on average wages and on employment in a covered sector with comparable impacts in the alternate sector where the disemployed, formerly covered sector employees, may seek new employment. In our case, the SIC two- and three-digit forest products industries form the covered sector and we can measure the minimum wage impacts on average wages in these industries directly. Measuring the employment impacts is more difficult. Forest products employees have a wide range of employment opportunities and we cannot empirically separate their uncovered sector alternatives from all other employment alternatives. The common solution to this problem is to observe relative forest products–aggregate economy employment impacts, where the measure of aggregate employment includes the sum of employment in all covered and uncovered sectors.

This understanding provides foundation for statistical estimations of the wage and relative employment impacts due to changes in the minimum wage in the forest products sectors. From these estimates we can determine changes in the wage bill caused by changes in the level of the minimum wage and, finally, we can reflect on distributive impacts. Our estimates show that both the minimum wage and the anticipated minimum wage have positive effects on average wages for the lumber and wood products and the paper and allied products industries and for all eleven SIC three-digit forest products industries. These effects are consistent with our expectations and generally are statistically significant at least at the 10 percent level. (Subsequent examination of the same wage impacts in three states with large forest products sectors conforms with these observations.)

Our observations of minimum wage impacts on relative forest products employment are more difficult to generalize with confidence. The net effect of the current and anticipated minimum wage parameters tends to be negative. This means that increases in the statutory minimum wage cause forest products industry employers to hire relatively fewer employees. Our aggregate employment regressions suggest confirmation of the hypothesis that the newly disemployed forest products workers seek employment in the uncovered sectors of the aggregate economy. A subsequent review of the relative forest products–agricultural employment suggests that disemployed lumber and wood products employees, in particular, seek new employment in agriculture. (The equations for the three states provide additional support for this observation.)

The industry wage bill is the sum of all wage payments made in that industry. We can use our regressions on average wages and on employment to inquire what would have happened to the wage bill in the forest products industries if the statutory minimum wage were increased $.25 in 1983. (Recall that all equations are in log form.) The $.25 increase is comparable to other recent increases in the minimum wage and 1983 is the most recent year for which there is a full data set for all independent variables.)

Table 5.7 shows the average wage and the total employment for each SIC two- and three-digit industry both before and after our hypothetical increase in the minimum wage. The second four columns of the table record the implied changes in employment and the wage bill. For example, the average wage in the lumber and wood products industry (SIC 24) increases $.11 (from $8.10 per hour to $8.21 per hour) while employment decreases 0.7 percent (from 545,095 to 541,028 employees). Firms pay a total of $26,570 more for their labor input after the increase in the minimum wage. Further examination of Table 5.7 shows that this is the general case. An increase in the minimum wage causes an increase in the wage bill in both SIC two-digit industries and in eight of the eleven three-digit industries. These eight three-digit industries employ 76 percent of all forest products workers.

The increase in the wage bill accrues, however, to 6384 fewer employees in the combined lumber and wood products and paper and allied products industries. (The number 6384 is the total is the total for row 6 of Table 5.7.) We have no direct evidence of the welfare impacts on either disemployed workers in the forest products industries or on those additional workers attracted to the forest products work force by the higher minimum wage, yet who are still searching for employment. We can project, nevertheless, that a share of the disemployed forest products workers find employment in other uncovered industries and, in particular, we know that former lumber and wood products employees are likely to find employment in agriculture. Agriculture has an average wage of $4.73 dollars per hour after the hypothetical increase in the statutory minimum wage. If the average disemployed lumber and wood products worker now receives this average

Table 5.7. Impacts of a $0.25 increase in the statutory minimum wage

SIC industry	Before increase		After increase		Changes				1983 Average annual income
	Average wage	Employment	Average wage	Employment	Employment		Wage bill		
					(#)	(%)	($1000)	(%)	
24	8.10	545,095	8.21	541,028	-4076	-.7	26.57	.6	$15,520
241	10.45	60,522	10.93	63,548	3026	5.0	62.12	9.8	20,027
242	8.60	168,868	8.71	168,589	-279	.2	16.15	1.1	16,548
243	7.75	166,638	8.11	169,431	2793	1.7	82.64	6.4	15,317
244	5.62	31,926	5.84	30,851	-1075	-3.4	.75	.4	10,651
245	6.95	56,233	7.12	52,782	-3451	-6.1	-15.01	-3.8	13,152
249	7.06	62,623	7.22	60,697	-1926	-3.1	-3.89	-.9	13,181
26	11.48	479,642	11.72	477,334	-2308	-.5	88.06	1.6	20,969
261,2,6	11.67	144,708	12.00	144,365	-343	-.2	43.64	2.6	25,777
262	12.01	127,867	12.32	121,104	-6763	-5.3	-43.68	-2.8	25,958
263	12.04	44,976	12.33	45,135	159	.3	15.00	2.8	26,027
264	8.80	152,136	8.87	151,024	-1112	-.7	.79	.1	17,910
265	8.50	139,032	8.67	137,203	-1829	-1.3	7.78	.1	17,751

agricultural wage, then the change in the minimum wage probably has a negative impact on his or her welfare. Surely this is not the socially desired impact of a regulation designed to improve distributive justice.

We can pursue the distributive point further by comparing wages in the forest products industries with some measure suggestive of the minimum level of social welfare acceptable in our society. The 1983 poverty level of $10,178 for a household of four people serves as such a measure (U.S. Department of Commerce 1985).

An additional column of Table 5.7 shows the average annual income of workers in each forest products industry.[12] Three of the forest products industries (wood containers, SIC 244; wood buildings, SIC 245; and miscellaneous wood products, SIC 249) show average annual incomes within 30 percent of the national poverty level. Marginal employees are paid less than average-wage employees and, perhaps, many marginal employees in these three industries could be well served by society's concerns to increase their minimum wage. These three industries, however, show negative employment effects in response to increases in the minimum wage. Indeed, they show three of the four largest percentage disemployment effects among any industries surveyed. Furthermore, two of these three industries show negative changes in their wage bills. In sum, workers in the most poorly paid industries are least well served by increases in the minimum wage and marginal workers in these industries, the workers whose income is very most likely at or below the national poverty level, are probably worst served yet.[13]

In conclusion, it is difficult to measure the social welfare costs of the minimum wage provision of the Fair Labor Standards Act. The use of supply and demand curves to display the welfare triangles, as in Figure 1.1, demonstrates that there must be net social costs to any such regulation. The important question has to do with whether the distributive gains from the regulation justify these costs. We can demonstrate some of the costs to employers in terms of the increase in their total wage payments. We can also demonstrate that these costs accrue as gains to those workers who remain employed in the covered industries. Finally, we can also provide evidence that strongly suggests that a small number of the lowest paid of those workers formerly employed in the forest products industries also bear heavy burdens. These workers lose some share of their forest products employment as a result of an increase in the minimum wage. They must seek new employment, often in lower paid sectors of the economy that are not covered by the minimum wage. These disemployed, former forest products workers are precisely those individuals whom society seeks to protect through its concerns with distributive justice. They are precisely the employees for whom increases in the statutory minimum wage are most distressing.

Appendix 5A: Structural Equations

The B&G supply and demand functions, in log form, for the covered (forest product industry) markets are

$$N^s_{j,t}/A^s_{i,t} = a^s_0 (N_{j,t-1}/A_{i,t-1}) - a^s_1(w_{j,t}/\Omega_t)$$
$$- a^s_2 E_t(w_{j,t+1}/\Omega_{t+1}) - a^s_3 E_t(w_{j,t+2}/\Omega_{t+2})$$
$$+ a^s_4 I_t + \epsilon^s_t \qquad (5A.1)$$

$$N^d_{j,t}/A^d_{i,t} = a^d_0 (N_{j,t-1}/A_{i,t-1}) + a^d_1(w_{j,t}/\Omega_t)$$
$$+ a^d_2 E_t(w_{j,t+1}/\Omega_{t+1}) + a^d_3 E_t(w_{j,t+2}/\Omega_{t+2})$$
$$+ a^d_4 I_t + \epsilon^d_t \qquad (5A.2)$$

where N_j, A_i, w_j, Ω_t, I_t and ϵ_t are as defined for equations (5.1)–(5.4). The superscripts s and d refer to supply and demand and E is a rational expectations operator. We anticipate that the elasticity coefficients a_0, a_1, a_2, and a_3 are positive and constant. (If coverage changes, then the sign of a^d_1 is ambiguous. Increases in the ratio of the average wage to the minimum wage $[w/\Omega]$ increase demand in the covered markets but, by assumption, decrease the number of covered markets. It is reasonable, however, that the sum of a^d_1 and a^s_1 is positive; that is, the net effect on coverage of increasing $w - \Omega$ is positive.) Furthermore, a^s_0 equals a^d_0 and a^s_4 equals a^d_4. These latter seem to be innocuous, but simplifying, assumptions.

Demand determines employment in the covered sector. Therefore,

$$N_t = N^d_t, \text{ and} \qquad (5A.3)$$
$$X_t = N^s_t/N_t \qquad (5A.4)$$

where X is the log of the ratio of supply to employment. The usual assumption is that X_t has been positive since the establishment of a federal minimum wage. A positive X indicates excess supply in the covered sector where this excess supply includes both nonparticipants in the labor force and those unemployed but actively searching for employment in the covered sector.

Notional supply is the number of workers who, given current and expected future wage rates, would supply labor services if they could obtain employment in their desired sector. Notional supply exceeds effective supply. We specify aggregate notional supply to grow at some exogenous rate (perhaps comparable to growth rates for the labor force or for the population as a whole) subject only to random disturbance. The log of aggregate notional supply is

$$A^s_t = b + c^s t + \zeta_t \qquad (5A.5)$$

where b and c^s are constants and ζ_t is a random variable with zero mean. Employment is demand-determined in the covered sector. Therefore, aggregate effective labor supply is aggregate notional supply less those workers disemployed from the covered sector who refrain from increasing effective supply in the uncovered sector. The log-linear expression for this is

$$A^{s'}{}_t = A^s{}_t - \eta X_t \qquad (5A.6)$$

where $A^{s'}{}_t$ is aggregate effective supply and η is the elasticity of the ratio of aggregate effective to aggregate notional supply with respect to the ratio of supply to employment in the covered sector. The coefficient η ranges from zero to $\exp(N_t/A_t)$. If η is zero, either disemployed covered workers find employment in uncovered sectors or, when they depart from the covered sector labor force, they are replaced by others who enter and find employment in the uncovered sector. If $\eta = \exp(N_t - A_t)$, then excess supply in the covered sector has no effect on effective supply in the uncovered sector. Rather, excess supply in the covered sector remains unemployed but searching for employment in that sector.

The aggregate demand equation in the B&G model specifies an equation in which employment velocity depends on productivity, the expected rate of wage inflation and random disturbances. Aggregate demand, then, is a function of employment velocity, the average wage rate, and the money stock. Specifically, the log-linear expressions are

$$A^d{}_t = M_t - w_t + V_t \qquad (5A.7)$$

with $V_t = c^d t + v(E_t w_{t+1}/w_t) + \phi_t$

where M = the money stock; V = employment velocity; c^d, v = constant coefficients; and ϕ = random variable with zero mean. Therefore, the aggregate market clearing assumption is

$$A_t = A^d{}_t = A^{s'}{}_t \qquad (5A.8)$$

which means that those desiring employment in the uncovered sector can find it.

Finally, the B&G model also specifies minimum wage policy and monetary policy. The minimum wage is always in nominal terms. Furthermore, Boschen and Grossman assert that amendments to it are frequent enough to anticipate. Amendments serve to set the minimum wage level at some target level, which is a function of the average manufacturing wage.

$$\Omega_{t+n} = E_{t+n-1} w_{t+n} + y + \omega_{t+n} \text{ for all } n = 2, 3, 4, \ldots \qquad (5A.9)$$

where y is a constant policy target for the log of the ratio of the minimum to the average wage and ω is a random variable with zero mean. Taking expectations of equation (5A.9) implies that $E_t(\Omega_{t+n}/w_{t+n}) = y$.

Monetary policy requires determinations of the money stock and future changes in that stock. B&G model it as an AR (1,1) process:

$$m_{t+2} = h + km_t + \lambda_{t+1} \qquad\qquad (5A.10)$$

where m_{t+1} is growth in the money supply measured as $M_{t+i} - M_{t+i-1}$, h and k are constants, and λ is a random variable with zero mean. Taking the expectation of equation (5A.10), we find that $E_t m_{t+1} = h + km_t$. Furthermore, $E_t M_{t+1} = M_t + E_t m_{t+1}$.

Equations (5A.1)–(5A.10) describe the B&G model as modified for our analysis of minimum wage effects in forest-based industries. Boschen and Grossman found a solution for w_t and applied this solution to derive aggregate employment and the ratio of covered to total employment, A_t and N_t/A_t, respectively. These derivations of equations (5.1)–(5.4) are lengthy and complex. The interested reader should refer to the original article. That article also carefully summarizes and discusses the reduced form coefficients — the α, β, γ and δ — in terms of the structural parameters. Table 5.8 repeats this summary in its most brief form.

Appendix 5B: Occupational Safety and Health Act

The major law concerned with safety and health in the working place is the federal Occupational Safety and Health Act of 1970 (OSHA). It mandates employers to protect employees from "recognized hazards that are causing or are likely to cause death or serious harm." OSHA provides for enforcement by the Department of Labor and for fines on firms found not in compliance with the act. The objective of this appendix is to examine the economic impacts of OSHA on the forest products industries, but a lack of adequate data restricts the analysis. Alternately, we can first review background data suggesting that injury, illness, and mortality in the forest products industries may justify special response, then organize the conceptual arguments for assessment of welfare impacts, and finally address the question of what data would permit such an assessment if available.

BACKGROUND DATA

Injury, illness, and mortality data can show us the danger associated with holding employment in a given industry. Figure 5.2 shows the inci-

Table 5.8. Reduced form coefficients

Variables		Reduced form	
Dependent	Independent	Definition[a]	Anticipated sign
w_i, w_j	Ω_{it}	$\alpha_1 = \gamma_1 = K_1\eta(n_1^s + n_1^d)$	if $\eta > 0$, then $1 > \alpha_1 > 0$
w_i, w_j	Ω_{t+1}	$\alpha_2 = \gamma_2 = K_1[(1-\eta)v\alpha_1 + \eta(n_2^s + n_2^d)(1-\alpha_1)]$	$\alpha_2 > 0$
w_i, w_j	M_t	$\alpha_3 = \gamma_3 = 1 - \alpha_1 - \alpha_2$	if $\eta > 0$, then $1 > \alpha_3 > 0$
w_i, w_j	m_t	$\alpha_4 = \gamma_4 = k(v\alpha_3 - \alpha_2)(1 + v - kv)^{-1}$	?: $E_t w_{t+1}$ has a positive effect on aggregate labor demand, therefore a positive effect on w_t. $E_t w_{t+1}$ also has a positive effect on demand in the covered market, therefore a negative effect on w_t.
w_i, w_j	I_t	$\alpha_5 = \gamma_5 = (c^d - c^s)\alpha_3$	?: offsetting demand and supply effects
A_i	Ω_t	$\beta_1 = -(1 + K_2)\alpha_1$	if $\eta > 0$, then $\beta_1 < 0$
A_i	Ω_{t+1}	$\beta_2 = -(1 + K_2)\alpha_2 + K_2\alpha_1$	if $\eta > 0$, then β_2?
A_i	M_t	$\beta_3 = \alpha_1 + (1 + K_2)\alpha_2$	if $\eta > 0$, then $\beta_3 > 0$
A_i	m_t	$\beta_4 = (1 + K_2)^2\alpha_2(1 + K_2 - kK_2)^{-1}$	if $\eta > 0$, then $\beta_4 > 0$
A_i	I_t	$\beta_5 = (c^d - c^s)\alpha_3 + c^s$	if $\eta > 0$, then β_5?
$N_j - A_i$	Ω_t	$\delta_1 = a_1^d(\alpha_1 - 1)$	$\delta_1 < 0$
$N_j - A_i$	Ω_{t+1}	$\delta_2 = a_1^d\alpha_2 + a_2^d(\alpha_1 - 1)$	if $\eta > 0$, then δ_2?
$N_j - A_i$	M_t	$\delta_3 = a_1^d\alpha_3 + a_2^d(1 - \alpha_1)$	$\delta_3 > 0$
$N_j - A_i$	m_t	$\delta_4 = a_1^d\alpha_4 + a_2^d k(\alpha_3 + \alpha_4)$	if $\eta > 0$, then δ_4?
$N_j - A_i$	I_t	$\delta_5 = (c^d - c^s)\delta_3 + a_3^d$	$\delta_5 > 0$
$N_j - A_i$	$(N_j/A_i)_{t-1}$	$\delta_6 = a_6^d$	$\delta_6 > 0$

Note: Refer to equations (5.1)–(5.4) and Appendix 5A. The α and γ have the same form.

[a]Where $K_1 = [(1 - \eta)(1 + v) + \eta(a_1^s + a_1^d)]^{-1}$
$K_2 = (\alpha_2 + \alpha_4)[\alpha_3 - (1 - k)\alpha_4]^{-1}$

dence of injury and illness per 10,000 employees by broad industrial category. Table 5.9 shows the additional risk of mortality for men in selected occupations. The forest products industries are part of the manufacturing and the agriculture, forestry, and fisheries industry categories in Figure 5.2. Manufacturing has a high injury and illness rate and agriculture, forestry, and fisheries have an intermediate rate among the nine industrial categories shown. Lumbermen, which means contract foresters, loggers, and sawmill employees, have a risk of mortality exceptionally greater than that risk for the average male in the average industry. Their risk of mortality is second

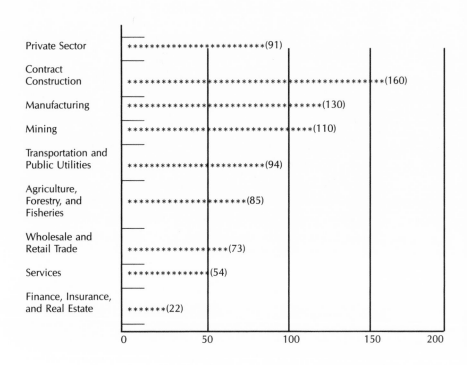

Figure 5.2. Injury and illness incidence rates by industry division, United States, 1975. Source: R. Freeman, *Labor Economics* (Englewood Cliffs, N.J.: Prentice-Hall, 1979), p. 167. Reprinted with permission.

Table 5.9. Additional mortality risk in selected occupations, 1966

Occupation	Additional mortality risk per 100,000 workers
Actors	73
Bartenders	176
Boilermakers	230
Cooks	132
Electricians	93
Elevator operators	188
Firemen	44
Fisherman	19
Guards, watchmen, and doorkeepers	267
Hucksters and peddlers	76
Longshoremen and stevedores	101
Lumbermen	256
Mine operatives	176
Power plant operatives	6
Railroad conductors	203
Sailors and deckhands	163
Taxicab drivers	182
Waiters	134

Note: Actuarial data were used to calculate the expected number of deaths per 100,000 workers in each occupation based on standard life tables and the age distribution of workers in that occupation. Expected deaths per 100,000 were then subtracted from actual deaths to yield the data for additional risk.

Source: R. Thaler and S. Rosen, "The Value of Saving a Life: Evidence from the Labor Market," in *Household Production and Consumption,* ed. N. E. Terleckyj, p. 288. (New York: Columbia University Press for the National Bureau of Economic Research, 1975). Reprinted with permission.

only to the additional risk in security-related occupations. Although these data are exceedingly general, they do encourage inquiry into the merit of either additional safety and health measures or additional compensation for workers in some parts of the forest products industries.

WELFARE IMPACTS OF OSHA

The impacts of OSHA can be described in a manner similar to the general discussion of regulations addressing market failure in Chapter 1. Figure 5.3A compares with Figure 1.1. The function D describes the industry's demand for labor in the absence of OSHA. The function S describes the supply of labor in the absence of OSHA. The equilibrium wage and employment are w and $N,$ respectively. The introduction of OSHA imposes costs on employers who, therefore, reduce their demand for labor by the incremental cost per employee of meeting OSHA standards. The function D' describes the new demand for labor in the presence of OSHA. Employees, once given the protection required by OSHA, no longer require the wage differential previously necessary to induce them to face the abnormal employment-related risk. The new labor supply function intersects D' at point a if—and only if—employees value OSHA-imposed protection equally, at the margin, to the employers' marginal costs of compliance. The new equilibrium wage w' varies from the old wage only by the risk compensation.

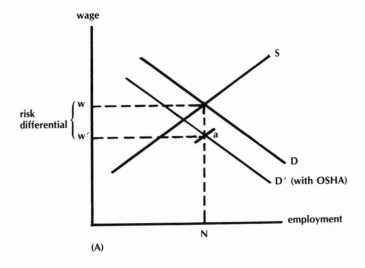

(A)

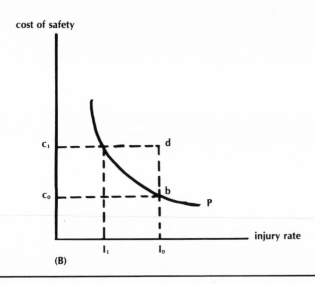

(B)

Figure 5.3. Welfare effects of OSHA.

The final condition, however, would be unusual. OSHA requirements in some cases, no doubt, cost more than the employees' marginal valuation for them. In such cases, employee supply intersects employer demand D' above point a in Figure 5.3A and OSHA has both wage and employment effects. There is associated substitution toward capital in the production process and OSHA causes an inefficiency in the labor market where the degree of inefficiency is a function of the cost of compliance with OSHA.

Figure 5.3B provides an alternate exposition of this problem, which is more common to the labor economics literature (e.g., Fleisher & Kniesner 1984). The cost minimizing firm observes a safety production function P describing the trade-off between injuries and the cost of their reduction. The firm finds its optimal injury rate at, say, I_0 where the cost of safety is c_0. Compliance with OSHA may require expenditures equal to c_1. If point b is cost minimizing, then the additional expenditure $c_1 - c_0$ is inefficient. Even when the expenditure of c_1 reduces injuries to I_1, the extra safety costs outweigh the financial benefits. Furthermore, there is some evidence that injury reduction may not occur. Rather, we may observe point d where compliance costs increase while the injury rate remains unchanged.

EMPIRICAL EVIDENCE

Viscusi's (1979) evidence, from a sample including 84 percent of covered workers shows no noticeable effect of OSHA on industrial injuries from 1972 to 1975. [Indeed, Viscusi (1979, 246; 1981, 289) and Thaler and Rosen (1975, 292) find that the full perceived difference in risk level between employment alternatives is absorbed either by additional worker compensation or by demographic differences in employees (e.g., education, race, age, job tenure).] Furthermore, Smith (1976) demonstrates that, for firms with more than 500 employees, compliance with OSHA costs approximately ten times the expected value of fines for noncompliance. It should not be surprising, therefore, that firms prefer to take their chances with the fine and that OSHA does little to improve occupational safety and health. Nevertheless, OSHA may have another impact that is beneficial. It requires the Department of Labor to assemble and distribute information about worker safety and job hazards. This information may assist unions and laborers in assessing the appropriate risk differential for their wage standards.

Our problem is that satisfactory data are unavailable for an assessment of OSHA for a particular forest products industry—or for any industry— within the framework of either figure. Mitchell (1982) cites the major data problems. First, no good data exist on worker exposure to risk. Second, data collected prior to 1970 are incompatible with post-OSHA data. Therefore, (1) there is limited opportunity to make empirical estimates based on time series data and (2) it is impossible to contrast the with- and without-OSHA scenarios. Third, reporting requirements are better for injuries than for illness. Finally, it is difficult to define or measure the dependent policy variable: Rather than safety costs, costs of compliance, or employee valuation of the safety measure, most studies focus on the probabilities of inspection or citation and use industrywide and plant-level data. They tend to use injury rates as the dependent variable affected by policy. Rosen (1981) argues that the important policy questions have to do with which workers are at risk. Furthermore, it is important to control for the endogeneity of inspections and to include control variables for union and management differences. Lack of data prevents research from focusing on the impact of OSHA on employment and wages.

In summary, OSHA has been an extensive and expensive piece of employment legislation. Its effects, as measured, have been small and there is no empirical evidence of either efficiency or distributive gains associated with it. OSHA may be necessary, but it is certainly not a sufficient condition for moving toward a safer and healthier work environment. OSHA's specific impact on the forest products industries is wholly indeterminate.

 Notes

1. Of course, these numbers reflect the reports of firms which are in compliance with the law. There always remain an unknown number of workers who are paid in cash and, therefore, who escape employer records. These workers avoid the constraint of the legal minimum wage (Altonji & Ashenfelter 1980).

2. The 1939 amendments to FSLA provided exemption from overtime coverage for small logging contractors for up to 56 hours per week for a 14-week period. Justifications for granting the exemption were (1) the difficulties that nonexemption created for log concentration yards, which had been forced to monitor compliance by contractors from whom they purchased; (2) the seasonality, therefore the transitory employment characteristic, of logging; and (3) the unsubstantiated argument that employment records are too difficult for small firms to maintain (MWSC 1981, vol. VI, 133).

A 1949 amendment granted minimum wage and overtime exemptions for logging operations employing twelve or fewer persons. A 1966 amendment reduced this limit to eight or fewer persons. A 1974 amendment repealed the minimum wage exemption but left in place the overtime exemption for logging contractors and small sawmills with eight or fewer employees.

3. We abstract from or hold constant across both sectors the incentive effects of unemployment insurance and other social welfare programs.

4. Wessels (1980, 33) notes that this same analysis applies to *an increase in* (rather than an initial imposition of) the minimum wage, although welfare implications cannot be inferred if D_c in Figure 5.1 is steeper than D_1 (measured at w_{m1}). He also presents evidence to suggest that D_c usually is steeper than D_1.

5. The lumber and wood products industries (SIC 24) are characterized by average wages below the average manufacturing wage for our entire sample period from 1947 to 1983. Average wages for paper and allied products (SIC 26) are marginally lower than those for all manufacturing from 1947 to 1960 and marginally greater than average manufacturing wages for the remainder of the sample period.

6. Boschen and Grossman also test for the effect of changes in the numbers of workers and industries covered by minimum wage legislation. We do not test for coverage as there was no significant change in coverage for workers either in the lumber and wood products or in the paper and allied products industries over our relevant time periods.

7. When Boschen and Grossman test for the effects of changing coverage, they also assume that the number of covered markets is a positive function of both the current ratio of the minimum wage to the average wage and the current ratio of covered to total employment.

8. We anticipate multicollinearity between the minimum wage and the anticipated minimum wage and there is no good way to avoid it. Multicollinearity poses no problem in our case, however, because it does not damage the usefulness of the model for prediction.

The usual correction for multicollinearity uses the change in the independent variable rather than the variable itself. This correction does not apply in our case because changes in the minimum wage occur less than annually, therefore there would be zeros for some annual observations of $\Omega_{t+1} - \Omega_t$. (Observations of zero cannot be entered in a meaningful way in log form.) The statistical effect of the anticipated multicollinearity is unbiased but inefficient estimates. Elasticities calculated from these estimates may be incorrect, but predictions of net effects of all independent variables on the dependent variable are unbiased.

9. The combined impact of the two minimum wage variables on relative employment is positive in only three industries: logging camps and logging contractors (SIC 241); which is relatively less covered by the statutory minimum wage than most other forest products industries; millwork, veneer, plywood, and structural wood members (SIC 243); and paperboard mills (SIC 263).

10. Boschen and Grossman's empirical estimates for other (nonforest) industries show the same unanticipated negative sign. They have no explanation.

11. We also examined the full set of wage and employment relationships in three states with high percentages of employment in the forest industries. We intended to choose one northwestern and one southern state as representatives of the greatest regional strengths of the forest products industries. Oregon is an obvious choice in the Northwest with 7.9 percent of its nonagricultural employment in the forest products industries. Mississippi is a good choice in the South with 3.5 percent of its nonagricultural employment in the forest products industries, but there is a lack of industrial data for the state of Mississippi. North Carolina is an alternate choice with 2.5 percent of its nonagricultural employment in the forest products industries but with more data for specific industries and for longer periods. The higher percentage of forest industries' employment in each of these states suggests that employment shifts between sectors should be more emphatic than in the national sample.

The data series are brief for all three states. Therefore, there are various statistical difficulties with the analyses. Nevertheless, we find that the signs on all independent variables in all equations in all three states conform with the national observations. The coefficients on Ω_t, M_t and I_t are often significant at the 10 percent level. This conformity suggests robustness for our national observations.

12. The average annual income is the sum of the fifty weekly average incomes (USDL Bureau of Labor Statistics 1984a). It is an overstatement to the extent that many forest products industry employees, particularly those in the lumber and wood products industries, do not work that regularly. Our distributive conclusions are conservative to the extent of this overstatement.

13. Our (much less reliable) state data reinforce these conclusions. Furthermore, the minimum wage impact is the most negative for the lowest average wage group in our entire sample (marginal lumber and wood products employees in the state of Mississippi).

 ## References

Altonji, J., and O. Ashenfelter. 1980. Wage movements and the labor market equilibrium. *Economica* 47(187):217–45.

Boschen, J., and H. Grossman. 1981. The federal minimum wage, employment, and inflation. In *The report of the minimum wage study commission,* vol. VI, pp. 19–42. Washington, D.C.: U.S. Government Printing Office.

Eccles, M., and R. Freeman. 1982. What: Another minimum wage study? *American Economic Review* 72(2):226–32.

Federal Reserve Board of Governors. 1984. *Federal Reserve Bulletin.* Washington, D.C.: author.

Fleisher, B. M., and T. J. Kniesner. 1984. *Labor economics: Theory, evidence, and policy.* 3d ed. Englewood Cliffs, N.J.: Prentice-Hall.

Freeman, R. B. 1979. *Labor Economics.* 2d ed. Englewood Cliffs, N.J.: Prentice-Hall.

Gallant, A. R., and J. J. Goebel. 1976. Nonlinear regression with autoregressive errors. *Journal of the American Statistical Association* 71:961–67.

Greber, B. J., and D. E. White. 1982. Technical change and productivity growth in the lumber and wood products industry. *Forest Science* 28(1):135–47.

Mincer, J. 1976. Unemployment effects of minimum wages. *Journal of Political Economy* 84(4):S87–104.

Minimum Wage Study Commission. 1981. *Report of the Minimum Wage Study Commission.* Washington, D.C.: U.S. Government Printing Office.

Mitchell, O. S. 1982. *The labor market impact of federal regulation: OSHA, ERISA, EEO, and minimum wage.* National Bureau of Economic Research Working Paper No. 844. New York: National Bureau of Economic Research.

Peterson, J. M. 1981. *Minimum wages: Measures and industry effects.* Washington, D.C.: American Enterprise Institute.

Rosen, S. 1981. Valuing health risk. *American Economic Review* 71(2):241–45.

Rottenberg, S., ed. 1981. *The economics of legal minimum wages.* Washington, D.C.: American Enterprise Institute.

Smith, R. 1976. *The Occupational Safety and Health Act: Its goals and its achievements.* Washington, D.C.: American Enterprise Institute.

Stevens, J. B. 1980. *Six views about the wood products labor force, most of which are wrong.* Corvallis: Oregon Agricultural Experiment Station Technical Paper.

Stier, J. C. 1980. Estimating the production technology in the U.S. forest products industries. *Forest Science* 26(3):471–82.

Tauchen, G. E. 1981. Some evidence on cross-sector effects of the minimum wage. *Journal of Political Economy* 89(3):529–47.

Thaler, R., and S. Rosen. 1975. The value of saving a life: Evidence from the labor market. In *Household production and consumption,* ed. N. E. Terleckyj. New York: Columbia University Press for the National Bureau of Economic Research.

U.S. Department of Commerce, Bureau of the Census. 1985. *Statistical abstract of the United States, 1985.* 105th ed. Washington, D.C.: U.S. Government Printing Office.

U.S. Department of Commerce, Bureau of Economic Analysis. 1978. *Business statistics 1977. Supplement to survey of current business.* Washington, D.C.: U.S. Government Printing Office.

_____. 1983. *Business statistics 1982. Supplement to survey of current business.* Washington, D.C.: U.S. Government Printing Office.

U.S. Department of Labor, Bureau of Labor Statistics. 1979. *Employment and earnings, United States, 1909-1978.* Bulletin 1312-11. Washington, D.C.: U.S. Government Printing Office.

_____. 1984a. *Employment and earnings, January-August 1984.* Washington, D.C.: U.S. Government Printing Office.

_____. 1984b. *Employment and earnings, August 1984.* Washington, D.C.: U.S. Government Printing Office.

_____. 1984c. *Supplement to employment and earnings, July 1984.* Washington, D.C.: U.S. Government Printing Office.

Viscusi, W. K. 1979. *Employment hazards: An investigation of market performance.* Cambridge, Mass.: Harvard University Press.

_____. 1981. Occupational safety and health regulation: Its impact and policy alternatives. In *Research in Public Policy Analysis and Management,* ed. J.P. Crecine. Greenwich, Conn.: JAI Press Incorporated.

Welch, F. 1978. *Minimum wages: Issues and evidence.* Washington, D.C.: American Enterprise Institute.

Wessels, W. J. 1980. *Minimum wages, fringe benefits and working conditions.* Washington, D.C.: American Enterprise Institute.

CHAPTER 6

The Jones Act

The Jones Act restricts shipments between U.S. ports to U.S. built, owned, and operated vessels. It exists in the name of national security and for the specific purpose of ensuring the continued existence of a viable U.S. merchant fleet. Its impact on forestry is to raise lumber shipment costs over what they would be were shipment permitted on less expensive, non-U.S. ships. This raises the delivered price of lumber to domestic U.S. consumers and causes substitution away from some less expensive sources of lumber. In particular, one argument has it that the Jones Act causes substitution by eastern U.S. consumers away from coastal producers in the U.S. Pacific Northwest and toward coastal producers in neighboring British Columbia. Therefore, according to this argument, the Jones Act abuses both U.S. lumber producers and consumers to the advantage of a select group of Canadian producers (Morgan 1980; also Austin & Darr 1975).

In terms of the discussion in Chapter 1, the Jones Act is a demand-side regulation. By raising the delivered price of lumber it decreases the derived demand for stumpage. Its justification is market failure, that is, the probable failure of the market to compensate the U.S. merchant fleet for its national security role, which presumably provides social value in addition to the value the merchant fleet provides as a peacetime shipper of goods.[1]

The purpose of this chapter is neither to debate the national security arguments nor to estimate the magnitudes of their associated social benefits. Rather, this chapter proposes to assess the welfare impacts of the Jones Act on U.S. and Canadian producers and on U.S. consumers of lumber. This purpose is narrowly consistent with the focus of this volume on the impacts of various public regulations affecting the forest industry. It refrains from judgements about the greater merit of the law, beyond its impact on forestry.

The following two short sections of this chapter provide further background and outline the analytical approach. The body of the chapter follows the problem formulation laid out in the latter short section as it derives the welfare effects of the Jones Act.

Background

The idea of protecting the coastal trade of a nation from foreign shipping originated with protection-minded mercantilists in seventeenth century Europe. It came to the United States in 1789 when the first U.S. Congress, in retaliation against similar European statutes, provided for discriminatory tonnage fees on all foreign ships operating between U.S. ports. In 1808, and again in 1817, Congress altered the law to completely exclude vessels of foreign registry from the U.S. coastal trade. Finally, since 1920, section 27 of the Merchant Marine Act requires that all domestic shipments be in U.S. built, owned, and operated vessels. This 1920 law is commonly referred to as the Jones Act after its author, Senator Wesley Jones.

The simplest domestic industry protection arguments for this particular market intervention are no longer used. Rather, a national security argument is more prominent. This latter argument is founded on the importance of merchant vessels and the unreliability of foreign fleets in time of war. Counterarguments that U.S. allies are among the world's foremost maritime nations and that the United States, at the outbreak of war, would surely seize those enemy merchant vessels docked in U.S. harbors have made little impression on lawmakers and have caused no revision of the 1920 law itself (Jantscher 1975).

The Jones Act has probably had an impact on the lumber industry since its origin in 1920, but this impact has been noticed most since 1950. More specifically, the Northeast became an important market for lumber from the coastal Pacific Northwest after the opening of the Panama Canal, and until the early 1950s this intercoastal trade was fairly prosperous. This trade declined dramatically, however, during the past thirty years. That is, overall West to East Coast lumber trade remains relatively stable at 1.6 billion board feet annually, but an ever-increasing share of this trade originates not from Oregon and Washington but from British Columbia.

The slow decline in U.S. import duties on Canadian lumber and arguably favorable Canadian stumpage pricing policies may be factors in the shift to British Columbian sources.[2] Nevertheless, the Jones Act generally is seen as the major factor behind this shift because the decline in U.S. waterborne lumber shipments has occurred while U.S. shipbuilding and operating costs have climbed high above competitive world prices (Gorter 1956, 12). Northwestern U.S. producers of lumber fall under the terms of the Jones Act whereas such restrictions do not apply to British Columbian producers. Therefore, with less expensive foreign merchant vessels at their disposal, Canadian producers enjoy a critical advantage in the intercoastal lumber trade. U.S. lumber producers periodically have requested relief from this burden, but the maritime industry has resisted successfully.[3]

Thus, we observe a regulation originally intended to protect one U.S. industry, merchant shipping, from foreign competition but which may have been more effective in allowing foreign competitors in another industry, lumber, to secure an advantage over their U.S. counterparts. No one has fully assessed the magnitude of the impacts of this law. Beginning with the following section, that is our objective.

Approach

Our analytical approach relies on Samuelson's (1952) extension of a Koopmans (1949; 1951) and Dantzig (1951) model explaining trade between two regions. This varies from the general market failure discussion in Chapter 1 (Figure 1.1) only in that the Jones Act affects not one, but multiple, regional markets. Figure 6.1 introduces the Samuelson approach. It displays markets for lumber in two different regions. The figure places the markets back to back such that the quantity of lumber increases in both directions from the origin. In the absence of trade, demand D_i and supply S_i equilibrate at price p_1 or where the excess supply functions ES_i intersect the vertical axis. If there were no transportation costs and trade were permitted, then the joint market would equilibrate at p_3 with the low cost producer, region 1, exporting a volume equal to q_3 to the high cost producer, region 2.

Of course, there are transportation costs of, say, c per Mbf of lumber shipped. Trade occurs only if the original price differential exceeds the transportation cost ($p_2 - p_1 > c$). Indeed, the trade flow continues from region 1 to region 2 until the price differential at equilibrium just equals the transportation cost. The equilibrium prices with trade are p_1' and p_2' for regions 1 and 2, respectively. Region 1 ships the volume q^* to region 2. The gains from trade for each region equal the area between the region's excess supply function and its market clearing price with trade.

The function U, representing the vertical distance between the excess supply functions, provides an alternate picture of the same interregional equilibrium. The net combined gains from trade between the two regions equal the area cde under this function yet above the transportation cost constraint. Clearly, increases in transportation cost (such as those created by the Jones Act) reduce this area. Therefore, the aggregate impact of the Jones Act on producers and consumers is the difference in this area of net social gain due to trade measured first with and then without the Jones

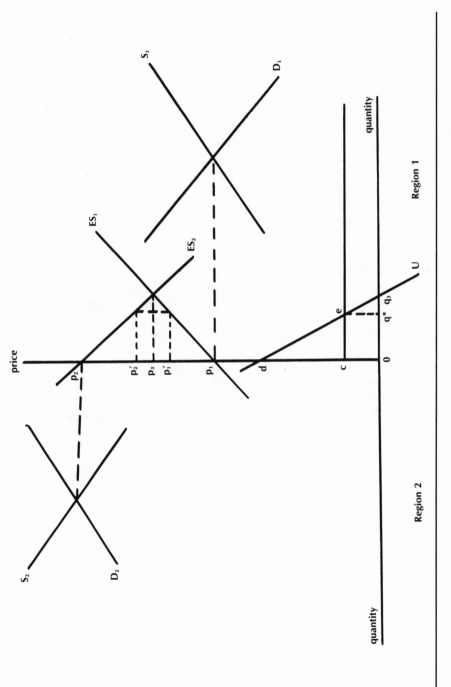

Figure 6.1. Trade between two regions.

Act–imposed transportation cost differential. Our empirical analysis follows this two-region graphical model extended to include numerous spatially distinct regions.

Subsequent sections of this chapter develop an empirical model using regional demand, supply, and transport cost data to generate the prices and interregional flows of lumber consistent with the spatial equilibrium described in Figure 6.1. There is a problem, however, in that lumber is not a homogeneous product. The lumber species shipped from the Pacific Northwest substitutes imperfectly for other species, with the relative prices of the species, therefore the impact of the Jones Act, affecting the degree of substitution between species. In order to understand the impact of substitution between species upon lumber demand, we develop a production function for construction, the final use of most lumber and the dominant use of Douglas fir, the species whose trade is most affected by the Jones Act. This production function permits imperfect substitution among variable lumber species and the demand for lumber of each species derives from it. The lumber supply functions originate from Adams and Haynes (1980).[4] The transportation cost estimates require independent derivation based on information obtained from shippers of lumber and from the Interstate Commerce Commission.

A quadratic programming package organizes the demand, supply, and transportation cost data and solves for the interregional prices and lumber flows that maximize social gain in 1977, the last year for which we have a full complement of necessary data. The programming package follows a procedure outlined by Tramel and Seale (1965, 67) for multiple products in multiple markets. Results consistent with actual (1977) prices and quantities verify the basic analysis and permit further examination with the different transportation costs, which would occur for 1977 if the Jones Act were repealed.

The final section of this chapter reports the regional price, quantity, lumber flow, and welfare differences observed for the two cases. That is, our conclusions are in the form of a comparative static snapshot indicating Jones Act impacts for the year 1977 only. The final section of this chapter takes the analysis a step further, however, and raises the question of Jones Act impacts under the reasonable conditions of more variable British Columbia or long-term U.S. supplies and an increasing impact for (exogenous) Japanese lumber demand.

Model Structure and Specification

Evaluation of regional as well as aggregate effects of Jones Act–imposed restrictions on trade requires division of the United States and Western Canada into the thirty-nine lumber demand and twenty-seven lumber supply regions identified in Figures 6.2 and 6.3, respectively. The regions are geographically distinct markets for which regional data are available or can be derived. The Jones Act affects U.S. producers and consumers, but U.S. consumers purchase from both U.S. and Canadian producers. Therefore, the Jones Act indirectly affects Canadian producers and our model must include U.S. demand regions and both U.S. and Canadian supply regions. The level of regional disaggregation both permits a fairly precise specification of export costs and enables interregional analysis of Jones Act impacts. The central cities identified in Figures 6.2 and 6.3 are the locations of major shipments to and from each demand and supply region; therefore, they provide the loci for transportation cost calculations.

DEMAND

Estimates for softwood lumber demand on a regional level must be derived from final product demand. The final use for 70–75 percent of Douglas fir, the primary West Coast species affected by the Jones Act, is construction, 78 percent of which is housing construction. Cycles in housing demand are the primary determinant of fluctuations in the demand for construction grade lumber. Therefore, knowledge of housing production is a reasonable source for derivation of the demand for Douglas fir and its substitutes.

The demand for housing is insensitive to the price of softwood lumber because lumber costs are a small component of total construction costs. That is, housing demand is exclusively a function of such factors as interest rates, credit conditions, and other nonlumber price factors. Therefore, the problem confronting each firm in the construction industry is to choose the least-cost combination of inputs, one of which is softwood lumber, to meet a level of housing demand specified by interest rates and credit factors. That is, firms take output as exogenously determined and maximize a function

$$Q = AK^{\alpha_K}Z^{1-\alpha_K} \qquad (6.1)$$

where Z is a composite input defined as

$$Z = [F^{(\sigma-1)/\sigma}\alpha_F + P^{(\sigma-1)/\sigma}\alpha_p]^{\sigma/(\sigma-1)} \qquad (6.2)$$

Equation (6.1) is a Cobb-Douglas production function that relates housing units Q to inputs of softwood lumber Z and capital K where capital, in this case, means all construction inputs other than softwood lumber and includes plywood and other wood fiber–based substitutes for softwood lumber. Equation (6.2) is a CES production function permitting substitu-

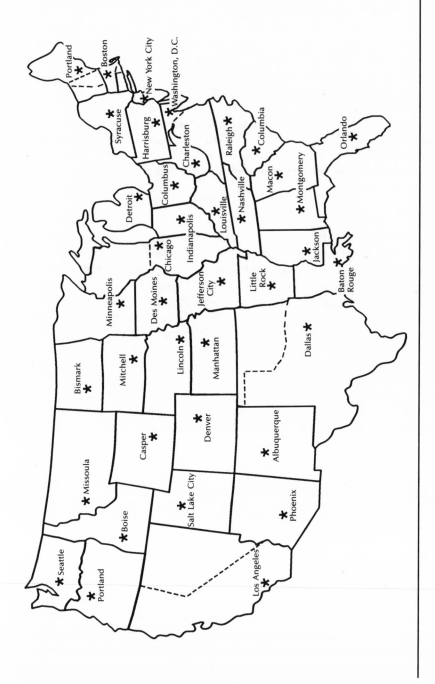

Figure 6.2. Demand regions and central points.

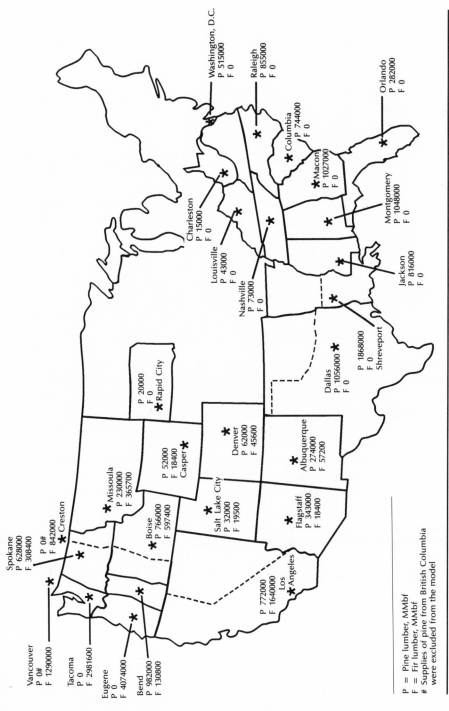

Figure 6.3. Regional supply allocation by species.

Vancouver
P 0#
F 1290000

Tacoma
P 0
F 2981600

Eugene
P 0
F 4074000

Bend
P 982000
F 130800

Spokane
P 628000
F 308400

Creston
P 0#
F 842000

Missoula
P 230000
F 365700

Boise
P 766000
F 597400

Salt Lake City
P 32000
F 19500

Flagstaff
P 343000
F 18400

Los Angeles
P 772000
F 1640000

Rapid City
P 20000
F 0

Casper
P 52000
F 18400

Denver
P 62000
F 45600

Albuquerque
P 274000
F 57200

Dallas
P 1056000
F 0

Shreveport
P 1868000
F 0

Charleston
P 15000
F 0

Louisville
P 43000
F 0

Nashville
P 73000
F 0

Jackson
P 816000
F 0

Washington, D.C.
P 515000
F 0

Raleigh
P 855000
F 0

Columbia
P 74000
F 0

Macon
P 1027000
F 0

Montgomery
P 1048000
F 0

Orlando
P 282000
F 0

P = Pine lumber, MMbf
F = Fir lumber, MMbf
# Supplies of pine from British Columbia
were excluded from the model

169

tion between Douglas fir F and pine P. This substitution is important because both pine and fir are used extensively in construction. Jones Act restrictions, however, directly affect only Douglas fir produced in the Pacific Northwest and not the pine species produced in the South and Southwest. Substitution between the two species groups is probably high but not perfect. The α_1 are factor shares, A is a Hicks neutral technology parameter, and σ explains the partial elasticity of substitution between fir and pine.

Equations (6.1) and (6.2) together with knowledge of a set of factor prices, w_F, w_P, and w_K for fir, pine, and capital, respectively, permit us to derive the demand equations for the two species of lumber. We can linearize these by means of a Taylor Series expansion. (Linearity is necessary because existing solution algorithms accommodate demand and supply functions only in fixed, linear, or log linear forms.) The results are demand equations for fir and pine lumber per housing start, each with arguments in own and cross prices.

The remaining steps in the demand specification are to specify these two functions and then to transform them into thirty-nine regional functions for each, fir and pine. Robinson's (1974) econometric model of the softwood lumber industry provides estimates for the own price coefficients, $\delta F/\delta w_F = \delta P/\delta w_P = -0.87$ per housing start. The cross-price coefficients, $\delta F/\delta w_P$ and $\delta p/\delta w_F$, are more problematic. They can be found with reference to equations (6.1) and (6.2) and a range of conjectures about the elasticity of substitution between fir and pine σ_{FP}. Substituting Robinson's own price coefficients, together with measures of the technology ($A = 0.25$) and factor share ($\alpha_K = 0.88$, $\sigma_F = \sigma_P$) parameters from Veltkamp (1981) and Mead (1966), into equations (6.1) and (6.2) yields a substitution elasticity of 2.73.[5] This elasticity estimate, in turn, provides an initial value for the cross-price coefficients, $\delta F/\delta w_P = \delta P/\delta w_F = 0.14$.

(Changes in the lumber market since the early 1970s may affect the validity of Robinson's estimates. Tests for extreme values of σ_{FP} equal to 1.8 and 10 reflect the impact of this possibility. We can also consider sensitivity to the ranges of factor shares $0.80 < \alpha_K < 0.95$ and $0.75\alpha_F < \alpha_P < 1.33\alpha_F$, although it will become apparent that the range of substitution elasticities dominates the ranges of factor shares with respect to impacts on cross-price coefficients.)

We now have estimates of all price effects per housing start. The final step in obtaining regional demand functions is to multiply these price effects by the number of housing starts in each demand region in order to obtain regional demand functions of the form

$$F_j = -\gamma_j w_{Fj} + \zeta_j w_{Pj} + \delta_{Fj} \tag{6.3a}$$
$$P_j = -\eta_j w_{Pj} + \zeta_j w_{Fj} + \delta_{Pj} \tag{6.3b}$$

for each of j = 1, . . . , 39 demand regions. The γ_j and η_j are own-price coefficients for fir and pine, respectively. The ζ_j are cross-price coefficients and the δ_j are residuals or constant terms. The Department of Commerce collects housing start data but in a form not fully satisfactory for our purposes. Appendix 6A describes our adaptation of the housing start data and reports observations on 1977 housing starts for each of the thirty-nine demand regions.

Finally, the eventual empirical tests require that equations (6.3a) and (6.3b) be rewritten as inverse demands. The inverse forms are

$$w_{Fj} = -\theta_j F_j - \nu_j P_j + \gamma_{Fj} \qquad \textbf{(6.4a)}$$
$$w_{Fj} = -\mu_j P_j - \nu_j F_j + \gamma_{Pj} \qquad \textbf{(6.4b)}$$

where the θ_j, ν_j, and μ_j are regional quantity coefficients and the γ_j are constants.

SUPPLY

The specification of regional lumber supply is somewhat easier. The regional pattern of lumber supply is highly associated with the inventory of standing timber because logs are bulky and hauling them is relatively expensive per unit of output value. Therefore, the production of construction grade softwood lumber takes place principally in the large timber growing regions of southern and western United States as well as in British Columbia. The principal species of the U.S. Northwest and British Columbia are Douglas fir and western hemlock. The principal species of the Rocky Mountains are Douglas fir and ponderosa pine. The principal species of the South and Southeast are longleaf, shortleaf, slash, and loblolly pines, four species generally grouped under the name southern yellow pine.

White pine from the Northeast and the Great Lakes states is ill-suited for general construction purposes. Redwood from the West, jack pine from the Great Lakes states, and the spruces and lodgepole pine from the U.S. West and from British Columbia are also ill-suited for general construction. We can exclude them all from our analysis for this reason.

The species groups fir-hemlock and ponderosa–southern yellow pine create independent supplies because, while good substitutes, they are not a homogeneous product. Using separate production data for the regions that supply both species groups yields, of the twenty-seven total supply regions in the empirical model, fourteen that supply fir and twenty-three that supply pine. Figure 6.3 identifies these regions, their central cities, and the level of 1977 shipments from them. As with demand, various conjectures regarding regional supply elasticities are possible. Initially the analysis holds all regional supplies F_K and P_K fixed at the 1977 levels $\overline{F}_K$ and $\overline{P}_K$ shown in Figure 6.3 (U.S. Department of Commerce 1978). Subsequently, it allows West Coast supplies to vary according to Adams and Haynes' (1980) regional estimates. In this latter case,

$$w_{FK} = \psi_K F_K = \omega_K \qquad (6.5)$$

for the West Coast fir regions, while F_K and P_K are constant everywhere else.

TRANSPORTATION COSTS

Three classes of carriers transport lumber within and between the United States and Canada: water, rail, and truck. Choice among the three depends on a number of factors and varies across regions. Truck and rail rates are important, although by no means exclusive, factors. Generally, truck rates are unregulated while rail rates are a hodgepodge of partial regulation and regional deregulation. In contrast with truck rates, rail rates tend to decline with distance, making rail shipment more competitive on longer hauls. Waterborne shipments impose very low variable costs per unit distance. Therefore, where there is access to ports, waterborne shipments become relatively more competitive as shipping distances increase.

Nonrate factors also affect relative transportation economies. Trucks generally are fastest on short hauls, but they are less flexible than rail in terms of routing because truckers prefer to haul to those demand centers from where backhauling is more likely. Furthermore, truckers may charge substantially lower rates on backhauls rather than return empty. Finally, road capacity limitations applied to truck loads sometimes skew the comparison in favor of rail shipment.

One geographic impact of these observations is for southeastern lumber shipments, most of which are short hauls of less than 300 miles, to go by truck. Pacific northwestern and Rocky Mountain lumber shipments, on the other hand, tend to cover greater distances and rail is more economical. The same logic accounts for extensive rail shipment by British Columbian producers. As the latter are uninhibited by Jones Act restrictions, they also find intercoastal water shipment attractive.

Our empirical approximations of transportation costs rely on truck, rail, and waterborne rates published by the Interstate Commerce Commission. In all cases it is necessary first to convert the rates into a cost of hauling a prescribed load-unit (Mbf) of softwood lumber between each pair of demand and supply regions. The trucking rate is straightforward (ICC, 1977). The waterborne rate is the cost of shipment from port to port plus the additional trucking cost for deliveries from the destination port to an inland demand center.[6]

Rail rates are not available between all demand and supply shipment centers. Indeed, the ICC seldom publishes rail rates and then only publishes a modicum of observations. The ICC (1978) provides a means for estimating rail rates, however. It provides thirty-five observations of rates per pound for shipment in 1974 between points fairly evenly spread between 171 and 4061 miles. Converting pounds to Mbf and 1974 rates to 1977 rates and regressing the resulting thirty-five converted cost observations on various functions of distance creates a rule for rail rates. The ICC rate-making rule is essentially unknown; therefore, there is no reason not to choose the best-fitting regression.[7]

We now have truck, rail, and waterborne shipment rates between all demand and supply regions. The operational assumption in the empirical tests that follow is that producers always choose the least of these three.

Solution Algorithm

Competitive producers from each supply region confront the previously identified regional demands and transportation costs. Their problem is to allocate their shipments so as to maximize profits. Or, more formally, fir (pine) producers in the ith supply region choose to ship to those demand regions with greatest fir (pine) prices net of export costs, $w_{Fj} - t^F_{ij}$ (or for pine, $w_{Pj} - t^P_{ij}$). Samuelson (1951) formulates the problem in a mathematical programming framework in order to yield a spatial equilibrium solution. Takayama and Judge (1964a, 1964b, 1971) classify and extend Samuelson's analysis.

The original Samuelson analysis considers only a single product as it maximizes total producer and consumer surplus net of transportation costs. It requires all incoming shipments to be nonnegative, all regional supplies to be at least as great as the same region's outbound shipments, and regional demands to be greater than or equal to the same region's incoming shipments. These requirements are consistent with real world observations. The Samuelson analysis further requires construction of a univariate integral for each geographical region and, within the region, calculates the area between demand and supply functions. In its second step, it sums across the integrals for both regions and subtracts total transport costs, thereby deriving a measure for the net social welfare from trade between the regions. Takayama and Judge (1971, 108) show that this welfare measure, under normal conditions, is strictly concave. Therefore, it represents a welfare maximum.

Takayama and Judge also expand the problem to more than a single product by means of a similar method that requires a multivariate line integral. The derivation of the welfare measure in this case is identical with the univariate case except that it requires that the cross-price effects be equal for each region. (This is not constraining on our analysis.)

Our analysis follows Takayama and Judge, but in two steps, corresponding to our two supply assumptions. Initially, it assumes that all supplies are fixed at their 1977 levels. Equations (6.4a) and (6.4b) are the regional demands. The Takayama-Judge welfare index W_j for the jth demand region is

$$W_j = \lambda_{Fj} + \lambda_{Pj}P_j - 1/2(F_j^2 + 2\nu_j F_j P_j + \mu_j P_j^2)$$
$$- \sum_{k=1}^{27}(c_{kj}^F x_{kj}^F + c_{kj}^P x_{kj}^P) \tag{6.6}$$

where x_{kj}^F and x_{kj}^P are the volumes of fir and pine transported between regions j and k. Summing across all demand regions yields a maximization problem in quadratic programming

$$W = \sum_{j=1}^{39} w_J = \sum_{j=1}^{39} \lambda_{Fj} F_j + \lambda_{Pj} P_j - 1/2(\theta_j F_j^2 + 2\nu_j F_j P_j + \mu_j P_j^w)$$
$$- \sum_{j=1}^{39}\sum_{j=1}^{27}(c_{kj}^F x_{kj}^F + c_{kj}^P x_{kj}^P) \tag{6.7}$$

subject to

$$x_{kj}^F > 0 \qquad x_{kj}^P > 0 \text{ for all } k \text{ and } j \tag{6.8}$$
$$F_k > \sum_{j=1}^{39} x_{kj}^F \qquad P_k > \sum_{j=1}^{39} x_{kj}^P \text{ for all } k \tag{6.8b}$$

$$F_j > \sum_{k=1}^{27} x_{kj}^F \qquad P_j > \sum_{k=1}^{27} x_{kj}^P \text{ for all } k \tag{6.8c}$$

Subsequently, we introduce variable regional supplies. Combining equation (6.7) with a set of demand and transport cost parameters permits determination of the maximum net welfare associated with any regional supply allocation. In particular, our interest is in expanding equation (6.7) to incorporate equation (6.5), the Adams-Haynes variable West Coast supply estimates for Douglas fir.

$$W = \sum_{j=1}^{39} \lambda_{Fj} F_j + \lambda_{Pj} P_j - 1/2(\theta_j F_j^2 + 2\nu_j F_j P_j + \mu_j P_j^2)$$
$$- \sum_{k=1}^{27}(w_k F_k + 1/2\psi_k F_k^2) - \sum_{j=1}^{39}\sum_{k=1}^{27}(c_{kj}^F x_{kj}^F + c_{kj}^P x_{kj}^F) \tag{6.9}$$

Solving the general problem is straightforward within the context of this quadratic programming model. Equations (6.7) or (6.9), together with Tramel and Seale's (1959; 1965) reactive programming algorithm, obtain a spatial equilibrium consistent with 1977 interregional export costs. Indeed, interregional prices and quantities consistent with actual 1977 observations of prices and quantities verify our model. Finding prices and quantities in absence of the Jones Act requires reapplication of equations (6.7) and (6.9) and the algorithm and then a search for the spatial equilibrium consistent with the new transportation costs prevailing after decreasing West Coast U.S. lumber shipment rates to the East Coast from the level of 1977 rail rates to the level of international waterborne rates. The welfare costs of the Jones Act are the differences between the two sets of outputs from the programming model.

 Results

The results of our analysis and the output of the model appear in terms of changes in shipment volumes and geographic patterns and in terms of welfare gains. First, however, we wish to assure ourselves that the model accurately reflects economic reality. Contrasting the model's 1977 projections of regional softwood lumber flows with the most comparable data on similar regional flows, 1974 data reported by the ICC (1978), provides a check on this. (There will be some discrepancy simply because the two years in question are not identical.)

The species of softwood lumber reported in the ICC data are virtually the same as those examined in our analysis. Both the ICC and our analysis confine shipments from the Southeast to southern yellow pine and both exclude redwood and the true firs from their western shipment totals. The ICC groups shipments by only nine regions instead of our twenty-seven. Table 6.1 shows these regions and their 1974 shipment totals for the sum of both Douglas fir and pine. Comparison of our predictions with the ICC data requires reassembly of our predictions for the many smaller regions to coincide with the nine larger ICC regions. Table 6.1 also shows these larger regional shipment totals, as our analysis predicts, for each assumption regarding the substitution elasticity between fir and pine. The final row of the table shows the correlation coefficients between actual 1974 shipments reported by the ICC and our 1977 predictions for each elasticity.

The correlation coefficients are high and their significance increases with higher values for the elasticity of substitution. They provide strong support for the predictive power of the model, support that is relatively

Table 6.1. Predictions and ICC data (MMbf) ($\alpha_K = 0.88$, $\alpha_F = \alpha_P$)

Regions	ICC	$\sigma_{FP} = 1.8$	$\sigma_{FP} = 2.7$	$\sigma_{FP} = 10$
B.C. and West to South	3538	3610	3364	2678
B.C. and West to Northeast	2338	2120	2037	2040
B.C. and West to Western North Central	1883	1319	1305	1468
B.C. and West to Eastern North Central	2313	1975	1788	1846
B.C. and West to Upper North Central	4597	3196	3151	3192
West to West	7396	7359	7741	8209
South to Western North Central	648	1149	1107	871
South to Eastern North Central	1165	2029	1844	1608
South to South	3005	4247	4232	4997
Correlation with ICC data		.9507	.9523	.9560

invariant even with large changes in the elasticity of substitution. This support is all the stronger if we acknowledge that some differences between the ICC data and our predictions are due to changes in the regional composition of the softwood lumber market between 1974 and 1977. First, the relative share of northeastern housing starts declined by 20 percent from 1974 to 1977. This accounts for a substantial decline in shipments from British Columbia and the U.S. West to the Northeast and helps to account for the differences between the ICC data and predictions for those regional flows. Second, the shares of housing starts in both the West and the South increased over the same period and they help explain our predicted increase in West to West and South to South shipments. Finally, post–World War II rotations of southern yellow pine were coming of harvest age by 1977. Increasing pine harvests enabled greater substitution of pine for fir and account for a greater predicted southern yellow pine share of the North Central market.

Table 6.1 confirms the model's ability to predict 1977 interregional softwood lumber flows. Nevertheless, we might continue this examination of the model's reliability with tests for the sensitivity of its results to changes in relative factor shares. Table 6.2 contrasts the ICC data with predicted 1977 shipments when $\sigma_{FP} = 2.7$ and for extreme values of the relative factor shares. The correlations are not as great as in Table 6.1, but they are not much smaller. Changing factor shares certainly does not alter either the nature of the results or our confidence in the model's ability to predict.

REMOVAL OF THE JONES ACT

The final step in the analysis is the simulation of Jones Act deregulatory impacts on the United States' softwood lumber markets. Let us initially consider the simulated impacts on volume of lumber shipments and then the implied decreases in aggregate U.S. and Canadian transport costs and social welfare.

Table 6.2. Predictions and ICC data (MMbf)—with variable factor shares ($\sigma_{FP} = 2.7$)

		Capital share		Fir-pine share	
Regions	ICC	$\alpha_K = 0.80$ $\alpha_F = \alpha_P$	$\alpha_K = 0.95$ $\alpha_F = \alpha_P$	$\alpha_K = 0.88$ $\alpha_F = 0.75\alpha_P$	$\alpha_K = 0.88$ $\alpha_P = 0.75\alpha_F$
B.C. and West to South	3538	3112	3679	3318	3422
B.C. and West to Northeast	2338	1963	2269	2024	2027
B.C. and West to Western North Central	1883	1316	1324	1280	1312
B.C. and West to Eastern North Central	2313	1807	2072	1824	1962
B.C. and West to Upper North Central	4597	3136	3220	3033	3164
West to West	7396	8192	7116	7810	7677
South to Western North Central	648	1041	1185	1123	1096
South to Eastern North Central	1165	1748	1673	1552	1525
South to South	3005	4627	4254	4400	4462
Correlation with ICC data		.9120	.9302	.9191	.9248

We shall find that the magnitudes of aggregate impacts of Jones Act deregulation are wholly consistent with Figure 6.1. That is, aggregate transportation costs decrease (*c* falls in Figure 6.1). Aggregate shipments show a small increase (from *q**), and aggregate welfare (*cde*) shows a corresponding small increase. The small volume and aggregate social welfare impacts can be important, however, from the perspectives of particular regions. The declines in both British Columbian shipments and welfare and the gains to U.S. coastal northwestern producers and northeastern consumers will be most notable.

LUMBER FLOWS. The level of total shipments between all thirty-nine demand and twenty-seven supply regions is in the neighborhood of 24.9 MMbf and only increases approximately 0.25 percent as a result of removing the Jones Act restriction. Regional impacts are more interesting, however, and perhaps the most interesting is the change in the source of lumber shipments to the U.S. Northeast.

Table 6.3 shows our prediction for this regional change. The table combines the coastal Douglas fir–growing regions of western Washington and western Oregon and compares their shipments to the U.S. Northeast with those of their primary competitor, tidewater British Columbia. The table shows simulated lumber flows both with and without the Jones Act restriction and for a range of supply and substitution elasticities. Coastal Washington and Oregon producers respond to the relaxation of the Jones Act restriction by expanding their shipments to the Northeast by more than 900 MMbf. Coastal British Columbian producers reduce their shipments between 730 ($\sigma_{FP} = 10$, variable supplies) and 915 MMbf ($\sigma_{FP} = 1.8$, variable supplies). The latter are particularly responsive to the supply price and substitution elasticities. Clearly, the effect on regional lumber flows of relaxing the Jones Act restriction is substantial—regardless of the supply and substitution elasticities. U.S. producers obtain large gains in the northeastern market at the expense of their Canadian counterparts.[8]

Increases in the substitution elasticity of fir for pine yield a smaller increase in total softwood lumber shipments to the various regional sources for the Northeast. Intercoastal shipments from Washington and Oregon decline as species substitution increases because an increase in substitution implies a demand increase for the relatively less expensive species. Fir becomes relatively less expensive in the Northeast after relaxation of the Jones Act restriction; therefore, total northeastern demand increases when there is a high degree of substitutability between species. Southern markets divert less coastal British Columbian fir, however, because pine remains relatively less expensive in the South. We conclude that when species substitution is low and supply varies with price, intercoastal shipments from Washington and Oregon (about 669 MMbf with the Jones Act) increase by

Table 6.3. Shipments to the Northeast (Mbf)

	From western Washington/Oregon	From western British Columbia
$\sigma_{FP} = 10$		
With Jones Act	604,908	1,290,000
Without Jones Act (fixed supplies)	1,520,582	610,919
Without Jones Act (variable supplies)	1,539,331	560,743
$\sigma_{FP} = 2.7$		
With Jones Act	610,452	1,290,000
Without Jones Act (fixed supplies)	1,552,823	469,073
Without Jones Act (variable supplies)	1,571,778	448,762
$\sigma_{FP} = 1.8$		
With Jones Act	668,817	1,290,000
Without Jones Act (fixed supplies)	1,636,435	395,911
Without Jones Act (variable supplies)	1,655,376	375,661

Note: The Northeast includes D.C., Delaware, Maryland, Virginia, Pennsylvania, New York, New Jersey, Massachusetts, Rhode Island, Connecticut, Vermont, New Hampshire, and Maine.

986 MMbf (to 1655 MMbf) while shipments from coastal British Columbia (about 1290 MMbf with the Jones Act) decrease by 914 MMbf (to 376 MMbf). On the other hand, as species substitution increases and supplies are held constant, then intercoastal shipments from Washington and Oregon increase by 916 MMbf (to 1521 MMbf, an increase of 70 MMbf less than with lower substitution and variable supply), whereas shipments from coastal British Columbia decline by only 679 MMbf (to 611 MMbf, 235 MMbf more than before).

The opportunity for substitution between fir and pine also means that relaxing the Jones Act restriction has secondary impacts on pine shipments from the South. The increase in fir shipments to the Northeast tends to depress the pine market there. In response, southern producers divert some shipments from the Northeast to the now more profitable markets in the Midwest and the South. The magnitude of this diversion varies considerably with market assumptions, but only becomes significant when fir-pine substitution is great. With easy substitution, southern pine shipments to the Northeast decline by 72 MMbf (to 886 MMbf) while southern shipments to the Midwest and the South increase by 58 and 14 MMbf, respectively (to 948 and 5011 MMbf).[9]

The mode of transportation is also important from a policy perspective. Currently, all lumber shipments from coastal British Columbia are waterborne. Rail shipments between British Columbia and the United States do exist, but they originate from interior eastern British Columbia. On the other hand, all current transcontinental shipments from coastal Washington and Oregon are hauled overland in boxcars. This situation would change sharply were the Jones Act to be repealed. All shipments from the U.S. Northwest to the Northeast would be waterborne. Shipments from coastal British Columbia to the Northeast would continue to be waterborne but a large percentage of coastal British Columbian shipments would divert to other regions for which rail is the more economical means of transportation.

TRANSPORTATION COSTS AND SOCIAL WELFARE. Welfare gains are composed of gains in consumers' and producers' surpluses, plus the gains from releasing shipping resources to provide higher valued services. The discussion of Figure 6.1 anticipated that shipping cost savings would dominate and that these savings would wholly accrue to U.S. producers and consumers.

Table 6.4 displays our projections for shipping cost savings plus gains in consumers' and producers' surpluses. These projections are consistent with expectations. Aggregate savings in transportation costs range from roughly $4.5 to $5.9 million annually, depending on the elasticities of supply and substitution. Where supplies vary with price, producers respond more efficiently to transportation cost changes. Therefore, cost savings increase with the supply elasticity. The substitution elasticity between fir and pine induces two counteracting effects. As fir and pine substitute more easily, producers adjust more efficiently to transportation cost increases and cost savings occur. As the substitution elasticity decreases, however, northeastern demand for all softwood lumber increases. Therefore, when waterborne shipment rates decrease, then more shipments are affected at low substitution elasticities and total shipping cost savings rise. Thus, Table 6.4 shows that transportation cost savings are greater when $\sigma_{FP} = 1.8$ or 10 and when one or the other of these effects dominates. When $\sigma_{FP} = 2.7$, then neither effect is great and transportation cost savings are lower.

The multicommodity extension of the levels of consumers' and producers' surpluses from equations (6.7) and (6.9) permits derivation of the

Table 6.4. Cost savings and welfare gains due to deregulation

	Cost savings	Surplus	Total welfare gains
$\sigma_{FP} = 1.8$			
With fixed supply	$5,473,374	$ 967,619	$6,440,993
With variable supply	5,916,050	1,163,669	7,079,719
$\sigma_{FP} = 2.7$			
With fixed supply	4,536,600	1,043,859	5,580,359
With variable supply	4,995,960	872,909	5,868,869
$\sigma_{FP} = 10$			
With fixed supply	4,845,780	1,045,971	5,891,751
With variable supply	5,314,610	595,343	5,909,953

surpluses associated with any well-behaved set of regional supplies, demands, and product allocations. The second column of Table 6.4 displays the results of this derivation both with and without the Jones Act and for each elasticity. The Table 6.4 results combine consumers' and producers' surpluses. In all cases, the surpluses, as anticipated, are small relative to the transportation cost savings.

Combining the surplus gains due to Jones Act deregulation with the simultaneous decrease in transportation costs yields the measure of total gain in economic welfare accruing to softwood lumber producers and consumers if waterborne shipping is a competitive user of resources. The international aggregate gain in economic welfare approximates $6 million of which approximately $5 million is transportation cost savings. These approximately $5 million cost savings vary somewhat in response to changes in the elasticities, but they are never truly great when viewed in the context of total construction grade softwood lumber shipment costs, approximately $700 million in 1977.[10]

This small aggregate impact for the Jones Act seems plausible, however, when we recognize that substantial gains are contingent upon a large housing market in the Northeast. Not only is the northeastern housing market a small share (less than 7 percent) of the total U.S. housing market, but this share is declining as the locus of U.S. population shifts toward the Sunbelt. Furthermore, the impact of the Jones Act decreases as southern yellow pine improves its substitution for Douglas fir. We might expect that the expanding production of pine in the past decade has cut into northeastern markets for fir and, thereby, has decreased the impact of the Jones Act. Moreover, we might anticipate that this trend will continue and that southern pine will be an even better competitor in the Sunbelt. Therefore, the aggregate significance of the Jones Act to the whole of the softwood lumber industry may decline further yet over time.

Finally, the impact of Jones Act deregulation on the transportation industry involves a substantial reallocation from its rail component to the waterborne shipping component. Waterborne shippers, most of whom are foreign, receive from $25,281,000 to $41,950,000 annually in added revenue, whereas U.S. rail losses are in the neighborhood of $30,697,000 to $46,296,000. These estimates make abundantly clear the overriding interest of the U.S. rail industry in opposing Jones Act deregulation. The fact that the gains to waterborne shipping are mostly non-U.S. further explains the lack of U.S. maritime interest in making lumber an exception to Jones Act regulation.

REGIONAL WELFARE EFFECTS. Repealing the Jones Act also leads to welfare redistribution among various U.S. and Canadian regions. Indeed, regional redistributive effects contrast with the aggregate effects discovered in previous sections in that regional effects are often substantial. Table 6.5 shows the most important regional gains and losses in welfare for the range of elasticities and for both fixed and variable supply assumptions. It continues to measure welfare gains as the sum of transportation cost savings plus the gains in consumers' and producers' surpluses. Table 6.5 is not strictly comparable with Table 6.4, however, because it disregards inland Canadian producers and their portion of the total welfare reported in Table 6.4. (Repealing the Jones Act would cause some increase in inland Canadian shipments to inland United States. These shipments would replace a share of current coastal U.S. shipments to inland United States, which divert to intercoastal U.S. with the repeal of the Jones Act.)

As anticipated, the large losers of deregulatroy action are British Columbian producers forced out of northeastern U.S. markets. Their welfare losses are in the range of $7,204,872–7,389,430 annually. Even this large amount, however, is only 0.4 percent of British Columbia's total external shipments (Statistics Canada 1977).

The sum of all U.S. producers and consumers, on the other hand, obtains gains roughly twice the aggregate welfare gains (regardless of national geography) shown in Table 6.4. Coastal northwestern U.S. producers are the chief beneficiaries of deregulation, gaining up to $9,819,175 annually, thereby increasing the value of their external shipments of Douglas fir by 6 percent (U.S. Department of Commerce 1977b). The ripple effects on other U.S. producers are somewhat ambiguous, however, and depend on how the new allocations affect their own individual shipments and lumber prices. For example, if deregulation causes southeastern pine producers to redirect their shipments away from the Northeast, then the economic welfare of southeastern producers could either rise or fall, depending on supply and substitution elasticities.

Consumers' gains also vary considerably across regions. Northeastern consumers gain between $10,671,620 and $11,416,880 annually in added welfare as northeastern lumber prices decline by $2–3/Mbf. These gains occur at the partial expense of consumers elsewhere in the U.S., however, because prices rise slightly in all regions outside the Northeast.

 Conclusions

This chapter assesses the annual welfare impacts of the Jones Act, a regulation affecting shipment of lumber between producers and consumers. It begins by simulating the various regional Canadian and U.S. markets that may be affected by the Jones Act and then examines — under alternate

Table 6.5. Regional welfare changes

Elasticities	Total U.S. welfare gains	West Wash./Ore. producer welfare gains	Canadian Pacific producer welfare losses	Southern producer welfare gains	Northeast consumer welfare gains
$\sigma_{FP} = 1.8$					
With fixed supply	$12,879,503	$9,122,970	$7,387,140	$ 6,560	$10,883,400
With variable supply	13,249,761	9,819,175	7,204,872	−60,890	10,671,620
$\sigma_{FP} = 2.7$					
With fixed supply	12,018,779	9,122,450	7,389,430	−328,840	11,416,880
With variable supply	12,116,195	9,562,158	7,251,197	−267,630	11,278,340
$\sigma_{FP} = 10$					
With fixed supply	12,348,821	9,147,790	7,325,320	−79,290	11,080,770
With variable supply	12,229,709	9,384,342	7,219,086	14,740	10,770,560

assumptions regarding relative factor shares, supply price, and substitution elasticities—how these markets would change were the Jones Act restriction to be removed.

The summary results are that deregulation would create small aggregate efficiency gains, but substantial redistributive gains for northwestern U.S. producers and considerable gains for northeastern U.S. consumers. The secondary effects on southern and southeastern producers mostly would be insignificant. Removing the present coastal lumber shipping restrictions would increase both revenues and waterborne lumber shipments for coastal northwestern U.S., opening new eastern markets for U.S. producers and improving the U.S. balance of trade. Major cost and shipment volume reductions would be borne by British Columbian producers.

Furthermore, the fact that deregulation would increase maritime shipments undermines the national security justification for the Jones Act. That is, if the Jones Act decreases maritime shipments—and even a small share of these shipments are or would be on U.S. vessels—then the substitution effect of the Jones Act does not support, rather it detracts from, a larger American merchant fleet and the nonmarket national security value attached to it.[11] It is clear that the impact of the Jones Act on the lumber industry yields no net social benefits, is actually disadvantageous to the coastal northwestern U.S. lumber industry and to consumers in the Northeast, and may yield net disadvantages to the maritime industry and to national security.

Nevertheless, two caveats to our analysis are necessary. One has to do with the reliability of our sample year, 1977, as a basis for policy generalizations, and the other has to do with further adjustments outside the analysis that might be made in the presence of deregulation. Regarding the first, the annual gains to deregulation would vary somewhat with the business cycle and, indeed, demand in the 1977 period studied was somewhat stronger than it has been in more recent years. Nevertheless, estimates such as those of Adams and Haynes (1980) indicate that demographic trends should create relatively high demands for housing and lumber in the latter part of the 1980s, thereby increasing the level of potential deregulatory savings. The second caveat is that adjustment to deregulation might be tempered by a temporary shortage of ships available to meet the waterborne shipping demands of coastal northwestern U.S. producers. This would raise short-run transportation costs and decrease short-run deregulatory gains.

Our analysis also points out the difficulty of confining the impacts of waterborne transport deregulation to any one industry or region. We have seen that regulations originally directed toward helping one industry (the merchant marine) actually may have damaged that industry and certainly have damaged another industry (the lumber industry). Our results also show, however, that deregulation would be quite harmful to Canadian lumber producers and U.S. rail carriers. Coastal Canadian producers might adjust (in a manner which we did not examine) by shifting to other foreign markets, perhaps in the Pacific Rim. Nonetheless, our findings suggest that removal of the present restrictions is likely to encounter stiff opposition from various industries and geographical regions, each acting in its own best interests.

 Appendix: Housing Starts

Robinson's econometric observations rely heavily on housing start data published in *Construction Review* (U.S. Department of Commerce 1977c) and *Construction Reprots* (U.S. Department of Commerce 1977a). The Department of Commerce derives these data from housing permit data and weighted estimates of miscellaneous construction activities. The housing start data are available, however, only for four large regions, rather than for the thirty-nine disaggregated regions of our demand analysis. The Department of Commerce also reports permit data by states and large SMSAs, which do correspond with our thirty-nine regions. Our problem, therefore, is to convert the permit data to annual housing start observations for each of our thirty-nine regions.

There are three steps to our general approach. The first postulates a free-form distributed-lag relationship for each of the four aggregate Department of Commerce regions wherein housing starts are a function of lagged permits. More formally,

$$Y_t = \xi_t + s_{1t} + s_{2t} + s_{3t} + \phi_1 X_t + \phi_2 X_{t-1}$$
$$+ \ldots + \phi_n X_{t-n} + \epsilon_t \qquad \text{(6A.1)}$$

where Y_t is the number of regional housing starts in the present period, the S_i are seasonal dummies, the X_i are permits issued in each period j, the ξ and ϕ are constants, and ϵ is an error term or residual. The second step produces regressions which estimate coefficients for each of the four aggregate regions. We correct for serial correlation where it is present.[12] The final step generates 1977 housing start estimates by combining the regression coefficients with permit data from the thirty-nine disaggregated regions. Consistency with Robinson (1974) requires inclusion of mobile home shipments in the regional totals. Therefore, we add mobile home shipments to the housing start estimates for each region in proportion to their share of total housing starts. Table 6.6 reports the final (rounded) total housing start estimates necessary to obtain equations (6.4a) and (6.4b).

Table 6.6. Housing starts by region

Region	Housing starts
1. Oregon	43,100
2. Washington	68,800
3. Idaho	13,700
4. Montana	7,000
5. Wyoming	6,500
6. Calif./Nevada	336,000
7. Utah	24,900
8. Arizona	49,100
9. New Mexico	14,800
10. Colorado	42,500
11. Kansas	20,800
12. Nebraska	13,400
13. South Dakota	7,800
14. North Dakota	8,100
15. Texas/Okla.	249,400
16. Arkansas	17,000
17. Missouri	38,700
18. Iowa	27,300
19. Minnesota	47,600
20. Ill./Wisc.	151,500
21. Michigan	77,200
22. Indiana	47,000
23. Ohio	80,600
24. Kentucky	27,200
25. W. Virginia	4,000
26. DC/Del./Va./Md.	151,800
27. Pennsylvania	60,100
28. N.Y. City/N.J.	52,400
29. N.Y. State	35,900
30. Mass./R.I./Conn.	53,400
31. Vt./N.H./Me.	16,400
32. North Carolina	52,300
33. South Carolina	31,300
34. Georgia	48,800
35. Florida	182,800
36. Alabama	40,800
37. Mississippi	13,600
38. Tennessee	42,100
39. Louisiana	38,800

 Notes

1. Scott (1983) reviews the conditions under which national security makes a sensible (or insensible) argument for encouraging resource production or conservation. See, particularly, his Chapter 6.

2. Cardellichio (1980, 73) argues otherwise and points instead to the increasing scarcity of privately owned timber in the U.S. Pacific Northwest. Canadian stumpage pricing policies were the source of a recent unsuccessful countervailing duty request brought before the International Trade Administration by the U.S. industry. They continue to be controversial.

3. Senator Maureen Neuberger of Oregon in 1962 introduced the most recent

Congressional action seeking relief from the Jones Act for lumber producers. It is interesting that both sides of this political battle feature senators from the Northwest and northwestern wood products and shipping interests in general. Both Senator Jones and the recent leading defender of merchant marine shipping interests, Senator Warren Magnuson, were from Washington.

4. Holland and Judge (1963) use a similar approach for assessing interregional lumber flows. Our approach extends theirs to permit variable regional supplies as well as substitution among lumber species.

5. The substitution elasticity derives from our equation (6.1) and (6.2) assumptions about functional form, knowledge that an average single-family dwelling requres 8 Mbf, and the other parameters discussed in the previous paragraph.

6. Drew Chad of the Transportation Division of MacMillan Bloedel, British Columbia's largest producer and shipper supplied the waterborne rates in personal communication, 25 January 1980.

$$7. \quad x = -15.7 - 0.0472m + 0.564m^{3/4}$$
$$(-2.50) \quad (-3.01) \quad (4.34) \quad R^2 = 0.916 \quad F = 175.0$$

where x = cost in \$/Mbf, and m = miles. The numbers in parentheses are t ratios. The regression apparently is valid for all rail shipments that cost in excess of \$5.48 per Mbf, the smallest observation in the ICC report. See Boyd (1981 pp. 124–27) for further discussion.

8. The model does not permit a similar comparison with total coastal British Columbian shipments because some British Columbian shipments may shift from the U.S. Northeast to eastern Canada or overseas. The model cannot estimate these shifts because it does not include eastern Canada and overseas consumption regions.

9. Changes in factor shares do not alter the nature of these results. The range of impacts on intercoastal shipments from Canadian and U.S. sources (in MMbf) is

	Canada	United States
$\alpha_K = 0.80$, $\alpha_F = \alpha_P$, supplies fixed	−750	+924
$\alpha_K = 0.95$, $\alpha_F = \alpha_P$, supplies variable	−938	+994
$\alpha_K = 0.88$, $\alpha_P = 0.75\alpha_F$, supplies fixed	−804	+936
$\alpha_K = 0.88$, $\alpha_F = 0.75\alpha_P$, supplies variable	−863	+970

Altering the capital share causes more variation than altering fir-pine shares. Predictions are more robust with regard to U.S. shipments, but this may only reflect greater existence of other Canadian markets outside the framework of our analysis.

10. Once more, changes in factor shares do not alter the nature of this result. Deregulatory cost savings range from \$4,086,150 ($\alpha_K = 0.80$, $\alpha_F = \alpha_P$, supplies fixed) to \$6,225,960 ($\alpha_K = 0.95$, $\alpha_F = \alpha_P$, supplies variable). Total welfare gains are slightly larger. They reach a maximum of \$7,313,210 ($\alpha_K = 0.95$, $\alpha_F = \alpha_P$, supplies variable).

11. An undetermined income effect may or may not exceed the substitution effect. Therefore, the net effect of the Jones Act on the size of the U.S. merchant fleet is unclear.

12. See Boyd (1981) for details.

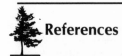

References

Adams, D. M., and R. W. Haynes. 1980. *The 1980 softwood timber assessment market model: Structure, projections, and policy simulation.* Forest Science Monograph 22.

Austin, J. A., and D. R. Darr. 1975. The Jones Act and the Douglas-fir region softwood lumber industry in perspective. *Journal of Forestry* 73(10):644–48.

Boyd, R. G. 1981. The effects of U.S. domestic shipping regulations on the North American lumber market. Ph.D. diss., Duke University, Durham, N.C.

Cardellichio, P. 1980. Can transportation rates explain the West's loss of lumber market share? *FORSIM Review* 4(3):73–78.

Dantzig, G. B. 1951. Application of the simplex method to a transportation problem. In *Activity analysis of production and allocation,* ed. T. C. Koopmans. New York: John Wiley and Sons.

Gorter, W. 1956. *United States shipping policy.* New York: Harper and Brothers.

Holland, I. I., and G. G. Judge. 1963. Estimated interregional flows of hardwood and softwood lumber. *Journal of Forestry* 61(7):488–97.

Interstate Commerce Commission. 1977. *Distance commodity rates.* MF-ICC No. 38. Washington, D.C.: U.S. Government Printing Ofice.

_____. 1978. *Investigation of the railroad rate structure—Lumber and lumber products.* Washington, D.C.: U.S. Government Printing Office.

Jantscher, G. R. 1975. *Bread upon the waters: Federal aids to the maritime industries.* Washington, D.C.: The Brookings Institution.

Koopmans, T. C. 1949. Optimal utilization of the transport system. *Econometrica* 17(7):136–46.

_____. 1951. Analysis of production and the efficient combination of activities. In *Activity analysis of production and allocation,* ed. T. C. Koopmans. New York: John Wiley and Sons.

Mead, W. J. 1966. *Competition and oligopsony in the Douglas-fir lumber industry.* Berkeley and Los Angeles: University of California Press.

Morgan, I. P. 1980. The impact of the Jones Act on selected United States industries. D.B.A. diss. Harvard University.

Robinson, V. L. 1974. An econometric model of softwood lumber and stumpage markets, 1947–1967. *Forest Science* 20(6):171–79.

Samuelson, P. A. 1952. Spatial price equilibrium and linear programming. *American Economic Review* 21(6):283–303.

Scott, A. 1983. *Natural resources: The economics of conservation.* Ottawa: Carleton University Press.

Statistics Canada, External Trade Division. 1977. *Trade of Canada: Exports by countries.* Catalogue 65-003.

Takayama, T., and G. G. Judge. 1964a. Equilibrium among spatially separated markets: A reformation. *Econometrica* 32:510–24.

_____. 1964b. An interregional activity analysis of the agricultural sector. *Journal of Farm Economics* 46:349–65.

_____. 1971. *Spatial and temporal price and allocation models.* Amsterdam: North-Holland.

Tramel, T. E., and A. C. Seale, Jr. 1959. Reactive programming of supply and demand relations—application to fresh vegetables. *Journal of Farm Economics* 41(12):1012–22.

_____. 1965. Reactive programming—Recent developments. In *Interregional competition research methods,* ed. R. A. Kind. Raleigh: North Carolina State University Press.

U.S. Department of Commerce, Bureau of the Census. 1977a. *Construction reports. Quarterly.* Washington, D.C.: U.S. Government Printing Office.

_____. 1977b. *U.S. exports, domestic merchandise, SIC-based products by world areas.* Publication FT-610, annual. Washington, D.C.: U.S. Government Printing Office.

_____. 1978. *Lumber production and mill stocks.* Current Industrial Report MA-24T. Washington, D.C.: U.S. Government Printing Office.

U.S. Department of Commerce, International Trade Administration. 1977c. *Construction Review.* Vol. 23 (bimonthly). Washington, D.C.: U.S. Government Printing Office.

Veltkamp, J. 1981. Forest summary. *FORSIM Review* 12(1):1–12.

CHAPTER 7

Taxation

The previous chapters examine regulations which usually derive from public laws imposing direct resource management constraints or incentives. Such market interventions are the focus of the public debate about regulation and their discussion is the main purpose of this book. Nevertheless, any discussion of regulation in forestry would be incomplete if it ignored taxation and public ownership. While these two issues are not the focus of the regulation debate they are important public interventions in the marketplace. Indeed, it may be that no regulations have greater welfare impacts on producers of timber or consumers of wood products than either preferential capital gains taxation of timber or restrictions on the market sensitivity of timber sales from public lands. This chapter and the next turn from the more typical topics within the regulation debate to those taxes and those restrictions on the public forestlands that cause departures from market solutions and welfare maximization.

This chapter focuses on taxation, an important issue in any industry, but a truly critical issue in forestry. One measure shows the forest products industry as the fourth greatest tax-paying industry, exceeded only by tobacco, rubber, and trucking. By this measure, forest industry taxes averaged 36.1 percent of net revenues in 1985 in comparison with an overall domestic industrial rate of 16.1 percent (Pease & Dorgan 1984). On the other hand, another measure claims that tax incentives provide 25 percent of the forest industry's after-tax profits and preferential capital gains treatment of timber alone may cost the U.S. Treasury $355 million in foregone annual tax revenues, or enough to finance the entire annual U.S. Forest Service budget (Russakoff 1985, A2ff).

One chapter alone does not provide sufficient opportunity to inquire into all the special tax provisions affecting timber. This would require a truly extensive effort and it would distract from the main thrust of a book on public regulations in general. Our alternative in this chapter is to examine two illustrative taxes, one federal and one local, for their welfare effects and their incidence.[1] These illustrations expand upon the forest taxation literature in that they are both empirical and based on general equilibrium models. Prior literature features partial equilibrium models and numerical examples.[2] The advantage of the general equilibrium approach is that it permits economywide estimates of welfare impacts and incidence. In contrast, the partial equilibrium approach only permits estimates of impacts within the timber sector itself. It disregards secondary impacts on the economy as a whole.

The key federal taxation issue is the capital gains provision of the income tax. At the time of this study, it permitted taxation of timber-derived income at a preferential rate equal to 40 percent of the ordinary rate for other corporate and individual income. There have been previous partial equilibrium empirical estimates of the welfare effects of this tax but no estimates of its incidence (e.g., U.S. General Accounting Office 1981; Sunley 1972).

The key local taxation issue in the literature has been the nonneutrality of property taxes and their substitutes: bare land taxes, yield taxes, and severance taxes. Specifically, attention has focused on the nonneutral effects of these taxes on rotation length and forestland use. This literature is particularly well developed (e.g., Klemperer 1982; Gaffney 1979). Indeed, its thoroughness justifies turning our attention elsewhere.

One contemporary property tax issue of interest is "current use" taxation. Favorable taxation of undeveloped and, often, forested land at its current use rate is designed to limit urban growth and to induce creation of green corridors within growing population centers. The development of Forsyth County (Winston-Salem), North Carolina, between 1960 and 1970 is the basis for an empirical model of the dynamic adjustments to a current use tax. The widespread acceptability of current use taxation in the United States (communities in forty-seven states now permit it) suggests that the findings from a Forsyth County example have generalizable implications beyond this county and beyond the state of North Carolina.[3]

 Capital Gains

The Revenue Act of 1943 extended capital gains treatment to income received from timber cut for sale or used in a business. This preferential tax treatment currently extends to corporations and individual purveyors of timber so long as they hold their timber in excess of six months. It includes those vertically integrated firms making implicit sales from their timber lands to their own mills as well as those loggers who purchase public agency stumpage prior to logging and transferring the logs to their own mills or to the mills of other firms. The U.S. Treasury estimates that preferential capital gains treatment of timber cost approximately $1.6 billion in tax revenue losses on real timber income in the five years from 1976 to 1980 (U.S. Government Accounting Office 1981).[4]

The preferential capital gains treatment of timber is the subject of frequent debate. Both of the 1985 tax simplification plans (Bradley-Gephart and Kemp-Kasten) proposed, and the 1986 plan (subsequent to our analysis) adopted its removal. There are periodic proposals of various intermediate alternatives, including extension of the six-month holding period, limitation of preferential treatment to only those who grow timber thereby eliminating the preferential treatment from loggers and from integrated firms who only have a contract right to harvest, and elimination of preferential treatment only from those who contract harvests on public lands.

In contrast, several arguments support preferential capital gains treatment of timber. Most are descriptive and only one generates even debatable economic support. The argument that timber is a long-term, therefore risky, investment deserving compensatory tax relief is denied if we admit that long-term, high-risk investments are not unique to timber production. Furthermore, the market manages investments with these characteristics more efficiently than does the tax code. A second argument has to do with incentives to reforest. Favorable capital gains taxation does not encourage reforestation except as it encourages all wise investments by making more after-tax income available to the landowner.[5]

A third argument supports capital gains on distributive grounds. Sunley (1972) responds that capital gains treatment of timber requires the firm to have 1972 taxable income in excess of $25,000 and that capital gains benefits increase with profitability, therefore with firm size and for vertically integrated firms. Furthermore, corporations, not individual landowners, retain approximately 75 percent of the foregone tax revenues (U.S. Government Accounting Office 1981). Thus, for individuals as well as for corporations, capital gains benefits increase with income, and low-income individuals receive little benefit.[6] In sum, even if a few small landowners receive capital gains benefits, these characteristic capital gains results are not those expected of a public policy designed for distributive purposes. The distributive argument for capital gains is unsupported.

The debatable argument in support of preferential capital gains treatment for timber is made on grounds of horizontal equity. That is, if preferential capital gains treatment were removed from the timber industry alone and not from other resource-based industries at the same time, then timber producers would be at a competitive disadvantage with producers of substitute products. Therefore, this argument prefers delay in any adjustment of the preferential capital gains rate for timber awaiting simultaneous adjustment for all competitive industries. The opposing argument, of course, is that tax reform must start somewhere. Why not start with timber. The analysis in this chapter sheds no additional light on the merit of this last argument. It considers the impact if preferential capital gains treatment were removed from timber alone. The analysis begins with the assembly of a conceptual model and continues with its empirical application assessing incidence and welfare. Finally, it draws conclusions and some further implications.

THE MODEL

Harberger (1962; 1966) introduces the standard two-sector, two-factor general equilibrium approach for evaluations of the corporate income tax. Mieszkowski (1967) and Shoven (1976) extend it. (In addition, Brittain [1972] and Boskin [1975] use this approach to study the incidence of the social security tax and the impact of having an untaxed household sector.)

Following Harberger, consider an economy that produces two outputs, timber X and the sum of all other products Y. Both producing industries are competitive and both operate under conditions of constant returns to scale. Both industries employ combinations of the same two factors of production, capital and labor, which are fixed in aggregate supply at K and L. Output prices are denoted by p_X and p_Y, the return of capital by r, and the wage by w. All consumers possess identical homothetic utility functions (i.e., the ratio of the demands is independent of income). Later, we can relax the assumptions of competitive markets and homothetic utility in order to observe their impacts on the empirical findings.

Under these assumptions the cost functions in each of the two industries may be written as

$$C_i = C_i\,(r,w)i \qquad i = X,Y \tag{7.1}$$

where C_i represents both marginal and average cost in the ith sector. Competition in all markets assures that prices equal marginal costs, therefore

$$p_i = C_i\,(r,w) \qquad i = X,Y \tag{7.2}$$

and the effects of input price changes on output prices can be written as

$$\hat{p}_X - \hat{p}_Y = (\theta_{LX} - \theta_{LY})\hat{w} - (\theta_{KY} - \theta_{KX})\hat{r} \tag{7.3}$$

or

$$\hat{p}_X - \hat{p}_Y = \theta^*(\hat{w} - \hat{r}) \tag{7.3a}$$

θ_{ij} is the share of total returns in the jth industry paid to the ith factor of production and the hats indicate percentage changes.[7] Not surprisingly, this formulation indicates that, if timber is the capital intensive sector (i.e., θ_{KX} > θ_{KY} and θ_{LY} > θ_{LX}), then a decrease in $w - r$ leads to an increase in the relative price of timber, $p_X - p_Y$. See the appendix to this chapter for derivation of general equilibrium conditions (7.3) and (7.3a) and also the general equilibrium condition (7.7).

Turning to the demand side, consumer preference for a given product i depends on relative output prices as well as consumer income. Therefore,

$$\hat{X} = \epsilon_{XX}\hat{p}_X + \epsilon_{XY}\hat{p}_Y + \eta_X(dU/M)e_u \tag{7.4a}$$

and

$$\hat{Y} = \epsilon_{YX}\hat{p}_X + \epsilon_{YY}\hat{p}_Y + \eta_Y(dU/M)e_u \tag{7.4b}$$

represent consumer demands for the outputs of each sector. The ϵ_{ij} are compensated demand elasticities, the η_i are income elasticities, M is income, U refers to utility, and e_u is the derivative of the expenditure function with respect to utility.

Multiplying equation (7.4b) by η_Y and equation (7.4a) by η_X and then subtracting the second from the first yields

$$\eta_Y\hat{X} - \eta_X\hat{Y} = (\eta_Y\epsilon_{XX} - \eta_X\epsilon_{YX})\hat{p}_X - (\eta_X\epsilon_{YY} - \eta_Y\epsilon_{XY})\hat{p}_Y \tag{7.5}$$

Homotheticity permits setting η_Y and η_X equal to 1, which implies that consumer demand is linear in income, probably a reasonable assumption for the sum of all demand for timber and certainly a good assumption for the sum of demand for all other products. Homotheticity, together with the additive properties of compensated demand elasticities, permits simplifying equation (7.5) to

$$(\hat{X} - \hat{Y}) = -\sigma_D(\hat{p}_X - \hat{p}_Y) \tag{7.6}$$

where $\sigma_D = -(\epsilon_{XX} + \epsilon_{YY})$.[8] Equation (7.6) relates changes in the demand for output quantities to changes in output prices, incorporating the extent of substitution in demand between the two outputs.

Finally, we must relate relative factor prices to the production of final goods in order to obtain the general equilibrium system of equations describing the interaction between all given prices and quantities. The final relationship, fully developed in the appendix, is

$$\tau^*(\hat{X} - \hat{Y}) = (\hat{w} - \hat{r})\,[\sigma_X(\theta_{KX}\tau_{LX} + \theta_{LX}\tau_{KX}) + \sigma_Y(\sigma_{KY}\tau_{LY} + \theta_{LY}\tau_{KY})] \tag{7.7}$$

where σ_X and σ_Y are the substitution elasticities in the two sectors, τ_{LX} and τ_{LY} are the physical shares of labor in the timber and nontimber sector, and τ^* is analogous to θ^* (see note 7). Equation (7.7) relates output quantities to input prices, incorporating substitution among inputs. Clearly, the greater the substitution elasticities, the more sensitive relative outputs are to changes in relative input prices. The magnitudes of these elasticities are critical to the magnitudes of our measures of incidence and welfare.

INCIDENCE. Government subsidies in the form of capital gains tax relief reduce the relative cost of capital and affect this analysis by altering the relative input prices confronting producers. That is, the application of a tax T_{KX} alters equation (7.3a) by adding $\sigma_{KX}\hat{T}_{KX}$ to the right-hand side and alters equation (7.7) by subtracting $\sigma_X(\theta_{KX} \tau_{LX} + \theta_{LX} \tau_{KX})\hat{T}_{KX}$ from the right-hand side.[9] These two equations, plus equation (7.6), form a system of three equations in three unknowns. Solving them for $(\hat{w} - \hat{r})$ provides the incidence equation

$$(\hat{w} - \hat{r}) = \frac{\sigma_X(\theta_{KX}\tau_{LX} + \theta_{LX}\tau_{KX})\hat{T}_{KX} - \sigma_D\theta_{KX}\tau^*\hat{T}_{KX}}{\sigma_D\theta^*\tau^* + \sigma_X(\theta_{KX}\tau_{LX} + \theta_{LX}\tau_{KX}) + \sigma_Y(\theta_{KY}\tau_{LY} + \theta_{LY}\tau_{KY})} \qquad (7.8)$$

which expresses the general equilibrium change in relative price entirely in terms of the exogenous factor shares and the elasticities. Clearly, for $\tau^* < 0$ the value of $(\hat{w} - \hat{r})$ increases with the value of the timber sector's substitution elasticity σ_X and its capital share σ_{KX}. Therefore, as capital intensity increases, capital owners capture a larger share of the tax subsidy.

WELFARE. The welfare loss due to distortionary taxation policies can be derived by the same approach. Harberger (1962) works in terms of production rather than cost relations. He manipulates the previous system of equations to produce a new system of three equations in the three unknowns $\hat{K}_X$, $\hat{L}_X$, and dr (the change in the demands for capital and labor and the change in the return to capital, respectively). Writing these three equations in our notation yields

$$\sigma_{KX}\theta_{KX}T_{KX} = \epsilon_{KX}(\sigma_{KY} - \theta_{KX})dr + \theta_{LX}\hat{L}_X + \theta_{KX}\hat{K}_X \qquad (7.9)$$

$$0 = \sigma_Y dr - (L_X/L_Y)\hat{L}_X + (K_X/K_Y)\hat{K}_X \qquad (7.10)$$

$$\sigma_X T_{KX} = -\sigma_X dr - \hat{L}_X + \hat{K}_X \qquad (7.11)$$

The comparative static results for a tax on timber can be derived by applying Cramer's rule. Harberger (1966) solves explicitly for $\hat{K}_X$:

$$\hat{K}_X = \frac{\epsilon_{XX}(\theta_{KY}\sigma_X(\tau_{LX}/\tau_{LY}) + \theta_{KX}\sigma_Y) - \sigma_X\sigma_Y\theta_{LX}}{\epsilon_{XX}(\theta_{KY} - \theta_{KX})(\tau^*/\tau_{KY})\tau_{LY} + \sigma_Y + \sigma_X[\theta_{LX}(\tau_{KX}/\tau_{KY}) + \theta_{KX}(\tau_{LX}/\tau_{LY})]} \qquad (7.12)$$

Substituting $\sigma_D r_Y$ for ϵ_{xx} yields equation (7.13), which explains the percent change in demand for the dependant variable due to preferential tax treatment.

$$\hat{K}_x = \frac{\sigma_D r_Y(\theta_{KY}\sigma_X(\tau_{LX}/\tau_{LY}) + \theta_{KX}\sigma_Y) - \sigma_X\sigma_Y\theta_{LX}}{\sigma_D r_Y(\theta_{KY} - \theta_{KX})(\tau^*/\tau_{KY})\tau_{LY} + \sigma_Y + \sigma_X[\theta_{LX}(\tau_{KX}/\tau_{KY}) + \theta_{KX}(\tau_{LX}/\tau_{LY})]} \quad (7.13)$$

where r_Y is the share of income not spent on timber. Extracting total timber capital K_x provides the measure of capital misallocation. The area of the deadweight welfare loss triangle (comparable to *abd* in Figure 1.1) equals this capital misallocation times one-half of the preferential tax treatment for timber, $T_X/2$.

This measure of welfare loss is similar to its partial equilibrium counterpart. Mieszkowski (1967) points out, however, that inclusion of the aggregate demand and factor share terms accounts for an *output* effect in addition to the traditional *substitution* effect. That is, we know that capital substitutes for labor and that the demand for capital rises when capital in the timber sector is subsidized and technology is flexible (i.e., $\sigma_X > 0$). Mieszkowski's point is that output in the timber sector also rises relative to the output of the nontimber sector. If timber is relatively capital intensive, then the output effect causes the demand for capital to increase still further, thereby reinforcing the initial distortion due to factor substitution.

EMPIRICAL ESTIMATES

Table 7.1 shows our actual parametric values for 1979. The timber industry is a small share of the aggregate economy, therefore the values for the capital and labor shares in all but timber (θ_{KY} and θ_{LY}, respectively) can be computed from data on total corporate profits, corporate employee compensation, proprietors' total income, and proprietors' employee compensation, which are found in the *Statistical Abstract of the United States* (U.S. Department of Commerce 1980). Capital and labor shares in the timber industry (θ_{KX} and θ_{LX}, respectively) are Daniels et al.'s (1985) esti-

Table 7.1. Parameter values for 1979

$\theta_{KY} = .15$	$\tau_{KY} = .992$
$\theta_{LY} = .85$	$\tau_{KX} = .008$
$\theta_{KX} = .25$	$\tau_{LY} = .996$
$\theta_{LX} = .75$	$\tau_{LX} = .004$
$\theta^* = .1$	$\tau^* = -.004$
$\sigma_Y = 1$	$\sigma_D = 1, .5$
$\sigma_X = 3, 2$	$r_Y = .99$

mates for North Carolina. Not surprisingly, these values of θ_{KX} and θ_{KY} indicate that timber is a relatively capital intensive industry. Values for labor's physical shares (τ_{LX} and τ_{LY}) can be calculated in a similar manner except that the calculation also requires a value for total timber income. This can be derived from receipts and material costs for the derivative industries, information which is available in the *1979 Statistics of Income* published by the IRS.

The elasticity of substitution in the timber industry σ_X is Daniels et al. (1985) estimate. The relatively large value for this parameter is a consequence of the long production period and ample substitution possibilities afforded timber growers. Nevertheless, since Stier (1980) shows that logging has limited substitution possibilities, it may be best to consider as well the lower value of $\sigma_X = 2$ and to present a range of plausible results. Parashevopoulos (1979) and Klein (1974) provide evidence of the other substitution elasticity, σ_Y. Uncertainty about the aggregate demand elasticity σ_D recommends that we vary its value from .5 to 1.0, as Harberger (1962) does.

The parameter r_Y is the share of income not spent on timber. It can be computed from national income data in *The Economic Report of the President* (U.S. Council of Economic Advisors 1980) and data on timber receipts from the *1979 Statistics of Income.*

The value of $\hat{T}_{KX}$ is the effective 1979 capital gains tax subsidy for corporate and noncorporate owners of forest capital. The division of corporate and non-corporate profits can be derived from Clawson (1979). Recipients' tax rates and tax brackets and the distributions of recipients within tax brackets originate from the *1979 Statistics of Income,* the *1979 IRS Tax Guide,* and findings by Royer (1981).

INCIDENCE. The incidence results in Table 7.2 indicate that, even with most conservative estimates, capital appropriates substantially more than 100 percent of the income tax subsidy due to the preferential capital gains treatment. This suggests that arguments justifying capital gains based on its employment effects have negative validity. That is, preferential capital gains treatment of timber encourages use of capital inputs and an absolute reduction in labor inputs.

Table 7.2. Capital incidence

	Elasticity assumptions		Incidence
Case 1	$\sigma_D = 1$	$\sigma_X = 3$	271%
Case 2	$\sigma_D = 1$	$\sigma_X = 2$	186%
Case 3	$\sigma_D = .5$	$\sigma_X = 3$	265%
Case 4	$\sigma_D = .5$	$\sigma_X = 2$	180%

WELFARE. The welfare results in Table 7.3 indicate that, even with most conservative assumptions about output demand and input substitution, the welfare loss due to preferential capital gains treatment of timber is quite large, ranging from $240.9 to $368.2 million. This finding is all the more striking in light of the fact that the timber sector only constitutes approximately 1 percent of total GNP, and its total corporate and noncorporate earnings for 1979 totaled only $2 billion.

Table 7.3. Welfare loss

Case 1	$368.2 million
Case 2	$259.4 million
Case 3	$349.9 million
Case 4	$240.9 million

We must emphasize that the magnitude of these welfare loss estimates closely relates to the importance of the Mieszkowski's output effect. Partial equilibrium analysis does not incorporate this particular effect. Moreover, the output effect would still exist, except on a smaller scale, if preferential capital gains treatment were removed from other resource-based industries that compete with timber (i.e., that produce substitute products).

SENSITIVITY. The results presented so far are based on a model that is subject to some fairly restrictive assumptions. We now seek to determine how sensitive the results are to the relaxation of these assumptions. Specifically, consider how incidence and welfare measures change

(1) with the presence of market power in the timber sector,
(2) with relaxation of the assumption of homothetic demands and uniform income elasticities, and
(3) with the introduction of other economic distortions caused by taxes on property and on corporate income.

Although the timber industry is generally considered highly competitive, there is the possibility of some market power in the form of mark-up pricing. This complicates the analysis. The critical difference is that with mark-up pricing the factor shares θ_{ij} refer to shares in the cost of output, not to factor shares in the value of output. Hence, the θ_{ij} may differ significantly from observed factor shares. Ballentine and Eris (1975) show that if $\sigma_D < \sigma_X$, then the calculations may overstate the incidence and welfare distortions. Using Ballentine and Eris' corrections and allowing for a monopoly markup of 20 percent reduces the incidence measure for Case 1 in Table 7.2 from 271 percent to 224 percent. Similar reductions occur in all cases considered (for both incidence and welfare). Therefore, the possibility of some market power should be taken into consideration when interpreting our earlier results, but market power does not alter the magnitude of the findings.

Other problems arise if the assumption of homothetic demand functions is withdrawn and the income elasticities η_{ij} take on values other than one. Under these conditions, the presence of other preexisting tax differences may bias the calculated results.[10] The corporate income tax, for example, puts an excess burden on corporate income. This means that if the timber sector has a higher proportion of corporate income than the economy as a whole, then the timber sector loses relative to other sectors. Furthermore, a large body of literature since 1935 suggests that the property tax negatively biases deferred yield operations such as timber production.[11] If corporate income taxes and property taxes indeed fall more heavily on the timber industry and if $\eta_x > 1$, then the welfare and incidence measures would again be overstated. Empirical evidence from Clawson (1979), the *1979 Statistics of Income*, and Royer (1981), however, indicates that this bias is likely to be small. Sensitivity analysis confirms this view. That is, (reasonably high) hypothetical values of $\eta_x = 1.2$ and an excess timber tax burden equaling 20 percent only change the incidence measure for Case 1 from 271 percent to 226 percent. Again, changes of a similar magnitude occur in all four cases — and the general nature of our results is unaffected.

CONCLUSIONS AND EXTENSIONS

The welfare losses and investment distortions due to preferential capital gains taxation of timber are considerable under the most cautious of estimates. They cannot be justified except on grounds that competitive resource-based industries also receive preferential capital gains treatment. To remove the capital gains advantage from timber could be interpreted as discriminatory toward timber relative to these other industries. Thus, this justification, together with the large welfare costs and incidence distortions, is a better argument for removing favorable treatment from all resource-based industries at the same time.

Reform, if it were to occur within timber income taxation, could be piecemeal in nature, however, and when we analyze the welfare impacts of more selective policies, we find that more cautious judgements need to be made. Increasing the required holding period for timber might reduce eligibility, thereby reducing capital gains losses somewhat. But this also extends the average rotation length of capital gains–eligible timber, thereby increasing capital's share of total returns to the timber sector θ_{KX} and increasing the welfare loss associated with any given level of foregone revenue. The final impact of extended holding periods on economic efficiency in this case is not obvious.

It seems that a more promising option would be to exclude large corporations from preferential treatment. This would significantly reduce the capital gains loss. This option might be less attractive to policymakers, however, if it leads to some decrease in reforestation effort. Distributive justice might be an additional justification for excluding corporations from this preferential treatment since, by and large, corporations now receive a larger tax break from preferential timber treatment than private individuals. If distributive arguments are used, however, then the policy debate should place less emphasis on economic efficiency.

Finally, our results strongly indicate that allowing capital gains treatment for publicly owned timber has little justification. If it turns out that this provision mainly affects corporations, then the welfare gains due to its removal may be initially overestimated. There would be no offsetting loss in conservation effort, however, because public agencies, not private loggers, are responsible for reforestation on public lands. Thus, a good argument can be made for abolishing preferential tax treatment of timber income in this particular case.

 Current Use Taxation

While capital gains is the most talked about income tax issue, probably current use taxation is the most talked about property tax issue facing forestry today. Its desired impact generally is on smaller forest landowners located near developing urban areas.

Property is most commonly appraised at the value associated with its highest and best use, and urban land use values are generally greater than agricultural and forestland values. Therefore, as time passes and the margin of development proceeds outward from urban areas, land values and, along with them, appraisals and property taxes generally increase. Higher land values are an incentive for agriculture and forest landowners to sell their land to developers. Where landowners prefer not to sell, then higher taxes and lower after-tax profits may alter their preferences.

Local citizens, however, collect aesthetic externalities from the remaining open land and green space. They prefer that some open space remains after development and they may be against development altogether. They may sympathize with the current farm and forest landowners who wish that economic forces would not coerce them to change their land use preferences. For whichever reason, the local community may adopt current use taxation, thereby leaving taxes unchanged for those agriculture and forestlands at the margin of urban development. The community intends the lower current use taxes to reduce the incentive to develop and to encourage leaving some lands in agriculture and forestry.[12]

This section shows that such current use taxes do not halt but only delay eventual development. Nevertheless, it also shows that, when certain restrictive conditions obtain, current use taxes provide welfare gains in addition to the aesthetic externalities. We begin by reasoning through contrasting conceptual models for highest and best use and for current use taxation. In each case, we contrast the transitional paths to equilibrium (short-run neutrality) and the comparative static results (long-run neutrality). We subsequently develop a measure of the differential welfare impacts of the two property taxes and then test the short- and long-term comparisons empirically in Forsyth County, North Carolina, for the period 1960–1970.

THE MODEL

Our analysis follows location theory as originally set forth by von Thunen (1826) and a two-sector linear property tax model formulated by Turnbull and Boyd (1985). The two sectors are an urban sector and a rural land use sector. Our attention focuses on the development margin at which the uses overlap. Competition and full employment prevail throughout.[13]

The general model is best understood with reference to Figure 7.1 where A is the total quantity of available land and $A(t)$ is the quantity of urban sector land at time t. The inverse demand function for urban or developed land at time t is

$$s(t) = p_0 + p_1 A(t) \tag{7.14}$$

in the northeast quadrant. The vertical axis measures value. The reservation land rent for development is the rural (agriculture and forest) land rent p_2 which is exogenous to the region. Long-run equilibrium in the land markets occurs at A, where $s = p_2$. This is the usual static land allocation.[14]

The development of rural land for urban uses is a dynamic market process. Therefore, we need to examine the time path $A(t)$ as the land market adjusts toward the steady state equilibrium. The marginal benefit $\Delta(t)$ for developing another acre of land is the urban–rural rent differential (or the urban opportunity rent) at that time

$$\Delta(t) = s(t) - p_2 \tag{7.15}$$

This marginal benefit is the vertical distance between the rural and the downward sloping urban land rent gradients in the northeast quadrant. The

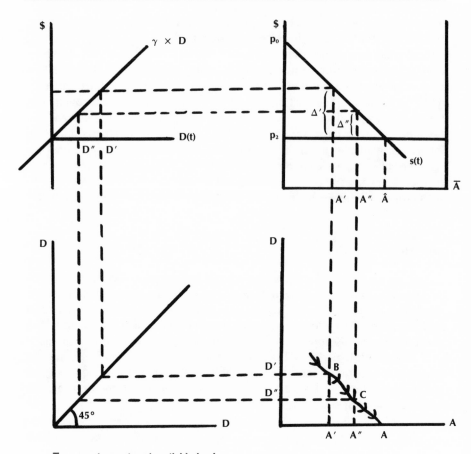

$\overline{A}$ = total quantity of available land
D(t) = level of new development undertaken at time t

Figure 7.1. The market for land development.

marginal benefit of development at any time t decreases as land development increases at that time.

The marginal cost of development at time t increases with the level of new development $D(t)$ undertaken.[15] The northwest quandrant shows this relationship.

Equating marginal benefit with the marginal cost provides the level of development undertaken at a moment in time

$$\Delta(t) = \alpha D(t) \tag{7.16}$$

For example, if the current state is A' and the marginal benefit of new development is Δ', then new development proceeds until its rate is D' and its marginal cost also is Δ'.

To solve the model algebraically, substitute equations (7.14) and (7.15) into equation (7.16) and substitute the result into the development definition.

$$dA(t)/dt = \dot{A}(t) = D(t) \tag{7.17}$$

This yields

$$\alpha\dot{A}(t) = \alpha D(t) = p_0 - p_1A(t) - p_2 \tag{7.18}$$

The solution for the differential equation (7.18) is

$$A(t) = [A(0) + (p_2 - p_0)/p_1]e^{-\rho t/\gamma} + (p_0 - p_2)/p_1 \tag{7.19}$$

where $A(0)$ is land allocation at time $t = 0$ and ϱ is the discount rate. Knowledge of equation (7.19) and the appropriate parametric values for any community enables replication of the time profile of rural to urban land reallocation.

The southeast quadrant depicts the nature of the land development process. In this quadrant the horizontal axis measures the total level of development A and the vertical axis measures new development D. The northeast and northwest quadrants show that each value for A determines a unique value for D. Therefore at A' there are D' units of new development and we are at point B on the arrowed development path. With the new development, then, total development increases to A'' and the differential decreases to Δ''. Smaller marginal benefits are now available, development activities in the next period decrease relative to D'', and we move to point C on the arrowed development path. This process continues until, in the limit, development reaches a steady state with no periodic increments at $\hat{A}$.

Figure 7.1 provides a basic framework for analysis. It remains to be seen how best use and current use taxation fit within this framework.

THE HIGHEST AND BEST USE TAX PROFILE. Any property tax decreases the after-tax property value. A neutral tax decreases the after-tax property value without altering resource use. In our case, any property tax decreases both the urban and rural land rents, $s(t)$ and p_2, and a neutral tax does it without altering the rural to urban land allocation.

There are two results, one having to do with long-run and one with short-run neutrality. There are two relevant questions. In the long run, after all resource adjustments and in whatever length of time, is land allocation different from what it would have been without the tax? This is a question of comparative statics. And, is land allocation different from what it would have been for any shorter period of time? This question has to do with the dynamic adjustment path of land allocation. The next paragraphs show the shifts in property valuation due to highest and best use property tax and argue that they are both long-run and short-run neutral.

Begin by assuming a tax rate of T and refer to Figure 7.2, which is a variation on the northeast quadrant of Figure 7.1. To the left of $\hat{A}$ both urban and rural land rents shift downward by Ts since urban is the highest use, or $s > p_2$. To the right of $\hat{A}$, both urban and rural land rents shift downward by p_2 since rural is the highest use, or $p_2 > s$.

Further reference to Figure 7.2 shows that the tax has no impact on development regardless of the amount of developed land, say A'. That is, there is no change in Δ', the rent differential. Therefore, there are no changes in either the arrowed development path or the equilibrium land allocation.[16] Therefore, both the long-run equilibrium at $\hat{A}$ and the time path to it, $A(t)$, are unchanged. Highest and best use taxes are both long-run and short-run neutral.

THE CURRENT USE TAX PROFILE. For the current use profile continue to assume a tax rate of T but refer now to Figure 7.3. The after-tax urban land rent shifts downward by Ts both to the left and to the right of $\hat{A}$, since current use taxation shows no preference for land's market value or opportunity rent. The after-tax rural land rent gradient shifts downward by Tp_2 for the same reason. At $\hat{A}$, both urban and rural land rent gradients shift by

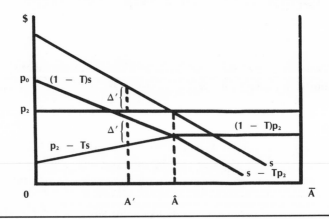

Figure 7.2. The market for land development under highest and best use taxation.

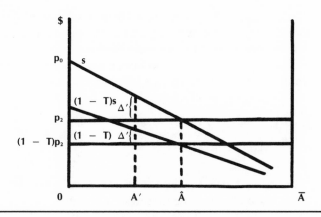

Figure 7.3. The market for land development under current use taxation.

the same amount ($Ts = Tp_2$). Therefore, $\hat{A}$ does not change as a function of the tax and current use taxation is long-run neutral.

Consider land allocation at A' a bit further. Current use taxation rotates the land rent differential $\Delta(t)$ downward to $(1 - T)\Delta(t)$. This lower after-tax marginal benefit for development reduces the rate of new development, thereby lengthening the time period necessary to achieve steady state equilibrium at $\hat{A}$. In conclusion, current use taxation is not short-run neutral. Rather, current use taxation has the desired dynamic bias against development.

These findings are only partially consistent with the desires and expectations of those who favor current use taxation. They are consistent in the short run to the extent that current use taxation decreases the rate of development but inconsistent in that it has no effect on the final urban–rural land use allocation. Any acre that was going to be developed will be developed — eventually. The remaining policy question is whether the delay in development is worth the foregone tax revenues plus the additional tax administration costs necessary to obtain it.

MEASUREMENT OF A WELFARE EFFECT. We have discussed the incidence but not the welfare effect of imposing current use taxation. Mills (1981) defines welfare for the static case as the sum of the areas under the two rent functions in the northeast quadrant of Figure 7.1 and evaluates the welfare effects of land taxes by measuring the differences they create in this area. We employ a dynamic analog of this measure in order to evaluate the intertemporal welfare effect of current use taxation.

Our dynamic measure calculates the present value of the area under the rent functions net of adjustment costs for a development period between some initial time 0 and a terminal time T. We assume that economic agents have static expectations and that they base their investments on the belief that the existing rent differential will not change in the next period.[17]

More formally, the dynamic measure of economic welfare is

$$W = \int_0^{t_1} \{ \int_0^{A(t)} (p_0{}^* - p_1{}^*)dg + [A - A(t)]p_2{}^* $$
$$- \int_0^{D(t)} \gamma g dg \} e^{-\rho t} dt \qquad (7.20)$$

where g is an operator, $*$ denotes the before tax parameter, and ϱ is the appropriate social discount rate. The first term in equation (7.20) describes the rents accruing to urban land use, the second term describes the rents accruing to agricultural and forestland use, and the final term explains the cost of urban land development. The relative efficiency of alternate land taxes can now be determined by calculating this measure of economic welfare under various empirical alternatives.

MEASURING IMPACTS OF CURRENT USE TAXATION

Forsyth County, North Carolina, is a 412 square mile area that surrounds its central city of Winston-Salem. There are three principal reasons why it is a good choice for displaying the incidence and welfare effects of current use taxation. First, the county is not completely urban. There is a sufficient mix of developed and undeveloped land to ensure an interior solution, that is, a solution in which some undeveloped land remains, or $A > \hat{A}$. Second, the review period, 1960–1970, was one of slow population growth, 0.7 percent per annum. This is evidence of relatively stable demand for land. Therefore, there is no need to complicate the analysis with exogenous growth considerations. Third, ten years of stable demand should be sufficient for the market to achieve a stable long-run equilibrium.

Forsyth County had 220 square miles of developed land in 1960. That is, $A(0) = 220$. The average annual return on undeveloped land p_2 was $98.90 per acre and the differential between undeveloped and marginal land $\Delta(0)$ was approximately 10 percent, although uncertainty about the precise differential leads us to vary it in the simulations that follow. Urban development claimed an additional 52 square miles by 1970, or $\hat{A} = 272$ (U.S. Department of Commerce 1977).

We can compute estimates of p_0 and p_1 from these measures together with equations (7.14) and (7.15) (and knowledge that $s(0) = p_0$). No information is available on the marginal cost of development but it can be calculated as a residual. That is, at $t_1 = 120$, terminal time in months,

$A(120)$ approximates $\hat{A}$ or 272 square miles. The estimate for γ of 36.387 derives from this information and equation (7.19). Uncertainty about the precise value of γ suggests the simulations that follow.

The next step is to calculate the land development time path under a best use tax. For expositional ease, we assume a best use tax without regular reassessment. Since best use taxation is completely neutral, the development path under best use taxation is identical with the development path in absence of any tax on land. To replicate this time path we apply the known parametric values to solve equation (7.19) for $A(t)$ once for each twelve-month interval over the ten-year (120 month) period 1960–1970. Table 7.4 shows the calculated land allocation profiles for various initial levels of the rent differential $\Delta(0)$.

Increasing the rent differential makes the urban rent gradient in the northeast quadrant of Figure 7.1 steeper (i.e., increases p_1). Furthermore, it expands the level of construction accompanying land development A and causes swifter convergence to the steady state level of development, where $A = 272$. Table 7.4 confirms these points. It also shows that the development paths differ less between higher initial rent differentials than between lower ones. That is, the land use profile associated with $\Delta(0) = 0.10$ is closer to that of $\Delta(0) = 0.15$ than to that of $\Delta(0) = 0.05$.

We repeat each development time path calculation using both one-half and double the value for the marginal cost of development in order to test for sensitivity to that variable. Table 7.5 compares with Table 7.4 for $\gamma = 18.193$. Table 7.6 compares with Table 7.4 for $\gamma = 72.774$.

Increasing the marginal development cost raises the cost function in the northwest quadrant of Figure 7.1. For a given rent differential, larger marginal development costs decrease construction and delay the convergence of development to $A = 272$. Tables 7.5 and 7.6 reveal that the effect of changing marginal costs is surprisingly small, however, and that

Table 7.4. Land development in square miles under best use tax, $\gamma = 36.387$

Month	$\Delta(0)$[a] $= 1\%$	5%	10%	15%
0	220	220	220	220
12	223.1583	233.9864	244.2108	251.6852
24	226.1248	244.2108	257.1493	264.0637
36	228.9111	251.6852	264.0637	268.8995
48	*231.5282*	*257.1493*	*267.7588*	*270.7887*
60	233.9864	261.1436	269.7335	271.5268
72	236.2952	264.0637	270.7887	271.8151
84	238.4638	266.1983	271.3527	271.9278
96	240.5007	267.7588	271.6541	271.9718
108	242.4139	268.8995	271.8151	271.9890
120	244.2108	269.7335	271.9012	271.9957

[a]Initial difference in the rate of return.

Table 7.5. Land development in square miles under best use tax, $\gamma = 18.1935$

Month	$\Delta(0)^a = 1\%$	5%	10%	15%
0	220	220	220	220
12	226.1248	244.2108	257.1493	264.0637
24	231.5282	257.1493	267.7588	270.7887
36	236.2952	264.0637	270.7887	271.8151
48	*240.5007*	*267.7588*	*271.6541*	*271.9718*
60	244.2108	269.7335	271.9012	271.9957
72	247.4840	270.7887	271.9718	271.9993
84	250.3716	271.3527	271.9919	271.9999
96	252.9191	271.6541	271.9977	272.0000
108	255.1665	271.8151	271.9993	272.0000
120	257.1493	271.9012	271.9998	272.0000

ᵃInitial difference in the rate of return.

Table 7.6. Land development in square miles under best use tax, $\gamma = 72.774$

Month	$\Delta(0)^a = 1\%$	5%	10%	15%
0	220	220	220	220
12	221.6039	227.5398	233.9864	239.4982
24	223.1583	233.9864	244.2108	251.6852
36	224.6648	239.4982	251.6852	259.3026
48	*226.1248*	*244.2108*	*257.1493*	*264.0637*
60	227.5398	248.2402	261.1436	267.0395
72	228.9111	251.6852	264.0637	268.8995
84	230.2402	254.6308	266.1983	270.0621
96	231.5282	257.1493	267.7588	270.7887
108	232.7765	259.3026	268.8995	271.2429
120	233.9864	261.1436	269.7335	271.5286

ᵃInitial difference in the rate of return.

the model is robust. Changing marginal development costs have little impact. Therefore, our subsequent discussion focuses on the intermediate value of 36.386 for this variable.

We might test the accuracy of our model by comparing the known intermediate and final developed land allocations, $A(48) = 243$ square miles and $A(120) = 272$ square miles, respectively, with the model's simulations for developed land allocation at these taxes. The final rows of Tables 7.4–7.6 show the mean absolute percentage error for these comparisons.[18] For Table 7.4, with an intermediate marginal cost of development, the mean absolute percentage error ranges from 6.6 percent to 14.9 percent with the lowest values where the initial rent differential is in a "reasonable" range of 5–10 percent. This implies confidence in the model's ability to replicate actual development.

This result is encouraging, although our primary purpose is not to provide extremely accurate simulations. Rather, our intent is to quantify the dynamic impact of nonneutral land taxes. The best use tax profile provided by the model is a benchmark for the analyses of incidence and welfare that follow.

INCIDENCE. The current use tax rate imposed in Forsyth County is 0.86 percent (North Carolina Department of Tax Research 1970). In order to measure the change in the development path in Forsyth County resulting from imposition of this preferential tax, we calculate the development paths for the same differential rent values used in Table 7.4 but in presence of this tax. Table 7.7 displays the results. It is apparent from a comparison of Table 7.7 with Table 7.4 that the predictions are accurate. Current use taxation retards development but does not alter long-run equilibrium. The magnitude of short-run changes in the development path is small, however, and in no period does current use taxation retard development by more than 1 square mile.

Tables 7.8 and 7.9 show land development paths under alternate current use tax rates. Table 7.8 halves the original rate to 0.43 percent and Table 7.9 doubles it to 1.73 percent. Not surprisingly, these tables show that higher current use tax rates retrard development more than lower current use tax rates. The impact of current use taxation remains quite small in all

Table 7.7. Land development in square miles under current use tax, equivalent tax rate (.86%)

Month	$\Delta(0)^a = 1\%$	5%	10%	15%
0	220	220	220	220
12	223.1353	233.8967	244.0795	251.5411
24	226.0815	244.0795	257.0086	263.9506
36	228.8502	251.5411	263.9506	268.8331
48	231.4518	257.0086	267.6780	270.7540
60	233.8967	261.0150	269.6794	271.5098
72	236.1941	263.9506	270.7540	271.8071
84	238.3530	266.1018	271.3310	271.9241
96	240.3817	267.6780	271.6408	271.9701
108	242.2881	268.8331	271.8071	271.9883
120	244.0795	269.6794	271.8964	271.9954

^{a}Initial difference in the rate of return.

Table 7.8. Land development in square miles under current use tax, high tax rate (1.73%)

Month	$\Delta(0)^a = 1\%$	5%	10%	15%
0	220	220	220	220
12	223.1096	233.7964	243.9323	251.3791
24	226.0332	243.9323	256.8501	263.8227
36	228.7820	251.3791	263.8227	268.7572
48	231.3665	256.8501	267.5862	270.7141
60	233.7964	260.8696	269.6176	271.4901
72	236.0809	263.8227	270.7141	271.7978
84	238.2289	265.9922	271.3059	271.9198
96	240.2484	267.5862	271.6253	271.9682
108	242.1471	268.7572	271.7978	271.9874
120	243.9323	269.6176	271.8908	271.9950

^{a}Initial difference in the rate of return.

Table 7.9. Land development in square miles under current use tax, low tax rate (.43%)

Month	$\Delta(0)^a = 1\%$	5%	10%	15%
0	220	220	220	220
12	223.1483	233.9474	244.1538	251.6226
24	226.1060	244.1538	257.0882	264.0147
36	228.8846	251.6226	264.0147	268.8708
48	231.4950	257.0882	267.7238	270.7737
60	233.9474	261.0878	269.7101	271.5195
72	236.2512	264.0147	270.7737	271.8117
84	238.4156	266.1565	271.3433	271.9262
96	240.4490	267.7238	271.6484	271.9711
108	242.3592	268.8708	271.8117	271.9887
120	244.1538	269.7101	271.8992	271.9956

a Initial difference in the rate of return.

cases, and it seems that substantially higher taxes are necessary before green space laws can have appreciable effects, even on short-run land allocation.

WELFARE. Turnbull and Boyd (1985) demonstrate that a tax on current land income may be more economically efficient than a uniform tax on anticipated income from the highest and best land use. Turnbull and Boyd begin with the assumption that investors and developers have static expectations, which means that they perceive the rent differential to be fixed over time. But we recall that urban development in one period reduces the rent differential in the next period. Therefore, investors with static expectations overestimate their future earnings and excessively employ all resources, including land, used by the development sector. In this event, a slower rate of development leads to a greater level of aggregate economic welfare. A tax on current use can bring about the required slower development.

The empirical results of Table 7.10 confirm this theoretical observation. The aggregate level of welfare W associated with a tax on highest and best use is, indeed, lower than that of an equivalent tax on current land income. Further, and as expected, the level of welfare increases as the current use tax rate increases and as the rate of development decreases. For example, for the case in which the rent differential $\Delta(0) = 0.10$ and the

Table 7.10. Welfare index values (in 1970 dollars)

Tax	$\Delta(0) = 1\%$	5%	10%	15%
Best use	6,145,834	5,652,090	5,075,741	4,521,562
Low rate income	6,146,141	5,653,576	5,078,705	4,526,044
Equivalent rate income	6,146,540	5,655,505	5,082,550	4,531,859
High rate income	6,147,328	5,659,310	5,090,143	4,543,336

Note: These figures are for the intermediate $\gamma = 36.387$. Values for high and low γ exhibit identical patterns.

marginal development cost $\gamma = 36.387$, the economic welfare associated with a best use tax is $6809 less than the welfare for Forsyth County associated with an equivalent tax on current use. This welfare loss increases substantially with increases in the rent differential and it increases slightly with decreases in the marginal development cost. Nevertheless, nowhere do the gains of switching from a best use tax to an equivalent current use tax exceed $13,000 or about $.05 per acre.

FINAL OBSERVATIONS

Conceptual arguments and simulations for Forsyth County, North Carolina, both indicate that current use taxation retards growth in the short run while leaving the final allocation between urban and rural land uses unchanged. Both the conceptual arguments and the simluations also show that there may be gains in economic welfare from using current use taxation in preference to highest and best use land taxation. These welfare gains are due to the assumption of static expectations on the part of investors and developers. Both Mills (1978) and Turnbull and Boyd (1985) point out that the welfare gains disappear entirely under the alternate assumption of rational expectations. With rational expectations, economic agents foresee the impact of their actions on the rent differential. This prevents overinvestment in development and nullifies any efficiency gains from current use taxation.

In conclusion, current use taxation has the impact its proponents desire, but in such small measure as to be inconsequential. Taken as a whole, our results indicate that current use taxation causes relatively small changes in the rate of land development and, at best, yields insignificant gains in welfare. Even a shift to the largest current use tax fails to alter these conclusions in a meaningful way. (Perhaps this recommends preference for alternatives to taxes, such as zoning in order to preserve green space.)

General Forest Taxation Conclusions and Further Implications

There are three general conclusions to draw from our observations of forest taxation. The first two pertain to the capital gains provision of the income tax and to current use taxation of forestland, the two specific taxes that we used as examples.

Favorable capital gains treatment of timber (under the law prior to 1987) yields a welfare loss to the economy as a whole (but welfare gains to owners of timber harvest rights) in the range of $240.9 to $368.2 million annually nationwide. The precise impact for the new law will depend on the true income elasticity of demand for stumpage, degree of market power in the industry, and the impact of related taxes. Under any assumptions about these industry characteristics, the impact of capital gains treatment is enormous. Furthermore, capital appropriates more than 100 percent of the subsidy.

Elimination of some capital gains treatment, like that accruing to private harvesters of public timber, is both justifiable and socially desirable. Complete elimination is more problematic, however, as it requires arguing for either elimination of capital gains for all industries or else unequal treatment of timber with respect to other competitive resource-based industries, which would continue to receive favorable capital gains treatment after this advantage were removed from timber. Clearly, this final point begs a three sector general equilibrium analysis in which those industries that compete with timber and also receive favorable capital gains treatment of their resource compose the third sector. Such an analysis could test for the magnitude of timber losses due to discriminatory removal of capital gains only from timber and not from its competitors.

Current use taxation is quite a different case from capital gains. The current use tax is a particular version of the property tax, one designed to retard economic growth and to maintain green space, particularly in urban and near-urban areas where large externalities may be associated with green space. Our observations indicate that current use taxation has the desired impacts but to such small and impermanent extent as to be meaningless. It is hard to imagine that the gains from current use taxation in Forsyth County outweigh the additional administrative costs they must impose. It is easy to understand why few landowners have taken advantage of current use taxation. Our observations are so extreme as to suggest confidence in extrapolating them to other areas in the United States where there are current use taxes.

Finally, the previous literature on forest taxation features partial equilibrium analyses and measures of the incidence of various land taxes on timber rotation lengths. A considerable amount remains to be learned from general equilibrium analysis of empirical cases designed to measure the welfare effects of the various taxes affecting forestry. This same approach can add further to our knowledge of the incidence of forest taxes on productive factors other than time and timber itself. Our analyses of capital gains and current use taxation demonstrate this approach.

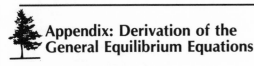

Appendix: Derivation of the General Equilibrium Equations

Total differentiation of equation (7.2) from the text yields

$$\hat{p}_X = \frac{w(\delta C_X/\delta_w)\hat{w}}{C_X} + \frac{r(\delta C_X/\delta_r)\hat{r}}{C_X} \qquad (7A.1a)$$

and

$$\hat{p}_Y = \frac{w(\delta C_Y/\delta_w)\hat{w}}{C_Y} + \frac{r(C_Y/\delta_r)\hat{r}}{C_Y} \qquad (7A.1b)$$

Defining factor shares as

$$\theta_{Li} = \frac{w(\delta C_i/\delta_w)}{C_i} \quad \text{and} \quad \theta_{Ki} = \frac{r(\delta C_i/\delta_r)}{C_i}$$

and subtracting equations (7A.1b) from (7A.1a) yields equations (7.3) and (7.3a) in the text.

Relating the changes in capital and labor use to relative factor prices, factor shares and substitution yields

$$\delta C_X/\delta w = -\theta_{KX}\sigma_X(\hat{w} - \hat{r}) \qquad (7A.2a)$$
$$\delta C_Y/\delta w = -\theta_{KX}\sigma_X(\hat{w} - \hat{r}) \qquad (7A.2b)$$
$$C_X/r = \theta_{LX}\sigma_X(\hat{w} - \hat{r}) \qquad (7A.2c)$$

and

$$C_Y/r = \theta_{LY}\sigma_Y(\hat{w} - \hat{r}) \qquad (7A.2d)$$

The constant returns to scale production function assures that factors are used such that

$$(\delta C_X/\delta_w)X + (\delta C_Y/\delta_w)Y = L \qquad (7A.3a)$$
$$(\delta C_X/\delta r)X + (\delta C_Y/\delta r)Y = K \qquad (7A.3b)$$

Differentiating equations (7A.3a) and (7A.3b), and inserting equations (7A.2a)–(7A.2d) provides

$$\tau_{LX}\hat{X} + \tau_{LY}\hat{Y} = (\hat{w} - \hat{r})(\tau_{LX}\theta_{KK}\sigma_X + \tau_{LY}\theta_{KY}\sigma_Y) \qquad (7A.4a)$$
$$\tau_{KX}\hat{X} + \tau_{KY}\hat{Y} = -(\hat{w} - \hat{r})(\tau_{KX}\theta_{LX}\sigma_X + \tau_{KY}\theta_{LY}\sigma_Y) \qquad (7A.4b)$$

Finally, subtracting equation (7A.4b) from (7A.4a) yields equation (7.7) in the text.

Notes

1. Incidence has to do with whom or what bears the burden or appreciates the gain from the tax relief in question. It is comparable to the distributive question in other chapters.

2. Boyd (1986) reviews the literature. He provides numerical examples and extensive citations.

3. Our findings may even be generalizable beyond U.S. borders. While writing this chapter, we came upon the same issue in the lead editorial of the *Sunday Statesman* (16 June 1985) in Delhi, India.

4. Sunley (1972) also elaborates on a number of administrative problems of capital gains taxation of timber.

5. That is, there is a positive income effect but it is undoubtedly dominated by a negative substitution effect. In the unusual empirical study on forest taxation, Chang (1983) finds little evidence that preferential capital gains taxation influences net reforestation among nonindustrial private forest landowners.

6. There is some speculation that small landowners may not report the income from timber sales. When they do report this income, there are some cases where neither they nor the consulting foresters who advise them may be aware of the capital gains provision. In neither case does the capital gains provision yield benefits to these small landowners. (We owe these points to J. Royer and J. Stier.)

7. The parameter θi_* defines the determinant $\begin{vmatrix} \theta_{LX} & \theta_{KX} \\ \theta_{LY} & \theta_{KY} \end{vmatrix}$

which expands as $\theta_{LX}(1 - \theta_{LY}) - \theta_{LY}(1 - \theta_{LX}) = \theta_{LX} - \theta_{LY}$.

8. $\epsilon_{ij} = -\epsilon_{ij}$ since the compensated demands are homogeneous of degree 0 in prices.

9. The cost of capital in sector X changes from r to rT_{KX}, where T_{KX} is defined as 1 plus the tax rate. We confine our attention to the infinitesimal tax. Therefore, all differentials (i.e., T_{KX}) are evaluated at an initial rate where $T_{KX} = 1$.

10. See Magee (1971) for evidence of this effect.

11. See Fairchild (1935), Manning and Thompson (1969), and Klemperer (1977) for evidence of time bias in the property tax. See Stier and Chang (1983) for evidence of the incidence of the property tax on timber.

12. Dunford (1980) provides a description of actual green space laws. Savage (1977) outlines the concerns that led to such laws.

13. This analysis ignores externalities and addresses only market inefficiencies. If aesthetic externalities are important, then the price of rural land should be adjusted accordingly.

14. See, for example, Bentick (1979) and Mills (1981).

15. Turnbull and Boyd (1985) derive this development cost from the underlying technology.

16. This finding holds both to the left and to the right of A' because, recalling equation (7.15), d is the difference (positive or negative) between s and p_2. This difference is everywhere identical with the difference between $(1 - T)s$ and $p_2 - Ts$ (to the left of A) or $1 - Tp_2$ (to the right of A).

17. These assumptions are consistent with previous literature. See, for example, Mieszkowski (1972) and Oates (1969).

18. The mean absolute error is defined as $\dfrac{1}{N} \sum\limits_{i=1}^{N} \left| \dfrac{Y_i^b - Y_i^a}{Y_i^a} \right|$

where N is the number of observations, Y_i^b is the simulated value, and Y_i^a is the actual value.

References

Ballentine, J. G., and I. Eris. 1975. On the general equilibrium analysis of tax incidence. *Journal of Political Economy* 83:633–40.

Bentick, B. L. 1979. The impact of taxation and valuation practices on the timing and efficiency of land use. *Journal of Political Economy* 87(4):859–69.

Boskin, M. J. 1975. Efficiency aspects of the differential tax treatment of market and household economic activity. *Journal of Public Economics* 4:1–25.

Boyd, R. G. 1986. *Forest taxation: Current issues and future research.* Report to the Southeastern Forest Experiment Station. Research Triangle Park, N.C.: USDA Forest Service.

Brittain, J. A. 1972. *The payroll tax for Social Security.* Washington, D.C.: The Brookings Institution.

Chang, S. J. 1983. Reforestation by nonindustrial private landowners: Does the capital gains tax matter? In *Nonindustrial private forests: A review of economic and policy studies,* ed. J. P. Royer and C. D. Risbrudt. Durham, N.C.: Duke University School of Forestry and Environmental Studies.

Clawson, M. 1979. *The economics of U.S. private nonindustrial forests.* Resources for the Future Working Paper R-14. Washington, D.C.: Resources for the Future.

Daniels, B. J., S. E. Daniels, and W. F. Hyde. 1985. *Capital–Labor Substitution in Timber Growing.* SCFER Working Paper No. 13. Research Triangle Park, N.C.: USDA Forest Service Southeastern Forest Experiment Station.

Dunford, R. W. 1980. A survey of property tax relief programs for the retention of agricultural and open space lands. *Gonzaga Law Review* 15(3):675–99.

Fairchild, F. R., and Associates. 1935. *Forest taxation in the United States.* USDA Miscellaneous Publication No. 218. Washington, D.C.: U.S. Government Printing Office.

Gaffney, M. 1979. *Taxation on yield, property, income, and site. Effects on forest resources and management.* Department of Economics Working Paper No. 39. Riverside: University of California.

Harberger, A. C. 1962. The incidence of the corporate income tax. *Journal of Political Economy* 70:215–40.

_____. 1966. Efficiency effects of taxes on income from capital. In *Effects of corporation income tax.* Detroit, Mich.: Wayne State University Press.

Klein, L. 1974. Issues in econometric studies of investment behavior. *Journal of Law and Economics* 13:43–49.

Klemperer, W. D. 1977. An economic analysis of the case against ad valorem property taxation in forestry—a comment. *National Tax Journal* 30:469.

_____. 1982. An analysis of selected property tax exemptions for timber. *Land Economics* 58:293–309.

Magee, S. P. 1971. Factor market distortions, production, distribution and the pure theory of international trade. *Quarterly Journal of Economics* 85:625–43.

Manning, G. H., and Thompson, E. F. 1969. Forest property taxation: Another look. *Journal of Forestry* 67:556–59.

Mieszkowski, P. M. 1967. On the theory of tax incidence. *Journal of Political Economy* 75:250–62.

_____. 1972. The property tax: An excise tax or profits tax? *Journal of Public Economics* 1:73–96.

Mills, D. E. 1978. Competition and the residential land allocation process. *Quarterly Journal of Economics* 92(2).

_____. 1981. The non-neutrality of land value taxation. *National Tax Journal* 34:125–30.

North Carolina Department of Tax Research. 1970. *Statistics of taxation.* Raleigh: Author.

Oates, W. E. 1969. The effects of property taxes and local public spending on property values: An empirical study of tax capitalization and the Tiebout hypothesis. *Journal of Political Economy* 77(6):957–71.

Parashevopoulos, C. C. 1979. Alternative estimates of the elasticity of substitution. *Review of Economics and Statistics* 61:439–42.

Pease, D. J., and B. L. Dorgan. 1984. *Study of 1983 effective tax rates of selected large U.S. corporations.* Washington, D.C.: U.S. Government Printing Office.

Royer, J. P. 1981. *North Carolina forest landowner survey.* Report to the Forest Service Southeastern Forest Experiment Station. Research Triangle Park, N.C.: USDA Forest Service.

Russakoff, D. 1985. Timber industry is rooted in tax breaks. *Washington Post* (24 March 1985), Section A.

Savage, H. 1977. Forest taxation: The power to destroy. *American Forests* 83(1):16–19.

Shoven, J. B. 1976. The incidence and efficiency limits on taxes on income and capital. *Journal of Political Economy* 84:1261–84.

Stier, J. C. 1980. Estimating the production technology in the U.S. forest products industries. *Forest Science* 26:471–82.

Stier, J. S., and S. J. Chang. 1983. Land use implications of the ad valorem property tax: The role of tax incidence. *Forest Science* 24:702–12.

Sunley, E. J. 1972. The federal tax subsidy of the timber industry. In *The economics of federal subsidy programs.* Washington, D.C.: U.S. Government Printing Office.

Turnbull, G. K., and R. G. Boyd. 1985. *Dynamic adjustment to land taxation policy: Neutrality and welfare implications.* SCFER Working Paper No. 11. Research Triangle Park, N.C.: Southeastern Center for Forest Economics Research.

U.S. Council of Economic Advisors. 1980. *Economic report of the President.* Washington, D.C.: U.S. Government Printing Office.

U.S. Department of Commerce, Bureau of the Census. 1977. *City and county data book, 1977.* Washington, D.C.: U.S. Government Printing Office.

_____. 1980. *Statistical abstract of the United States 1979.* Washington, D.C.: U.S. Government Printing Office.

U.S. Department of the Treasury, Internal Revenue Service. 1980. *1979 statistics of income.* Washington, D.C.: U.S. Government Printing Office.

U.S. General Accounting Office. 1981. *New means of analysis required for policy decisions affecting private forestry sector.* Report to the Congress by the Comptroller General EMD-81-18. Washington, D.C.

von Thunen, J. H. 1826. *Isolated state.* English edition ed. by Peter Hall, 1966. London: Pergamon Press.

CHAPTER 8

Public Ownership of Forestlands

Our greater focus in this book is on private lands, but we cannot ignore public ownership. Public ownership is a market intervention, and an important one when we consider that public agencies manage 482.5 million acres or 28 percent of the commercial forestland in the United States (USDA 1982, 349). There are well-established justifications for public ownership, both in concept and in practice. The conceptual argument is that a price responsive market alone cannot provide for public goods and external values in accordance with their social valuation. In practice, we know that recreation and water, for example, are important social outputs of our forests. Often they are produced on land with no higher productive value, yet often they are produced either jointly or in competition with market valued goods like timber. In neither case do recreation or water quality trade regularly in a fully responsive market. Therefore, regulation, perhaps including public ownership of their source, is necessary for their provision at a level corresponding to their social valuation.

Our concern is less with the justification for public ownership than with its impact. Therefore, our questions in this chapter have to do with whether regulations restricting the responses of public land managers to market signals have positive or negative impacts on social welfare. Furthermore, do these regulations improve distributive justice?

As we cannot examine all private regulations, similarly we cannot examine all restrictions on public land managers. We might consider as illustrative, however, the management of four goods or services provided on or by public lands. The first, timber, is a good that the market values accurately, but one whose output is severely constrained by the various regulations on public managers. There may be considerable efficiency gains to relaxing these constraints. Relaxing these constraints, however, may create sharp distributive impacts on the many small rural communities with tim-

217

ber-based economies. The U.S. Forest Service, manager of one-fifth of the commercial forestland and one-third of the standing timber in the United States, is keenly aware of these potential distributive impacts. Its intention to satisfy the distributive objective of providing long-term community integrity by guaranteeing a constant volume flow of timber is the second public land management restriction that we examine in this chapter.

The public lands also provide a multiple of nonmarket valued goods and services. Indeed, their very reason for existence, both originally and today, is the contention that nonmarket valued goods and services are too important to ignore. Perhaps the most obvious of these today is recreation. The difficulty of excluding recreational users from most forestland makes public goods of many forms of recreation. Nevertheless, it does not remove all market and market proxy data from the knowledge of forest managers. Our third case uses such data to consider the efficiency gains and allocative differences if the U.S. Forest Service campgrounds, in one illustrative valley in western Montana, were managed in accordance with efficiency criteria — given the data and managerial skills currently available. Our efficiency approach is generalizable to other forms of recreation, other public agencies, and other locations. Therefore, our results for this western Montana valley also have generalizable implications. Our discussion features the supply derivation because supply is an essentially unexamined topic in the recreation literature.

Finally, the public lands provide important nonmarket, nonuser specific services. Watershed management and wildlife protection are examples. Endangered species protection is another example and one with a particularly high policy profile. Our fourth case considers what information even an incomplete economic analysis can lend to good decision making in one specific endangered species case, the management of the red cockaded woodpecker in the pinelands of the Croatan National Forest in North Carolina. This case does not provide definitive solutions to what is a very difficult problem. It does suggest, however, a general approach that displays the least-cost method for satisfying a regulatory constraint on, and thereby clarifies some management options for, the woodpecker case and any endangered species management program. Used properly, this approach can help to improve the quality of policy discourse regarding tradeoffs between endangered species management and production of other highly valued outputs of the forest.

The remainder of the chapter examines each of the four examples in turn, then concludes with a summary statement regarding efficiency criteria and public land management.

Public Timber Management

Our discussion of the marketing of the public timber resource begins with a review of the current U.S. Forest Service harvest decision criteria. These criteria are similar to those for the Bureau of Land Management, the Bureau of Indian Affairs, and many state agencies including the Washington State Department of Natural Resources, the largest state forest management agency. These criteria cause substantial variation from market efficiency results for timber management. The second part of this section considers one method for measuring these variations. Finally, a third part discusses the results of our measurement in both efficiency and distributive terms.

The public agencies, both federal and state, produce 22 percent of the annual softwood harvests in the United States. The national forests produce 15 percent of these harvests themselves (USDA 1982, 424). (The national forest share of total public production provides justification, in addition to the justification provided by the similarity between the U.S. Forest Service and other public agency harvest decision criteria, for building our analysis on a foundation of Forest Service timber management planning.) On a regional basis, the public sector share of the total softwood production ranges from 66 percent in the Rocky Mountains to 6 percent in the Northeast. Therefore, we might anticipate that the regional impact of public management can range from substantial to inconsequential.

The decision regarding the annual timber volume offered for sale by the U.S. Forest Service originates from the ten-year plan for each of the 154 individual national forests. A constrained volume maximization rule determines planned harvests. Its objective is sawtimber volume maximization over time given the current timber stand ages, volumes and anticipated growth. The Forest Service constrains the solution volume such that planned harvests in future decades never fall below those of the current decade although (planned) annual harvests may fluctuate within the range of plus or minus 10 percent from one-tenth of the ten-year total. Neither production costs nor market prices play a role in this harvest calculation. (Adams and Haynes [1981] address the absence of market *price*, but not the absence of *production costs*.) Clearly, we anticipate Forest Service results quite different from those determined by market efficiency.

ANALYTICAL APPROACH

The economics literature generally models public agency timber supply as fixed at the predetermined planned level. This is not wholly consistent with reality but it is consistent with the Forest Service objective to produce a constant timber volume regardless of market conditions. An assumption of fixed supply departs from reality in that the offered volume is not always either bid upon or sold and that, even if the offered volume is sold, the logger with the winning bid may delay the harvest operation up to five years while waiting for better market conditions. Nevertheless, our analysis is concerned as much with the advisability of pursuing the Forest Service objective as with its previous success. Therefore, we remain consistent with the majority of the literature and take public agency production as fixed and invariant with the market. We inquire how public agency success at meeting the fixed timber harvest volume objective varies from social efficiency.

Our procedure begins with the choice of 1977 as the year for comparative market analysis. The year 1977 is the most recent year for which we can be confident of the coincidence of our data with the needs of our analytical model. We examine supply and demand for softwood sawtimber under current harvest decision criteria and contrast our results with those occurring under a simulated alternative scenario where the public sector follows market decision criteria. We are interested in the contrasting market clearing prices, the public and private sector harvest levels and relative producer surpluses, and a measure of contrasting consumer welfare. Regional knowledge of contrasting market equilibria permits regional as well as national estimates of these differential consumer and public and private producer impacts.

We must emphasize that this approach yields results that are one-time (1977) effects only. They suggest, but only suggest, directions of change for longer-term effects. A true longer-run analysis would require dynamic linkages of both the demand and supply models through time as well as investment and inventory feedbacks from one year to subsequent year supplies.

Our empirical measures rely heavily on the macroeconomic timber modelling of Adams and Haynes (1981) as revised (1985). The Adams-Haynes (AH) model is the best known econometric model of the forestry sector and the only model in the public domain. It is the model that the U.S. Forest Service uses for its projections of the aggregate timber economy. Adams and Haynes provide softwood stumpage supply functions for eight regions and two private sectors, the forest industry (FI) and other private (OP) forest landowners. Our assessment of the impact of current public timber management policies follows the AH model in initially taking public supply as fixed at the observed 1977 level.

Our estimate of total public timber management and harvest costs equals the sum of the 1977 Forest Service timber management budget, the K-V (reforestation) budget, and one-half the road and trail budget plus 10 percent overhead. This sum is adjusted upward proportionally for the non-

Forest Service share of 1977 public harvests. The final cost estimate is conservative to the extent that other Forest Service activities are inputs to timber management (e.g., fire control, insect and disease protection, some research). It also is conservative to the extent that the Forest Service budget is largely an input to anticipated harvests many years in the future, yet we compare this current budget with current, not anticipated future, receipts. If expenditures and receipts remain constant over time, then this is equivalent to assuming a zero discount rate.[1]

Adams and Haynes derive stumpage demand for all but two regions from the demand for lumber and wood products and incorporate into their model a sophisticated understanding of opportunities for interregional flows of various intermediate products. Stumpage demand from the Northeast and North Central regions is small and the AH model treats it as a constant.[2] We disregard these two regions in our analysis because their public harvest share is insignificant at our level of detail.

Equilibrating the Adams-Haynes–derived demand functions from the remaining six regions with their private sector supply functions and the exogenously fixed public harvests provides a basis for reasonable estimates for the producer and consumer welfare arising from current public timber management practice. Table 8.1 summarizes the functions underlying these calculations. All functions are of linear form. AH chooses between two basic specifications for the supply functions. Their criterion is best statistical fit. Table 8.1 continues the AH pattern of reference to stumpage prices in 1967 dollars per Mbf and output in MMcf. (This means that all final observations occurring in value terms must be inflated to 1977 dollars using the same producer price index that Adams and Haynes use.)

The preceding paragraphs explain our base case estimates of actual 1977 public prices, costs and harvest levels. We turn now to our simulation of a market sensitive public supply. Deriving public supply functions for each region is a difficult problem and our first generation effort is admittedly ad hoc. We are looking for supply functions that reflect the costs of growing and harvesting timber. The AH private sector functions do this. This suggests beginning with the AH direct supply functions (from Table 8.1) and transforming them into indirect functions that display price intercepts and price (cost) responses to harvest and inventory levels. The new problem is to modify these functions until their intercepts and the coefficients on their response terms resemble those of cost sensitive public functions. We consider adjustments for the intercept and coefficients in turn.

The scant evidence available suggests a public equilibrium price at a level perhaps $20 per Mbf (1977) in excess of private stumpage prices. This may be due to greater public timber production costs, including the costs of managing a large bureaucracy, not replicated in smaller private operations. It may also be due to multiple use constraints or even to something else that

Table 8.1. Base case: stumpage demand and supply

Derived demand equations: $Q = Q_d(P)$

Region	Intercept	Price (1967$/Mbf)
Southeast	912.8	−1.5466
South Central	1554.1	−3.0857
Rocky Mountains	864.2	−0.1426
Pacific Southwest	798.0	−2.5127
Pacific Northwest-West	2795.6	−4.5153
Pacific Northwest-East	561.5	−1.7226

Supply equations: private sector $Q = Q_s(P,I)$, $Q/I = Q_s(P)$
public sector $Q = \bar{Q}_s$, $Q/I = \bar{Q}_s$

Region Landowner	Dependent variable	Intercept	Price (1967$/Mbf)	Inventory (MMcf)	Trend (1/t)
Southeast					
FI	Q	−434.517	4.03927	.049082	
OP	Q	273.313	2.96201	.002691	
Public	Harvests = 57.79 MMcf	Costs = $11,697,237			
South Central					
FI	Q	−434.517	4.03927	.0949082	
OP	Q	273.313	2.96201	.006329	
Public	Harvests = 127.93 MMcf	Costs = $17,335,861			
Rocky Mountains					
FI & OP	Q/I	.0093917	.0003513		
Public	Harvests = 546.92 MMcf	Costs = $54,192,925			
Pacific Southwest					
FI	Q/I	.0252454	.0004464		
OP	Q	−1863.03	.732612	.108447	69250.9
Public	Harvests = 369.37 MMcf	Costs = $27,566,929			
Pacific Northwest-West					
FI	Q/I	.024569	.0006436		
OP	Q/I	−.0081291	.0007948		
Public	Harvests = 1032.17 MMcf	Costs = $56,695,406			
Pacific Northwest-East					
FI	Q/I	.0252322	.0000775		
OP	Q/I	−.0007838	.000287		
Public	Harvests = 370.01 MMcf	Costs = $23,496,576			

FI = Forest industry
OP = Other private
Q = Quantity harvested (MMcf)

we cannot anticipate. For whatever reason, a price differential apparently exists. The level of the public supply function, therefore the price intercept, must be adjusted accordingly.[3]

The public sector response to harvest quantity changes might reasonably mimic marginal production costs for the more similar of the two private sectors. For this reason, we identify the private sector in each region that most closely resembles that region's public sector in land quality and market share and choose the AH specification of its supply function for the underlying function from which we make (intercept and coefficient) adjustments in order to obtain a public supply function. This AH function for each region provides the coefficient of price response to harvest changes.

Finding an appropriate public inventory coefficient is a more complex problem. Inventory is exogenous in the AH supply functions although potentially harvestable timber is actually a function of market price. This point is less important for the stable market conditions that Adams and Haynes model, but it becomes very important if that market suddenly is destabilized. Throwing a large public inventory on the market creates just such a destabilizing effect — and we will see that throwing a large public inventory on the market is just what demand-sensitive public harvest criteria recommend. Therefore, our simulation must make two inventory adjustments, one to reflect the expected relative differences between the public sector and the mimic-private sector with respect to both inventory per acre and inventory quality and the other to modify the measure of public inventory itself to reflect price.

The first adjustment in the inventory coefficient reflects the relative differences between public and mimic-private sector inventory per acre and inventory quality. Harvest costs per unit of volume decrease in response to improvements in each of these. Per acre inventory data are readily available from Forest Survey (USDA 1978). Site-class midpoints are our indicators of inventory quality. Our argument is that site class is a measure of biological quality and, in general, lands of poorer biological quality may be managed less well and harvested less frequently. Therefore, a larger share of their standing timber may be decaying, inadequately spaced, etc., all of which creates poorer quality. The full adjustment multiplies the relevant region's FI or OP inventory coefficient by:

$$\frac{\text{public inv./acre}}{\text{FI-OP inv./acre}} \times \frac{\text{quality adj. pub. inv.}}{\text{quality adj. FI-OP inv.}}$$

The final adjustment converts inventory from a purely physical measure into a term with economic meaning. Marginal stands (and marginal forestlands) now (implicitly) enter the inventory when stumpage prices increase and depart when stumpage prices decrease. Even if the

Forest Survey measure of inventory does not reflect this adjustment, the bidding of those loggers who compete for public timber sales does. We assume that physical and economic inventories are in balance for the 1977 base year under current management. There is a direct relation between economic inventory and price. Therefore, the greater the difference between simulated and actual equilibrium prices, the greater the difference in economic inventories. Following this reasoning, our final adjustment multiplies 1977 Forest Survey inventory for public lands by the ratio of the eventual simulated equilibrium price to the actual 1977 AH equilibrium price.

Our new simulated public supply functions must be transformed back to direct supply functions in order to bear comparison with the AH functions. Table 8.2 shows these simulated market responsive public supply functions and the new regional AH-derived demand functions appearing in response to them.[4] Equilibrating the supply and demand functions and contrasting the results with those that we obtain for the base case permits one estimate of the first year welfare effects arising from market responsive public softwood timber supplies. The nature of the derivation of our simulated public supplies causes us to feel more confident of the direction of changes in welfare effects than in the absolute levels of these effects. Nevertheless, we show welfare effects as indicative of the magnitude of importance of this policy issue.

Table 8.2. Fully market responsive stumpage demand and supply

Derived demand equations: $Q = Q_d (P)$

Region	Intercept	Price (1967$/Mbf)
Southeast	904.8	−1.5466
South Central	1529.1	−3.0857
Rocky Mountains	903.6	−2.7106
Pacific Southwest	768.9	−2.5127
Pacific Northwest-West	2752.9	−4.5153
Pacific Northwest-East	551.2	−1.7226

Supply: FI and OP equations unchanged from base case.

Region	Public supply equations Equation
Southeast	$Q = 273.313 + (P - 10.299)(2.96201 + .0000073I)$
South Central	$Q = 273.313 + (P - 10.299)(2.96201 + .00258I)$
Rocky Mountains	$Q/[I(P - 10.299)/26.09] = .00349 + .00021P$
Pacific Southwest	$Q/[I(P - 10.299)/20.45] = .01968 + .00042P$
Pacific Northwest-West	$Q/[I(P - 10.299)/20.74] = .03107 + .00111P$
Pacific Northwest-East	$Q/[I(P - 10.299)/19.94] = .0350 + .000111P$

RESULTS

Tables 8.3 and 8.4 show our estimates for the 1977 price and quantity changes and the consumers' and producers' surplus changes due to introducing market sensitive public timber harvest criteria.

Our results are conjectural — and heavily dependent on both the inventory term and the decrease in public production costs associated with the introduction of the new public supply mimic from private supply. We anticipate no debate over the direction or order of effects for our public inventory and production cost terms. Therefore, we anticipate that the price, quantity, and surplus measures in Tables 8.3 and 8.4 also are of correct sign and approximate magnitude.

Our greatest confidence is in the results for the four western regions, where the public presence is the greatest and where Adams and Haynes have the greatest confidence in their own model. The public producers' surpluses for the Pacific Southwest and the Pacific Northwest-East are ambiguous. (That is, public supply in these regions is highly price inelastic. The inelasticities prevent the model from finding a stable solution within a small number of iterations.) Both the directions and rank orders of all

Table 8.3. Differences between 1977 actual and simulated market clearing quantities and prices

| | Harvest levels | | | | Stumpage price (1977$/Mbf) actual–simulated |
| | % Changes by ownership | | | Total (in MMcf) actual–simulated | |
Region	FI	OP	Public		
SE	−17	−5	+425	837.07–1016.73	95.06–76.75
SC	−7	−5	+183	1387.40–1541.10	104.89–83.54
RM	+25[a]	−[a]	−19	861.94–832.93	30.41–50.67
PSW	−4	−14	+8	711.65–717.53	66.71–39.71
PNW-W	−34	−74	+70	2565.33–2651.30	99.04–40.28
PNW-E	−3	−35	+6	511.01–516.89	56.96–38.72

[a]FI and OP combined in Rocky Mountain region.

Table 8.4. Efficiency and distributive gains from fully market responsive timber harvest criteria (in millions of 1977$)

| | Consumers' surplus | Producers' surpluses | | |
Region		FI	OP	Public
SE	40.2	−21.4	−57.5	179.8
SC	45.3	−74.2	−76.5	128.2
RM	−30.9	45.8[a]	−[a]	41.0
PSW	20.6	−69.5	−11.9	−
PNW-W	689.8	−398.3	−68.6	996.8
PNW-E	21.8	−12.2	−3.3	−
Total	786.8	−592.8	−217.8	

[a]FI and OP combined in Rocky Mountain region.

other changes conform with expectations based on the size of existing public inventories and their accessibility.

Reference to Table 8.3 shows that the most notable shifts are (1) the southern increases in public sector harvests and (2) the western increases in public sector harvests and relatively comparable decreases in combined forest industry and other private harvests. Current large public inventories (per acre) and very long public rotations probably explain the opportunity for public sector harvest increases in the South. (The forest products industry does not argue for expanded public harvests in the South, as it does in the West, because the southern industry is more dependent on its own land, and expanding public harvests would depress private values.)

The Rocky Mountains are an exception to the second notable shift. The only truly substantial western shift, however, is the very large public harvest increase (and corresponding forest industry decrease) in the Douglas-fir region (PNW-W). There are stumpage price decreases in all western regions except the Rocky Mountains. The signs and the orders of magnitude for these quantity and stumpage price shifts fit our impression of the consensus intuition of policy analysts working in these three regions.

The Rocky Mountain region displays the opposite price and quantity effects. Public harvests decrease substantially, private harvests increase sharply but not enough to offset the public decrease, and the regional stumpage price increases sharply. Table 8.4 shows net welfare gains for both private and public producers. Private producers gain from both price and harvest increases. Public producers gain by decreasing ineffective production activities. The direction of these Rocky Mountain effects satisfies our impression of consensus intuition for all but that share of the local forest products industry dependent on public timber as a resource input. We personally anticipate that a more careful analysis would suggest even more substantial public harvest decreases in this region.

The U.S. aggregate (public and private) 1977 harvest shift is not large, only a 5.8 percent increase, but the regional price adjustments are meaningful. The price adjustments in each region are greater than we expect within a normal year. They are not as great, however, as the adjustments we observe in the most recent ten years (a turbulent time for the industry) and they are not as great as observed price variations within regions but across quality, species, access, and ownership classes at any moment in time.

The general price decrease across the aggregate of all regions suggests that consumers obtain the greatest gains from a public agency shift to market-sensitive harvest criteria. Price decreases should also cause some counterpart losses by producers, losses that would be further emphasized for private producers in all regions except the Rocky Mountains, because private producers also lose market shares to the public sector. This is exactly what Table 8.4 shows. (Recognize that consumer gains in Table 8.4

refer to gains for consumers of timber produced in the identified region. The intermediate and final good consumers, themselves, may not live in the producing regions.)

We anticipate large public sector efficiency gains due to both the public harvest level shifts and the change to market responsive public cost functions. The ad hoc nature of our public cost estimates for both the base case and the simulated market solution yield less confidence in our estimates of public surplus gains. Nevertheless, our large estimates (greater than six times actual 1977 public timber management expenditures) strongly suggest that there are great gains for the public treasury to be found in more market-sensitive public timber management.[5] In conclusion, shifting public timber management criteria to reflect market sensitivity obtains a large aggregate social gain and a large gain for the public treasury. There are also underlying losses for many private timber producers and perhaps for both timber producers and consumers in one region, the Rocky Mountains.

We might anticipate the question of possible environmental damages due to such large shifts in timber harvests. It is not a necessary fact that nonmarket forest values must always trade off against the anticipated general social gain from following market timber criteria. Furthermore, our conclusions depend more on a redistribution of timber harvests than an overall expansion. Therefore, they probably imply more for the redistribution of environmental effects than the aggregate impact. Indeed, in the more fragile forests of the Rocky Mountains, there should be a substantial by-product gain in nonmarket forest outputs as a result of following market timber criteria.

Our results refer to 1977, but they also suggest price and inventory destabilizing effects and social welfare gains in the near term after 1977. Although these near-term adjustments are large, we expect that the long-term price and inventory effects of shifting to market-sensitive public harvest criteria may be less important. Long-term market pressures will deplete the public inventory surplus in a market responsive case. Long-term market and political pressures may force a gradual administrative release of public inventories even if current public timber management criteria persist. Long-term welfare gains are more difficult to anticipate. They can persist, regardless of price and inventory levels, to the extent the public sector becomes responsive to production costs. Permitting marginal production costs to determine supply is less expensive than current public agency practice.

The dramatic market impacts suggested by our analysis argue for a change from market constraining public management policies. They also (implicitly) argue against rapid policy changes of great magnitude. The result of rapid change would be precipitous for some communities, even if it would benefit the American economy as a whole. Any policy change toward market criteria on public lands in the neighborhoods of these select communities would have to be tempered. The next section of this chapter addresses a Forest Service policy partly intended to protect timber-based communities from just such precipitous market impacts.

 ## Community Stability

Community stability is the U.S. Forest Service expression for its objective to maintain the integrity of those small communities scattered throughout the West that are dependent on public timber harvests. This is a noble objective consistent with aggregate public policies designed to minimize the social costs of a cyclic economy and consistent with general public concern for the welfare of local populations caught in the boom-and-bust towns frequent in the history of the American West.

The Forest Service approach to community stability is through the availability of public timber harvests. The Forest Service anticipates that in the presence of externally generated instability, perhaps a cyclical national construction industry, then a constant flow of public timber guarantees not only the continued and stable existence of the local mills that consume public timber but also the continued and stable existence of the local community for which the mills are a major industry. Our discussion shows that the Forest Service policy has a stabilizing impact only in the narrowest sense. Generally, the policy impact is small and destabilizing, although its magnitude varies depending on just which community variable is measured: employment or the wage bill for forest products workers only; or income, employment, or the wage bill for the community as a whole. Furthermore, the success of the Forest Service policy comes only at a considerable cost to the public timber management budget and, therefore, to the federal treasury.

Our discussion begins by considering the various possible definitions of community stability and continues by introducing a conceptual framework and then a case study for analysis. The conceptual framework relies on a two-sector, three-factor general equilibrium model first introduced by Harberger (1966, 1962) and later extended by Atkinson and Stiglitz (1980, 167–99). The eight most western counties in the state of Montana and the years 1968–1981 provide evidence for the case study. Wood products provide 7 percent of Montana's gross product and probably three times that for the western counties where the Forest Service presence is truly substantial. Our empirical analysis relies on Wear's (1985) translog estimates of the wood products industry's production function for Montana to specify a modified Harberger model. We use this specification to contrast the impacts of simulated market-sensitive public timber harvests with known and fixed Forest Service harvests that are invariant with the large local lumber price changes, changes that vary as much as 18 percent from the mean during our fourteen-year period.

DEFINITION

The Forest Service displays its community stability objective in its national forest management plans, where it may design even flows of harvest volumes for periods in excess of 150 years. It chooses the communities deserving of this attention according to the definition that

> Dependent communities are areas with common social and economic interests bounded by established daily marketing and work force commuting patterns, and encompassing one or more primary wood products manufacturing facilities located within or adjacent to a specific area of National Forest timber upon which it is dependent for its timber supply and where 10 percent or more of the community work force is employed in the primary manufacturing of wood products, including logging and log transportation, and National Forest timber accounts for at least 30 percent of the timber used in the primary wood products manufacturing facilities in the last five calendar years (Federal Register 42(106); 28258. Thursday, June 2, 1977).

The objective may be noble but it must fail in most cases. First, the opportunities for taste and technological changes in 150 years are so great as to make the volume of one specific resource input like stumpage unlikely to be an important determinant of expected community welfare in that time—regardless of the current significance of that specific resource. Second, even if the specific input retains its current importance, then it must account for much more than 3 percent of community employment before its production can claim a meaningful impact on the community.[6] Third, planning an even harvest flow does not ensure an even flow of resource inputs to the processing facility. There is usually a private source for some timber and this source responds to the market, thereby absorbing any cyclic variation the public sector fails to absorb (Waggener 1977). Even in the unusual case where there is no significant private supply, there remain too many opportunities to store inventories between planned public harvests and mill inputs (i.e., on the stump both before and after an effective timber sale and also in the mill's log yard). Indeed, total storage time can be indefinite if a planned Forest Service timber sale attracts no bidders. Even if the sale goes as planned, market conditions can easily slow the actual harvest until the period between the timber sale and log input to the head saw exceeds five years.

These criticisms might not be nearly so damaging, however, if the

Forest Service were to alter its periodic harvest plans to reflect the intermediate run of perhaps three to fifteen years, shorter than the lifetime of the
mill and at least as long as a building cycle or business cycle. This is a
period in which existing capital in the wood products industry is relatively
inflexible and labor may be mobile between sectors within a community but
tends to be immobile from community to community. These conditions, as
well as a small, often insignificant private supply, characterize many of the
Rocky Mountain communities that the Forest Service intends to protect.
Good redistributive and stabilization arguments can be made for a public
policy that removes cyclic instability during a market adjustment period in
this case.

This is the reasonable case for the Forest Service policy we examine in
this chapter. We assume, furthermore, that the community in question sells
its wood products in an external market and that its particular wood products industry is a stationary or declining industry. (The Forest Service has
no interest in restraining expanding industries and such restraint is not a
timely issue for us.) An externally originating and unanticipated downward
adjustment in demand confronts the community's wood products industry.
The Forest Service responds by attempting to ease the burden of adjustment by maintaining a fixed flow of stumpage inputs, thereby intending to
absorb a large share of the cyclic economic adjustment costs itself.[7]

A MODEL OF THE COMMUNITY

We follow the modelling approach of Caves and Jones (1981), which
considers the elements of the single community's general equilibrium system characterized by its equations of change. Thus, we consider changes in
demand for the product relative to changes in product prices, and on the
supply side, changes in product supply relative to changes in factor shares
and changes in factor inputs relative to changes in factor prices.

Citizens of the aggregate economy consume two goods, wood products
X and a generalized all-other-goods Y. Prices of both are set in the external
economy. The local economy is a price taker with respect to each.

$$\hat{p}_Y = 0, \hat{p}_X = -c \qquad (8.1)$$

The hats signify logarithmic differentiation (i.e., $p_Y = dp_Y/p_Y$). The market
for all goods other than wood products is stable and the market for wood
products has just received a destabilizing price shock.

On the supply side, our community produces the same two goods, X
and Y: X with three factors, capital K, labor L, and Forest Service stumpage S; and Y with only capital and labor. Both producing industries are
competitive and operate under conditions of constant returns to scale.

These common and reasonable assumptions permit us to write the conditions for changes in product supply relative to changes in factor shares

$$\hat{X} = \theta_{KX}\hat{K}_X + \theta_{LX}\hat{L}_X + \theta_{SX}\hat{S}_X \tag{8.2}$$

and

$$\hat{Y} = \theta_{KY}\hat{K}_Y + \theta_{LY}\hat{L}_Y \tag{8.3}$$

where θ_{ij} is the initial share of factor i in the total cost of producing output j (e.g., $\theta_{KX} = r_X K_X/X$).

The conditions of competition and production functions which are homogeneous of degree 1 also permit us to determine the changes in factor inputs relative to changes in factor prices.

$$\frac{d(K_Y/L_Y)}{(K_Y/L_Y)} = -\sigma_{KL\text{-}Y}\frac{d(r_Y/w)}{(r_Y/w)} \tag{8.4a}$$

where $\sigma_{KL\text{-}Y}$ is the substitution elasticity between capital and labor in the production of Y and r and w are the unit costs of capital and labor, respectively. Equation (8.4a) can be rewritten as

$$\hat{K}_Y - \hat{L}_Y = -\sigma_{KL\text{-}Y}(dr_Y - dw) \tag{8.4b}$$

Similarly,

$$\hat{L}_X - \hat{K}_X = (1 - \theta_S)\sigma_{LK\text{-}X}(\hat{r}_X - \hat{w}) + \theta_S\sigma_{LS\text{-}X}(\hat{s} - \hat{w})$$
$$- \theta_S\sigma_{KS\text{-}X}(\hat{s} - \hat{r}_X) \tag{8.5}$$

$$\hat{L}_X - \hat{S}_X = (1 - \theta_K)\sigma_{LS\text{-}X}(\hat{s} - \hat{w}) + \theta_K\sigma_{LK\text{-}X}(\hat{r}_X - \hat{w})$$
$$- \theta_S\sigma_{SK\text{-}X}(\hat{r}_X - \hat{s}) \tag{8.6}$$

and

$$\hat{K}_X - \hat{S}_X = (1 - \theta_L)\sigma_{KS\text{-}X}(\hat{s} - \hat{r}_X) + \theta_L\sigma_{KL\text{-}X}(\hat{w} - \hat{r}_X)$$
$$- \theta_L\sigma_{SL\text{-}X}(\hat{w} - \hat{S}_X) \tag{8.7}$$

where s is the unit stumpage price. Factor and product prices are normalized. Equation (8.7) is the difference between equations (8.5) and (8.6). Therefore, these three equations are linearly related and we can use any two of them.

We also know that, under conditions of competition with constant returns to scale, factor payments just exhaust total receipts in each industry.

$$p_Y dY + Y dp_Y = w dL_Y + L_Y dw + r_Y dK_Y + K_Y dr_Y \tag{8.8a}$$

Furthermore, we know that the marginal products of the factors equal the factor costs divided by the output prices (e.g., $MP_{L\text{-}Y} = w/p_Y$).

$$p_Y dY = w dL_Y + r_Y dK_Y \qquad\qquad (8.8b)$$

Subtracting equation (8.8b) from (8.8a) and dividing by Y yields

$$dp_Y = (L_Y/Y)dw + (K_Y/Y)dr_Y$$
or
$$dp_Y = \theta_{LY}dw + \theta_{KY}dr_Y \qquad\qquad (8.8c)$$

Similarly,

$$dp_X = \theta_{LX}dw + \theta_{KX}dr_X + \theta_{SX}ds \qquad\qquad (8.9)$$

Finally, the expression for Forest Service stumpage supply is

$$\hat{s}e_S = \hat{S}_X \qquad\qquad (8.10)$$

where e_S is the supply elasticity.

We now have eight equations (8.2–8.6 and 8.8c–8.10) and eleven unknowns (dX, dY, dK_X, dL_X, dS_X, dK_Y, dL_Y, dr_X, dr_Y, dw, and ds). The underlying assumptions about the community provide conditions explaining three of these unknowns:

$$\begin{aligned} dr_Y &= 0 \\ dK_X &= 0 \\ dL_X &= dL_Y \end{aligned} \qquad\qquad (8.11)$$

The external market determines r_Y. The community is a price taker with respect to it. Capital facilities, such as sawmills, in the wood products industries are immobile in the intermediate-run period of an economic cycle. This means that K_X is fixed and constant but r_X can vary in the community over this period. Community labor supply is constant and freely mobile between the two sectors. (If community labor supply were mobile, then it could respond to a cyclic economy by finding employment outside the local area and the community stability problem would be much less important.) Labor mobility between sectors, as between logging and ranching, is consistent with observed behavior.

Our final count is eight equations and eight unknowns. We can estimate changes in payments to the community's factors of production. These payments are important measures of community stability and social welfare. Changes in them measure the community response to external economic stimuli.

The second step in our analysis contrasts these market responsive results with those deriving from Forest Service harvests constrained so that the supply elasticity e_s is equal to zero. This is the extreme case where Forest Service policy is perfectly effective in maintaining an even annual harvest flow.

The differences between the factor use and factor payment estimates from the two steps in the analysis measure the policy impacts on community stability.

DATA

Western Montana provides a reasonable base for displaying the empirical effects of this model. Its economy is heavily dependent on timber production and processing and the bulk of its timber resource originates from public, and particularly Forest Service, lands. Therefore, a sudden and large external change in the price of wood products like lumber might sharply affect the western Montana economy and the Forest Service might reasonably anticipate that its timber harvests can meliorate this impact. The availability of Wear's (1985) three-factor model of the empirical relationships for Montana's wood products industry is additional reason for using western Montana to display our arguments.

Table 8.5 reports our data sources. It emphasizes our reliance on Wear's own input data and the results of his translog production estimates.[8] Banskota, Phillips, and Williamson's (1985) results provide confidence in Wear's estimates. They derive elasticity and factor share estimates for the sawmill industry in the neighboring Canadian province of Alberta. The sawmill industry is a large share of Montana's wood products industry and Wear's estimates for the latter fall within the range of the Banskota et al. estimates.

Our output measures are gross receipts because value-added data are not available for all sectors. Uniform use of gross receipts in all cases yields unbiased results. The basic output data are statewide. We multiply them by the state population share of the western timber-producing counties to obtain a measure of total output in these counties alone and then subtract the total state output of the wood products sector, virtually all of which occurs in these counties, to obtain the western Montana output for all other (nonwood products) sectors.

The stumpage supply elasticity is Adams and Haynes (1985) private sector elasticity for the Rocky Mountain region. The AH private sector elasticity is preferable because, unlike the public sector elasticity, it is unbiased by the community stability policy we wish to examine. Nevertheless, the AH public sector elasticity exceeds their private sector elasticity and we might expect an unconstrained public sector elasticity to be greater yet. Therefore, we examine the range $0.24 < e_s < 1.0$.

The remaining data are either explicit assumptions, equations (8.1) and

Table 8.5. Data sources: The western Montana economy

Parameter	Source
X = wood products output	Value of shipments SIC 24, USDC Bur. Census 1967–1982
Y = all other output	Value of shipments in mfg, USDL Bur. Labor Stat. 1971, 1976, 1981, 1984; USDC Bur. Census 1967–1982 (noncensus years); plus total cash rcpts to farmers, USDA 1969–1983; plus annual sales of retail stores, USDC Bur. Census 1969–1982
K_X, L_X, S_X = capital, labor, stumpage in X	As in Wear 1985
θ_{iX} = share of factor i in total cost of X	Derived from Wear 1985
$r_X = r_Y, w$ = return on capital, wages	Derived from θ_{iX}, and $X = r_X K_X + w L_X + s S_X$
θ_{iY} = share of factor i in total cost of Y	Derived from knowledge of w, r, K_Y, L_Y, Y
K_Y, L_Y = capital, labor in Y	Derived from θ_{iY} and $Y = r K_Y - w L_Y$
σ_{ij-X} = factor substitution elasticities in X	Wear 1985
σ_{KL-Y} = factor supply elasticities in Y	Klein 1974, Parashevopoulos 1979
e_s = stumpage supply elasticity	Adams and Haynes 1985
$dK_X = 0$, no change in capital used in X	Assumption: short-run capital immobility in the declining industry
$dL_Y = -dL_X$	Assumption: full employment; labor mobile within the local community
dp_X = exogenous change in lumber price	Ponderosa pine boards (no. 3, random lengths, FOB mill), USDC BEA 1980, Western Wood Products Association 1986
$dp_Y = 0$, no change in price of all other goods	Assumption: stable external economy in all other sectors

(8.11), or common estimates of the factor substitution elasticity for the aggregate economy. The several steps in the derivation of factor shares in the all-other-goods sector and the imposition of a U.S. aggregate factor substitution elasticity on what may be a very different Y sector in western Montana cause us to question their reliability. Closer inquiry, however, shows our eventual results to be insensitive to differences in the ranges 0.25 < θ_{KY} < 0.45 and 0.75 < σ_{KL-Y} < 1.25. Therefore, we accept the derived factor shares and the aggregate factor substitution elasticity as sufficient for our purpose.

RESULTS AND CONCLUSIONS

Table 8.6 reports the direct results from introducing these data into the eight-equation conceptual model. The western Montana economy is increasingly responsive to higher stumpage supply elasticities. That is, all variable factors and products diverge further from their initial values in response to the given change in lumber prices and more elastic stumpage supplies. In any market sensitive case, decreasing lumber prices cause both decreasing demand for the final output of the wood products sector and decreasing demands for its factors of production. Therefore, stumpage demand decreases and stumpage prices also decrease. Some capital facilities in the wood products sector become underemployed and the return on capital facilities in this sector drops sharply. Some local labor shifts to the Y sector and that sector expands absolutely, absorbing some new capital from outside western Montana.

When Forest Service policy constrains the market response by holding stumpage supply constant, this policy also forces a compensating decrease in the stumpage price. This price decrease is additional to the market-induced adjustment. The larger-than-market stumpage supply combines with some otherwise underutilized capital facilities and some labor that would otherwise transfer to the Y sector. Together, these factors restrict the

Table 8.6. Response of the western Montana economy to an 18 percent decrease in the price of wood products (1977$)

Parameter and initial value	Market sensitive timber supply		Constant timber supply
	$e_s = 0.24$	$e_s = 1.0$	$e_s = 0$
X (million$) = 406	294.7	286.7	313.5
Y (million$) = 1928	1978	1994	1965
L_X (million hrs) = 19.3	15.45	14.21	16.48
L_Y (million hrs) = 149	152.8	154.1	151.8
K_X (billion$) = 1.202	1.202	1.202	1.202
K_Y (billion$) = 4.999	5.128	5.170	5.094
S_X (million Mbf) = 1.12	1.04	0.934	1.12
$r_X = 0.135$	-30%	-37%	-23%
$s =$	-31%	-17%	-43%

full market-responsive decline in wood products output, but they also prevent the full potential increase in Y sector output.

Table 8.7 shows the impact of these various changes on several measures of community stability. The first measure is the apparent Forest Service measure of community stability, timber harvests that, by policy decree, are constant regardless of the supply elasticity. The remaining measures display the social impact of this policy. The policy clearly expands timber harvests and the employment of labor in the wood products sector. It has no impact on the aggregate employment of labor as labor only moves locally between sectors in response to changing sector demand. Equation (8.8c) shows that the average wage in the community must remain constant. A constant wage and unchanging aggregate employment together imply a constant wage bill regardless of policy.

A satisfactory measure of aggregate community welfare is difficult to define. We might consider payments to factors that remain in the community; that is, the aggregate wage bill plus most returns to capital. Stumpage receipts leave the community for the general federal treasury but the treasury returns one-quarter of them to local counties as a payment in lieu of local taxes from the public lands. The sum of community factor payments decreases by one-quarter of the decrease in stumpage receipts as a result of the Forest Service policy. Thus, policy has a very small negative net effect on the community.

Nevertheless, the public cost of this policy is great. Policy holds public harvests constant, which implies it also holds public timber costs constant at the previous market equilibrium level. The policy creates higher than (new) market equilibrium costs and lower stumpage prices, therefore, lower than market equilibrium receipts. In sum, the public treasury pays a large fee (approximately one-half the original stumpage bill) in order to create a small negative impact on western Montana.

In conclusion, the Forest Service has a well-placed concern for the social hardship faced by resource-based communities as their final goods prices fluctuate widely. Translating this concern into a remedy is more difficult. Providing a constant flow of the basic resource is no remedy in the intermediate period of an economic cycle with labor showing mobility only from job to job within the local community. A constant harvest policy improves employment and total wage income in the wood products sector but foregone gains in the rest of the local economy offset these wood products gains. Furthermore, the policy requires large public management costs. At best, we can say that this policy is well-intentioned but misguided and expensive.[9]

Table 8.7. Community impacts from holding stumpage supply fixed

Measure of community stability	Elasticity assumption	
	$e_s = 0.24$	$e_s = 1.0$
Timber harvests (S_X)	+0.08 million Mbf (+7.7%)	+0.19 million Mbf (+20%)
Wood products employment (L_X)	+1.03 million hrs (+6.7%)	+2.27 million hrs (+16%)
Total employment ($L_X + L_Y$)	no change	no change
Wood products wage income (wL_X)	+$8.61 million (+6.7%)	+19.1 million (+16%)
Total wage income [$w(L_X + L_Y)$]	no change	no change
Factor payments which remain in the community [$\sum_i(wL_i + r_i K_i) + sS_X/4$]	−$1.5 million (< 0.1%)	−$0.75 million (< 0.1%)
Public timber budget:		
receipts foregone	−$5.9 million	−$10.6 million
additional costs	−$29.4 million	−$24.7 million
total (initial $81.2 million)	−$35.3 million	−$35.3 million

Recreation Supply

Supply is the focus of the next two sections, both of which consider nonmarket values provided on public forestlands. Nonmarket values usually suggest focus on demand estimation, and there is an extensive literature on this topic. This means, however, that the supply side of efficient resource allocation is somewhat overlooked. Yet we can show that supply data are readily available in the form of public agency budget and expenditure records and we can reasonably argue that land managers possess the insight to make judgements about supply more easily and confidently than judgements about demand. Furthermore, accurate supply information alone encourages least-cost decisions and can often prevent egregious errors in resource allocation.

Our objective in this section is to consider recreation resource allocation, in particular allocation of the recreation resource defined by U.S. Forest Service campgrounds but common to various federal and state agencies and even some private operations.[10] The magnitudes of public agency recreation budgets and levels of visitor use alone suggest the significance of possible errors in recreation resource allocation and the potential importance of improving our understanding of it. In fiscal year 1984, the Forest Service spent $99 million providing 229 million visitor days of outdoor recreation (G. Elsner, USDA Forest Service, personal communication). The National Park Service spent another $1,049 million providing another 108 million visitor days (USDI National Park Service 1984, 1986). Clearly, errors in recreation resource allocation can have large social impact even if our insights are limited to suggesting small adjustments in either these budgets or their distributions.

Our approach to the question of recreation resource allocation is through a case study of national forest campgrounds in the Seeley-Swan Valley (SSV) in western Montana. The Seeley-Swan is a long narrow valley bordered by the Mission and Swan Mountains to the east and west, respectively. The Swan River flows the length of the valley and drains the several lakes, which are focal attractions for four relatively similar Forest Service campgrounds. The valley is a popular recreation spot within easy access of 42 percent of Montana's population. It is relatively unknown, however, to out-of-state campers, who travel the interstate highways just north and south of it and who are more likely to visit Glacier and Yellowstone National Parks, respectively. In sum, we might characterize the SSV as providing an important, although not a unique, recreation opportunity for a regional market.

The resource allocation problem confronting SSV managers is illustrative of the general problem facing on-the-ground public agency managers. The important constraints on the problem are the physical boundaries of agency jurisdictions, not the greater market area, and the agency's budget appropriations. Our important perspectives are those of the agency's local recreation manager in the off-season, say December, in planning the next year's operation from the base of whatever campground facilities are already in place.[11] Expansion is unlikely under current public agency budgets; but at this time the manager has the options of altering use patterns, some reduction in facilities, various maintenance activities and even the possibility of contracting for private operation of the campgrounds. Our approach to the problem is through marginal analysis, where incremental expenditure options define supply schedules for the four SSV campgrounds and aggregate consumer preferences define a single demand schedule for all four.

The remainder of this recreation discussion concentrates on constructing the supply schedules and drawing conclusions. The current Forest Service recreation management decision begins with an arbitrary fee for campsite use. (Three of the SSV campgrounds charge $4 per campsite per night. The fourth, which has flush toilets, charges $5 per night.) The local recreation manager has discretion only with respect to cost allocation. The contrast between the current level of campground operation under these arbitrary prices and the optimal improvement made after considering our supply information and the implicit demand schedule is the feature of our conclusions.

SUPPLY SCHEDULE CONSTRUCTION

The annual planning perspective of this analysis suggests that the existing level of permanent Forest Service personnel and the four existing campgrounds each with its current number of campsites are sunk costs. It is not within the discretion of recreation managers to alter either in the forthcoming year. Discretion pertains only to the fixed costs of opening each campground for annual operation and the variable costs associated with the level of campground use. Fixed costs may be constant across campgrounds or they may vary according to the number of existing and identifiable campsites within each campground. Variable costs are functions of the number of recreation-visitor-days (RVD, where one RVD equals one camper for one twelve hour period) of campground use.

Data for our analysis originate from the Program Accounting and Management Attainment Reporting System (PAMARS). These data are for the specific SSV campgrounds in question and have the advantage of reflecting actual 1984 expenditures rather than ex ante budget allocations. Interpretive assistance from the local recreation staff helped us divide the PAMARS data into twelve recreation activity groups from which we can develop twelve underlying cost functions. Together these form the cost function for each campground.

Table 8.8 summarizes the functions and we discuss each in turn. The campground is the observational unit for the table. Read across the table to identify first the fixed cost, then the variable cost coefficients associated with each activity in the campground. (Our regressions repress the intercept term.) Fixed costs, to repeat, can be functions of either (opening) the campground or the number of campsites per campground. All campsites in each campground are independent and well marked. Variable costs are functions of the 1984 use levels. Table 8.8 also reports three tests for statistical fit. The t-statistic appears under each fixed or variable cost coefficient. The R^2 and equation F-statistics appear in the right-hand columns. The F-tests all reject, at least at the 10 percent level, the hypothesis that all equation coefficients are equal to zero.

The small sample sizes require that we construct, rather than statistically estimate, four underlying total cost functions (for utilities, replacement of physical deterioration, fee management, and vehicle use). Table 8.8 also shows the results of these constructions. The assistance of the local SSV recreation staff improves our confidence in them.

OPENING THE CAMPGROUND. Two activities involve only the single and permanent costs associated with opening the campground: land use and electricity. The cost of assigning the lands in these campgrounds to recreation rather than to some other use is an implicit cost equal to the net value of its forgone next best use. Timber and water production are the likely alternatives for the SSV campgrounds. These campgrounds are all in fragile riparian areas where Forest Service policy seeks to protect water quality by requiring longer timber rotations and, even then, restricts harvests within some distance of streams and lakesides. This suggests that harvests would seldom, if ever, occur on the 68 acres in the four campgrounds and the expected timber value, which is also the campground opportunity cost, is effectively zero. The Forest Service managers judge that SSV campground use does not limit water quality. Therefore, this potential opportunity cost is also zero.

The local electric utility sends a monthly bill for each campground but each bill is close to the minimum charged to provide service to that facility. That is, once the electricity is turned on and the campground is open for visitor use, then the level of use is seldom sufficient to raise the electricity bill above the minimum fee. Therefore, this fee is equivalent to a one-time-only annual fee. (There are no significant statistical relationships between the electric bill and either RVD's of use or numbers of campsites.)

COMPLEX COST FUNCTIONS. Estimating the cost functions for the remaining ten activities is a more complex task: Most of these activities have both fixed cost and variable cost components, two are joint costs. The Forest

Table 8.8. Recreation activity total cost functions for four SSV campgrounds in 1984

Activity	Fixed costs			Variable costs	
	Campground	Campsite	RVD	R^2	F
Land	0		—		
Utilities	[c]		—		
Toilet pumping	—	5.1387 (15.099)[b]	0.00135 (1.036)	.999	890.4[b]
Garbage collection	—	3.8005 (0.474)	0.0418 (1.362)	.919	11.31[a]
Maintenance: user-induced	—	2.4757 (4.409)[b]	0.0103 (4.792)[b]	.997	281.2[b]
Physical deterioration: Labor	—	−19.9448 (−1.346)	0.3191 (5.624)[b]	.985	67.07[b]
Facilities	—	2.578 (0.558)	0.0794 (4.487)[b]	.989	86.55[b]
Replacement	—		—		
Compliance checks	—	3.9364 (1.020)	0.08268 (5.595)[b]	.993	145.1[b]
Fee management	—		[c]		
Law enforcement	—	29.9695 (2.254)	0.0197 (0.387)	.959	23.63[a]
Vehicle use	[c]				
Overhead	0	0	0		

[a]Significant at the .10 level.
[b]Significant at the .05 level.
[c]Constructed costs.

Activity	Lake Alva	Big Larch	River Point	Seeley Lake
Utilities per campground	120.00	137.60	103.57	289.00
Replacement per campground	5300.60	9018.16	3397.64	7692.28
Fee management/RVD	0.0791	0.0709	0.0715	0.0309
Vehicle use per campground	1668.62		2669.07	
per RVD	0.0869	0.0210	0.0267	0.0142

Service also contracts two activities to private firms, which means the cost reporting for these two activities is different. The activities themselves feature campground cleanup, maintenance, and repair (six activities) and camper management (three activities).

Recreation managers strategically place toilets and garbage dumpsters near groups of campsites within each campground. They then contract both the toilet pumping and the garbage collection activities to private firms. The fee for each activity is a function of the number of trips the contractor makes. Contractors make new trips and empty every toilet or dumpster within a campground each time one toilet or dumpster within that campground becomes full. Therefore, it is reasonable that toilet pumping costs and garbage collection costs are functions both of the fixed number of campsites (which relate to the number of toilets and dumpsters) and the variable number of RVDs of use (which dictate the frequency of trips) within each campground.

Maintenance includes two accounting activities: user-induced maintenance and clean-up, and normal physical deterioration. The user-induced maintenance and clean-up cost is a function of the time spent on maintenance times the Forest Service wage ($0.857/hr) for the summer volunteers who provide this service. User-induced maintenance is distributed according to the number of campsites and the level of use within each campground. (Some capital facilities require periodic maintenance even if only used once, plus additional maintenance depending on their use levels.)

Whether maintenance against normal physical deterioration is a fixed or variable cost could be the subject of reasonable debate. Forest Service policy restricts physical deterioration and requires maintenance of all capital in a high quality condition. This means that local recreation managers do not have the option to permit even an unused campground to deteriorate and that the costs incurred to prevent normal deterioration are fixed costs. Conversely, our regressions show highly significant relationships between these costs and the use level. This significance might reflect only a coincidental relationship between (1) normal deterioration and fixed campground size and (2) the use level. Therefore, the relationship could be consistent with the fixed cost argument. Table 8.8 records the statistical results. Our later analysis treats maintenance to prevent deterioration as a fixed cost but examines the change in optimal resource allocation if we treat it as also having a variable component. The allocation decision for this cost is important because the variable component is 60 percent of total variable costs for the sum of all activities.

Maintenance against normal physical deterioration has both labor and capital components and the capital component further divides into facility repair and replacement costs. We estimate the labor costs as the residual Forest Service labor expenditures after deducting for labor used in for all other recreation activities. The statistical distribution of these residuals across campgrounds is a function of both general campsite aging (or the number of campsites) and the campground use level. The statistical distribution of facility repair costs is similar.

Replacement cost is the value of existing capital in place depreciated at the Forest Service rate of 4 percent per annum. The estimates in Table 8.8 derive from the capital inventory for each campground and the Forest Service replacement cost for each inventory item. Variation across campgrounds in terrain and access affect large cost items such as roads and water systems, thereby preventing any obvious relationship between replacement costs and numbers of campsites.

There are three camper management activities: compliance checks, fee management, and law enforcement. Compliance checks are the activity of inspecting the campground to ensure that campers use only assigned campsites and are otherwise in compliance with the regulations for campground use. The cost of this activity is equal to the time spent on it times the wage for (nonvolunteer) seasonal Forest Service employees ($7.23/hr). Time is a function of campground size and camper use. That is, larger campgrounds require longer for the employee to traverse and more campers mean more occupied campsites to check.

The Forest Service dispenses envelopes in which campers deposit user fees. The envelopes also contain survey questions about the users. Fee management is the act of emptying these envelopes and sorting their user data. Clearly,

$$\text{fee management cost/RVD} = \text{cost/envelope} \div \text{RVDs/party}$$

where there is one envelope but perhaps many RVDs per party. The cost per envelope is the $7.23 hourly wage for regular hourly employees times the five minutes spent on each envelope. RVDs per party is one of the survey questions on each envelope. Seeley Lake campground, perhaps due to its flush toilets, attracts more users and for longer periods. Therefore, it accumulates more RVDs per party but lower incremental fee management costs per RVD than the other three campgrounds.

Law enforcement is a heavy cost item conducted by other Forest Service personnel and charged against the recreation budget. The Forest Service recreation staff cannot provide us with good arguments for the determining factors behind allocation of the cost to particular campgrounds. Our weak statistical relationship suggests that the number of sites, each of which must be patrolled whenever the campground is open, and the use level each may have impacts.

Finally, there are two costs that are joint to many of these activities: vehicle use and overhead. The Lolo National Forest charges its recreation budget a total vehicle cost for use in association with all recreation activities except the contracted activities. The recreation staff recommends a division of this cost across all four campgrounds such that a larger share accrues to Lake Alva, the most distant campground. Finally, we somewhat arbitrarily divide the share for each campground into fixed and variable components according to the fixed-variable share of the sum of all noncontracted activities and further divide each variable share by the use level for that campground. The fixed-cost shares for the three campgrounds that are adjacent to one another are truly a joint cost because Forest Service personnel normally travel to all of these three in the same trip.

The Lolo National Forest supervisor's office and the Forest Service regional office charge overhead to the Ranger District as a share of total field expense for personnel and systems support. We argue that this charge is a sunk cost, irrelevant to our objective of examining recreational operations for a single season. The supervisor's office and the regional office do alter the magnitude of their staffing, therefore the magnitude of their total overhead charges, but only in response to demands of a term longer than one season.

EMPIRICAL RESULTS AND CONCLUSIONS

We can combine our supply information with knowledge of consumer demand in order to learn about the socially optimal price and use levels and to compare the social welfare and recreation management differences between these optimal levels and 1984 actual levels.

Demand information originates from the user survey data (postal zip code of user origin) on the reverse side of the fee envelopes. The specification for the inverse travel cost demand function for the aggregate of all four campgrounds is

$$Q = e^{\alpha}(TC + F)^{-\beta}$$

where Q = RVDs/1000 population in the origin zone; TC = implicit travel cost/RVD (composed of the round trip mileage cost and the values of both travel time and on-site time); F = implicit campsite fee/RVD; Q_c = actual 1984 RVDs (37543); and α, β are parameters.

The term α is normalized so that it defines a function passing through observed values for Q and $TC + F$ for the 1984 season. The estimated values for α and β are 40.9073 and 6.5136, respectively. The standard error on β is 0.7350.

This demand function is conceptually identical to that developed by Wilman (1980) and its results fall within the range of the Sorg and Loomis (1984) survey. Furthermore, the statistical evidence strongly supports our hypothesis that the four campgrounds are homogeneous in their demands. That is, the estimated parameters for the four independent campground demand functions all fall within 1 standard error of each other and within 1 standard error of the estimated parameter for the aggregate demand function.[12]

Our first results derive from the joint allocation of the vehicle use cost. They imply a sequence to the annual opening of campgrounds. If it is optimal to open only one campground, then Lake Alva is the least expensive to operate. If more than one campground is optimal, then two or more of the other three are least expensive. This is not a major issue for SSV recreation, however, because all annual use levels under any reasonable pricing scenario recommend opening all four campgrounds.

The other results derive from setting the sum of marginal costs equal to the implicit campground user fee (Table 8.9). The 1984 implicit fee per RVD was $0.81 at Lake Alva and in the range $0.71-$0.77 at the other three campgrounds. The aggregate use level was 37,543 RVDs and the net economic value, including consumers' and producers' surplus was $609,820. Setting the implicit fee equal to the marginal cost changes the use level to somewhere in the range of 37,673-38,695 RVDs and the net economic value to somewhere in the range of $612,829-628,063. (The treatment of maintenance to prevent deterioration as either a fixed or variable cost determines these ranges.)

It is clear that there is some improvement in social welfare from decreasing the fee and increasing use until the fee equals the marginal cost. It is also clear, however, that a large percentage decrease in the fee has only a small impact on the use rate and on social welfare. This is because the fee is only a small share of the implicit travel cost (approximately $106 per RVD). Furthermore, while setting the fee equal to the marginal cost has a small impact on social welfare, it has a large negative impact on Forest Service recreation receipts. It may be a wise public agency administrative and political choice to set the fee above marginal cost, thereby obtaining receipts much closer to the total costs of the recreation operation and making SSV recreation much less subject to the whims of the federal budget process.

Regardless of the administrative and political advisability of the choice of fee level, marginal cost is constant per RVD and changes in the demand price have little impact on the optimal use level. (The supply function is

Table 8.9. Comparison of actual and optimal SSV recreation use levels

	Lake Alva	Other campgrounds	Use level	Net economic value
Actual fee	$0.81	$0.71-$0.77	37,543	$609,820
Low optimal fee	$0.32	$0.25	38,695	$628,063
High optimal fee	$0.72	$0.65	37,673	$612,829

elastic and the demand function inelastic.) Furthermore, the optimal and actual use levels are similar. This is clearly one of those satisfying cases where analysis suggests that society is doing well by relying on the manager's intuition.

This first generation research shows the usefulness of recreation supply and demand analysis and the sources of both data and managerial skills regarding supply. It also raises interesting questions about optimal pricing schemes once we generalize to other recreation opportunities. The SSV facilities are similar and the supply and demand elasticities are uniform across them. Generalizing to other recreation opportunities, ranging from undeveloped wilderness camping to resort communities, changes the uniformity of elasticities. This range of opportunities can occur even within the management responsibility of one Forest Service Ranger District. Therefore, this new pricing problem can be a real problem even for local managers.

Consider multiple classes of recreation opportunities and, for example, a management decision to constrain operations such that revenues exceed some share of total costs. (This constraint is similar to apparent management behavior on the SSV.) Efficiency criteria and social welfare maximization remain the guiding characteristics within the constraint. The optimal pricing scheme—and a measure of its variation from the current price policy—becomes an interesting question for the next generation of public recreation policy analysis.[13]

Endangered Species Management: The Case of the Red-Cockaded Woodpecker

This section of the chapter considers one endangered species problem, red-cockaded woodpecker (RCW) management on the Croatan National Forest in North Carolina, as an example of the broader class of nonmarket resource services provided to all consumers without exclusion, yet often provided with a substantial impact on the resource management agency's budget.[14] The RCW is on the national endangered species list and, although its survival throughout its range is no longer in grave doubt, its occurence remains unusual and its management is a contentious issue for the U.S. Forest Service and the Fish and Wildlife Service.

We show that even an incomplete analysis, with no demand assessment and using only readily available cost data, can help managers and policy makers understand the relevant tradeoffs. We also show, in this special case, that there is great variation in costs depending on where and how RCW management proceeds. This is important information considering the highly speculative, and often inflammatory, statements made by both proponents and opponents of endangered species protection.

The economics literature on preservation focuses on either maximizing a social welfare function that includes both development goods and natural assets or else satisfying a safe minimum standard. As yet, there are no successful empirical applications of the welfare maximization approach that feature actual endangered species (Miller 1981; Smith & Krutilla 1978; Fisher & Krutilla 1974). The literature on safe minimum standards accepts a normative decision to preserve (provided costs are within socially acceptable limits) and then searches for the minimum viable population given irreversibility and uncertainty (Bishop 1978; 1979; 1980; Ciriacy-Wantrup 1968). This literature also includes no well-developed empirical examples.

Our approach is intermediate. Given the normative decision to preserve, we ask what is the least-cost management alternative for preserving any population level, implicitly including the level of the safe minimum standard. Our discussion begins with an introduction to the important characteristics of RCW biology and habitat. It continues with development of an economic model that emphasizes the trade-off between RCW habitat and timber production, the highest-valued alternate use of most RCW habitat. This model permits managers and policymakers to make cost-effective endangered species decisions at the margin. It also shows the critical RCW management variables and suggests where further biological research can provide information useful to managers. Finally, we test the model with data from the Croatan National Forest and discuss our results.

BIOLOGICAL BACKGROUND

The red-cockaded woodpecker inhabits mature (50–150-year-old) pine forests in the South. It lives in population units called *clans,* each of which consists of a mated pair and its (up to seven) helpers. Clans roost in areas known as *colonies* and mated pairs nest in cavity trees within these colonies. Cavity trees are mature live pines in which the woodpeckers excavate cavities for nesting. The existence of cavities is essential because males without cavities cannot attract mates.

Colony sites must include a replacement stock of cavity trees because woodpeckers abandon nests in dead trees. Woodpeckers also abandon nests in live trees when the hardwood and sapling pine undergrowth reaches the height of the cavity (Hooper, Robinson, & Jackson 1979). Prescribed burning can control the undergrowth, thereby preventing this cause of abandonment.

Colony sites on the Croatan range from 7 to 90 acres. Clans defend territories ranging from 100 to 250 acres around colony sites and forage on live pines of all ages within this territory. Clans make little use of pine saplings or pure hardwood stands within their territories because the active flow of resin restricts insect infestation within pine saplings and pure hardwood stands do not tend to occur in mixture with the mature pines that provide cavity trees.

ECONOMIC ANALYSIS

Our analysis assumes an exogenous demand (that is, there is a public law requiring endangered species management) and searches for the least marginal cost management alternative that satisfies this demand. The most important costs for RCW management are the implicit costs of foregone timber opportunities. The only direct RCW management costs are those for prescribed burning to maintain understory height below the cavity level. The cost management unit is the clan, which may be of varying population. Therefore, the marginal cost function measures the timber opportunity cost per clan or per colony site. No change in timber management is necessary on woodpecker foraging territories as foraging and timber management are compatible.

Figure 8.1 explains this marginal cost approach. The twin horizontal axes show the 1:1 relationship between clans and colony sites. If the number of clans, say C_1, is known, then the acreage in colony sites H_1 also is known, and conversely. Demand is fixed regardless of cost, at some exogenously determined number of clans, say C^*. The marginal cost function, reading from the origin, ranks preservation costs per clan from least to most expensive (or from least to most profitable timber opportunity). The total cost of RCW management is the area under the marginal cost function and to the left of C^*. The marginal cost of protecting any given clan or preserving a specific colony site is the vertical difference between the marginal cost function and the point on the horizontal axes identifying that clan and colony site.

The management and policy implications of this approach should be clear. First, there are social gains to following the obvious ranking and preserving the least expensive clans first — given the choice. Second, alternate management practices shift the marginal cost function, thereby changing the cost of protecting a given number of clans. Furthermore, better information regarding management impacts on the woodpecker increases confidence in the marginal cost function. Thus, learning how to decrease marginal costs and how to increase biological and managerial certainty would be important contributions of biological research. Third, varying the legal requirement C^* shifts the specified demand left or right, thereby altering total costs of RCW management and the marginal cost of the last clan or colony site saved. Good biological understanding argues for a de-

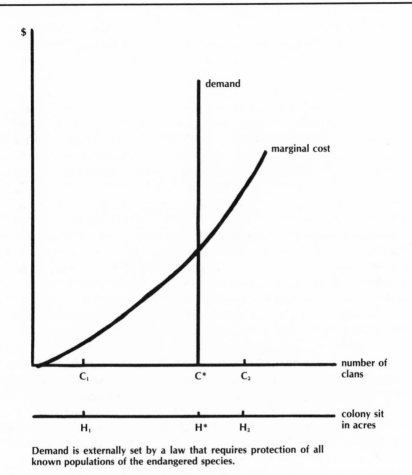

Demand is externally set by a law that requires protection of all
known populations of the endangered species.

Figure 8.1. Endangered species modeling.

mand function far enough to the right to guarantee a safe minimum biological population.

The Croatan National Forest manages its important timber species,
loblolly and longleaf pine, on seventy-year rotations in accordance with
multiple use–sustained yield criteria and the National Forest Management
Act of 1976. RCW biologists recommend average ages of ninety-five for
longleaf and seventy-five for loblolly, although there are woodpeckers nesting in Croatan loblolly stands as young as forty-six years (M. R. Lennartz,
USDA Forest Service, personal communication).

The costs of delayed harvests imposed by the biological recommendations are not constraining everywhere on the Croatan, however, because not all timber stands in the forest are commercially productive. The noncommercial stands tend to be biologically mature and RCW preservation occurs on them without competing with timber management. The marginal cost function, in this case, runs along the horizontal axis in Figure 8.1.

Where the timber stands are commercial, there are two alternate approaches to extending timber management rotations for woodpecker management: (A) permanent cessation of all timber harvesting on currently occupied colony sites; or (B) extended rotations and harvests on a sequence of timber stands recruited as colony sites. Neither alternative is a perfect preservation solution. The first fails to consider the 4–9 percent annual mortality rate among occupied cavity trees and makes no provision for their future replacement (Hooper et al 1979).[15] The understory is unlikely to provide replacements because pines tend to grow in even-aged stands with large gaps between the older age classes. The second alternative assumes that clans costlessly relocate upon harvest of their colony sites, although there is no empirical evidence supporting this assumption. Thus, in the short run, the second alternative provides uncertain results. In the long run, however, we can expect that as biologists learn more about colony establishment the second alternative may become more attractive.

ALTERNATIVE A: PRESERVING EXISTING COLONIES IN PERPETUITY. Current woodpecker management on the Croatan corresponds to this alternative. Current colony sites are insulated from timber management but there is no provision for future colony replacement. Foregone net timber receipts V_1 can be calculated according to the familiar Faustmann equation modified to include revenues from a sequence of harvests $Q(t)$, including both thinnings and final harvests that vary in diameter and, therefore, value; increasing relative stumpage prices $p(t)$; costs $c(t)$ from a sequence of inputs; and the number of acres A composing the known colony site.

$$V_1 = A[\sum_{t=0}^{T} p(t)Q(t)e^{-rt} - \sum_{t=0}^{T} c(t)e^{-rt}]/(1 - e^{-rt}) \tag{8.15}$$

Equation (8.15) describes the present value of an infinite series of rotations beginning now. Table 8.10 describes the empirical data used to estimate this value.

Further modification of the equation is necessary to include the value of currently standing timber on an existing colony site. The present value of standing timber is equal to

$$V_2 = A[\sum_{t=0}^{T-a} p(t)Q(t)e^{-rt} - \sum_{t=0}^{T-a} c(t)e^{-rt}] \tag{8.16}$$

Table 8.10. Abbreviated cost–revenue stream used in the calculation of perpetuity rents:

$$v_2 = A \left[\left(\sum_{t=0}^{T} p(t)Q(t)e^{-rt} - \sum_{t=0}^{T} c(t)e^{-rt} \right)/(1 - e^{-rT}) \right]^a$$

Year[b]	Treatment[b]	Output [Q(t)] by site index (SI)[c]					Costs [c(t)]	Revenues[d,e]
Loblolly pine		SI: 70	80	90	100	110		
0	Site preparation	—	—	—	—	—	$130/acre	$ 0.00
0	Fertilizer	—	—	—	—	—	$ 30/acre	$ 0.00
1 – T[f]	Annual management	—	—	—	—	—	$ 2/acre/year	$ 0.00
30	Commercial thin (cordwood)	0.98	4.03	6.63	11.10	13.44	$ 6/cord	$ 7.75/cord
50	Commercial thin (cordwood)	11.55	15.62	22.00	29.44	33.57	$ 6/cord	$ 7.75/cord
70[g]	Harvest (sawtimber)	22.55	29.50	36.60	44.95	53.10	$ 10/Mbf	$148.00/Mbf
78[h]	Harvest (sawtimber)	23.65	30.60	37.95	46.10	54.70	$ 10/Mbf	$148.00/Mbf
Longleaf pine		SI: 50	60	70	80			
0	Site preparation	—	—	—	—		$130/acre	$ 0.00
0	Fertilizer	—	—	—	—		$ 30/acre	$ 0.00
1 – T[f]	Annual management	—	—	—	—		$ 2/acre/year	$ 0.00
40	Commercial thin (cordwood)		0	1.47	4.84		$ 6/cord	$ 7.75/cord
60	Commercial thin (cordwood)	0	4.09	9.74	15.24		$ 6/cord	$ 7.75/cord
80[i]	Commercial thin (cordwood)	0	7.50	14.71	25.05		$ 6/cord	$ 7.75/cord
70[g]	Harvest (sawtimber)	5.40	12.35	20.40	28.30		$ 10/Mbf	$148.00/Mbf
98[h]	Harvest (sawtimber)	9.60	18.50	27.35	36.55		$ 10/Mbf	$148.00/Mbf

[a]For discussion of formula, see text: r = 4%, 7%, or 10%.
[b]Various sources: Asheville Office, National Forests of North Carolina.
[c]Source: USDA (1929, revised 1976).
[d]Source for prices: Norris (1979, 1980, 1981).
[e]Price sensitivity tested by assuming (1) constant prices and (2) rising relative prices in separate runs. See text for discussion.
[f]T denotes the final year of the rotation. Thus T = 70 for 70-year rotation, T = 78 for loblolly extended rotations, and T = 98 for longleaf extended rotations.
[g]Projected cut under current rotation.
[h]Projected cut under extended rotation.
[i]Commercial thinnings in the eightieth year only occur under the longleaf extended rotation management alternative.

where the revenues and costs generated by the current stand are calculated from the present ($t = 0$) to the time of their final harvest ($t = T - a$ where $T = 70$ and $a = $ the current stand age).

The combined value of the standing timber V_2 plus the value of all future rotations V_1 equals the total value of the colony site V_3 where

$$V_3 = V_2 + V_1 e^{-r(T-a)} \tag{8.17}$$

V_3 is the full timber opportunity cost associated with permanent removal of the existing colony site from timber production.

ALTERNATIVE B: ROTATING RECRUITMENT STANDS. The cost of implementing management alternative B is the difference in net revenues between current seventy-year timber rotations and the extended rotations. Its calculation depends on two important assumptions, one having to do with the length of RCW habitation in recruitment stands and the other having to do with current stand age structures and harvest scheduling.

For the first, we accept biological evidence that suggests woodpeckers mate in their second year and inhabit colony sites until their eighth year when they die, the site then can be harvested, and descendants of the mated pairs relocate to adjacent recruitment stands (Ligon 1970). We combine this assumption with Lennartz's (1982) recommendation of stands averaging seventy-five years for loblolly and ninety-five years for longleaf. Together, these recommend sequences of thirteen loblolly and seventeen longleaf colony sites.

In addition, we assume each colony site is 11.7 acres, the average size of current RCW colonies on the Croatan, and that the various loblolly and longleaf sites on the Croatan have sufficient adjacent acreage to allow such sequences of stands.[16] (We know from the Forest Survey that there exists sufficient acreage within each site quality index but we do not know whether it is distributed adjacently.) Conversion from seventy-year rotations to extended rotations poses no immediate stand age problems because the Croatan has an excess of mature and noncommercial timber stands that can fill the RCW management gap until current commercial stands reach ages seventy-five and ninety-five for loblolly and longleaf, respectively.

With this background we can consider the equations for modeling management alternative B. Make the (generous cost and conservative RCW management) assumption that all recruitment stands must grow from currently idle timberland. The present value of the perpetual net revenue stream from 11.7 acres of loblolly on a seventy-year rotation is

$$L_{70} = [11.7/(1 - e^{-70r})]\{p(70)Q(70) - c(70) + [p(30)Q(30) - c(30)]e^{-30r} + [p(50)Q(50) - c(50)]e^{-50r}\} \tag{8.18}$$

for stands currently seventy years old. (Recall from Table 8.10 that thinning occurs at ages thirty and fifty for loblolly. Initial-year site preparation and fertilization costs enter as final harvest costs for the previous rotation. Annual management costs are compounded, summed, and entered at years thirty and fifty.) Similarly, the present value of the perpetual net revenue stream from 11.7 acres of loblolly on seventy-eight-year rotation is

$$L_{78} = [11.7/(1 - e^{-78r})]\{[p(78)Q(78) - c(78)]e^{-8r}$$
$$+ [p(30)Q(30) - c(30)]e^{-38r} + [p(50)Q(50)$$
$$- c(50)]e^{-58r}\} \qquad (8.19)$$

Subtracting L_{78} from L_{70} provides the loblolly opportunity cost for providing a single extended rotation RCW colony site.

Recall, however, that a six-year sequence of thirteen sites is necessary. Therefore, opportunity costs totaling $L_{70} - L_{78}$ occur every six years on each 200 acre RCW habitat. The discounted total opportunity costs for maintaining an RCW clan in perpetuity are

$$C_L = L_{70}(1 + e^{-6r} + e^{-12r} + \ldots + e^{-72r}) - L_{78}(e^{-8r} + e^{-14r}$$
$$+ \ldots + e^{-80r}) \qquad (8.20)$$

An analogous expression describes longleaf opportunity costs for maintaining RCW clans in perpetuity.

EMPIRICAL RESULTS AND CONCLUSIONS

Table 8.10 shows our harvest projections, prices, and costs. There are two modifications and two sensitivity analyses worthy of comment. (1) Hopkins (USDA Forest Service, personal communication) provides data on the stocking of current stands. We make the generous assumption that all future stands will be fully stocked. This assumption raises our timber opportunity costs an undetermined amount, perhaps as much as 100 percent. (2) Prescribed burning is a timber management practice in addition to those shown in Table 8.10. Managers normally apply it to fully managed timber stands on the Croatan. Therefore, it adds to timber management costs. It also is a requirement of RCW management. One impact is to decrease the flammability of the forest floor thereby decreasing the risk of wildfire and decreasing the cost of stewardship of all forestlands, commercial or otherwise. Therefore, it is not an incremental cost for RCW management and it does not appear in either Table 8.10 or in our empirical estimates.

Our analyses may be sensitive to increases in relative stumpage prices over time and to various costs of capital. Real sawtimber stumpage prices have been increasing at a 3 percent annual rate and cordwood prices have been increasing at a 1.5 percent annual rate (Dutrow, Vasievich, & Conklin 1982). Some evidence, however, suggests these rates may decline early in the next century. Other evidence suggests that competing environmental amenity values also may be increasing in real value. Nevertheless, we test for real annual rates of 0, 1.5, and 3.0 percent for sawtimber and 0, 0.75, and 1.5 percent for cordwood. Finally, the U.S. Forest Service uses a 4 percent discount rate, but only on appeal from the general federal agency rate of 10 percent. We test for both rates as well as for the intermediate rate of 7 percent. The social opportunity cost of funds probably falls within this range.

The first-order results from our equations and data yield timber values and RCW opportunity costs that are generous for various reasons already identified, and because we disregarded the large expenses of access to the timber management sites (including building the logging roads themselves). One measure of the overestimate is our projection of 14,745 Mbf of mature timber on the Croatan in 1982. Yet timber managers harvested only 2804 Mbf or 14 percent of this. If we assume that the managers' judgments were rational, then only the 14 percent was commercial and the remaining 86 percent, in fact, had no timber opportunity cost. This 86 percent of timber sites was free for RCW management. In terms of Figure 8.1, this means that the RCW marginal cost function departs from the horizontal axis only for RCW sites occurring on the commercially valuable 14 percent of timberland.

Consider how this observation alters the final cost estimates for preserving fifty-two RCW habitat sites under either management alternatives A or B. First, assume that the ordered ranking of sites is correct and the generous timber opportunity costs, which constitute the first-order results, are correct for the most valuable 14 percent of all sites. The actions of timber managers have shown us that this opportunity cost is zero on the remaining sites.

Under alternative A the best twenty-two timber sites fall on longleaf site indices 70 and 80 and loblolly site indices 100 and 110. These sites provide 2983 Mbf annually, or more than a sufficient volume to satisfy the 1982 harvest level for the Croatan. There are no foregone timber opportunities on the remaining thirty RCW colony sites. The large number of low-quality timber sites with RCW colonies suggests that low-quality sites were left undisturbed by timber management before RCW protection became an issue. It also suggests a rational tendency for timber managers to harvest good sites first. Of the twenty-two sites with valuable timber opportunities, six have timber stands currently over age eighty-five. Timber managers apparently found these sites unprofitable for timber, even before recent discoveries of the woodpecker and requirements for its protection. Subtracting these six sites leaves sixteen RCW sites on which the Croatan must forego a viable timber option. Table 8.11 is the marginal cost schedule for these remaining sixteen sites under each price and discount rate scenario. It leads us to the observation that total perpetuity costs for preserving the fifty-two existing sites (at a 4 percent discount rate and 0 rate of stumpage price increase) are $220,422. The annual payment associated with this level of protection is $8816.88. (More than one-fourth of the costs are for one highly productive loblolly site that is almost of harvest age now.)

There are fifty-four 200-acre preservation units on longleaf site index 50 and loblolly site index 70. These each satisfy the alternative B requirement for rotating recruitment stands in perpetuity. They are the poorest sites and the least likely ever to become commercially viable for timber. If current timber management is an indication, they are not viable for commercial timber production and preserving fifty-two of them requires no timber opportunity foregone.

In conclusion, the costs of preserving the fifty-two existing RCW colonies is relatively small. There is no cost at all for the fifty-two recruitment colonies. Indeed, the costs of timber opportunities foregone are probably lesser problems of RCW management than is the uncertainty clouding the efficiency of either preservation management alternative.

Finally, a summary note is in order regarding our application of marginal cost analysis for endangered species management in general. Outlining the costs associated with the anticipated preservation of discrete biological units does provide the resource manager with the total cost information necessary for choice between management alternatives with various associated risks of species extinction. (It provides supply information but no demand information.) Furthermore, our marginal cost analysis determines the relative costs of preserving various potential individual habitat sites and provides a means of evaluating alternate approaches for satisfying an exogenous preservation constraint.

Nevertheless, the tool is not without its limitations. It is important to bear in mind that this analysis presents the costs of providing *habitat* for the species. This may or may not result in preservation of the *species* or even its *individual* members. Preservation of the individual occurs when the individual's niche requirements are satisfied throughout its natural life span. Preservation of the species requires not only preservation of the individual, but also preservation of a sufficient number of individuals to maintain genetic diversity throughout the geographic range of the species. This compounds uncertainty: We know neither the specific habitat requirements of the individual nor the population level and distribution necessary to guarantee the genetic stock. Further biological research may answer these questions. With the answers, we can redefine the colony site, or the horizontal axis in Figure 8.1, and the safe minimum standard below which population preservation is not viable. Subsequently, we can apply the same

Table 8.11. Marginal costs: Costs of preserving individual existing colony sites where timber management is a viable option

Case	Species	Site index	Acreage	Age	Discount rate and rate of price change[a] scenarios								
					r = .04			r = .07			r = .10		
					0.00 0.00	.015 .0075	.03 .015	0.00 0.00	.015 .0075	.03 .015	0.00 0.00	.015 .0075	.03 .015
47	Longleaf	70	7	52	$ 3264	5218	8374	1598	2346	3363	884	1294	1831
16	Longleaf	70	7	59	4434	6355	9545	2739	3482	4434	1930	2410	2983
31	Longleaf	70	7	64	5495	7309	10531	3974	4585	5373	3277	3699	4173
52	Longleaf	80	7	52	5566	8405	13187	2812	3979	5561	1583	2226	3070
15	Longleaf	70	7	67	6241	7947	11194	4951	5375	6015	4475	4762	5080
49	Longleaf	70	7	69	6791	8403	11670	5726	6008	6478	5498	5627	5780
30	Longleaf	70	15	64	11776	15662	22566	8515	9824	11513	7021	7927	8942
6	Loblolly	100	7	52	12906	18770	27785	6816	9350	12761	3896	5311	7170
10	Longleaf	80	15	54	12985	19263	29274	6998	9538	12908	4213	5687	7568
8	Longleaf	80	15	56	14130	20360	30347	8116	10662	13975	5215	6769	8697
11	Longleaf	70	15	74	15177	18515	25539	13192	13853	14403	13053	13102	13203
12	Longleaf	70	15	74	15177	18515	25539	13192	13853	14403	13053	13102	13203
13	Longleaf	70	15	74	15177	18515	25539	13192	13853	14403	13053	13102	13203
50	Longleaf	70	15	74	15177	18515	25539	13192	13853	14403	13053	13102	13203
9	Longleaf	90	15	52	19597	28920	43420	10221	14150	19446	5818	8004	10875
46	Loblolly	110	15	57	56529	74452	100862	35798	44762	56025	24015	29823	36912
Total cost					220422	295124	420911	151032	179473	215464	120037	135947	155893

[a]Rate of price change: First entry for sawtimber, second entry for cordwood.

marginal cost analysis as demonstrated in this section except with superior confidence in the precision of the marginal cost estimates.

 ## Conclusions and General Implications

Public land management is probably the most thoroughly reviewed and analyzed topic in all the literature having to do with natural resource management. This chapter makes no attempt to repeat this literature or to be comprehensive in its own review. Rather, it samples four unresolved and contemporary public land management issues with the intent of raising the quality of analysis and the level of discourse regarding each.

The first two issues have to do with public timber management policies. The market fully values and freely exchanges timber yet public agencies in general prefer nonmarket criteria for timber harvest decisions. We examine the costs of their departure from market criteria. One reason the U.S. Forest Service departs from market timber harvest criteria reflects its concern for the stability of small timber-based communities. We also examine whether current Forest Service harvest policies can have the desired welfare impacts on such communities. Our other two issues have to do with nonmarket values provided on the public lands: recreation and the protection of endangered species. We review a specific case for each with the joint intentions of displaying improved analytical methods and learning whether the general policy discussions of these topics feature their most important social welfare considerations.

The public lands produce 22 percent of our annual softwood timber harvests. Their timber management objective resembles the production of an even flow of annual sawtimber harvests regardless of local market criteria. Special interest groups widely discuss the resulting departures from market results but there has been no general analysis and there is no consensus of opinion. Our approach to this problem begins with the simulation of market responsive public supply functions for six regions of the country. We introduce these functions into the Adams-Haynes macroeconomic model of the timber sector. The revised model permits us to contrast regional prices, costs, harvest levels and consumers' and producers' surpluses occurring under conditions of either current or market-sensitive public timber management criteria.

Our analysis is impressionistic and should not be taken as conclusive. It represents a one-year harvest shift and incorporates no dynamic effects, no local variations (which might dominate political judgments about regional solutions), and no adjustments for nonmarket values that may compete with timber production. We mean to leave no impression of precision.

Nevertheless, our results are truly large and emphatic. They suggest substantial harvest increases on the public lands for all regions except the Rocky Mountains. These increases cause stumpage price decreases, large consumer gains, large gains for the public treasury, and some offsetting harvest and profit decreases for private timberland owners. (See Table 8.4.) The welfare shifts are large enough, if accurate, to dominate impacts of most other forestry regulations for either public or private lands discussed in this book. While we make no claim for accuracy in the magnitude of our results, we do believe they emphasize the importance of this policy issue. The departure of public timber management from market harvest criteria deserves further serious inquiry.

Our second issue is community stability. The Forest Service attempts to protect small local communities with timber-based economies from the local hardship caused by a fluctuating macroeconomy. The method of protection is through a guaranteed flow of public harvests to the local mills. It is questionable whether this Forest Service policy can succeed in the presence of many opportunities for local adjustments in stumpage and log inventories, from both public and private lands. We overlook these opportunities for adjustment and inquire whether, in the best of cases, the Forest Service policy can be effective.

Our analysis features a general equilibrium model and data from western Montana. Our results are sensitive to the stumpage supply elasticity. Different elasticities create different factor shares and different final output levels for the different sectors of the local economy (see Tables 8.6 and 8.7). Nevertheless, the impact on either employment or total factor payments is negligible in any case. The smaller the elasticity, the less the impact on any specific industry or any factor of production. As the elasticity increases, the Forest Service policy has a greater impact. That is, policy succeeds in maintaining employment in the wood products industry, but it has no impact on overall community employment or wages. The policy does extract a substantial toll, however, from the public treasury. Thus, we can say that the Forest Service's current community stability policy is noble but misguided.

We have no knowledge of the total social costs of this policy across all forests and communities. We doubt, however, whether any Forest Service policy to stabilize small local communities can be effective. There are too many opportunities for economic response beyond Forest Service control. If we are correct, then the unquestionably noble community stability objective provides no justification by itself for departure from market timber harvest criteria.

Our two inquiries into nonmarket value management are very localized. Our recreation analysis focuses on the Seeley-Swan Valley (SSV) in western Montana. It searches for an optimal demand–supply equilibrium, but its feature is the estimation of a local recreation supply function, something the bulk of the recreation economics literature overlooks but a key item for on-the-ground recreation managers. Supply may be the only factor their management can alter. They certainly have a difficult time altering demand.

Our demand analysis uses the common travel-cost method. Our supply analysis depends on cost functions constructed from local Forest Service data with the considerable assistance of the local managers themselves. Our results are very satisfying for both managers and analysts. (See Table 8.9.) They show that equilibrium price and quantity levels for the four camp-grounds are close to the actual price and quantity levels and the small deviation of the actual from the optimal makes good budgetary sense. This means that SSV recreation managers perform well by social criteria. It may also be that recreation supply has not been a critical analytical problem and that the absence of an abundant literature reflects this. Of course, it is impossible to generalize from our small sample of four campgrounds, but our analysis should leave both managers and analysts with a satisfying feeling.

Our final inquiry regards a single endangered species, the red-cock-aded woodpecker, in a single location, the Croatan National Forest in North Carolina. We do not have the means to estimate demand for en-dangered species protection and the biological information necessary for the most satisfying supply estimation is also lacking. We can take the bio-logical data available and estimate the costs of RCW protection in terms of other land use opportunities foregone. These costs vary with the biological management assumptions and the number of colonies protected. In no case is protection cost very large. Indeed, the first 86 percent of all colony sites require no foregone land opportunity costs in any case we examine.

The importance of this analysis is that (1) it provides evidence that RCW management costs society less than much of the political discussion would have us believe and (2) it demonstrates a mechanism for arraying costs and management choices in a manner that makes resource tradeoffs clear. The low-cost result causes us to ponder whether the costs of activities to protect other endangered species may be less than often anticipated. Application of this method and these results should help focus scientific research for the RCW, and for other endangered species as well, on topics having large impacts on either management costs or species survival. The method and results beg clearer analysis of endangered species problems in general and before any further political decisions are made.

In conclusion, none of these four analyses provides universal evidence of a high degree of confidence regarding the welfare impacts of any public land management policy. They all, however, provide emphatic statements about some phase of public land management. These results show us good reason why resource analysts have put great effort into understanding public land policy. They also suggest that market-valued resource outputs from the public lands are less well-managed for society's best interests than are those other resource outputs that do not exchange in the market. Perhaps public land policy is a more critical issue than many private resource policy questions and perhaps the potential social costs of mismanaging the public's lands, particularly its timber resource, are greater than the social costs of the private regulations discussed in the previous chapters.

 Notes

1. That is, our analysis compares current expenditures with current receipts, yet the correct comparison is between current expenditures and the discounted future receipts which managers anticipate those expenditures will create. If planned harvest volumes remain constant over time and ouput prices and factor costs retain their current relative relationship, then current receipts are a reasonable proxy for discounted future receipts only if capital has a zero opportunity cost. Our true 1977 public sector estimate is conservative if the actual cost of capital exceeds zero.

2. Adams and Haynes include more sophisticated intermediate product demand functions for these two regions. To a large extent intermediate product demands in these regions are originally satisfied by stumpage supplies from the other six regions.

3. D. Jackson (personal communication) finds a $12 per Mbf difference between state and private stumpage in Montana. The federal-private difference is probably greater. Furthermore, it is our observation that the federal accounting procedure underestimates timber harvest and production costs on public lands. Regardless of this observation, overestimating the public-private difference causes *under*estimation of the anticipated social welfare losses due to public agency constraints on market timber criteria—and, thereby, strengthens our eventual conclusions.

4. D. Adams and J. Kincaid assisted in our Table 8.2 revision of the AH model. The interpretation of results remains our own.

5. Public sector gains are measured as

1977 actual: price (Table 8.3) times harvest quantity (Table 8.1) minus costs (Table 8.1).
Simulated: the area below equilibrium price (Table 8.3) and above the supply schedule (Table 8.2).

The 1977 actual net public timber revenues can be negative. The public producers' surplus calculated in the simulated case is due to the fixity of capital where capital is the standing timber inventory. Table 8.4 shows the difference between the 1977 actual net gains and the simulated market-sensitive net gains.

6. See the quotation. If the total timber input accounts for 10 percent of community employment, then 30 percent of total timber input must account for approximately 3 percent of community employment, depending on elasticities.

7. This policy may be wise if the demand shift is temporary. If the shift is permanent, then a wiser policy would introduce a smooth decline in Forest Service

timber inputs, thereby easing the transition to a permanently lower level of wood product output. Otherwise, the Forest Service can only succeed in either introducing a permanent subsidy for a declining industry or postponing an eventual precipitous adjustment. It is a point of fact that easing transitions and smoothing declines are not actions consistent with the current Forest Service policy that this chapter examines.

   8. Wear's factor share estimates are

$$\theta_{KX} = 0.7381 + 0.0730\ln r_x - 0.0285\ln w - 0.0445\ln s$$
$$\qquad (0.1050) \quad (0.0246) \quad\quad (0.0149) \quad\quad (0.0288)$$
$$\theta_{LX} = 0.4281 - 0.0285\ln r_x + 0.0970\ln w - 0.0684\ln s$$
$$\qquad (0.0063) \quad (0.0149) \quad\quad (0.0232) \quad\quad (0.0338)$$
$$\theta_{SX} = -0.1662 - 0.0445\ln r_x - 0.0684\ln w + 0.1129\ln s$$
$$\qquad (0.1052) \quad (0.0288) \quad\quad (0.0338) \quad\quad (0.0742)$$

where the numbers in parentheses are the standard errors. Wear derives the substitution elasticities: $\sigma_{KL} = 0.8221$; $\sigma_{LS} = 0.1285$; $\sigma_{KS} = 0.4491$.

   9. We also examined an alternative specification (1) restricting the wage in the unionized wood products sector so that it is inflexible downward yet permitting a market responsive wage in the Y sector and (2) holding the community's aggregate level of capital facilities constant but permitting some capital, like pickup trucks and personally owned tools, to shift between sectors. The results are much the same as those reported in Tables 8.6 and 8.7. All variables change in the same directions as previously reported. Forest Service policy holds down the average wage, therefore, the community's wage bill. Local capital owners gain at the expense of labor. Surely, this is an undesirable policy result. There is no net effect on factor payments but the costs for the public treasury are $69.8 million, almost double those reported in Table 8.7.

   10. This section relies on preliminary insights from the Steven E. Daniels' dissertation (1986). Daniels also considers other functional forms, other time periods for decision making and the option to contract for private provision of recreational services on national forestlands.

   11. All four campgrounds fall within bounds of the Seeley Lake Ranger District. The district itself extends beyond the Seeley-Swan Valley and includes five other, similar campgrounds in neighboring supply-sheds.

   12. The specification of the demand function is log linear generalized least squares. Unequal zonal populations cause heterscedasticity, therefore we weight the regression by the square root of zonal population. This is equivalent to generalized least squares and, as such, is unbiased and efficient. Travel time is valued at 35 percent of the average wage rate. On-site time is 100 percent of the average wage rate. (These valuations are consistent with Wilman's (1980) theoretical recommendations.) Travel is at 50 mph, and the average wage rate within each zone of recreator origin is from *Local Personal Income 1977–1982* (USDC 1984). We derived α because otherwise the regressions produced statistically insignificant estimates of it and also yielded meaningless consumers' surplus values.

   13. Steven Daniels discussed this question with us. Kerry Smith clarified and modified it.

   14. Judge, Strait, and Hyde (1984) discuss the analysis in abbreviated form. Much of the data in both that paper and this section are the same because of a common author and research director.

   15. With an average of 1.5 cavity trees per colony on the Croatan, all existing

cavity trees will be dead in seventeen to thirty-eight years. Clearly, an alternative for preservation of existing stands must be found and must be implemented soon.

16. The 200-acre foraging areas recommended for the Croatan National Forest are not constraining as 11.7 acres for each of thirteen loblolly or seventeen longleaf stands implies only 152.1 or 198.9 acres per colony, respectively.

 References

Adams, D. M. and R. W. Haynes. 1981. *The 1980 softwood timber assessment market model: Structure, projections and policy simulation.* Forest Science Monograph 22. (Results revised, 1985, personal communication from D. M. Adams.)

Atkinson, A. B. and J. E. Stiglitz. 1980. *Lectures on public economics.* New York: McGraw-Hill.

Banskota, K., W. Phillips, and T. Williamson. 1985. Factor substitution and economies of scale in the Alberta sawmill industry. *Canadian Journal of Forest Research* 15(6):1025–30.

Bishop, R. C. 1978. Endangered species and uncertainty: The economics of the safe minimum standard. *American Journal of Agricultural Economics* 60:10–18.

———. 1979. Endangered species, irreversibility and uncertainty: A reply. *American Journal of Agricultural Economics* 61:376–79.

———. 1980. Endangered species: An economic perspective. In *Forty-fifth North American wildlife and natural resource conference, transactions,* K. Sabol, ed. pp. 208–18. Washington, D.C.: Wildlife Management Institute.

Caves, R. E. and R. W. Jones. 1981. *World trade and payments: An introduction.* Boston: Little, Brown.

Ciriacy-Wantrup, S. V. 1968. *Resource conservation: Economics and policies.* 3d ed. Berkeley: University of California.

Daniels, S. 1986. Efficient provision of recreational opportunities: The case of U.S. Forest Service campgrounds. Ph.D. diss., Duke University, Durham, N.C.

Dutrow, G. F., J. M. Vasievich, and M. E. Conklin. 1982. *Economic opportunities for increasing timber supplies. An assessment of the timber situation in the United States, 1952–2030.* Forest Service Report No. 23. Washington, D.C.: U.S. Department of Agriculture.

Fisher, A. C. and J. V. Krutilla. 1974. Valuing long run ecological consequences and irreversibilities. *Journal of Environmental Economics and Management* 1:96–108.

Harberger, A. C. 1962. The incidence of the corporate income tax. *Journal of Political Economy* 70:215-40.

———. 1966. Efficiency effects of taxes on income from capital. In *Effects of corporation income tax.* Detroit: Wayne State University Press.

Hooper, R. G., A. F. Robinson, Jr., and J. A. Jackson. 1979. *The red-cockaded woodpecker: Notes on life history and management.* USFS General Report SA-GR7. Washington, D.C.

Judge, R. P., R. Strait, and W. Hyde. 1984. The economics of endangered species preservation: The red-cockaded woodpecker. In *Transactions: North American wildlife and natural resources conference 49,* pp. 375–81. Washington, D.C.: Wildlife Management Institute.

Klein, L. 1974. Issues in econometric studies of investment behavior. *Journal of Law and Economics* 13:43–49.

Ligon, J. D. 1970. Behavior and breeding biology of the red-cockaded woodpecker. *The Auk* 87:255–78.

Miller, J. R. 1981. Irreversible land use and the preservation of endangered species. *Journal of Environmental Economics and Management* 8:19–26.

Norris, F. M. 1979–81. Timber-Mart South. Highlands, N.C.: Timber-Mart South and Data Resources Incorporated.

Parashevopoulos, C. C. 1979. Alternative estimates of the elasticity of substitution. *Review of Economics and Statistics* 61:439–42.

Smith, V. K. and J. V. Krutilla. 1978. Endangered species, irreversibilities, and uncertainty. *American Journal of Agricultural Economics* 61(2):371–79.

Sorg, C. F. and J. B. Loomis. 1984. *Empirical estimates of amenity forest values: A comparative review*. USDA Forest Service General Technical Report RM-107. Fort Collins: Rocky Mountain Forest and Range Experiment Station.

U.S. Department of Agriculture. 1929, revised 1976. *Volume, yield and stand tables for second growth southern pines*. Miscellaneous Publication No. 50.

_____. 1969–1983. *Agricultural statistics*. Washington, D.C.: U.S. Government Printing Office.

U.S.D.A., Forest Service. 1978. *Forest statistics of the U.S., 1977*. (Review draft.) Washington, D.C.: U.S. Government Printing Office.

U.S. Department of Commerce, Bureau of the Census. 1967–1982. *Annual survey of manufacturers*. Washington, D.C.: U.S. Government Printing Office.

_____. 1969–1982. *Current business reports: Monthly retail trade*. Washington, D.C.: U.S. Government Printing Office.

_____. 1971, 1976, 1981, 1984. *Census of manufactures*, Vol. III, *Area statistics*. Washington, D.C.: U.S. Government Printing Office.

U.S. Department of Commerce, Bureau of Economic Analysis. 1980. *Business statistics, 1979*. (Biennial supplement to the *Survey of current business*.) Washington, D.C.: U.S. Government Printing Office.

_____. 1984. *Local personal income, 1977–1982*. Washington, D.C.: U.S. Government Printing Office.

U.S. Department of the Interior, National Park Service. 1984. *133 report on budget execution*. Washington, D.C.: Author.

_____. 1986. *National park statistical abstract, 1985*. Denver, Colo.: National Park Service Denver Service Center.

Waggener, T. R. 1977. Community stability as a forest management objective. *Journal of Forestry* 75:710–14.

Wear, D. 1985. A comparison of dual approaches to estimating production technology: The wood products industry in Montana. Unpublished manuscript, School of Forestry, University of Montana, Missoula.

Wilman, E. A. 1980. The value of time in recreational benefit studies. *Journal of Environmental Economics and Management* 7(3):272–86.

CHAPTER 9

Summary, Conclusions, and Policy Implications

Regulation is an important public policy issue for natural resources much as it is for the economy as a whole. A battery of public market interventions affect resource scarcity and resource allocation and most of us hold strong opinions about these interventions. Yet our opinions often lack substantiating empirical content. This is surely the case in forestry where regulation of U.S. forestlands has been a motivating issue of public policy for at least a century, yet there are almost no empirical studies measuring the impacts of the special public regulations and other policies affecting forestry. The objective of this book is to provide some of the empirical evidence missing from the popular debate on public policy and regulatory reform in this sector.

The regulatory history of American forestlands begins with timber harvest restrictions first imposed by the King of England in order to preserve a stock of shipbuilding material for the Royal Navy. The young American republic showed similar concern in its efforts to ensure a continued flow of naval stores from the southern pine resource. These concerns, based on anticipated shortages of specific forest products, are prologue to the strongest and most long-lasting regulatory effort in American forestry, the government effort to prevent an anticipated future timber famine. In the late nineteenth century, this concern became the original justification for federal ownership of what is now one-quarter of all American forestlands.

Even federal ownership was not perceived as sufficient protection. Continuing concern for an anticipated timber famine raised policy questions about private land management. Federal regulation of private forestlands became, in the 1930s, probably the most divisive issue in the history of American forestry. The forest industry avoided sweeping federal regulations at this time only by arguing that the states are the proper institutions to introduce forest regulations. Subsequent laws in sixteen states mandate minimum timberstand volumes and seek to ensure early regeneration following harvest. The federal government also began, at this time, a long and continuing policy of market interventions that provide forestry incentives for nonindustrial private landowners.

Public ownership, state regulations and publicly funded incentives remain features of national forest policy today. In addition, the environmental awareness of the 1970s encouraged a new round of state forest practice acts to regulate harvests on private lands with the intent of protecting environmental and aesthetic values.

The political values of the 1980s raise questions about many of these regulations. The Sagebrush Rebellion questions public ownership, industrial interests question the production costs imposed by environmental regulations and federal budgetary problems raise doubts about public expenditures for private forestry incentives. Nevertheless, thorough empirical tests of the social and economic impacts of regulation in forestry are restricted to three papers on international trade in logs or lumber (Wiseman & Sedjo 1981; Sedjo & Wiseman 1983; Gallagher 1980).

This book examines the economic impacts of several politically important regulations in an attempt to overcome this absence of empirical evidence. The standard economic arguments for public intervention in the marketplace, therefore for regulation, are market failure, distribution, and stabilization. We cannot examine every regulation affecting forestry today. We can choose example regulations that (1) rely on each of these three economic arguments as justification and (2) affect either the supply (timber production) or demand (wood processing) sides of the stumpage market. We anticipate that these examples may provide generalizable evidence about the impacts of other production and processing regulations dependent on the three standard arguments. It rapidly becomes clear, however, that the economic justification for each individual regulation is elusive. For example, what was originally justified on grounds of perceived market failure may now find greater support for its distributive impacts. This means that we must examine both, and perhaps stabilization impacts as well, for each regulation. For this reason, our subsequent empirical analyses select market regulations on basis of their initial justifications, but the analyses themselves always extend to other arguments for public intervention.

If the term *regulation* can be understood to mean "market intervention," then it should also be clear that this classification easily overlooks two important groups of market distortions: nonneutral taxes and public ownership. We add chapters with representative examples from each. Our analyses show that the economic impacts of two of these taxation and public ownership "regulations" are greater than the sum of all the other market distortions that we examine.

Our analyses rely on general equilibrium models wherever possible because these improve on common partial equilibrium models by also picking up effects on the rest of the economy external to the forestry sector. Our summary measure of economic impact is the sum of discounted benefits minus discounted costs, including nonmarket benefits and costs. We make an effort not to overlook administrative costs, an effort that we also think improves on much of the general regulation literature.

The twenty-two data sets applied in these analyses each yield results that satisfy the usual tests for statistical reliability. The data at hand are not always sufficient to determine the net economic impact with precision. They are sufficient, however, to discern whether the net impacts are positive or negative. The data also are sufficient to identify general classes of beneficiaries for redistributive payments. Together, these efficiency measures and distributive statements provide strong evidence of the merit of each example regulation.

The following sections of this final chapter first summarize our specific results as they apply to each of five general public market interventions plus two nonneutral taxes and four market distorting policies for the public lands. We subsequently draw general conclusions and policy implications. Our conclusions and policy implications look to the (previously unidentified) stumpage price impacts of the various regulations as additional benchmarks. We also include a final comment on the aggregate impact of forest regulation on economic growth in the sector.

 A Summary of Policy Impacts

The first two regulations, state forest practice acts and forest incentive programs together with technical assistance, affect forestry from the supply side of the stumpage market. The third, price reporting, is an attempt to decrease price instability in the stumpage market itself. The fourth and fifth, the minimum wage and the Jones Act restrictions on intercoastal lumber shipments, affect forestry from the demand side of stumpage. Our inquiries into the impact of nonneutral taxes (focusing on capital gains and current use taxes) and public ownership (focusing on timber harvest scheduling, community stability and two nonmarket values: recreation and endangered species protection) follow.

SUPPLY-SIDE REGULATIONS

STATE FOREST PRACTICE ACTS. SFPAs provide the focus for most recent discussions of regulation in forestry. They are examples of regulations justified by market failure arguments. Sixteen states introduced forest practice legislation as early as fifty years ago in order to protect against the timber market's perceived failure to reflect anticipated future scarcity. More recent forest practice legislation (nine states) reflects the belief that markets fail to value environmental and aesthetic losses due to timber harvests. Both groups of forest practice legislation approach their different objectives in the same general manner. They mandate a minimum standing inventory of timber (in the form of either seed trees or other rapid reforestation) in the period immediately subsequent to each timber harvest.

It is difficult to contrast the impact of forest practice legislation on standing inventory with what that inventory would have been without the legislation. One alternative is to contrast the inventory in neighboring states with similar biological and economic characteristics but only one of which has an SFPA. Virginia, which has had forest practice legislation since 1950, and North Carolina are two such states. The thirty-five-year history of the Virginia law is approximately the period of one timber rotation for the predominant commercial species in these states. Therefore, it is sufficient time for the Virgina law to have had an inventory impact on most of its commercial timberlands.

Our analysis regresses a measure of standing inventory per acre in 199 counties in both states on biological, market, and ownership variables and an indicator variable that distinguishes between the two states. The biological, market, and ownership variables permit statistical removal of cross-state differences due to these variables and permit isolation, in the indicator variable, of any difference due only to state administration (i.e., the forest practice act). The equations perform well and all important coefficients, except the coefficient on the state indicator, both have the anticipated sign and are significant at the 1 percent level. Furthermore, there is no evidence of variation across within-state regions. The coefficients on the state indicator are small and never significant in four variations on the regressions. Therefore, we cannot reject the hypothesis that Virginia's forest practice act has had no measurable impact on standing timber inventory over the law's thirty-five-year existence.

Either Virginia's seed tree law does not produce an inventory different from that which landowners would maintain in absence of the law, or else Virginia's enforcement of this law is not effective. In either event, the absence of a measurable impact on current standing inventory precludes any effect on future timber supply and, therefore, any desired social benefit. If there is no additional inventory, then there also can be no additional landowner costs for holding additional inventory. Yet there are administrative costs of approximately $150,000 per year for Virginia's law. In sum, there are no apparent redeeming features in Virginia's legislation, as currently implemented, and North Carolina has been the wiser for avoiding the public expenditures of a similar law.

A different, and more effective, Virginia law might be designed. Perhaps because of industry opposition, it has not been. The facts of industry and other opposition, existing laws, and our empirical evidence all suggest a burden of proof for proponents of other SFPAs. We made additional empirical inquiry into the correlates of standing timber inventory in Oregon and Washington, two states with recent environmentally induced forest practice legislation. Their legislation is too new (1971 and 1974, respectively) to produce measurable effects on forest inventory and our final judgement of these laws must await the collection of new data. Nevertheless, our inquiry into measurable inventory adjustments for a longer (thirty-year) period in these two states does raise additional skepticism regarding potential SFPA gains from careful monitoring of industrial landowners with good timberlands who already have market incentives to reforest rapidly, thereby preparing by themselves for anticipated future timber demands and mitigating environmental and aesthetic losses from the harvest operation. Yet these landowners receive much of the enforcement attention from administrators of the new laws.

In sum, the Virginia–North Carolina analysis raises doubts regarding the social advantages of forest practice legislation in general. The Oregon–Washington analysis supports forest industry arguments that forest practice legislation is ineffective in its objective and adds potential costs to the production process. The Oregon–Washington analysis raises doubts about any legislation that does not sharply focus on those nonindustrial landowners in locations of least likely forest regeneration. Even this focus may have its drawbacks. While it may be attractive for nonmarket environmental and aesthetic values, it may also be unattractive for distributive reasons if these less productive nonindustrial lands are managed by poorer landowners.

THE FORESTRY INCENTIVE PROGRAM AND TECHNICAL ASSISTANCE. After SFPAs, FIP is probably the best-known market intervention in forestry today. It is the latest in a succession of federal programs beginning in 1924 that provide financial encouragement for nonindustrial private forest management (planting, growing, harvesting) through public cost sharing agreements. Originally, FIP was another example of a market intervention justified on the market failure grounds of impending timber shortage. In recent years, however, FIP has received some justification on the distributive grounds that its recipients are among the rural poor.

Our analysis of FIP features a general equilibrium model of nonindustrial private landowner behavior and Royer's (1981) survey of North Carolina landowners. The general equilibrium model introduces nonconsumptive landowner objectives like recreational forest use in addition to the market timber production objective. Our statistical analysis pairs characteristics of timber producing landowners, determined from the general equilibrium analysis, with Royer's survey questions. One characteristic is participation in FIP. The analysis searches for the likelihood that these characteristics predict either timber stand improvement (TSI) or timber harvests. TSI includes investments in both tree planting and timber growing although the vast majority of TSI cost-sharing investments are in the former.

Receipt of technical assistance (TA) is another landowner characteristic. TA in forestry, much like extension in agriculture, provides forest management advice to small landowners. It has the same market failure justifications as FIP and its inclusion in Royer's survey permits comparison of the effectiveness of cost-sharing programs like FIP with extension programs like forestry TA.

Our TSI and harvest equations for both FIP and TA all are highly significant. The coefficients on the independent variables are generally significant and their signs all coincide with anticipations from the conceptual model. Our analysis shows FIP to have a statistically significant impact on TSI but we cannot reject the hypothesis that FIP has no impact on timber harvests. TA has a larger impact than FIP and, unlike FIP, it has a significant impact on both TSI and harvests. This difference between FIP and TA is not surprising. FIP provides a specialized incentive not relevant to some landowner objectives and it creates a timber supply impact only through capital cost sharing. TA is factor neutral. Therefore, it creates a timber supply impact through all three inputs: capital, labor, and management. For this reason, TA is a more successful means than FIP of increasing both standing inventories and timber harvests, thereby increasing both future and current timber supply.

These observations, together with knowledge of North Carolina's demand and supply for stumpage, permit measures of the net social gains due to FIP and TA. The statistical tests from Royer's data show that TA shifts current harvests directly and that both FIP and TA shift future harvests through an inventory variable in the anticipated supply function. For North Carolina, both FIP and TA are socially inefficient investments made all the more so by heavy administrative costs (approximately $150,000 and $100,000 annually in North Carolina for FIP and TA, respectively) and by losses in the form of payments and assistance to landowners with nontimber objectives. These landowners may never harvest their timber.

The magnitude of total social inefficiency exceeds $947,800 per year for the federal FIP program in North Carolina and $303,000 per year for the TA program. The exact level of these inefficiencies depends on the share of landowners who never harvest. The additions to inventories and harvests created by FIP and TA may cause small decreases in eventual equilibrium stumpage prices ranging up to $8.18 per Mcf—depending on the production level or, specifically, on the share of North Carolina landowners who never harvest.

Distributive arguments also fail to justify either FIP or TA in North Carolina. Indeed, Royer's survey shows that the distribution of nonindustrial private landowner incomes is higher than the distribution of all-household incomes. Furthermore, the distribution of incomes for landowners *informed* of TA or FIP is greater, that for landowners *receiving* TA is still greater, and that for landowners *receiving* FIP is even greater yet. Thus, neither recipients of FIP or TA nor nonindustrial landowners in general are among the lower wealth group for which society usually intends redistributive assistance.

In sum, our analysis rejects both FIP and TA in North Carolina on both social welfare and distributive grounds. Neither can satisfy the market failure justification, either in North Carolina or elsewhere, without evidence of positive externalities sufficient to exceed the net social losses due to the current programs. We have no evidence that the timber market fails and we have heard no claims for other nonmarket values originating from these public programs. (The landowners with recreation or multiple objectives internalize their personal nonmarket benefits by being both the producers and the consumers of the services originating from their own timber stands.) We also suspect that our rejection of the distributive argument is valid beyond North Carolina's borders. Forest landowners generally are wealthier than nonlandowners and landowners informed of or receiving FIP or TA are probably wealthier yet. Thus, we have no evidence that either FIP or TA are socially satisfying programs and FIP is probably less satisfying in general than TA.

PRICE STABILIZATION

Stabilization is infrequently used as an argument for market intervention in private forestry. Support for Timber Mart-South (TMS), a recently established (1976) stumpage price reporting service for thirty-eight substate regions throughout the South and Southeast, is the only example to our knowledge. TMS reports monthly pulpwood and sawtimber stumpage prices, thereby providing previously unavailable information for timber landowners, increasing their certainty of local markets and stabilizing stochastic prices by narrowing the frequency distribution around the mean values of equilibrium regional stumpage prices.

There is a reasonable literature describing the gains to producers and consumers from price stabilization.[1] Empirical measurement poses a problem, however, in that it requires comparable price information both before and after introduction of the stabilizing mechanism. "Before" information comparable to that provided by TMS does not exist. If it did, then there would be no justification for TMS.

Our alternative attempt to understand the social welfare gains due to TMS has two features. First, we review both the supply- and demand-related arguments for price instability in forestry and then search for empirical evidence that price instability in forestry is either abnormal or causes unusual hardship. Second, we seek other (southwide and annual) evidence on price variation, find the decrease in this variation necessary to offset the known public costs of support for TMS and then inquire whether this decrease is a reasonable expected result of TMS. The evidence for this second step depends on (1) demand and supply regressions for both sawtimber and pulpwood stumpage and (2) Turnovsky's (1974) measure of welfare gains due to decreases in the error terms in these regressions.[2]

A review of the conceptual arguments regarding price variation reminds us that only unpredictable price variation causes producers and consumers to misestimate the market and, thereby, creates social welfare losses. (Producers and consumers anticipate and adjust for predictable price variation in advance of its occurence. Therefore, predictable variation causes no social hardship.) Various empirical tests on two different sets of historical price data show lumber prices to be less predictable than pulp prices but the data provides little justification for arguing that stumpage prices are more unpredictably volatile than the prices of comparable natural resource or agricultural commodities.

On the other hand, the public costs of TMS approximate only $17,000 annually. Very small decreases of less than 1.5 percent in either unpredictable pulpwood or sawtimber price variations are sufficient to offset these TMS costs. A preliminary examination of the first three years' experience with TMS suggests that it may cause a decrease in the unpredicted price variations greater than thirty times that sufficient to generate net social benefits, thereby justifying the public investment. Furthermore, TMS has a favorable distributive effect, decreasing the relative market advantage of generally well-informed millowners and other stumpage processors by providing market information to generally less well-informed, less wealthy small private forest landowners.

Apparently TMS is a socially efficient public investment, even if we have a difficult time arguing that price instability is an important problem in forestry. The small public costs and strong likelihood of positive net social gain together with positive distributive effects encourage consideration of stumpage price reporting services for other regions of the country.

DEMAND-SIDE REGULATIONS

THE FAIR LABOR STANDARDS ACT. The FLSA mandate for a statutory minimum wage has its largest forestry effects on workers involved in processing timber after its harvest. Therefore its primary effect is on the demand side of the stumpage market. It has covered workers in the forest products industries since the law's introduction in 1935. The standard justification for the minimum wage is distributive: It intends to provide a minimum level of well-being for the poorest, least-skilled workers in our society.

Given (1) labor mobility, (2) opportunities for substitution of labor for other factors of production within the forestry sector, and (3) opportunities for labor substitution between forestry and other sectors of the economy not fully covered by the minimum wage, then increasing the minimum wage may have both wage and employment effects in the various forest products industries — all of which are covered by the minimum wage. Our analysis searches for empirical measures of these effects in thirteen two- and three-digit SIC code forest product industries as well as in the aggregate economy and in the agricultural sector. The aggregate economy and agriculture include uncovered sectors that offer alternative employment for forest products workers affected by the minimum wage. Therefore, they provide a measure of employment substitution in response to minimum wage impacts in covered industries.

Our equations regress average wages and employment on minimum wage and the anticipated minimum wage and correct for monetary effects and aggregate production or business cycle effects. These equations are generally significant at the 5 percent level and all important independent variables have the anticipated signs. Coefficients in the wage equations tend to be statistically significant but those in the employment equations tend not to be. Perhaps the employment effects of increasing the minimum wage are less reliable or perhaps our time series data (from ten to thirty-five years, depending on the industry) are too brief. In any case, our results are consistent with the literature for other industries and the signs are consistent with our more brief empirical examinations of minimum wage impacts on forest product industries in Oregon, Mississippi, and North Carolina, three states with large forest products sectors.

The analysis demonstrates that both the minimum wage and anticipated minimum wage have positive effects on the average wage in all thirteen forest product industries. The net effect of the minimum wage and the anticipated minimum wage on employment in these industries generally is negative. These empirical results are consistent with results for the aggregate economy and for the agriculture sector. Together, they suggest the hypothesis that increases in the minimum wage disemploy some forest products workers and those who are newly disemployed seek employment in uncovered sectors of the aggregate economy. Lumber and wood products workers, in particular, seek employment in agriculture.

If we accept these wage and employment effects of minimum wage increases as accurate, then we can measure the impacts on the wage bill in each forest product industry and comment on distributive effects. In general, a $0.25 increase in the minimum wage creates up to a 9.8 percent increase in the wage bill and up to a 6.1 percent decrease in employment (depending on the specific forest product industry). Thus, wages increase for those forest products workers whose employment in the industry continues — but wages decrease for the newly disemployed who now seek employment in lower-paying sectors of the ecomony, not covered by the minimum wage. Furthermore, both the wage bill and employment decrease in two of the three lowest-paying forest products industries. (That is, former wages of the generally lower-income newly disemployed workers in these two industries exceed the wage increases of continuing workers.) Thus, workers in the lowest-paying industries are least well served by increases in the minimum wage and those previously marginal workers in these industries who seek new employment in agriculture are probably so poorly served that their new incomes may fall below the federally established poverty level. In sum, despite certain weak statistical results, it is difficult to justify the minimum wage in the forest product industries with the standard distributive argument that it helps that segment of society that is least well off.

THE JONES ACT. The Jones Act restricts shipments between U.S. ports to U.S. built, owned, and operated vessels. Its purpose is to protect a perceived national security interest in a viable merchant ship fleet, an interest which is not valued in the market. Therefore, the Jones Act is a market failure regulation in our taxonomy. It affects forestry by making lumber shipments between U.S. ports more expensive and it places U.S. lumber producers at a comparative disadvantage in their own domestic market competition with foreign, particularly Canadian, producers who have access to less expensive shipping.

Our empirical inquiry relies on a lumber trade model with thirty-seven demand and twenty-seven supply regions in the United States and Canada and transportation cost estimates between regions via truck, rail, ship, or their combination. Demand derives from regional housing demand and permits substitution between fir and pine. Supply includes supply of both fir and pine at various conjectured substitution and price elasticities. We first simulate annual regional shipments in presence of the Jones Act and then simulate shipments under the new transportation cost scenario, which would prevail under deregulation (i.e., in the absence of the Jones Act). The difference between the two scenarios provides a measure of the social costs imposed by the Jones Act. The model performs well. That is, it predicts actual annual shipments with a high degree of accuracy regardless of substitution and price elasticities or factor share assumptions.

The analysis projects moderate aggregate annual gains ($12–13 million in the United States) from deregulation but large redistributive gains for northwestern producers (up to $9.8 million or 6 percent of the current shipment value) and northeastern consumers (up to $11.4 million). There are only minimal secondary impacts on the South and Southeast due to shifting trade patterns. Outside the United States, British Columbian producers lose (up to $7.3 million) but they may receive some compensation from Pacific Rim markets in which northwestern U.S. producers no longer compete. U.S. rail carriers lose $30–40 million in gross shipping revenues and the maritime shipping industry (now mostly foreign) increases its gross revenues by $25–41 million.

This final observation that deregulation increases maritime shipments throws some doubt on the national security justification for the Jones Act. That is, if the Jones Act decreases maritime shipments, then it does not support, rather it detracts from, a larger international merchant fleet, some of which would be American and much of which (American or not) would be available to satisfy the nonmarket U.S. national security interest. It is clear that the Jones Act impact on the lumber industry yields no net social benefit, is actually disadvantageous to the U.S. lumber industry and to consumers in the northeast. In fact, it may yield net disadvantage to the maritime industry and to U.S. national security. It also is clear, however, that large special industry interests are affected by it and would probably resist any changes in it.

OTHER MARKET INTERVENTIONS IN FORESTRY

NON-NEUTRAL TAXATION. There clearly exist a variety of taxes from several levels of government that all affect forestry. Some are nonneutral; that is, they distort market scarcity values, therefore they distort social welfare and are interesting to us on those grounds. This is not a book on taxation. Therefore, we focus our analyses on only two example nonneutral taxes; current use property taxation and preferential capital gains treatments of timber by the federal income tax. Both affect the stumpage market from its supply side.

Current use taxation provides preferential treatment for existing land uses, like agriculture or forestry, in their market competition with land development opportunities. The exact form of current use taxation varies across tax jurisdictions. In general, foresters' interests are in those current use taxes that provide favorable tax rates for forested land on the argument that the existence of such land satisfies the aesthetic nonmarket values of citizens from neighboring communities. Our analysis of current use taxation develops from a two-sector, rural and urban, land model in which the urban area is expanding and the rural land has a nonmarket value worth protecting. The model incorporates simulated values and expansion rates corresponding to those for Forsyth County (Winston-Salem), North Carolina.

We find that current use taxation delays, but does not prevent, development. That is, current use taxation protects aesthetic values only in the intermediate run before full adjustment to the new current use tax structure. Subsequent adjustment to increasing urban land use values continues to occur just as it did before a one-time change in tax structure to favor forestland. Our simulations suggest that potential social welfare gains in Forsyth County are less than $13,000 or $.05 per acre for the ten-year period, 1960–1970. Observations of the generally expensive and confusing administration of current use taxation across the entire U.S. further suggest that the net social gains from current use taxation are nearly always smaller than in Forsyth County. They may even be negative, although they may also be meaningful and positive in a few localities.

The capital gains provisions of the federal corporate and personal income taxes permitted (until 1987) preferential taxation of timber-derived income at 40 percent of the rate for ordinary income. Various arguments are made for this preferential treatment but the argument with the most general appeal to us claims that industries in similar markets should be taxed similarly and, furthermore, points to other basic resource industries that receive favorable capital gains treatment.

We examined the welfare effects and the incidence of the capital gains provision from the perspective of a general equilibrium model with two industrial sectors, timber and a general nontimber (all-other goods) sector, each with two inputs, capital and labor. Our data originate from various generally accepted sources regarding the timber sector of the U.S. economy and the U.S. economy as a whole. Our findings show that the capital gains provision imposes social costs of $240–386 million annually (depending on the demand elasticity and the elasticity of substitution between factors of production in the timber sector) and that capital appropriates more than 100 percent of the tax subsidy. The latter implies that the tax has negative employment effects.

These impacts from preferential capital gains are larger than those of any of the more commonly referred to regulations of private forestland examined in the rest of this volume. Justification on either efficiency or distributive grounds is difficult but it is also difficult to refute the argument that similar industries should be treated similarly.

PUBLIC LANDS. Public ownership of 482 million acres or 28 percent of the commercial forestland in the United States is a major market intervention. Its justification depends on market failure arguments, generally either market failure to account for environmental and aesthetic values or the perceived market failure to anticipate future timber shortage (again).

Public lands are the subject of the largest economics and policy literature in forestry and it is not our intention to repeat that literature here. Rather, we examine four specialized policies impacting the public lands: recreation management, provision for endangered species, concern for the stability of small communities dependent on public timber harvests, and departures from market timber criteria.

We cannot determine aggregate net welfare impacts in the first two cases. Alternately, we can examine the opportunity costs of endangered species management and the efficiency of recreation resource allocation in special cases, which provide impressions and methodological examples for measuring the impact of public intervention. For red-cockaded woodpecker (RCW) preservation on the Croatan National Forest, timber is the greatest opportunity value foregone but in no case is this opportunity cost large. For more than thirty-six of fifty-two current RCW colonies, there are no viable timber opportunities foregone under any reasonable management scenario. For outdoor recreation in the Seeley-Swan Valley of western Montana, demand is insensitive to changes in Forest Service pricing policy. Futhermore, recreation supply (for which there is no previous literature to our knowledge) also is price insensitive and current resource allocation is close to the economic optimum. The RCW and the Seeley-Swan Valley examples only provide the briefest insights to two large public land management issues. Despite their brevity, they suggest the hypotheses that (1) endangered species protection probably does not cost as much as sometimes argued and (2) the efficiency of recreation management should satisfy most analysts and planners. Existing public interventions may be both justified and efficient in these cases of market failure to provide for environmental or aesthetic values.

Public timber management is a different case. Few deny that there is a satisfactory market for timber, yet public land managers in general (state and federal) depart from market criteria in their management and harvest of timber. We make a broad and general attempt to estimate the aggregate costs of this departure nationwide. Our analysis begins with the best-known econometric model of the U.S. forest products sector (Adams & Haynes 1981), a model that includes two classes of private timber producers and one summary public sector. The public sector is responsive to neither prices nor production costs in the Adams-Haynes model. We contrast the aggregate and regional welfare projections under this model with those occurring under a revision of the model that substitutes a market sensitive public sector. The market sensitive public sector mimics that class of private producers it most closely resembles in each of six regions of the country, after adjustments for standing inventory differences and public agency cost differences.

Our analysis suggests that public land departures from market timber criteria generally raise stumpage prices and cost consumers $786 million nationwide in one year. Departures transfer a benefit of similar amount to private producers in general but this redistribution is uneven, creating large private gains in western Washington and Oregon and small private losses in the Rocky Mountains. The cost to the public treasury is an even larger amount than the cost to consumers or similar net transfer to private producers. The net social loss is substantial.

Market timber criteria suggest substantial increases in public timber harvests in all regions except the Rocky Mountains. The U.S. Forest Service is concerned with community stability in this region and it attempts to stabilize small timber dependent communities by guaranteeing a fixed harvest flow regardless of declining market conditions. Our fourth analysis examines this policy. In this analysis, a two-sector general equilibrium model with approximate input data from western Montana argues that, in conditions most favorable to this policy (no inventory substitution, no public–private harvest substitution), the Forest Service has no net effect on community welfare. The Forest Service may protect local forest products employment but only at a compensating cost to the local economy as a whole. For example, the Forest Service policy, when confronted with an 18 percent decrease in external lumber prices, restricts the decrease in wood products employment by 7 percent from that which would occur were the Forest Service a price-responsive producer unconcerned with community stability. Forest Service policy also trickles through the local economy to restrict potential employment increases in the general economy. Policy also creates net losses in the sum of factor payments received by the community. Finally, it extracts a heavy toll on the U.S. Treasury. Thus, at best, the community stability policy as currently designed has no impact and, at worst, it has a negative impact on local community welfare. Community stability may be a noble public agency concern, but the current Forest Service policy is misguided.

In sum, public land timber management causes substantial social welfare losses that cannot be justified on basis of either timber market failure or stability arguments. These timber management losses are so large as to be of questionable justification on the basis of environmental and aesthetic market failures. Indeed, the latter are not the agencies' original justifications for either current timber harvest criteria or the community stability policy and at least three other studies (Hyde 1980; 1981; Kutay 1977) show public agency timber harvest criteria to conflict with, rather than promote, environmental and aesthetic values.[3] Furthermore, neither our endangered species example nor our forest recreation example suggest that large shifts from market timber criteria are necessary in order to produce environmental or aesthetic gains. The endangered species and recreation examples are highly selective. Nevertheless, they show Forest Service

management results that are remarkably similar to our anticipated efficiency results — yet they require almost no competition with timber production.

We must be very clear that our public land results are impressionistic at
best. Nevertheless, we find it difficult to deny the impression that potential
social losses on the public lands exceed the net social costs of all regulations
affecting the private sector on which we concentrate in this book. These
social losses probably justify the greater attention that planners and policy
analysts have directed to public land questions over the years.

 Conclusions

What can we learn from all this? Can we reasonably generalize from
these analyses of specific regulations and other policy-induced distortions
in the forestry sector of our economy? Tables 9.1 and 9.2 summarize our
results for regulations affecting private forestry and for taxation–public
ownership policies, respectively. They may help answer these questions.
The tables show the welfare and distributive effects previously discussed for
each regulation or other market distortion. They also show the stumpage
price impacts, another general point of reference which may be of particular interest to foresters.

Table 9.1 shows that the welfare effects are negative for all public
market interventions in private forestry except for Timber Mart-South.
Similarly, the distributive effects are the opposite of what U.S. society generally prefers for all cases except TMS. Wealthier landowners, higher-wage
employees, and Canadian producers gain from these interventions. Small
private producers, lower-wage employees, U.S. consumers, and the public
treasury bear the burdens of these interventions. That is, each intervention
fails its own test. Interventions justified to overcome market failure actually further distort the market — and have negative distributive effects as a
corollary. Interventions justified on distributive bases actually redistribute
away from the generally needy segments of society, and impose administrative burdens on the public treasury as well. This is true regardless of our
taxonomic distinction between demand-side and supply-side, or wood processing and timber growing, interventions.

These interventions cause small stumpage price effects both individually and cumulatively. For example, the cumulative effect in western Washington and Oregon is little different from the small regional impact of the
Jones Act because the state forest practice act impact is very small and
because the FIP program itself is small in these two states. In North Carolina, for another example, the ripple effect from the Jones Act is negligible

Table 9.1. Summary impacts of regulation of the private market

Regulation	Social welfare effects	Distributive effects	Stumpage price effects	Restrictions on analysis
State forest practice acts	−$150,000/yr or −$.01/acre/yr	Cost effective enforcement suggests burden on nonindustrial landowners, poorer quality lands, lower price markets	Negligible	Virginia, 1985 Supporting evidence: Washington and Oregon, 1985
FIP (cost sharing)	−$947,800/yr, more if some recipients have nontimber objectives causing them to never harvest	Favors larger landowners Some redistribution to intermediate and final consumers	−$6.38/Mbf for future harvests, less if some recipients never harvest	North Carolina, 1980
Technical assistance	−$303,000/yr, more if some recipients have nontimber objectives causing them to never harvest	Negative, but not as negative as FIP	−$8.18/Mbf for future harvests, less if some recipients never harvest Negligible decrease for current harvests	North Carolina, 1980
Timber Mart-South	>$520,000/yr	Increase market information of nonindustrial landowners	Unknown small price increase Decrease price variation	Southwide, 1977 & 1980
Minimum wage	Not estimated	All forest products industries: wage bill −$114,000 or 1%, −6354 employees or <1%, disemployed move to lower wage industries 3 lowest wage forest industries: 2 of 3 wage bills −2%, −6452 employees or −4%, disemployed may drop below poverty level	Very small and statistically insignificant	Hypothetical $.25 increase in minimum wage in 1983 Wage effects statistically reliable, employment effects not
Jones Act	Costs: $5.6–7.1MM in U.S. and Canada combined, $12.2–13.2MM in U.S. alone Benefits: no national security gain	Western WA/OR producers: −$9.1–9.8MM Northeastern consumers: −$10.7–11.4MM Canadian producers: +$7.2–7.4MM Shipments: rail +$30.7–40.6MM sea −$25.3–42.0MM	<$1.09/Mbf in western WA/OR Smaller and of uncertain sign in other regions	U.S. and coastal western Canada, 1977

Tax or public land policy	Social welfare effects	Distributive effects	Stumpage price effects	Restrictions on analysis
Current use taxation	Benefits: <$13,000 or <$.05/acre/10 years Costs: potentially large administrative costs	Unknown	Negligible	Forsyth County, North Carolina, 1960–1970, 1970s
Preferential capital gains	−$240.9–368.2MM or 12–18% of all earnings for timber sector of U.S. economy	>180% incidence on capital Negative employment effects	33–49% decrease (potentially substantial decrease)	Federal tax, 1979
Red-cockaded woodpecker	Benefits: unknown Costs: <$221,000 in perpetuity or <$8820 annually for all 52 habitat sites, zero opportunity costs for 36 individual sites	Unknown	Negligible	Croatan National Forest 1982
Developed campground recreation	$610,000–628,000 current policy yields $3,000–18,000 less than optimal policies	Unknown, generally local users	Zero	Seeley-Swan Valley, Lolo National Forest, 1984
Departures from market timber criteria	Perhaps −$13MM	Consumers −$786.8MM (−$689.8MM in western WA/OR) Industrial producers +592.8MM (+398.3MM in western WA/OR) NIPF producers +$217.8MM (mostly in South and western WA/OR) Public treasuries −$1300MM Rocky Mtns: harvest increases, environmental losses	Increase $20/Mbf everywhere except western WA/OR (+$49/Mbf) and Rocky Mountains (−$20/Mbf)	U.S.-wide, 1977
Community stability	Negligible decrease in factor payments remaining in community (annual community generated income) £ h t ti l t t U S	Increase wood products wage income <17% No effect on community-wide wage or employment	Decrease 12–26%	W. Montana, 1968–1981 Assume: −18% lumber price, no private stumpage response, no i t b tit ti

and there is no state forest practice act. Therefore, the small impact of the FIP program essentially measures the full change in North Carolina stumpage prices.

Timber Mart-South is an interesting exception to these emerging rules. The justification for its public support is a stabilization argument and our evidence suggests that TMS probably succeeds in its intention. It yields net gains in social welfare. It may even create positive distributive effects in the form of information gains for nonindustrial private forest landowners who are in poor competitive position relative to the generally wealthier mill-owners who purchase their timber. TMS is also interesting, however, in that it probably has the lowest public profile and generates the least policy analytic interest of any of our example regulations.

A full appreciation of Table 9.2 requires that we separate the cases of intervention for clear nonmarket and aesthetic values (current use taxation, red-cockaded woodpecker, recreation) from timber market interventions (capital gains taxation, timber harvest policy, community stability). The timber interventions all produce negative welfare effects and all cause unattractive distributive effects. That is, they favor capital over labor and generally well-off timber landowners rather than consumers or the general public. The individual stumpage price impacts of the timber interventions are substantial and important but of uncertain net magnitude as the decrease in stumpage prices caused by favorable capital gains taxation counters the general increase in stumpage prices caused by public timber harvest departures from market criteria.

The environmental and aesthetic interventions probably generate relatively small benefits, but their costs are small as well. Therefore, we anticipate that environmental and aesthetic interventions yield potential net welfare gains. Their distributive impacts are unknown and their stumpage price impacts are negligible and of uncertain sign. (These are good topics for further research.) In our judgement, the public land provision for these environmental and aesthetic values does not appear to have substantial impact on the timber sector of the aggregate U.S. economy.

In general, these analyses consider the most discussed and probably the largest impact public regulations of private forestry. Except for the isolated case of Timber Mart-South, existing regulations of the private sector all fail to accomplish their objectives and all have maldistributive effects on society—although these distributive effects may not be intended. Regulations of market-valued goods provided by the public forestlands are no better. Better regulations might be designed but it is a fact that better regulations do not exist among our examples. Our results are remarkably consistent and this consistency causes us to ponder whether we can generalize to other regulations that we have not examined.[4] It causes us to hypothesize that deregulation of private forestry in general may be a good thing.

On the other hand, the welfare and distributive effects of these regulations are uniformly small relative to either the forest products industry or
the affected regional economies. It is conceivable that the reluctance of
special interests may create greater transactions costs for deregulation than
deregulation of private forestry can reasonably yield in long-term efficiency
or distributive gains.

Whichever hypothesis one accepts is consistent with a third hypothesis
originating from this same evidence. This third hypothesis states that, as a
nation, we do a poor job of designing forest sector interventions and that
there are probably few good justifications in the future for additional selective and specific regulations of private sector forestry. Existing markets
apparently are more efficient and also allocate better. We expect that such
additional regulations would have small impacts and negative results and
they might stay with us for a long time. Only strong prior evidence to the
contrary could alter this general opinion and encourage our support for
selective regulations of either private forestlands or satisfactory forest
product markets in the unforeseen future.

Our general observations on taxation and public ownership, however,
are different. The capital gains tax provision alone accounted for 12–18
percent of earnings in the timber sector of our economy (until its revision in
1987) and one public land distortion alone causes a welfare loss as large as
that of the most important regulation of private sector forestry. These
observations suggest justification for further analysis, greater precision,
much care in formulating broad general policies, and greater general attention on taxation and public land policies than on specialized regulations.
The politics of private deregulation have less impact on private forestry or
on the forestry sector of the economy than do the politics of taxation and
public ownership. That is, while we might argue for deregulation of private
markets, we might argue even more strongly for the simplification and
neutrality of taxation and public management, as well as for privatization
of those publicly owned forest resources with satisfactory markets.

Harberger (1959) and Schultz (1964; 1978) invite taking this analysis a
step further by inquiring whether regulation is sufficient to affect economic
growth. Harberger finds that the elimination of resource misallocation in
Chile "would raise national welfare by no more than 15 per cent." Schultz
finds regulation a greater deterrent to growth in developing countries but
finds technical advances and improvements in human capital more important in developed countries like the United States and greater contributors
to growth in general.

Our observations of regulation in the forestry sector of the U.S.
economy are in partial agreement with Harberger and Schultz. Favorable
capital gains treatment of timber alone creates a misallocation equal to 12–

18 percent of sector earnings—but it is a misallocation that provides incentive for forestry sector growth. It is distortionary from the entire U.S. economy's perspective and favorable from forestry's perspective. FIP and technical assistance, when we consider their impacts on all fifty states, add considerably to this misallocation favoring forestry. Public timber management and the Jones Act misallocate away from U.S. forestry in general but public timber management also misallocates in favor of private timber producers.

In sum, resource misallocation may exceed 20 percent of private sector forestry earnings. This is a substantial misallocation and we think it must surely distort private sector growth. Distortion of the entire forestry sector, including both its public and private components, is much less likely because the large public timber management contribution to private sector growth is largely a transfer within the aggregate forestry sector. Our combined public and private forestry results probably conform with Harberger's and Schultz's findings.

We are less certain of the net distributive effects of this distortion and we cannot argue about its weight relative to gains from technical advances and improvements in human capital applied in forestry. No doubt the aggregate distortion favors capital and decreases market inducements for labor-saving technical change and training. Forestry sector investments in technology and human capital are less than they would be without the distortion. Nevertheless, there is no generalizable empirical evidence known to us on these latter topics in forestry. The topic invites future investigation.

 Notes

1. See Turnovsky (1974) or Newbery and Stiglitz (1981) for surveys.

2. All four equations display good statistical fit. Autocorrelation is not a problem. The signs on the independent variables satisfy expectations, the coefficients are generally significant at least at the 10 percent level, and the price elasticities are consistent with previous literature.

3. Various actions of major environmental groups also support this contention. Consider, for example, active research by Kaid Benfield and his colleagues at the Natural Resources Defense Council or the Wilderness Society–Colorado Open Space Council administrative appeal of various U.S. Forest Service timber management plans in 1978.

4. The previously cited articles on log trade by Sedjo and Wiseman (1983), Wiseman and Sedjo (1981), and Gallagher (1980) support our conclusions. They find that trade restrictions cause aggregate welfare losses and regional transfers from public producers (and the U.S. treasury) to private producers.

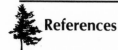

References

Adams, D. M., and R. W. Haynes. 1981. *The 1980 softwood timber assessment market model: Structure, projections, and policy simulation.* Forest Science Monograph 22. (Results revised, 1985, personal communication from D. M. Adams.)

Gallagher, P. 1980. *An analysis of the softwood log trade between the United States and Japan.* University of Minnesota Agricultural Experiment Station Technical Bulletin 330. Forestry Series no. 4.

Harberger, A. C. 1959. Using the resources at hand more effectively. *American Economic Review* 49:134–46.

Hyde, W. F. 1980. *Timber supply, land allocation and economic efficiency.* Baltimore: Johns Hopkins University Press for Resources for the Future.

———. 1981. Timber economics in the Rockies. *Land Economics* 57(4):630–39.

Kutay, K. 1977. *Oregon economic impact assessment of proposed wilderness legislation. Oregon omnibus wilderness act.* Hearings before the Subcommittee on Parks and Recreation of the Committee on Energy and Natural Resources. U.S. Senate, 95 Cong., 1 sess., 1977. Publ. 95-42 pt. 2:29–63.

Newbery, D. M. G. and J. E. Stiglitz. 1981. *The theory of commodity price stabilization: A study in the economics of risk.* New York: Clarendon Press.

Royer, J. P. 1981. North Carolina nonindustrial private forest landowners survey. Unpublished manuscript. Duke University School of Forestry and Environmental Studies, Durham, N.C.

Schultz, T. W. 1964. *Transforming traditional agriculture.* Chicago: University of Chicago Press.

Schultz, T. W., ed. 1978. *Distortions of agricultural incentives.* Bloomington: Indiana University Press.

Sedjo, R., and A. C. Wiseman. 1983. The effectiveness of an export restriction on logs. *American Journal of Agricultural Economics* 65(1):113–16.

Turnovsky, S. J. 1974. Price expectations and the welfare gains from price stabilization. *American Journal of Agricultural Economics* 56:706–16.

Wiseman, A. C., and R. Sedjo. 1981. Effects of an export embargo on related goods: Logs and lumber. *American Journal of Agricultural Economics* 63(3):424–29.

INDEX OF SYMBOLS AND ABBREVIATIONS
In order of their appearance

Chapter 1

NIPF = nonindustrial private forests
Mbf = thousand board feet

Chapter 2

SFPA = state forest practice act
π = profits
p = price
Q = quantity
K = capital
L = labor
r = return on capital
w = wages
λ = a Langrangian multiplier, the shadow price of the capital constraint
MP = marginal product
$VMP, SVMP$ = value, social value of the marginal product
S = renewable resource stock (i.e., timber inventory)
I = investment
PI = productivity index
A = acres
M = midpoint of the productivity index
$VOL, VOLP$ = volume per acre (public and private, private only)
SD = state dummy

PR = price
TX = property tax
IND = percentage of land industry owned
PUB = percentage of land publicly owned
HW = percentage hardwood
$\alpha_1, \alpha_2, \alpha_3$ = mountains, piedmont, coastal plain

Chapter 3

TSI = timber stand improvement
FIP = forest incentive payments
U = NIPF landowner utility
x_1 = household produced consumption
x_2 = value of personal timber harvests
y = money income
M = exogenous income
β_i = Hicks neutral technology parameters
T_K, T_L = taxes (or subsidies) on K, L
$\hat{}$ (hat) indicates logarithmic differentiation or percentage change
θ_L, θ_L = output share of L, K
$x = x_1 + x_2$ = total landowner produced output
μ = expenditure share
η, σ = income and substitution elasticities
s = supply elasticity
γ_i = impact of relative input taxes (subsidies) on ith output sector
y^*_{iH}, y^*_{iI} = propensity of landowner i to harvest timber, invest in TSI
HST = harvest probability
IMP = TSI (including reforestation) probability
INC = income
ED = years of education
TEC = technical assistance
$DIST$ = distance in miles from forestland
FRM = dummy for farm-nonfarm distinction
FOR = acres of forest
Q_D, Q_S = quantity demanded, supplied
P_S, P_F = stumpage, final good price
I = inventory
T = time in years

Chapter 4

TMS = Timber Mart South
ϵ = random term, uncorrelated overtime
N = number of firms in the industry
V = present value
C = cost
$\sim$ indicates expectation
* indicates optimality
η = forecast error
R = resource stock
PPI = producer price index
Q_s, p_s = quantity, price of saw timber stumpage
Q_p, p_p = quantity, price of pumpwood stumpage
p_1, p_u = lumber, paper prices
$w_1, w_u; r_1, r_u$ = wages, cost of capital in lumber, paper
u, v = error terms in demand, supply

Chapter 5

OSHA = Occupational Safety and Health Act
FLSA = Fair Labor Standards Act
$D_c, S_c; D_u, S_u$ = demand, supply in covered and uncovered sectors
$L_c, L_u; w_c, w_u$ = employment, wage in covered, uncovered sectors
w_m = minimum wage
s = reservation return to search
w = ln of average wage in all manufacturing i or in industry j
A_i = ln of actual employment in total economy
Ω = ln of statutory minimum wage
M, m = ln of money supply, growth in money supply
I = ln of index of industrial production
BLS = Bureau of Labor Statistics
SIC = Standard Industrial Classification
E = rational expectations operator
X = ln (N^s/N)
V = ln of employment velocity
y = policy target for ln (w_m/w)
η = elasticity of X_i/X_j

Chapter 6

ES = excess supply

Q = residential construction industry production function

Z = softwood lumber, a composite of fir and pine

CES = constant elasticity of substitution

F, α_F = fir, factor share in fir

P, α_P = pine, factor share in pine

A = Hicks neutral technology parameters

σ = partial elasticity between fir and pine

w_F, w_P, w_K = factor prices for fir, pine, all other inputs

δ, η, ζ = inverse regional demand quantity coefficients for fir, pine, cross-price

θ, μ, v = inverse regional demand quantity coefficents for fir, pine, cross-quantity

ICC = Interstate Commerce Commission

t^F_{ij}, t^P_{ij} = fir, pine transportation costs from supply region i to demand region j

W_j = welfare index for demand region j

x^F, x^P = shipments of fir, pine between regions

B.C. = coastal British Columbia

Chapter 7

C = industry cost function = marginal cost in sector

X, Y = timber, all other products

θ_{ij} = share of total returns to factor i in sector j

ϵ_{ij} = demand elasticities

η = income elasticities

M = income

U = marginal utility of expenditures

$\sigma_D = - (\epsilon_{xx} + \epsilon_{yy})$

σ_X, σ_Y = sector x, y substitution elasticity

τ = physical factor share

s = demand for developed land

A = acres

p_2 = price of undeveloped land

Δ = marginal benefit of development

D = level of new development
γ = cost of a unit of development
T = tax
ϱ = discount rate

Chapter 8

AH = Adams-Haynes
FI = forest industry
OP = other private
I = inventory
SE = Southeast
SC = South Central
RM = Rocky Mountains
PSW = Pacific Southwest
PNW-W = Western Washington and Oregon
PNW-E = Eastern Washington and Oregon
X, Y = wood products, all other goods
K, L, S = capital, labor, stumpage inputs
θ = factor share of total inputs
σ = factor substitution elasticity
e_x = stumpage supply elasticity
SSV = Seeley-Swan Valley
RVD = recreation-visitor-days
V = present net value
a = age of current stand
T = U.S. Forest Service rotation age
L_{70}, L_{78} = loblolly present net value for seventy, seventy-eight-year rotation
C_L = loblolly timber opportunity cost

INDEX

Allocation, 4
  examples of, 15–17
  justification for market intervention, 7–9,
    20
  justification for OSHA, 120
American Enterprise Institute (AEI), 122

Bureau of Labor Statistics (BLS), 128
Bureau of Land Management, and regulation, 6–7, 18

Camping. *See* Recreation; Travel cost model
Capital gains tax. *See* Tax, capital gains
Capital-labor substitution
  in timber production, 196
  in wood products industries, 129, 231
Clarke-McNary Act of 1924
  authorization of forestry extension, 48
  passage of, 25
Community stability
  definition of, 228–30
  impact of stumpage supply policies on,
    235–36, 258, 277
Cost sharing, impact of
  on nonindustrial private forest land-
    owners, 66
  on timber harvests, 66
  on timber stand improvement, 67
Current use tax. *See* Tax, current use

Demand. *See* Stumpage demand
Distribution
  effects of Jones Act, 181–82, 184, 274
  examples of, 16–17
  gains from minimum wage laws, 149
  gains from price reporting services, 91,
    271

general impacts of, 13–14
justification
  for capital gains taxation, 192, 200
  for FIP, 49, 73, 76
  for market intervention, 9–10, 20
  for minimum wage, 120
  for OSHA, 120

Economic cycles
  impact of price reporting on, 91
  impact of stabilization on, 14
  impact on community stability, 229–30,
    236
  impact on stumpage prices, 93
  relation to lumber production, 142
Elasticity
  of demand and income, tax model, 194–
    99
  of demand and supply, minimum wage
    model, 132–33
  of substitution
    lumber demand model, 170, 175–76,
      178–80
    tax model, 194–95
    timber-dependent community model,
      231–33
  of supply
    FIP model, 59–61, 77–78
    lumber supply model, 171, 178–79
    timber-dependent community model,
      232, 233, 236
Endangered species. *See* Red-cockaded
  woodpecker
Environmental Protection Agency
  and forest practices legislation, 26
  and market failure, 6
Externality
  causes of, 8–9
  in a competitive market, lack of, 75

Externality (*continued*)
  definition of, 8
  of green space, 200, 212
  from timber harvesting, 27–30

Fair Labor Standards Act, and minimum
    wage, 122–28, 145–46, 271–72
FIP. *See* Forestry Incentives Program
FLSA. *See* Fair Labor Standards Act
Forestry extension, impact on timber sup-
    ply, 63
Forestry Incentives Program
  budgets, 48, 69
  history of, 48
  impact in North Carolina, 67–71, 269
  impact on industrial timber owners, 69,
    73, 76
  impact on timber output, model of, 60–
    61
  justifications for, 49
  public costs of, 51, 70–71, 73, 269
  welfare and distributive impacts, 50–51,
    69–71, 269–70
Forest Service. *See* U.S. Forest Service

General equilibrium model
  of forest products industry, 134–36, 150–
    52
  of landowner behavior, 53–66
  reasons for use, 266
  supply equations, 78–79
  of tax effects on timber production, 193–
    96, 213
  of timber-dependent community, 230–32

Housing starts
  impact on lumber demand, 181
  in lumber demand model, 167–71, 176,
    185–86

Input-output equations, 59
  derivation of, 77–79

Jones Act, 4
  history of, 163–64
  impact on Canadian producers, 167,
    176–85
    impact on U.S. producers and consumers,
      162–63, 167, 170, 175–85
    impacts on trade, model of, 164–66

Labor mobility
  in forest products industry, 129, 133
  impact of minimum wage on, 130–33,
    138–43, 147–49
  in timber-dependent community model,
    232, 236
Lumber
  Canadian industry, 162–64, 171, 274
  shipment
    Canadian, to U.S., 163, 176–85, 273
    costs, 172, 178, 180–85
    by rail, 172–73, 179–80
    restrictions on, 162–64
    by truck, 172–73
    by water, 163, 172–73, 178, 180–81,
      184

Market failure, 6, 7
  definition of, 8, 11
  examples of, 6, 19
  justification
    for FIP, 49, 268
    for Jones Act, 162, 273
    for public land ownership, 275
    for SFPAs, 27, 266
    for technical assistance, 269
  and report on Forest Credit, 50
Market intervention. *See also* Allocation;
    Distribution; Stabilization
  classification of, 16–19
  justifications for, 7–11, 20, 265
  optimal, 11–16
  summarization of, 278–81
Mills
  coverage by minimum wage laws, 128
  impact of minimum wage laws on, 142–
    43
  impact of OSHA on, 120
  market power of, 93–94
  and price reporting services, 107–9
Minerals
  price variation of, 105
  production model for, 97–99
Minimum wage law
  coverage in forest-based industries, 122,
    128

current wage, 122
distributive impacts of, 146–49, 273
exemptions from, 128, 158 n.2
history of, 122–23
impact
  on employment, 121, 128, 133
  on forest-based industries, 139–43,
    146–49, 273
  on production, 127–28
  reports on, 122–29
  theoretical model of impacts of, 130–
    33
  on wage bills, 121, 127, 129, 132
Minimum Wage Study Commission
  (MWSC), report on effects, 122–27
Money supply
  and business cycles, 93
  impact on forest products industry em-
    ployment of, 138–39
  impact on minimum wage, 134–36
  in model of forest products industry,
    150–52

National Park Service, recreation provision,
  238
National security, justification for Jones
  Act, 163, 274
Nonindustrial private forest (NIPF) landowners
  and cost sharing and technical assistance
    programs, 48–76
  description of, 53
  distributive effects of, 68–71, 73
  income classes of, 73
  and investments in forest lands, 8, 32–34
  model of behavior of, 54–66
  North Carolina survey of, 62–63, 68, 73,
    84–85

Occupational Health Safety Act (OSHA),
  121
  costs of compliance with, 157–58
  economic impacts of, 152–58
  and employee protection, 120, 152, 157
  impact on forest-based industries, 154,
    158
  justifications for, 120

Paper and pulp industry

employees, covered by minimum wage,
  122, 128
employment, related to agricultural
  employment, 144
impact of minimum wage law on, 129,
  139–43, 146–49
price volatility in, 102–4, 112
producer price indexes for, 101–3
stagnation in, 143
Price forecasting
  and harvest decisions, 94, 100
  and price variation, 103
  and production models, 94–100
Price reporting services
  description of, 90–91
  impacts on stumpage market, 106–9, 112
  public support of, 90–91, 109, 111
  welfare gains from, model of, 114–16,
    271
Price volatility
  in agriculture, 102–6
  in efficient stumpage market, 227
  in lumber and wood products, 100–106
  in paper and pulp, 102–6
  and price reporting services, 108–9, 111–
    14
  and social welfare, 91, 111
  in stumpage markets, 91–94, 271
Production
  decisions, models of, 94–100
  function for construction, 167–71
Protection, justification for Jones Act,
  163–64

Quadratic programming, model of shipping
  costs, 173–75

Recreation
  camping, costs of, 239–44
  demand and supply model of, 239–46
  optimal pricing of, 245–46
  provision by U.S. Forest Service, 238–39
Red-cockaded woodpecker
  biology of, 247–48, 252
  management, costs of, 248–49, 254–56
  management, impact on timber harvest,
    254–57
  management alternatives, 250–53
Reforestation
  impact of FIP on, 68–69

Reforestation (*continued*)
  impact of SFPAs on, 36, 40
  required by SFPAs, 26, 32
  tax incentives for, 192
Regulation
  classification of, 17
  historical background of, 5–7, 264–65
  justifications for, 18, 265
  summary rule for, 13

Seed tree laws, 25
  in Virginia, 31–33, 36–37
Social efficiency, 8, 220
Social welfare, effects
  of capital gains taxation, 199–200, 211–12, 275
  of community stability policies, 235–37, 258, 277
  of cost sharing, 68–71
  of current use taxation, 210–11, 275
  of decreased campground fees, 245
  of Jones Act, 180–82, 274
  of minimum wage laws, 137–44
  of preserving endangered species, 248, 259
  of price reporting services, 111–14, 271
  of public agency harvest decisions, 226–27, 258, 277
  of seed tree laws, 36–37, 268
  of SFPAs, 40–42, 269–70
  of technical assistance, 71–73, 269–70
Stabilization
  examples of, 16–17
  impacts of, 14
  justification for market intervention, 10–11, 20, 90–91, 106
State forest practice acts
  effects on stumpage price of, 32–36, 38
  enforcement of, 37, 40–42, 267
  history of, 24–27, 264–65
  impacts of, 24–27, 41–42, 267–68
  in Oregon, 27–43
  in Virginia, 31–37, 41
  in Washington, 37–43
Statistical Abstract of the United States, 196
Stumpage demand
  community-based model of, 230–32
  derived model, 220–24
  impact of Jones Act on, 175–80
  impact of minimum wage on, 143

impact of OSHA on, 158
  North Carolina model, 79–83
  regional model, 171–75
  South-wide, 109–11
Stumpage price
  in efficient market model, 225–27
  impacts of price reporting services on, 112–13
  impacts of SFPAs on, 32–36, 38
  impacts on endangered species management, 254–55
  in production decision model, 94–96
  variation in, 91–94, 100–106
Stumpage supply
  impact
    of cost sharing on, 68–71
    of FIP on, 64–66
    of price reporting services on, 112
    of public land ownership on, 225–27
    of SFPAs on, 36, 38–40
    of stabilization policies on, 235–36
    of technical assistance on, 71–73
  model
    of North Carolina, 79–83
    of public, 220–24
    of regional, 171–75
    of U.S. Forest Service, 232
  South-wide, 109–11
Subsidy
  and capital gains tax, 197, 212
  description of, 50
  impact on timber output, 61, 67, 75
  output vs. input, 75
  and taxes, in general equilibrium model, 195
Substitution
  effect, in tax model, 196
  of inputs in timber growing, 196
  of inputs in wood products production, 231
  between lumber species, 167–72, 176, 178–80
  between wood products, 167
Supply. *See* Stumpage supply

Tax
  capital gains
    description of, 191–93
    incidence effects of, 197, 275
    model of effects, 193–96
    rate, 191, 193

welfare effects of, 198, 275
corporate income, 193, 199
current use
    description of, 200–201
    incidence effects of, 209–10
    model of, 201–6, 207–11, 275
    welfare effects of, 210–11
forest industry, extent of, 190
in general equilibrium model, 56–59
non-neutrality of, 191, 209–11, 274–75
property, 32–36, 199, 200–211
Technical assistance
    distributive effects of, 70–73, 76
    impact on timber harvest, 67, 71–73, 269
    impact on timber stand improvement, 67, 71, 269
Technology
    in general equilibrium model, 57
    impact on timber output, model of, 60–61
    in lumber demand model, 170
Timber. See also Stumpage demand; Stumpage price; Stumpage supply
Timber famine, 6, 21 n, 25, 49, 264, 275
Timber Mart-South (TMS)
    assessment of, 91–92
    description of, 90
    model of effects of, 106–9, 112, 114–16
    public support of, 90–91, 109, 111
    report of stumpage prices, 33, 63
Timber stand improvement (TSI)
    and Forestry Incentives Program, 48, 68–69
    impacts of cost sharing and technical assistance on, 66–67
    landowner probability of, 62–66
Trade

impact of Jones Act on, 175–85
interregional model of, 164–66
Transactions costs, of market intervention, 11–14
Travel cost model, demand for camping, 244–45

U.S. Forest Service, 34
    bulletins, 32, 34
    and community stability objective, 228–30, 235–37, 258
    and efficiency of harvest decisions, 227, 277
    and harvest planning, 219
    and market failure, 6
    model of regional harvests, 220–27
    recreation provision, 238, 240, 243
    and regulation on private lands, 25
    share of U.S. softwood harvest, 219
    and stabilization, 18

Welfare. See Social welfare
Wood products industry
    employees, covered by minimum wage, 122, 128
    employment, related to agricultural employment, 143–44
    impact of minimum wage on, 121, 129, 134–43, 146–49
    markets, 93, 230–33
    in Montana, 228, 233–36
    and price volatility, 102–6
    producer price indexes for, 101–3
    production, capital-labor substitution in, 129